The Soviet Maritime Arctic

5 June 1991

To: Dr. Craig Dorman
Director
Woods Hole Oceanographic
Institution

Craig, my sincere thanks are
extended to you and your
entire staff for the support
I received as a Fellow.
I am very pleased that this
contribution to the Western
polar literature was conceived
and accomplished at the
Oceanographic!

Respectfully,

Lawson W. Brigham

Captain, U. S. Coast Guard

Polar Research Series

edited by Bernard Stonehouse

L. W. Brigham, **The Soviet Maritime Arctic**

C. Harris and B. Stonehouse, **Antarctica and Global Climatic Change**

R. D. Massom, **Satellite Remote Sensing of Polar Regions**

other titles are in preparation

The Soviet Maritime Arctic

edited by
Lawson W. Brigham

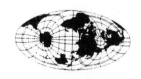

Belhaven Press, London
in association with the
Scott Polar Research Institute,
University of Cambridge

© Woods Hole Oceanographic Institution, 1991

WHOI Contribution No. 7609

First published in Great Britain in 1991 by
Belhaven Press (a division of Pinter Publishers),
25 Floral Street, London WC2E 9DS

British Library Cataloguing in Publication Data
A CIP catalogue record for this book is available from the British Library

ISBN 1 85293 169 8

Cover illustration by E. Paul Oberlander

Typeset by Communitype Communications Ltd
Printed and bound by Biddles Ltd, Guildford and Kings Lynn

Contents

Contents

List of figures

List of tables

Biographies of the editor and contributors

Editor:

Lawson W. Brigham edited this book while a Research Fellow at the Marine Policy Center, Woods Hole Oceanographic Institution. He has published widely on the Soviet Arctic, US Arctic policy, polar ship technology and polar navigation. A Commander in the American Coast Guard, he is currently a member of the Strategic Planning Staff at US Coast Guard Headquarters, Washington, DC.

Contributors:

Alexander I. Arikaynen is a leading Soviet researcher and Head of the Systems Analysis Laboratory for the Strategy of Arctic Development, Institute for Systems Studies, Moscow. In over 20 years of arctic research he has over 100 publications, including 10 books.

Terence Armstrong is a Researcher at Scott Polar Research Institute, Cambridge University, United Kingdom and an internationally recognized authority on the history, geography and development of the Soviet North. He has extensive publications on the Soviet Arctic and has made 12 visits to the USSR including several to Siberia.

Donald Barnett has been a Senior Analyst at the Joint Navy–NOAA Ice Center (formerly the US Navy Polar Oceanography Center) at Suitland, Maryland for more than 25 years. He is the leading American ice analyst for the Arctic and Antarctic.

William Barr is Professor and Head of the Department of Geography, University of Saskatchewan, Saskatoon, Canada and co-editor of *Soviet Geography and Geology*. He has extensive publications on the history of the exploration of the Arctic and Siberia, and the development of the Northern Sea Route.

William Butler is a Professor of Comparative Law, University of London and Director of the Centre for the Study of Socialist Legal Systems, University of London, United Kingdom, and the leading Western scholar on Soviet legal systems. He is also author of *Northeast Passage* and other major works on Soviet views on the Law of the Sea.

James Clarke is a Researcher in the World Energy Program of the US

Geological Survey, Reston, Virginia and a specialist in assessing undiscovered oil and gas in the USSR.

Ivan Frolov is a leading Soviet sea ice researcher and Head of the Ice Regime Laboratory, Arctic and Antarctic Scientific Research Institute, Leningrad. He was leader of the Scientific-Operational Group during the *Sibir*'s expedition to the Arctic in May-June 1987.

Franklyn Griffiths is Professor of Political Science, University of Toronto and formerly Senior Policy Advisor to Canada's Secretary of State for External Affairs. He is the editor of *Politics of the Northwest Passage* as well as editor and author of various works on Soviet affairs, arms control and arctic international policies.

Christopher Joyner is Associate Professor of Political Science at George Washington University, Washington, DC and a former Senior Research Fellow at the Marine Policy Center, Woods Hole Oceanographic Institution. He is the author of numerous papers on antarctic politics, the Law of the Sea and disarmament.

Robert North is Associate Professor of Geography, University of British Columbia, Canada. He is a specialist in Soviet and East European transport and communications policy on which he has written widely. He is author of *Transport in Western Siberia: Tsarist and Soviet Development.*

Gail Osherenko is a lawyer and researcher at the Institute for Arctic Studies at Dartmouth College, Hanover, New Hampshire and a specialist in environmental, natural resources and Native American law. She was formerly on the staff of the US Department of Justice and the US Council on Environmental Quality.

Willy Østreng is Director of the Fridtjof Nansen Institute, Lysaker, Norway. He has published widely on polar politics, security and strategy, resource management and the Law of the Sea. He is co-author of *Soviet Oil and Security Interests in the Barents Sea* and *International Resource Management.*

Alexei Y. Roginko is a Research Fellow at the Institute of World Economy and International Relations, USSR Academy of Sciences, Moscow. He has published widely on arctic and environmetal issues.

Walter Slipchenko is Director of Circumpolar Affairs for the government of the Northwest Territories in Ottawa, Canada. He was formerly Chief, Circumpolar Affairs Division, Department of Indian and Northern Affairs, where he coordinated Canadian–USSR arctic science exchanges for 20 years.

Gordon Watson is President of East–West Technical Services, Montreal, Canada and a retired Royal Navy officer. He is a naval engineer, linguist and specialist on Soviet arctic engineering and technology.

Oran Young is a political scientist and currently Director of the Institute for Arctic Studies at Dartmouth College, Hanover, New Hampshire. He is an expert on international conflict, international regimes for natural resources and the environment and has published widely on arctic issues for the past 15 years.

List of acronyms

ANSR   Administration of the Northern Sea Route
ATCP   Antarctic Treaty Consultative Party group
AVHRR   Advanced Very High Resolution Radiometer
ASW   anti-submarine warfare
AASRI   Arctic and Antarctic Scientific Research Institute
CANSR   Chief Administration/Northern Sea Route
CASC   Conference on Arctic Security and Cooperation
CITES   Convention on International Trade in Endangered Species
CPSU   Presidium of the Central Executive Committee of the USSR
DEW   Distant Early Warning
EEZ   exclusive economic zone
FESCO   Far Eastern Shipping Company
FRG   Federal Republic of Germany
GIUK   Greenland–Iceland–United Kingdom
IAND   Indian Affairs and Northern Development
ICBM   intercontinental ballistic missiles
IMO   International Maritime Organization
IWC   International Whaling Commission
ICJ   International Court of Justice
IUCH   International Union for Circumpolar Health
IASC   International Arctic Science Committee
LOS   Law of the Sea
LASH   lighter-aboard-ship
NRDC   Natural Resources Defense Council
NATO   North Atlantic Treaty Organization
NSR   Northern Sea Route
NWT   Northwest Territories
SSBN   nuclear-powered ballistic missile submarines
SARSAT   satellite-assisted search and rescue
SDI   Strategic Defense Initiative
START   Strategic Arms Reduction Talks
UNCLOS   Third United Nations Conference on the Law of the Sea
WHO   World Health Organization
WMO   World Meteorological Organization

Foreword

At the approach of the 21st century, the Soviet Union finds itself in a stunning political, economic and cultural transition. The chapters which comprise this book—interdisciplinary investigations into a full range of Soviet interests in maritime Arctic regions—must be read within the context of the pervasive upheaval whose magnitude seems to be building on an almost daily basis. At what point will that wave of political and economic change break upon arctic shores? To what extent has it begun to affect Soviet life and institutions in their northern regions? While answering these questions may be premature, this book is evidence that North American, European and Soviet scholars have already begun grappling with these and related policy issues.

To provide an opportunity for arctic specialists from varying disciplines to conduct research and report on their findings, the Marine Policy Center of Woods Hole Oceanographic Institution has acted as facilitator and coordinator, offering research fellowships, organizing a workshop on relevant topics and building upon that effort through the compilation of the additional research that is reflected in this volume. As the inaugural volume in a new series on polar studies, the following chapters offer the fruits of scholarly research in history, geology, law, environmental affairs, oceanography, political science and transportation studies. In its entirety, it provides not only the historical backdrop for investigating change in the Soviet maritime Arctic but also insights into the up-to-date developments that are contributing directly toward it.

Soviet (and Russian) progress in exploring and developing their maritime arctic regions has outpaced that of the other arctic states. The Russian presence in the Arctic dates back some 500 years. While it may be argued whether the Soviet Union is the pre-eminent geopolitical presence in the regions of the North, it is by no means presumptuous to argue that their physical presence has been the longest-standing, with the greatest commitment of resources. The record of Russian and Soviet achievement in maritime arctic ventures is unparalleled. Not surprisingly, however, the record of this achievement is largely unknown in the West.

The primary contribution of this book, then, is to bring that record to light for Western readers and provide information on the current status of Soviet scientific and technical progress in adapting to the demands of their maritime Arctic. How to structure such an immense undertaking is a tricky business, particularly since it is difficult to identify a single national priority that has driven Russian and Soviet activities. Unlike the Canadian experience, for example, a wide range of national priorities have motivated Russo–Soviet arctic ventures since Tsar Ivan III pushed the borders of his kingdom to the shores of the White Sea in 1478. This multiplicity of driving forces is virtually unique among the arctic states. The significance of various commercial, political, strategic and even cultural factors—at times distinct and at others interwoven—serves to distinguish Russo–Soviet experiences in the Arctic.

The Soviet maritime Arctic confronts with the very forces of nature those who are its natives, those who seek access to its secrets and particularly those who seek to conquer it. And yet, the region is not simply a physical enigma where the sea behaves like land and land like the sea; rather, its significance goes well beyond the realm of the natural sciences. It is a region that is home for more than 1 million people, holds immense potential as a source of hydrocarbon and mineral resources, serves as patrol area for nuclear submarines and remains one the few pristine natural environments remaining on earth. However striking that snapshot may be, it is still a static one which fails to press the point that the maritime regions of the Soviet Arctic are also undergoing pervasive, systemic change. The emergence of a fledgling Soviet environmental consciousness, the sweeping impacts of economic accountability, the expression of ethnic and regional identities in far-flung Soviet republics and a not-so-subtle swing toward multilateralism in Soviet international relations have all begun to leave their imprint on the Arctic.

James M. Broadus
Director, Marine Policy Center
Woods Hole Oceanographic Institution
Woods Hole, Massachusetts

Acknowledgements

This interdisciplinary volume was conceived and initiated during 1986–9 while I was a Guest Investigator and subsequently Research Fellow at the Marine Policy Center of Woods Hole Oceanographic Institution. I am very grateful to Dr James M. Broadus, Director of the Center, for his support and encouragement in allowing me to pursue my professional and personal curiosity regarding the Soviet maritime Arctic. I am also indebted to the United States Coast Guard for not only providing career opportunities to experience polar operations, but also for supporting my fellowship in residence at the Marine Policy Center. The academic experience enabled me to conduct independent research, lecture and collaborate with a host of arctic specialists in North America, Europe and the Soviet Union. In large measure, this book is the product of that collaboration.

Coordinating the contributions of 17 authors from 5 countries became a challenging undertaking. No editor can possibly do this alone and I especially thank Matthew J. LaMourie and Ellen M. Gately of the Center for their outstanding and untiring research and editorial support. Christine Kuethe and Laura T. Praderio provided extensive editorial assistånce, and their efforts markedly enhanced the overall work. The entire graphics team at the Institution provided expert artistic guidance and produced superb illustrations for the book. Ian Stevenson and Jane Evans of Belhaven Press were instrumental in guiding the manuscript to press from their vantage point in the United Kingdom.

My appreciation is extended to Dr Bernard Stonehouse, editor for this new series of polar books, and Dr Terence Armstrong, both of Scott Polar Research Institute, for providing me with wise counsel and continuous encouragement during this endeavor. Finally, my sincere gratitude is passed to the distinguished contributors to this volume — British, Canadian, Norwegian, Soviet and American — for their commitment to this project.

Financial support for the 1987 Soviet Maritime Arctic Workshop at Woods Hole and preparation of this book was provided through a grant from the John D. and Catherine T. MacArthur Foundation. I am grateful for this generous support and additional funding for my work provided by the Marine Policy Center.

Lawson W. Brigham
Commander, US Coast Guard
Woods Hole, Massachusetts
May 1990

1

Introduction

Lawson W. Brigham

The history of Russian and Soviet involvement in the Arctic Ocean spans more than 5 centuries. Owing to this rich history and a vast northern coastline, it is not too surprising that Soviet domestic and international policies play such a significant and influential role in the North. Soviet arctic programs and policies are, with little doubt, inexorably linked to the future of the entire Circumpolar North, a region of increasing political, scientific, environmental and strategic importance. However, the dynamic changes taking place today within the Soviet Union and its republics make any emerging Soviet policies toward the North uncertain at best. The major role of this volume, therefore, is to serve as a bridge between today's uncertainties and the remarkable record of exploration and development that has already been made in the Soviet maritime Arctic.

The entire northern coast of the USSR that borders on the Arctic Ocean — the Soviet maritime Arctic — stretches more than 160 degrees from the Kola peninsula east to the Bering Strait. Big Diomede Island, or Ostrov Ratmanov, can be considered the eastern extremity of this maritime region. A look at any globe from the top, or the view on any azimuthal polar projection (of the Arctic Ocean), will show the true nature of the immense Soviet territory and coastline covered by this expanse. The region also encompasses 11 of 24 of the world's designated time zones. While approximately four-fifths of the Soviet Union lies north of 60 degrees N, a better measure for the purposes of this volume is that more than one half of the Soviet Arctic coast lies above 70 degrees N! This, of course, has a number of significant environmental implications.

The geographical focus of this volume's theme is presented in Figure 1.1, the first in a series of 'base' maps for the region. Illustrated are the main marine transportation routes that make up the 5000 kilometer Northern Sea Route (NSR), and the major bodies of water that border the Soviet Arctic coast. Also shown are the northward flowing Siberian rivers that serve as the major link between the NSR, the interior of Siberia, and the railroads located along the southern tier of the USSR. What is striking in this part of the Arctic is the high level of human activity represented by the major industrial sites and principal ports on the map. It is the scale of this development in the Soviet maritime Arctic, and Siberia as a whole, that is unknown to most Westerners.

In order to gauge the state of modern progress and make informed predictions about the future, one must recognize the historical context within which exploration of the Soviet maritime Arctic has been undertaken. Chapter 2 provides this perspective with a thorough review of Russian, Russian–sponsored, foreign and Soviet exploratory voyages between 1478 and 1941. What is extraordinary is that the Northern Sea Route across the top of Eurasia was in commercial use by the early 1600s. Much of the Russian coast had also been explored and charted with considerable accuracy by 1743. Nothing compares to this legacy in the North American Arctic. The modern era of arctic exploration is likewise represented in Chapter 3 with a detailed account of the 1987 Soviet expedition of the nuclear icebreaker *Sibir'* to the North Pole. The leader of the expedition's hydrometeorological-scientific support group presents an 'insider's view' of the tactical planning that made *Sibir's* voyage a success. The technological and operational aspects of reaching the North Pole by surface ship are striking reminders of present day Soviet polar capabilities.

Throughout the first two chapters, the ever-present force of arctic ice appears consistently as the paramount environmental concern of explorers and traders. Thus, perhaps it is appropriate that the volume's section on the natural arctic environment ('Man and the Natural Setting') begins with an in-depth review of the seasonal and geographical distribution of the Soviet maritime Arctic's dominant physical feature, sea ice. This is followed by an eclectic group of 3 chapters which reintroduces the theme of Soviet man's relationship with the arctic regions. Current issues of environmental conservation in Soviet Arctic seas are raised in Chapter 5, which include the Soviet author's call for an Arctic Action Plan, a cooperative regional framework for protecting the arctic marine, coastal tundra, and forested tundra environments. Concrete progress by the 8 arctic states toward such a framework has already begun to materialize in the form of 2 Consultative Meetings on the Protection of the Arctic Environment, the first held in Rovaniemi, Finland (September 1989) and the second in Yellowknife, Canada (April 1990).

The discovery and exploitation of oil and gas resources in Western Siberia and several discoveries in the Barents and Kara seas have provided much of the impetus behind Soviet activities in their maritime Arctic during the past

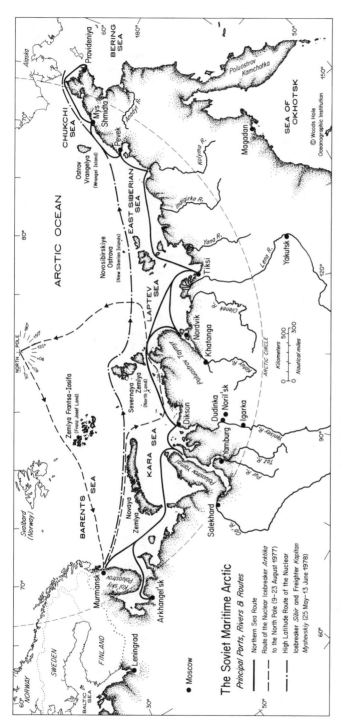

Figure 1.1 Principal ports, rivers, and routes of the Soviet maritime Arctic.

3

two decades. Chapter 7 provides profiles of the subsurface geology of those regions of the Soviet maritime Arctic where seismic surveys have been conducted. While many areas of the continental shelves have yet to be adequately surveyed by petroleum geologists, there remains the promise of new oil and gas discoveries. For example, the characteristic geology of the onshore areas of Western Siberia (particularly the Yamal and Gydanskiy peninsulas), when extended northward into the Kara Sea, strengthens the likelihood of potentially rich offshore gas deposits in that basin. Additionally, gas and oil deposits have been found in the Barents Sea and it is likely that new discoveries will be found in other offshore basins to the east. The harshness of the environment, extraordinarily high costs of development and overall global energy markets will all, as a matter of course, interplay and drive Soviet willingness to exploit future arctic finds. Western partners have, and will in the future, provide technology and much-needed capital.

'Man and the Natural Setting' also includes a thought-provoking chapter that accesses the significance of intrinsic northern identifications within the context of the Russian national identity and in terms of Soviet progress in the Arctic. Specifically, to what extent are Russian and Soviet accomplishments in the Arctic a function of cultural attachments to their northern landscape that make it easier for them to persevere and succeed in extreme polar conditions? Is that a valid hypothesis or might we attribute these Russian/ Soviet accomplishments to other, more tangible factors, such as the momentum of Soviet industrialization or coordinated plans to 'control' development in the Arctic? Chapter 6 speaks to these and other culturally related questions.

Marine transportation technology and the management of Soviet Arctic shipping become the predominant themes throughout the middle of the volume within the section entitled 'Challenges of Arctic Marine and River Transport'. Chapter 8 traces the evolution of modern Soviet icebreakers and projects the course of the USSR polar fleet — acknowledged widely as the world's largest — through the 1990s. Technological advancement, adaptation to unusual environments and technology transfer for the West have each played significant roles in the development of this diverse fleet during the past 4 decades. Despite the proven success of recent design improvements in polar icebreakers and icebreaking cargo carriers, it will remain difficult for the Soviets to attain the goal of year-round navigation across the entire Soviet maritime Arctic. While certain key sectors of the Northern Sea Route are maintained on a year-round basis (the best example being the route across the Barents and Kara seas to Dudinka), other sectors are not (the Laptev and East Siberian seas), even with substantial icebreaker support. The focus of the topic shifts from technology to management in Chapter 9. A straightforward critical analysis of the current organization charged with administering the Northern Sea Route is more than subtle proof that openness is penetrating the Soviet bureaucracy. The Soviet author chronicles many of the organizational changes that have influenced the effectiveness of the Administration of the Northern Sea Route (ANSR) since its establishment in 1970. Furthermore, many of the problems that

4

remain to be resolved before the promise of year-round arctic navigation can be made truly viable are highlighted. Despite these obstacles, however, the chapter concludes with a powerful statement that it is now time for a 'full payoff' of what the Soviet government has invested in the development of the NSR.

Is that payoff likely to appear soon? Chapter 10, a review of the 1986–87 Soviet Arctic shipping season, provides the most credible glimpse that can be found outside (and many would say inside) the USSR. Noted in this comprehensive review are the political and technical developments which may serve to increase overall NSR traffic volumes in future years, even if natural conditions worsen along many of the NSR's key sectors. The concluding chapters review the specifics of three important components of the overall Soviet Arctic marine transportation system: namely, operational icebreaking techniques, arctic port facilities and Siberian river transport. Several significant points come to light in Chapter 11, including the notion that Soviet ice specialists apparently are much more familiar with polar ship design work done in the West than Westerners are knowledgeable about Soviet problems and achievements in the Arctic. The author not only presents an array of icebreaking techniques used in Soviet ice convoys but also discusses how Soviet port managers make rational use of the maritime Arctic's prevailing natural material — ice — to serve their structural needs. Chapter 12 ends the marine transportation section with evidence suggesting that the effects of *perestroika* have begun to impact arctic shipping. The high costs of Siberian river operations and those characterizing the NSR have historically served to limit freight growth rates throughout the Soviet Arctic. In 1989, river traffic volumes started to fall as shippers, now faced with the realities of President Gorbachev's *khrozrachet* (economic accountability) policies, have become 'less prodigal' in their ordering. Sea traffic costs in the Arctic Ocean, normally higher than river costs, are also beginning to drive freight away from the NSR as both shippers and carriers attempt to justify the total costs of their transport operations. Nevertheless, the overall high level of marine and river transport in the Soviet Arctic is remarkable considering the severity and extent of seasonal sea ice along the NSR. Soviet technical and operational innovations in arctic shipping, including such unique events as nuclear icebreaker voyages to the North Pole (see Figure 1.2), are among the most noteworthy achievements in modern arctic history.

The final section of the volume is a collection of 5 chapters that address various strategic, legal and geopolitical interests of the USSR in the Arctic Ocean. The first concentrates on the geostrategic conditions of deterrence in the Barents Sea, concluding that this sea serves both strategic and defense purposes for the Soviet Union. Natural features of the Barents, such as the winter ice cover, restrictive depths and the presence of icebergs, present unique and formidable operational challenges to the submarines of the Soviet Navy's Northern Fleet. These constraints may force submarines to choose particular routes through the shallow reaches of the region, thereby making them potentially vulnerable to detection. A key question arises amid this analysis: do these same constraints make more preferable the stationing of submarines in the central Arctic Ocean rather than the shallow seas along

5

Figure 1.2 Soviet crewmember from the nuclear icebreaker *Sibir'* sets an anchor post in multi-year ice, at the North Pole, May 1987 (*Soviet Life*).

the Soviet northern coast? Whatever the answer is to this specific question, it is clear that the entire Arctic Ocean is an important military and security theater for the Soviet Union.

The legal regime of the Soviet maritime Arctic has for many years been construed (and frequently misunderstood) in the West as a curious blend of historic doctrines and statutes often at odds with international norms. However, a review of the current situation (Chapter 14) suggests that Soviet legislative enactments which indicate the balance of political, economic, legal, strategic and other interests embodied in the Law of the Sea (LOS) Convention are largely acceptable to the Soviet Union. This linkage to the LOS Convention has significant implications for all arctic rim states and for future development in the Arctic Ocean. Evidence shows that the more extreme doctrinal characteristics of the legal status of the seas north of the Soviet coast, such as the use of sector lines extending to the North Pole as state boundaries, do not enjoy support today in Soviet law or state practice. The USSR has adopted a body of international and national legal rules regarding environmental protection and the exclusive economic zone that are perhaps more consistent with future uses of the maritime Arctic. However, some key legal issues remain unresolved such as the right of innocent passage through waters landward of Soviet straight baselines.

Prior to 1987 it was widely believed that the Soviet Union considered the Arctic much too sensitive, primarily because of national security, to be an appropriate forum for international cooperation. This view has changed swiftly and in some sense radically since President Gorbachev's speech on arctic affairs in Murmansk on 1 October 1987 (see Appendix I). But was the original notion of a reluctant USSR arctic partner a myth or reality? Is there a legacy from which future cooperation can be built? Chapters 15 and 16 provide substantial support pointing to such a legacy, noting that the USSR has pursued a host of bilateral and multilateral arctic exchanges and agreements over the past 7 decades. Canada and the USSR, as one example, have steadfastly pursued the promise of bilateral cooperation in arctic sciences since the 1970s. During a flurry of activity between 1984 and 1987, 12 Canadian and 12 Soviet delegations were exchanged. They concentrated on 4 broad themes: geoscience and arctic petroleum, northern and arctic environments, northern construction, and ethnology and education. A significant protocol was signed in 1987 extending and expanding scientific and technical cooperation. Finally in November 1989, a mature and broad agreement was signed that heralds a new era of Canadian-Soviet relations in the Arctic (see Appendix III).

For many decades the USSR has belonged to conservation regimes involving fur seals and polar bears, the management of the Svalbard archipelago (the 1920 Treaty of Spitsbergen), and an array of broader multilateral regimes applicable to the Arctic Ocean (an example being the International Whaling Commission of 1946). Recent bilateral initiatives, particularly those related to the protection of the marine environment, have been signed with Norway, Sweden, Finland, Canada and the United States. Thus, in many respects, the Soviet record of cooperation in the Arctic — in terms of both bilateral and multilateral agreements — is perhaps indistinguishable from other states with polar interests.

A final chapter complements the geopolitical aspects of the Soviet maritime Arctic with a comparison of Soviet arctic and antarctic policies. While the USSR has multiple polar interests in both the Arctic and Antarctic, there are apparent, substantial contradictions in Soviet approaches to the 2 polar regions. In Antarctica the Soviet Union does not recognize the validity of other states' claims (as is also the case for the United States); it favors absolute freedom and complete access on the continent, in support of the Antarctic Treaty. Soviet policy on scientific activities in the Arctic Ocean, however, is governed by a restrictive consent system within the Exclusive Economic Zone. In Antarctica the USSR also insists that all circumpolar waters are high seas with complete access to fishing and shipping opportunities. By contrast, Soviet policy in the Arctic Ocean favors maintaining a nationalistic regime to regulate individual arctic states' coastal regions. Such disparate policies are perhaps inherent (and unavoidable) when a large polar state such as the USSR attempts to maintain an influential role in controlling its multi-faceted interests. Not to be lost in such a comparison is the considerable synergism of scientific effort and operational expertise which is an outgrowth of Soviet arctic and antarctic endeavors.

The issues framed and interpretations presented throughout the chapters of this volume will hopefully stimulate speculation and debate about the future of the Soviet maritime Arctic. Like Mikhail Gorbachev's historic speech in Murmansk, the contributors raise many more questions than they answer. These questions are woven into this interdisciplinary and international review that, at first glance, lacks a certain homogeneity. However, one strong and consistent theme is apparent throughout — Soviet concerns in their maritime Arctic represent an amalgam of key interests including economic, environmental, resource, political, cultural and strategic. It is extremely difficult to select a single interest as predominant to the exclusion of the others. Whereas in past decades national security interests might have dominated Soviet actions and attitudes in the Arctic Ocean, this does not appear to be the situation today.

The fundamental purpose of this volume is to improve Western understanding of the marine regions of the Soviet Arctic. It provides a broad background from which one might frame answers to key questions that are likely to arise in the future: what is the overall significance of this remote and often harsh marine area of the globe? What are the factors which may affect Soviet decision-making with regard to the Arctic Ocean? Is there a future economic potential for the Soviet offshore Arctic and, if so, what part will foreign investment and technology play in its development? How will the USSR and the Russian Republic balance the competing interests of the environment with the necessary development of Siberian resources? Can the Northern Sea Route become a viable, international waterway? The pressing political changes in the Soviet Union during the coming decade will surely give rise to a broad range of surprising prospects for the Arctic Ocean.

Part I
Exploration: past and present

2

The Arctic Ocean in Russian history to 1945

William Barr

The most compelling aspect of Russian involvement in the Arctic Ocean and its peripheral seas is that it spans five centuries. As early as 1478, the armies of Ivan III conquered Novgorod and expanded the territories of Muscovy to the White and Barents seas, giving Russia its first access to a sea coast. By the end of the 15th century, travel from the White Sea to Western Europe was standard practice for Muscovite merchants and diplomats. The protracted wars between Russia and Sweden eliminated the Baltic as a transit route for Russians and by the mid-16th century the White Sea Route was well established.

Exploration in the sixteenth and seventeenth centuries

By mid-century Russian craft were operating at least as far east as Ostrov Vaygach. In June 1556, Stephen Burrough of the English Muscovy Company called at Kol'skiy Zaliv and found 20 Russian vessels about to sail to the waters east of the Pechora River in order to fish and hunt walrus. Reaching Ostrov Vaygach, Burrough heard from the local Nentsy and from the Russians of the existence of the Ob' River farther east (Belov 1956; Neatby 1973). A few decades later, when Willem Barents sailed north in 1594 along the coast of Novaya Zemlya to Mys Zhelaniya, he noted the wreckage of ships and grave crosses at many points indicating that the Russians had been there before him (Belov 1956:82).

By about this same date a commercial route had been established via the

Arctic Ocean to the booming fur-trading center of Mangazeya on the Taz River in Western Siberia. M.I. Belov (1956) has left us a traveller's description of the Mangazeya route, compiled by a trader called Leontiy Ivanov Stubin (nicknamed Plekhan) who travelled the route in 1601. From the mouth of the Severnaya Dvina the route ran coastwise, through Yugorskiy Shar, into the Kara Sea to the west coast of the Yamal peninsula. To avoid the difficult ice conditions, the shallow-draft vessels crossed the peninsula travelling first along the Mutnaya and then the Zeleya rivers, with an intervening portage between them (Belov 1956:110–11).

Use of the Mangazeya Route was officially prohibited by Tsar Mikhail Fedorovich in 1616 and 1619. This was, in part, a defense measure against foreign interlopers and, in part, a means to greater control of the trade. The overland and river routes to Mangazeya could be controlled (and taxed) more easily by the government.

This same period witnessed the phenomenal Russian overland expansion eastward from the Urals to the Pacific. Yermak crossed the Urals and conquered the Tatar kingdom of Kuchum in 1582 (Lantzeff and Pierce 1973:95). In the summer of 1641, a detachment of Cossacks led by Ivan Yur'yev Moskvitin descended the Okhota to the Pacific. The desire for furs, extracted in the form of *yasak* or tribute from the indigenous peoples, was the driving force behind this phenomenal eastern surge. The routes used were mainly river routes — by boat in summer and by sledge in winter. Nevertheless, during or shortly after this eastern expansion, attempts were apparently made to utilize the central section of the Northern Sea Route around Poluostrov Taymyr as a commercial route.

In September 1940 a survey party found a wide range of artefacts (copper pots, silver coins, rings, crosses, beads, an axe, scissors and a rusted musket) on one of the Ostrova Faddeya. The following spring the same party found the remains of a log hut on the mainland coast in Zaliv Simsa (Dolgikh 1948:117; Okladnikov 1951:7; Barr 1974), along with a similar range of artefacts and some human bones. In 1945, both sites were excavated by an expedition led by A.P. Okladnikov. He recovered a remarkable collection of artifacts including parts of a boat, firearms, bows and arrows, substantial numbers of cloth fragments, leather garments and footwear and 3,482 Russian coins. Most importantly, both sites revealed abundant remains of furs: over half were arctic fox and most of the rest, sable.

Okladnikov interpreted the artifacts as evidence that a seaborne expedition coasting along the arctic coast had been stranded either by shipwreck or by the vessel becoming beset; the log hut was assumed to be the winter quarters of the expedition. It was clearly a Russian expedition and, based on the dates on the coins, Okladnikov (1951:28) placed the date of the event around 1619. Since, by this date, Russians had not yet penetrated east of Taymyr by the overland route, Okladnikov argued that the expedition had been eastward bound and had rounded Mys Chelyuskina. This meant that the nameless Russian expedition had passed this crucial point on the Northern Sea Route some 260 years before Nordenskiöld's expedition in *Vega*.

V.A. Troitskiy (1973) carried out some further excavations at both sites from 1971 to 1972. Based on his finds and some logical arguments, he refutes the idea that the expedition had been eastward bound. Most significantly, he questioned why a trading expedition heading east would have been transporting such a large quantity of furs. He argues that the expedition occurred around 1640, by which time the Russian occupation of the Lena Basin was well established. In his view the expedition that was shipwrecked had been bound westward from the Lena to European Russia.

Interestingly, there are only vague references in the literature to such an expedition. As Belov (1969a:109) has suggested, the reason that it is not better documented was that prohibition of the use of the sea route to Mangazeya was not unique. As the 17th century advanced, travel by traders and hunters to the Anabar, Ostrov Begichev, and the Yana, Indigirka and Kolyma basins was prohibited to prevent private trading (thus reducing the chances of extracting *yasak*). Similar prohibitions applied to overland routes. Repeated reminders of these travel restrictions in the literature suggest that infractions were common. It seems natural that clandestine attempts were made to circumvent these restrictive measures by using the Northern Sea Route. Certainly participants in such voyages would not wish to advertise their activities. Thus the archaeological record, as well as hints and rumors in the archival record, indicate that in the early 17th century Russian seafarers were making determined efforts to round Mys Chelyuskina, possibly in both directions. There is still no solid evidence, however, that they were successful.

By the mid-17th century there was already substantial use farther east of the Lena–Kolyma section of the Northern Sea Route. In 1633, the year of the founding of Yakutsk, a group of Cossacks, led by Il'ya Perfirev, descended the Lena to the delta (Belov 1956:150; Lantzeff and Pierce 1973:184; Armstrong 1965:23). Here the party split into two: one sailing west to the mouth of the Olenek, the other east to the mouth of the Yana. By 1643, the entire coast from the mouth of the Olenek to the mouth of the Kolyma had been explored. By 1645, the first trading vessels were plying between the Kolyma and Zhigansk on the middle Lena, and over the next few decades there was a regular movement of shipping along this central section of the Northern Sea Route.

By the 1680s, however, voyages between the Kolyma and the Lena had dropped off drastically and by the end of the century had nearly ceased. The cause was, in part, a shift in the emphasis of the fur trade from the northern river basins to more southerly ones such as the Penzhina, Gizhiga and Okhota and to Kamchatka (Belov 1956:181). These areas, of course, were better served by the more southerly overland routes and hence use of the Northern Sea Route declined.

The final chapter in this story of developments along the Northern Sea Route in the mid-17th century concerns the controversy surrounding Semen Dezhnev's voyage eastward from the Kolyma, through the Bering Strait and south into the Bering Sea in the summer of 1648. Scholars such as J. Burney (1819), F.A. Golder (1914) and L. Neatby (1973) claim for a variety of reasons that Dezhnev could not have passed through the Bering Strait but reached the Anadyr' Basin (his final destination) by some overland route from the arctic coast to the north. Despite these arguments, the evidence presented by scholars such as R.H. Fisher (1981) in support of Deshnev's voyage through the Bering Strait is all but unassailable.

Deshnev's voyage began in the summer of 1648, when seven vessels under his command started down the Kolyma from Nizhnekolymsk bound for the Anadyr' basin which, according to rumors, was rich in fur. Running into a storm east of Chaunskaya Guba, four vessels were driven ashore and wrecked and the survivors mostly killed by the Chukchi people. Around 1 September the three remaining vessels reached 'Bol'shoy Kamenniy Nos' (Mys Dezhneva), the easternmost point of Eurasia. One of the three ships was wrecked on the cape and its crew distributed between the other two. Coasting south in the Bering Sea, the two ships became separated in foul weather; Dezhnev's vessel finally landed at Mys Olyutorskiy, south of Anadyr'skiy Zaliv. From there, Dezhnev and 24 companions travelled overland north to the Anadyr', where they wintered. Thus, in 1648 Russian vessels coasted east from the Kolyma and passed through the Bering Strait into the Pacific. By the mid-17th century, therefore, a very considerable portion of the Northern Sea Route had already been explored by Russian seafarers; attempts were even being made to travel the middle section of the route from the Lena to the Yenisey around Taymyr. The available evidence of such attempts, however, is rather vague and open to a variety of interpretations.

The early eighteenth century

A rather abortive operation, aimed at exploring Chukotka and Kamchatka in the period 1716–20 and known as the Great Kamchatka Command, set the scene for an even more ambitious operation: the First Kamchatka Expedition of 1725–30, organized by direct orders from Peter the Great. The main objective of the expedition was to determine the geography of the Bering Strait area since the documentation of Dezhnev's voyage was still filed in the obscurity of archives in Yakutsk or Irkutsk. The leader of the new expedition was the Dane, Vitus Bering. By July of 1728, after 3 years of travel and preparations, Bering and his companions were ready to put to sea from Nizhnekamchatsk in the ship *Sv. Gavriil*. Coasting north Bering discovered St. Lawrence Island and pushed farther north toward the Bering Strait. At 67° 18'N, 167°W, well north of the strait, indeed in the mouth of Kotzebue Sound and only some 130 kilometers south of Point Hope, Alaska, Bering decided to turn back. Neither on the outward or homeward passage did he sight the Alaskan mainland, although he did sight and name the Diomede Islands. Thus, the existence of the Bering Strait still remained contestable; the 2 continents might conceivably be joined at a latitude farther north than that reached by *Sv. Gavriil*, and Bering could not have known positively that he was in the Arctic Ocean. In the summer of 1728, Bering made a second rather half-hearted attempt at sailing east to locate the Alaskan coast — without success. By 1 March 1730, he was back in St. Petersburg.

It was not until 2 years later that Russians first sighted Alaska. They were Ivan Fedorov and Mikhail Gvozdev, again using Bering's *Sv. Gavriil* as part of a military expedition aimed primarily at subduing the Chukchi. The vessel reached Mys Dezhneva on 5 August 1732; heading east, Fedorov and Gvozdev again sighted the Diomede Islands and also King Island. On 21 August 1732, they dropped anchor off Cape Prince of Wales and coasted east to the vicinity of Nome before turning back.

The Great Northern Expedition: 1733–43

The next chapter in the history of exploration of the Russian Arctic was an undertaking such as had never been seen before and perhaps not since then: the Great Northern Expedition of 1733–43. Once again under the command of Vitus Bering, it was on a vastly greater scale than his first expedition. It consisted of 7 independent detachments (not counting the scientific and support teams), totalling some 977 men. Its objectives were to investigate the feasibility of a Northern Sea Route, to explore the American coast, and to reconnoiter a sea route from Kamchatka to Japan (Belov 1956).

Space does not permit a detailed description of the activities of the five detachments that were dispatched to explore and chart the various sections of the Northern Sea Route. Suffice it to say that the activities of these various naval parties under such leaders as Stepan Malygin, Dmitriy Leon'tevich Ovtsyn, Fedor Minin, Vasiliy Pronchishchev, Kharitons Prokop'yevich Laptev, Dmitriy Yakovlevich Laptev, Semen Chelyuskin and Petr Lasinius were quite remarkable and deserve to be better known. What emerges clearly from the reports of the Great Northern Expedition is that, along the entire arctic coast, ice conditions in the period 1733–43 were vastly worse than at present and significantly worse than a century earlier. The different vessels were repeatedly blocked by ice and were forced to winter in the Arctic or return to their starting points and try again the following year. Thus it took 3 years for one detachment to sail from the White Sea to the Ob'; 3 years for another detachment to sail from the Ob' to the Yenisey. For 2 years yet another detachment was unable to get beyond Mys Sterlegova while attempting to sail from the Yenisey eastward past Taymyr to the Khatanga. One detachment, in 8 years of effort, was unable to reach Mys Chelyuskina by sea in trying to sail from the Lena west to the Yenisey. Here the crucial gap, from just east of Mys Chelyuskina to Mys Sterlegova, was filled in by groups travelling by dog sledge. Semen Chelyuskin had the honor of reaching the cape named after him, the most northerly tip of Eurasia. The detachment entrusted with sailing from the Lena to the Kolyma took 5 years to achieve that task, while 2 attempts at pushing east from the Kolyma were foiled by ice at Mys Bol'shoy Baranov.

Almost all the parties involved endured extreme hardships, and there were numerous deaths from scurvy. At least 2 detachment leaders, Lieutenant Vasiliy Pronchishchev and Petr Lasinius, died of scurvy as did

Pronchishchev's wife, Mariya Pronchishcheva, one of the earliest female arctic explorers to lose her life. From 1735 to 1736, 37 men of Lasinius's group of 52 died of scurvy while wintering at the mouth of the Khara Ublakh, just east of Tiksi. Other groups mutinied, and 2 officers, Pavlov and Murav'yev, had to face a court martial.

The Great Northern Expedition represented a remarkable achievement in terms of organization, perseverance and courage. It resulted in an outstanding compilation of knowledge. The entire arctic coast was surveyed and charted from Arkhangel'sk to Mys Bol'shoy Baranov, and Dmitriy Laptev's final overland trip from Nizhnekolymsk to the Anadyr' contributed extremely valuable information about the Chukchi, quite apart from the magnificent and probably better-known achievements of the Pacific detachment under Bering and Chirikov. In tangible terms, the expedition produced 62 maps and charts of the arctic coast and of Kamchatka, generally of a remarkably high standard. It is interesting to contrast the general chart of the Russian Arctic resulting from the great Northern Expedition (published in 1746) with what was known of the arctic coast of North America at the same date. By that time, William Baffin's voyage into Baffin Bay had been largely forgotten or discredited, and the only part of the Arctic reliably known and charted was Hudson Bay and Strait; the farthest north point known with any precision was Repulse Bay, reached by Christopher Middleton in 1742. Everything north and west from there to the Bering Strait was a gaping void.

In terms of the history of the Northern Sea Route, however, the Great Northern Expedition was a two-edged sword. The charts, soundings and sailing directions compiled during the expedition proved invaluable to later navigators. The endless problems encountered by all the detachments due to ice, however, and the failure, despite repeated attempts, to round Poluostrov Taymyr or to travel along the arctic coast of Chukotka, led to the conclusion in government circles that navigating the Northern Sea Route was totally impracticable.

Not surprisingly, there followed a period of inactivity in exploration. In the 1760s, however, M.V. Lomonosov, in one of the most daring endeavors in arctic experience, attempted repeatedly to sail across the Pole. Lomonosov was a strong proponent of the development of the Northern Sea Route and also believed firmly in the existence of an open polar sea. In 1764 he submitted his plan for sailing across the Pole to the Admiralty College (Belov 1956:363); it was approved by them and by Catherine the Great, and preparations began under a shroud of secrecy. The expedition commander was Vasiliy Yakovlevich Chichagov. In 1764, 6 vessels established an advance base at Bellsund in Svalbard and a year later the 3 expedition ships sailed north. They were blocked by ice at 80° 26'N and were forced to retreat. The following year Chichagov reached 80° 30'N before being forced to withdraw. Perhaps the most interesting aspect of this entire operation was its remarkable similarity 7 years later to John Constantine Phipps's efforts aboard *Racehorse* and *Carcass*. Mounted by the British Admiralty in the same area and with the same objectives, it met with no greater success.

The closing decades of the 18th century and the opening years of the 19th century brought no further attempts at exploring the Northern Sea Route *per se*, but a number of important undertakings were mounted, both by the Russian Navy and by private individuals, aimed at exploring various offshore islands or at investigating rumors of offshore land masses. For example, one thinks of Lieutenant Fedor Rozmyslov's expedition which surveyed Matochkin Shar, the strait bisecting Novaya Zemlya from 1768 to 1769; the trader Ivan Lyakhov's discovery and extensive exploration of the Novosibirskiye Ostrova from 1770 to 1774; Stepan Andreyev's journeys north across the ice from the mouth of the Kolyma to search for 'Bol'shaya Zemlya', a search which resulted in the discovery of the Medvezh'i Ostrova, during 1763–4; Lieutenant I. Leont'yev's more reliable survey of those same islands from 1769 to 1771; Yakov Sannikov's discovery of Ostrov Faddeyevskiy and Novaya Sibir' in the Novosibirskiye Ostrova during 1805–6; and finally, M.M. Gedenstrom's government-sponsored scientific expedition to survey all aspects of the Novosibirskiye Ostrova over the period 1808–12.

During this same period, one area of the arctic mainland also was receiving considerable attention, namely Chukotka, in particular the troublesome gap on the map of its arctic coast. In 1762, the trader Nikita Shalaurov (with the blessings of the Senate), having taken 3 years to reach the Kolyma from the Lena, tried sailing east from the mouth of the Kolyma but was foiled by ice at Chaunskaya Guba. In 1764 (now with government funding), he again sailed from the Kolyma in his ships *Vera*, *Nadezhda*, and *Lyubov'* and disappeared. The Chukchi later told of finding the expedition's wintering site, littered with skeletons.

Captain James Cook's foray into the Chukchi Sea in *Resolution* and *Discovery* in 1778, when he penetrated as far west as Mys Shmidta, provoked Catherine the Great into mounting an expedition finally to explore Chukotka. She recruited Joseph Billings, who had been with Cook as Assistant Astronomer; second in command was Gavriil Andreyevich Sarychev. When an initial attempt at sailing east from the Kolyma was blocked by ice at Mys Bol'shoy Baranov in 1787, Billings decided to explore the coast overland, starting from the Bering Strait. After a side trip in 1790 into the Gulf of Alaska, the following year, Billings, with a party of 7 men, was dropped off at Bukhta Lavrentiya (Belov 1956:428). In view of the reputation of the Chukchi, this was an extremely brave undertaking. From here Billings travelled west overland across Chukotka, reaching Nizhnekolymsk on 22 February 1792. An independent party under Gilev, travelling by reindeer, skirted the coast from Mys Dezhneva to Chaunskaya Guba; thus closing the final gap in the map of the arctic littoral with some degree of accuracy.

Just as in the case of the British Navy, cessation of hostilities against Napoleon in 1815 meant that a vast number of ships, officers and men became redundant. The Russian Admiralty tried to take up some of the slack in two main directions: circumnavigatory voyages aimed at exploration and scientific work; and arctic exploration. Two of the circumnavigatory operations combined both objectives, that is they also included an arctic component. Thus, in July 1816, O.E. Kotzebue passed the Bering Strait, northward bound in *Ryurik*, in an attempt at the Northwest Passage. Having discovered and explored the sound now named after him, he was prevented by ice from pushing farther north and retreated south to continue his circumnavigation. Similarly in 1820 and 1821, M.N. Vasil'yev and G.S. Shishmarev in *Otkrytiye* and *Blagonamerennyy* penetrated into the Chukchi Sea and each season pushed some distance along both the Chukchi and Alaskan coasts before being blocked by ice. In both years Vasil'yev penetrated a few tens of kilometers east of Icy Cape, Cook's farthest point north on the Alaskan coast. These naval operations aimed purely at arctic exploration coincide quite strikingly in terms of time with John Franklin's and especially William Edward Parry's efforts in the North American Arctic.

During Gedenstrom's expedition to the Novosibirskiye Ostrova, there had been several 'sightings' of land north of that archipelago, especially by Yakov Sannikov, a trader/trapper who had been roaming the islands since the turn of the century. These sightings, as well as persistent rumors of a landmass north of Chukotka, led the Admiralty to mount 2 major expeditions in the early 1820s; between them they were to survey the coast from the Lena to Bering Strait and also search for new lands. One expedition was led by Lieutenant F.P. Anzhu, the other by Lieutenant F.P. Vrangel'. Anzhu's work focused on the Novosibirskiye Ostrova. During the three winters of 1820–3, Anzhu and his companions, travelling by dog sledge, carried out a thorough survey of the Novosibirskiye Ostrova and made at least three attempts at searching for the alleged landmass north of the archipelago — all without success. A detached party, led by P.I. Il'in, surveyed the mainland coast from the Yana to the Olenek, including a traverse of the Lena delta.

Lieutenant Vrangel' was even more active during the same period; his mandate was to survey the Chukchi coast east from Mys Shelagskiy and to investigate rumors of land to the north. Over the period 1821–3, using a system of support sledges and cached depots similar to that which was to be used by Robert Peary in his attempts at the Pole some 90 years later, Vrangel' resurveyed the Medvezh'i Ostrova, surveyed the coast east to Kolyuchinskaya Guba and made determined efforts to locate the land alleged to lie north of Mys Shelagskiy. In 1823, prompted by local reports that land was visible to the north from Mys Yakan in clear weather, Vrangel' struck north until stopped by open water; he was then only 25 kilometers from the southwest tip of Ostrov Vrangelya. Altogether Vrangel's contribution was a major one: he had finally surveyed the last gap on the map of the arctic littoral and he had honed the techniques of exploration using dog sledges to a very fine art. When he set off from Nizhnekolymsk in February 1823, his expedition consisted of 21 dog sledges!

During this period the Admiralty also invested considerable time and effort in further explorations of Novaya Zemlya. Grigoriy Pospelov's expedition aboard *Pchela* had resulted in the mapping of the coast from Kostin Shar to Matochkin Shar, but the charts of the island were still very inaccurate and incomplete. Nothing whatever was known of the east coast. In 1819, to remedy the situation, the Admiralty dispatched Lieutenant

Andrey Petrovich Lazarev in the brig *Novaya Zemlya*. Lieutenant Fedor Petrovich Litke was also dispatched to mount three expeditions between 1821 and 1824. Both Lazarev and Litke were hampered severely by difficult ice conditions. However, Litke was able to survey the west coast as far north as Mys Nassau and to resurvey Matochkin Shar.

Subsequent expeditions to Novaya Zemlya, namely those of P.K. Pakhtusuv, in 1832–5, the Academy of Sciences led by K.M. Baer in 1837 and A.K. Tsivol'ka, 1838–9, all encountered very difficult ice conditions, but all made some contribution to charting the coasts or studying the interior (notably Baer's expedition in the latter case). Most significantly, Pakhtusov circumnavigated the south island in 1833, but nobody had managed to sail around the north island. These gains had been made at great cost: Tsivol'ka and eight of his men died of scurvy during their wintering at Krestovaya Guba between 1838 and 1839.

The remainder of the century is noteworthy as a period of almost total inactivity in Russian exploration of the Northern Sea Route. It is fair to note, though, that major advances were being made exploring and surveying the northern interior, especially by A.F. Middendorf, A.L. Chekanovskiy and I.D. Cherskiy. Two Russian stations of the International Polar Year 1882–3, namely those at Malyye Karmakulyy on Novaya Zemlya and on Ostrov Sagastyr' in the Lena Delta, were also active at this time (Barr 1985).

Northern Sea Route: foreign endeavors

In spite of Russian inactivity at this time, however, foreign endeavors led to a vast increase in knowledge of the Northern Sea Route. The first of these foreign contributors was Captain Henry Kellett who discovered Ostrov Geral'da and sighted Ostrov Vrangelya while searching for the missing Franklin expedition in his ship *Herald* in 1849 (Seemann 1853:114).

In 1862 in the west, Mikhail Konstantinovich Sidorov, a Siberian mine-owner, convinced of the importance of developing the Northern Sea Route in order to encourage the development of Western Siberia, sponsored a Russian-named expedition. Pavel Kruzenstern, led the expedition and sailed from Arkhangel'sk for the Yenisey in the schooner *Yermak* in August 1862. The vessel was crushed by the ice in the Kara Sea and its crew barely managed to make it to shore on Poluostrov Yamal. This disaster only strengthened the official opposition to Sidorov's schemes. Litke, now president of the Imperial Russian Geographical Society, had refused to support Sidorov's project and wrote that a sea link with the mouths of the West Siberian rivers 'belongs in the realm of impossible things' (Pinkhenson 1962:68). K.M. Baer, now an academician, who had earlier hung the label 'ice-cellar' on the Kara Sea, also ridiculed Sidorov's efforts.

At this point the rather unlikely figure of Captain Joseph Wiggins entered the picture. An experienced, widely read English sea captain, Wiggins was convinced that the Kara Sea ought to be navigable in summer (Johnson 1907). In the summer of 1874 he took the steamer *Diana* into Obskaya Guba but made no contact with shore. The next year (1875) in the little fishing sloop *Whim* he was forced to turn back owing to bad weather near Ostrov Kolguyev. But that same year, in collaboration with Sidorov and A.E. Nordenskiöld, Wiggins took the steamer *Pröven* as far east as Dikson at the mouth of the Yenisey and ascended the river in a motor launch.

Funded by foreign capital, there followed a period of commercial navigation to the mouths of the Ob' and Yenisey Rivers. In 1876, backed by British and Siberian investors (the latter the merchant A.M. Sibiryakov), Wiggins took the steamer *Thames* to the mouth of the Yenisey. The same year Nordenskiöld, also with Sibiryakov's backing, took the steamer *Ymer* and a cargo of freight to Gol'Chikha at the mouth of the Yenisey. In 1877 the steamer *Luise* took a cargo from Germany and England to the mouth of the Ob', then ascended the river to Tobol'sk. And in 1878, Wiggins's steamer *Warkworth* successfully reached Obskaya Guba where it transshipped its cargo to barges. The same year a German steamer *Neptune* hauled a cargo to the mouth of the Ob'. These efforts would continue, with increasing momentum and with Wiggins heavily involved, until the end of the century.

Exploration and scientific efforts also were advanced substantially through foreign initiatives during this period (see Figure 2.1). In August 1873, the Austro-Hungarian North Pole Expedition aboard *Tegetthoff*, under the command of Karl Weyprecht and Julius Payer, discovered the archipelago of Franz Josef Land (Payer 1876); the following year a sledge party led by Payer explored a considerable part of the archipelago. Farther east, George W. De Long, Commander of the American ship *Jeannette*, discovered the remote islands of Ostrov Zhannetty and Ostrov Genrietty in 1881 while drifting northwestward with the ice from the vicinity of Ostrov Vrangelya. After the ship was crushed, its crew discovered Ostrov Bennetta while en route to the Lena delta by sledge and boat (De Long 1884). That same year parties from 2 vessels searching for *Jeannette*, *Rodgers* and *Corwin* made the first landings on Ostrov Vrangelya and also on Ostrov Geral'da. And finally during 1878–9 Nordenskiöld made the first transit of the Northern Sea Route from west to east in *Vega* (Nordenskiöld 1881); he wintered en route at Kolyuchinskaya Guba. The steamer *Lena*, accompanying *Vega* as far as the Lena delta, began a career on that river which would last over 50 years. *Vega* returned to Stockholm in April 1880 after completing the first circumnavigation of Eurasia.

Also in that year, the Englishman Benjamin Leigh Smith sailed north in a purpose built steamer, *Eira*, to explore Franz Josef Land (Credland 1980). He explored a considerable part of the western islands of the archipelago. Returning again the following year, *Eira* was crushed and sank near Mys Flora; after wintering in an emergency shelter Leigh Smith and his crew sailed the ship's boats south to Matochkin Shar on Novaya Zemlya.

In the summer of 1893, the Norwegian Fridtjof Nansen took his purpose built ship *Fram* eastwards through the Northern Sea Route. In September, he deliberately put his ship into the ice to the northwest of the Novosibirskiye Ostrova. According to his calculations, the ice drift would carry his ship right across the Arctic Basin. Indeed, on 3 January 1896, *Fram* emerged into open water just northwest of Svalbard; en route its crew had collected a vast amount of valuable scientific data during its three-year

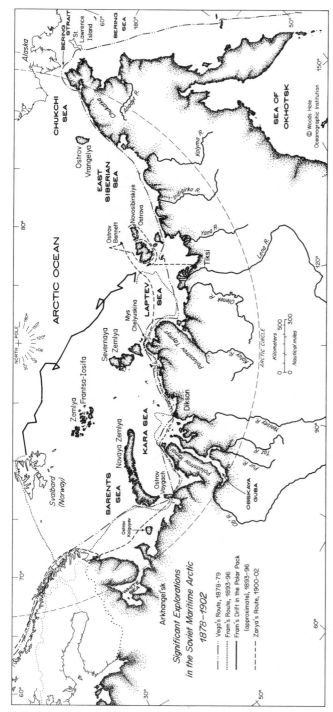

Figure 2.1 Significant explorations in the Soviet maritime Arctic, 1878–1902.

ice-drift (Nansen 1897). During this same period an English expedition was filling in the substantial gaps which still existed in the map of Franz Josef Land: Frederick G. Jackson spent 3 years on the archipelago (1894–7), operating from a base at Mys Flora (Jackson 1899).

Russian interest rekindled

No doubt provoked to some degree by all this foreign activity, the Russian authorities finally began to show some renewed interest in the Arctic in the closing years of the century. In January 1894, the Central Hydrographic Administration (a branch of the Navy), in collaboration with the Committee for the Trans-Siberian Railway, on which construction was about to start, proposed a detailed survey of the mouths of the Ob' and the Yenisey and the whole southern part of the Kara Sea. They hoped to use the Northern Sea Route to import materials for the railway to Siberia. A series of surveys followed which lasted 3 years (1894–6). Working from the steamer *Leytenant Ovtsyn* and the sailing vessel *Leytenant Skuratov*, Captain A.I. Vil'kitskiy made a thorough survey of the estuaries of the two great rivers; the outcome was the first pilot of the river mouths, published in 1899 (Pinkhenson 1962:204–5).

The sequel to this was the Arctic Ocean Hydrographic Expedition, 1898–1904 (Pinkhenson 1962:208) sponsored and financed again by the Committee for the Trans-Siberian Railway. Working from the steamer *Pakhtusov* and commanded variously by A.I. Vil'kitskiy, A.I. Varnek and F.K. Drizhenko, the expedition surveyed and sounded from the south end of the White Sea north to Matochkin Shar, and from Obskaya Guba west to the Norwegian border. A comprehensive set of charts and pilots was developed which rendered the Kara Sea route accessible to a conventional vessel with a normal degree of caution.

The first polar icebreaker, *Yermak*, the creation of Admiral Stepan Osipovich Makarov, was built by Armstrong Whitworth of Newcastle in 1898. The ship was 98 meters long, with a displacement of about 9,000 tonnes and engines of 10,000 horsepower and possessed such 'modern' design features as a rounded hull, cutaway bow and heeling tanks and pumps. Makarov intended it primarily for arctic research work and development of the Northern Sea Route, but he was strongly opposed by powerful bureaucrats in the Finance and Navy departments. Nevertheless, in 1899, *Yermak* made its maiden arctic voyage to the Svalbard area. Although attaining a latitude of 81° 28'N in very heavy ice, *Yermak* sustained some damage to its hull and Makarov's opponents seized upon this to cast doubt on the ship's suitability for arctic navigation. Instead *Yermak* was posted to the Baltic for the next 2 winters; there, it greatly lengthened the shipping season to Revel, Riga and St. Petersburg.

Nevertheless, in the summer of 1901, Makarov was able to persuade the Finance Minister, Witte, and the Naval Minister, Tyrtov, to send *Yermak* north again on a scientific cruise. Despite heavy ice conditions it made a very valuable cruise to Novaya Zemlya and Franz Josef Land but was unable to round Mys Zhelaniya into the Kara Sea. Despite or perhaps because of this cruise, the opposition gained even more strength, and for the remainder of the Tsarist period *Yermak* was assigned to the Baltic. Without any doubt Tsarist Russia thereby threw away the chance of becoming the world leader in arctic navigation and research.

Despite this setback, at the turn of the century, a major scientific expedition was mounted elsewhere in the Arctic but by the Imperial Academy of Sciences rather than by the Navy. This was Baron Eduard von Toll's Russian Polar Expedition 1900–2, aboard *Zarya* (Toll 1909; Barr 1981). The expedition was to focus on the Laptev Sea, the Novosibirskiye Ostrova and on any land which might lie north of that archipelago. During the first season *Zarya* was brought to a halt by heavy ice at Bukhta Kolin Archera off the west coast of Taymyr and was forced to winter there. The wintering was used for systematic meteorological and magnetic observations and for some far-ranging sledge trips to clarify the geography of this very intricate coast. The following season (1901) *Zarya* reached the Novosibirskiye Ostrova and settled down for a second wintering on the west coast of Ostrov Kotel'nyy. In the spring of 1902, Baron Toll and three companions set off by sledge and boat for Ostrov Bennetta; *Zarya* was to pick them up after the ice broke up. But the ship was unable to reach the island owing to heavy ice, and when a rescue party finally reached the island in 1903 it found only a message to the effect that the missing party had started back south in October 1902. Despite its tragic ending, this expedition was of great significance both in surveying and mapping the coasts and in making major contributions to meteorology, geology, geophysics, botany and zoology.

Russian activity in the eastern Arctic at this period was matched by foreign endeavors in the extreme west, namely on Franz Josef Land. In rapid succession Wellmann's American Expedition of 1898–9, the Duke of Abruzzi's Italian North Pole Expedition of 1899–1900, Baldwin's American Expedition of 1901–2, and Fiala's American Expedition of 1903–5 all added something to the knowledge of the archipelago. The results achieved by the American expeditions in particular were decidedly not commensurate with the vast amounts of money, materials and effort invested in these operations.

Russo–Japanese War

The outbreak of the Russo–Japanese War in 1904 provided the stimulus for renewed interest on the part of the Imperial government in developing the Northern Sea Route. To attempt to relieve the enormous congestion on the single-track Trans-Siberian Railway, it was decided to send a fleet of steamers via the Kara Sea to the Yenisey. The Russian authorities invited Joseph Wiggins to act as pilot for this fleet. Although intimately involved in the preparations, Wiggins fell ill in May 1905 and died in September. In the interim, a flotilla of 7 tugs, 11 lighters, 4 steamers and 2 icebreakers sailed into the Kara Sea and reached the mouth of the Yenisey. Cargoes were transshipped to the lighters, and while tugs and lighters headed up the Yenisey to Krasnoyarsk, the steamers returned safely to the west. This expedition clearly demonstrated the feasibility of the Kara Sea route and vindicated Joseph Wiggins.

The Russian defeat in the Russo–Japanese War, and especially the debacle of the Battle of Tsushima, led to even more far-reaching results with regard to the Northern Sea Route. It was argued that, if the Baltic squadron could have been sent to the Far East by way of the Northern Sea Route, it would have arrived at Vladivostok in much better condition and would have caught the Japanese off guard. The validity of this argument is doubtful (Novikoff-Priboy 1936; Westwood 1970), but the outcome was the Arctic Ocean Hydrographic Expedition, 1910–15, which represented a major and remarkably successful effort at surveying the whole of the Northern Sea Route. Two small icebreaking steamers, *Taymyr* and *Vaygach* were built expressly for the expedition in St. Petersburg in 1909 (Starokadomskiy 1976:7–8). After proceeding to the Far East via Suez and Singapore, in the fall of 1910 they made a reconnaissance foray into the Chukchi Sea. Then over the next three seasons they pushed progressively farther west along the arctic coast, sounding and surveying as they went and returning each winter to Vladivostok (see Figure 2.2). In 1913 they made the remarkable discovery of an archipelago north of Taymyr, which was named Zemlya Nikolaya II — now Severnaya Zemlya. In 1914, the 2 ships started west from the Pacific, intending to complete the through-passage to Arkhangel'sk but were forced to winter on the west coast of Taymyr. They completed the through-passage in the summer of 1915.

One final development prior to the Russian Revolution was the appearance of a remarkable Norwegian entrepreneur, Jonas Lied (Lied 1960). In June 1912, he founded his Siberian Company, whose main focus was trade with Siberia via the Kara Sea route, with cargoes being transshipped at the mouth of the Ob' and the Yenisey. An initial attempt in 1912 was unsuccessful because the captain of the solitary steamer, on encountering the ice, faltered and turned back. Over the next few years, however, the company annually sent steamers to the mouths of the Ob' and/or Yenisey, there transshipping inbound cargoes such as cement, for outbound Siberian cargoes such as hides, flax, hemp and butter. In 1917, the company's steamer *Obi* was forced to abort its voyage because of political rather than navigational difficulties.

The chaos, and especially the disruption of the railway system, which resulted from the Russian Civil War and the allied intervention in Northern Russia, led to an attempt by the White Russian authorities to use the Kara Sea route in 1919. By that summer the food situation in the north of European Russia was disastrous, yet in West Siberia, also under White Russian control, there was a surplus of grain. It was, therefore, decided to ship cargoes of grain down the Ob' by river craft to a rendezvous with seagoing vessels. They would then haul the grain to Arkhangel'sk. A motley collection of freighters and icebreakers was assembled for the task. In fact, the operation had only limited success: with the defeat of Kolchak's troops

Figure 2.2 Local inhabitants of Bukhta Provideniya shown with crewmembers on the deck of the Russian icebreaking steamer *Taymyr*, 1910.

in Western Siberia the transshipping operation at the mouth of the Ob' had to be abandoned when only half-completed.

The following summer (1920), with the railway system in an even worse state and the food situation in the Arkhangel'sk area also worse, the Bol'sheviks (now in complete control in both European Russia and West Siberia) organized another grain-hauling expedition to the Kara Sea. This time the operation was much more successful. During the 1921 season a serious effort was made to place the Kara Sea operation on sounder footing. Emphasis was placed on importing manufactured goods such as agricultural and mining machinery from Western Europe and on exporting products such as graphite, hides and wool; the movement of grain from the Ob' and Yenisey to the White Sea was also a priority. Eleven freighters were involved, with 4 icebreakers as escort (Belov 1959:161–72). Throughout the 1920s, the Kara Sea operation steadily increased in scale. With the restoration of the Soviet railway system, the coastwise movement of grain to Arkhangel'sk was phased out and greater stress was placed on importing machinery and exporting grain, timber and raw materials to Western Europe. In 1929, 26 freighters were involved; exports amounted to 60,000 tonnes and imports to 13,500 tonnes (Armstrong 1952:120).

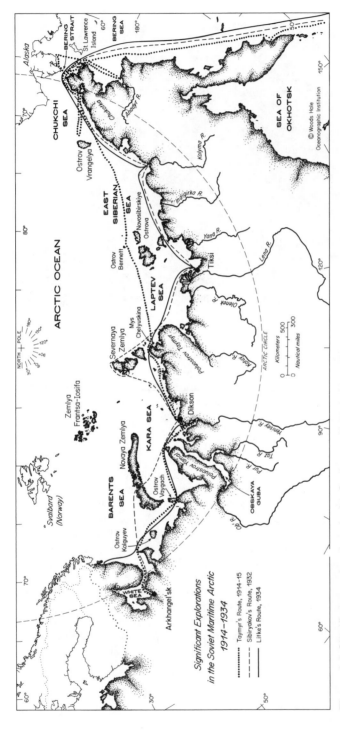

Figure 2.3 Significant explorations in the Soviet maritime Arctic, 1914–1934.

Early Soviet efforts

The initiation of Soviet activities (see Figure 2.3) in the High Arctic seems to have been almost accidental, a result of the crash of Nobile's airship *Italia* to the north of Svalbard in the summer of 1928. Apart from the involvement of the icebreaker *Krasin* which finally rescued the survivors from their camp on the sea ice, *Malygin* and *Sedov* were also detailed to assist in the search (Barr 1977). *Sedov's* contribution was to search the south coasts of Franz Josef Land. In the following year (1929), *Sedov* returned to Franz Josef Land and established a weather station at Tikhaya Bukhta (Shmidt 1962; Vize 1929), in part to buttress the Soviet claim to sovereignty over the archipelago in the face of substantial Norwegian activity on and around the archipelago.

In 1930, geographical exploration of the Soviet Arctic entered its final phase. Although Severnaya Zemlya had been discovered by the expedition aboard *Taymyr* and *Vaygach* in 1913 (Starokadomskiy 1976), the westward and northward extent of the landmass remained totally unknown. Hence in the summer of 1930, a four-man survey party, led by G.A. Ushakov, was landed on Ostrov Domashnyy off the west coast of the archipelago with instructions to explore and map the archipelago over the following 2 seasons (Barr 1975; Urvantsev 1935).

During the 1932 season 2 crucial operations were mounted. The first was an attempt at the first one-season passage of the entire Northern Sea Route by the icebreaker *Sibiryakov*. The operation was less than entirely successful because the ship lost its propeller in the ice just short of the Bering Strait and emerged from the ice under improvised sails to be taken in tow by a trawler dispatched to its aid (Barr 1978; Vize 1946; Shneyderov 1963). Also in 1932, the first attempt was made at sending a convoy of ships to the mouth of the Kolyma; the icebreaker *Fedor Litke* escorted 7 freighters, 2 river tugs and 3 barges to the mouth of that river from Vladivostok. Unfortunately, owing to heavy ice conditions, unloading had to be interrupted, and the convoy was forced to winter in Chaunskaya Guba to complete unloading in 1933 (Barr 1979).

But perhaps an even more important event in 1932 was the formation of the *Glavnoye Upravleniye Severnogo Morskogo Puti* (Directorate of the Northern Sea Route), whose primary function was to develop the Northern Sea Route as a regularly operating transport system. Over the next few years it became an amazingly powerful body, responsible for every aspect of development of the islands in the European Arctic and in the whole of the Asiatic part of the USSR north of 62°N (Armstrong 1952:55).

With this powerful administrative structure in place, development accelerated. In 1933 a convoy of 3 freighters, a tug and barges reached the Lena from the west (Barr 1982). In 1934, *Fedor Litke* (see Figure 2.4) made the first accident-free transit of the Northern Sea Route in one season (Vize 1946; Nikolayeva and Sarankin 1963:128–45). The following year the same icebreaker escorted the first freighters, *Vantsetti* and *Iskra*, through the entire route from west to east. In 1936, 12 freighters made the through-passage from west to east and 2 from east to west. The first warships, the destroyers *Voykov* and *Stalin*, also made the transit of the route from west to east, escorted by *Fedor Litke*.

In 1937 Glavsemorput' mounted an ambitious and highly successful air-supported high-latitude research initiative, namely the establishment of *Severnyy Polyus I* (North Pole I), the first Soviet arctic drifting station (Belov 1969b:304–32). Flying from an intermediate base on Ostrolf Rudol'fa, on 21 May 1937, 4 heavy aircraft landed on skis on the unprepared surface of an ice floe at the North Pole. When the planes took off again they left a four-man party led by I.D. Papanin and a fully equipped scientific station. Over the next 9 months, as the station drifted south down the east coast of Greenland, the party carried out a full program of meteorological and oceanographic observations. The 4 men were evacuated from their floe near the mouth of Scoresby Sund by the icebreaker *Taymyr* on 19 February 1938. This remarkably successful pioneer effort at establishing a scientific drifting station would stand the Soviets in very good stead when a much more ambitious program of similar activities was initiated after World War II.

During this time the tempo of activity on the Kara Sea section of the route was also steadily building. But in 1937 this expanding activity was brought to a rude halt; at the end of the season 26 ships, including most of the serviceable icebreakers, were caught by freeze-up and forced to winter at various points in the Arctic. When it became light in the spring of 1938, successful (but expensive) aerial evacuations were mounted to remove surplus personnel from 2 groups of ships adrift in the ice. In the summer of

Figure 2.4 In 1934, *Fedor Litke* made the first accident-free transit of the Northern Sea Route in one season.

1938 the primary effort was focused on freeing all the ships. This was successfully achieved, with the exception of the icebreaker *Sedov*: adrift in the ice in the northern Laptev Sea, its rudder had been so badly damaged by ice pressures that it could not be extricated. Hence, it was designated a high-latitude drifting research station and with a 'volunteer' crew of fifteen drifted across the Pole on its famous drift which lasted 812 days (Badigin 1950; Buynitskiy 1945).

In 1939 and 1940, the tempo of activity again began to pick up, so that by the outbreak of the war in 1941, the Soviet authorities had come close to fulfilling their intent of making the Northern Sea Route a regularly operating transport artery. Some measure of its status is that a total of 120 ships carried some 450,000 tonnes of lend-lease goods from American West Coast ports to Soviet arctic ports via the Northern Sea Route over the period 1942–5 (Armstrong 1952:123). The largest number of these ships (54) were bound for Tiksi at the mouth of the Lena, but 13 rounded Taymyr to reach the Yenisey ports, and one even continued west to Arkhangel'sk.

Conclusion

The half-millennium of history of Russian involvement with the Arctic Ocean displays some intriguing patterns. In the late 16th and early 17th centuries major portions of the Northern Sea Route were used for commercial purposes. In the early 18th century, through the efforts of the officers and men of the Russian Navy engaged in the Great Northern Expedition, almost the entire length of the Northern Sea Route was mapped with remarkable accuracy, despite enormously difficult ice conditions that were associated with the height of the Neoglacial. These difficulties, and similar ones encountered by officers such as Fedor Litke in exploring Novaya Zemlya waters in the early 19th century, led to a striking lack of interest or activity by the Russian government for most of the second half of the 19th century; indeed almost all significant developments during this period, whether in terms of exploration or commerce, were made by foreign expeditions or entrepreneurs. The belatedly renewed interest of the Imperial government in the Northern Sea Route was epitomized by the Arctic Ocean Hydrographic Expedition, 1910–15.

Under the Soviet regime commercial navigation in the Kara Sea built up steadily throughout the 1920s and 1930s. Exploration of the landmasses of the Arctic was completed with the exploration and mapping of Severnaya Zemlya during 1930–2. By the outbreak of World War II, following the voyages of *Vantsetti* and *Iskra* in 1935, regular, reliable movement of freight along the entire length of the Northern Sea Route had become a reality.

William Barr

References

Armstrong, T.E. 1952. *The Northern Sea Route. Soviet Exploitation of the Northeast Passage*, 55, 120-23. Cambridge:Cambridge University Press.
— 1965. *Russian Settlement in the North*, 23. Cambridge:Cambridge University Press.
Badigin, K.S. 1950. *Tri zimovki v l'dakh Arktiki* [Three Winterings in the Arctic Ice]. Moskva:Izdatel'stvo Ts. K. VLKSM Molodaya Gvardiya.
Barr, W. 1974. 'First ship to round Mys Chelyuskina?' *The Musk-Ox* 14:30-36.
— 1975. 'Severnaya Zemlya: the last major discovery.' *Geographic Journal* 141:59-71.
— 1977. 'The Soviet contribution to the *Italia* search and rescue, 1928.' *Polar Record* 18(117):561-74.
— 1978. 'The voyage of *Sibiryakov*, 1932.' *Polar Record* 19(120):253-66.
— 1979. 'First convoy to the Kolyma: the Soviet Northeast Polar Expedition, 1932-33.' *Polar Record* 19(123):563-72.
— 1981. 'Baron von Toll's last expedition: the Russian Polar Expedition, 1900-1902.' *Arctic* 34(3):201-224.
— 1982. 'The first Soviet convoy to the mouth of the Lena.' *Arctic* 34(3):201-24.
— 1985. *The Expeditions of the First International Polar Year, 1882-1883*. Arctic Institute of North America Technical Paper, No. 29. Calgary:Arctic Institute of North America.
Belov, M.I. 1956. *Arkticheskoye moreplavaniye s drevneyshikh vremen do seredinu XIX veka. Istoriya otkrytiya i osvoyeniya Severnogo Morskogo Puti, tom I* [Arctic Navigation from the Earliest Times to the Mid-Nineteenth Century. The History of the Discovery and Exploitation of the Northern Sea Route, Vol. 1], 82, 110-11, 150-8, 363, 428. Leningrad:Izdatel'stvo 'Morskoy Transport'.
— 1959. *Sovetskoye arkticheskoye moreplavaniye 1917–1932 gg. Istoriya otkrytiya i osvoyeniya Severnogo Morskogo Puti, tom III* [Soviet Arctic Navigation 1917-1932. The History of the Discovery and Exploitation of the Northern Sea Route, Vol. 3], 161-72. Leningrad:Izdatel'stvo 'Morskoy Transport'.
— 1969a. *Mangazeya*, 109. Leningrad:Gidrometeoizdat.
— 1969b. *Nauchnoye i khozyaystvennoye osvoyeniye Sovetskogo Severa 1933-1945 gg. Istoriya otkrytiya i osvoyeniya Severnogo Morskogo Puti, tom IV* [Scientific and Economic Exploitation of the Soviet North, 1933-1945. The History of the Discovery and Exploitation of the Northern Sea Route, Vol. 4], 304-32. Leningrad: Gidrometeorologicheskoye Izdatel'stvo.
Burney, J. 1819. *A Chronological History of North-Eastern Voyages of Discovery*. London:Payne and Foss and John Murray. Facsimile edition, 1969. Amsterdam and New York:Israel/Da Capo.
Buynitskiy, V.Kh. 1945. *812 dney v dreyfuyushchikh l'dakh* [812 Days in the Drifting Ice]. Moskva and Leningrad:Izdatel'stvo Glavsevmorputi.
Credland, A.G. 1980. 'Benjamin Leigh Smith: a forgotten pioneer.' *Polar Record* 20(125):127-45.
De Long, G.W. 1884. *The Voyage of the Jeannette. The Ship and Ice Journals of George W. De Long ... of the Polar Expedition of 1879-81*. Boston:Houghton and Mifflin.
Dolgikh, B.O. 1948. 'Novye dannye o plavanii russkikh severnym morskim putem v XVII veke' [New data on a Russian voyage along the Northern Sea Route in the Seventeenth century]. *Russkiye polyarnye morekhodi CVII veka u beregov Taymyra* [Seventeenth Century Polar Seafarers on the Shores of Taymyr], ed. O.P. Okladnikov, 117-57. Leningrad and Moskva:Izdatel'stvo Glavesevmorputi.

Fisher, R.H. 1981. *The Voyage of Semen Dezhnev in 1648*. London:The Hakluyt Society.

Golder, F.A. 1914. *Russian Expansion on the Pacific , 1641-1850*. Cleveland:Clark Co.

Jackson, F.G. 1899. *A Thousand Days in the Arctic*. New York and London:Harper and Bros.

Johnson, H. 1907. *The Life and Voyages of Joseph Wiggins, F.R.G.S.* London:John Murray.

Lantzeff, G.V., and R.A. Pierce. 1973. *Eastward to Empire: Exploration and Conquest on the Russian Open Frontier to 1750*, 95, 184. Montreal and London:McGill-Queen's University Press.

Lied, J. 1960. *Siberian Arctic. The Story of the Siberian Company*. London:Methuen and Co. Ltd.

Nansen, F. 1897. *Farthest North*. Westminster:Archibald Constable and Co.

Neatby, L. 1973. *Discovery in Russian and Siberian Waters*. Athens:Ohio University Press.

Nikolayeva, A.G., and V.I. Sarankin. 1963. *Sil'nee l'dov* [Stronger than the Ice], 128-45. Moskva:Izdatel'stvo 'Morskoy Transport'.

Nordenskiöld, A.E. 1881. *The Voyage of the Vega around Asia and Europe*. London:Macmillan and Co.

Novikoff-Priboy, A. 1936. *Tsushima*. London:George Allen and Unwin Ltd.

Okladnikov, A.P. 1951. 'Archaeological finds on Ostrov Faddeya and on the shores of Zaliv Simsa,' *In* : *Istoricheskiy pamyatnik russkogo arkticheskogo moreplavaniya XVII veka* [A Historical Memorial to Seventeenth Century Russian Arctic Navigation], 7-40. Leningrad and Moskva:Izdatel'stvo Glavsevmorputi.

Payer, J. 1876. *New Lands within the Arctic Circle*. London:Macmillan.

Pinkhenson, D.M. 1962. *Problema severnogo morskogo puti v epokhu kapitalizma. Istoriya otkrytiya i osvoyeniya severnogo morskogo puti, tom II* [The Problem of the Northern Sea Route During the Capitalist Era. The History of the Discovery and Exploitation of the Northern Sea Route, Vol. 2], 68, 204-5, 208. Leningrad:Izdatel'stvo 'Morskoy Transport'.

Seemann, B.C. 1853. *Narrative of the Voyage of H.M.S. Herald during the Years 1845-51*, Vol. 2, 114. London:Reeve and Co.

Shmidt, O.Yu. 1962. 'From the diaries and articles of O. Yu. Shmidt.' *Letopis' Severa* 2:15-57.

Shneyderov, V. 1963. *Velikim severnym* [With the Great Northerners]. Moskva:Gosudarstvennoye Izdatel'stvo Geograficheskoy Literatury.

Starokadomskiy, L.M. 1976. *Charting the Russian Northern Sea Route. The Arctic Ocean Hydrographic Expedition 1910-1915*, ed. and trans. W. Barr. Montreal and London:Arctic Institute of North America and McGill Queen's University Press.

Toll, E., ed. 1909. *Die Russische Polarfahrt der Sarja 1900-1902 aus den hinterlassenen Tagebüchern von Baron Eduard von Toll* [The Russian Polar Voyage of *Zarya* 1900-1902, from the Diaries Left by Baron Eduard von Toll]. Berlin:George Reimer.

Troitskiy, V.A. 1973. 'New finds on Ostrov Faddeya.' *Izvestiya Vsesoyuznogo Geograficheskogo Obshchestva* 105(1):62-67.

Urvantsev, N.N. 1935. *Dva goda na Severnoy Zemle* [Two Years on Severnaya Zemlya]. Leningrad:Izdatel'stvo Glavsevmorputi.

Vize, V.Yu. 1929. 'The expedition of the icebreaker *Sedov* to Franz Josef Land for the purpose of building a meteorological radio-station.' *Arktis*, 2:126-28.

— 1946. *Na* Sibiryakove *i* Litke *cherez ledovitye morya* [On Board *Sibiryakov* and *Litke* through Icy Seas]. MoskvaLeningrad:Izdatel'stvo Glavsevmorputi.
Westwood, J.M. 1970. *Witnesses of Tsushima*. Tokyo:Sophia University.

3

The 1987 expedition of the icebreaker *Sibir'* to the North Pole

Ivan Frolov

The main aims of the May 1987 expedition of the nuclear icebreaker *Sibir'* were to carry out multidisciplinary studies of a scarcely investigated area of the Arctic Basin, including the North Pole area, and to satisfy a practical objective — to evacuate the North Pole-27 Drifting Station and set up the North Pole-29 Drifting Station. The expedition program included studies in the fields of oceanography, sea ice, meteorology, geophysics, marine geology and geodesy.

Over the course of the voyage, a large number of hydrometeorological and geophysical field measurements were made over an extensive area. Of the scientific problem areas studied under the expedition program, main emphasis was given to the operational hydrometeorological information services of the voyage. The navigation strategy was based on ice and weather forecasts as well as probabilistic characteristics of the drift, deformations and fractures of the compact ice cover.

The 1987 expedition was the first time that a high-latitude voyage was made in spring, employing a navigational strategy of motion which utilized major fractures in the ice cover. Several factors contributed to the implementation of the expedition's comprehensive program:

1. Existing knowledge of the nature of the region, its ice and hydrometeorological conditions, obtained for a multi-year period from drifting stations, ships, radio markers, buoys, Soviet 'North' expeditions and satellites;

2. the establishment of a reliable system of hydrometeorological operational and prognostic information services; and
3. the availability of powerful nuclear icebreakers with navigational experience along the Northern Sea Route.

Expedition chronology

The expedition was organized by the Arctic and Antarctic Scientific Research Institute (AASRI) and led by Dr A. Chilingarov, deputy chairman of the USSR State Committee for Hydrometeorology and Dr B. Krutskikh, director of AASRI. The entire 1987 expedition can be divided into three stages:

Stage I: 8–20 May. At the end of this stage polar explorers from the North Pole-27 Drifting Station were evacuated.

Stage II: 20 May–3 June. During this stage the North Pole was reached (25 May); at the end of this stage, the icebreaker *Sibir'* arrived at Dikson Island.

Stage III: 4–19 June. The North Pole-29 Drifting Station was set up in the northern Laptev Sea (10 June).

The *Sibir'* research expedition departed the port of Murmansk on 8 May 1987 and crossed the ice edge of the Barents Sea on 9 May. From that date until 17 June, *Sibir'* was navigated entirely through ice of different concentrations, thicknesses, and hummocking. The ship sailed through ice cover under pressure in the central Arctic Basin and in the Barents, Kara and Laptev seas (see Figure 3.1).

After leaving Kola Bay, specific hydrometeorological observations, ozone and aerosol studies and ionospheric soundings were begun aboard *Sibir'*. As the icebreaker advanced farther north, other studies were conducted: IR radiometry; geological and geophysical studies; and testing of methods for soundings of the Barents Sea ice shelf and of the ocean slope. On 10 May, in the area of Franz Josef Land, the first gravimetric observations were made, radar measurements of the fast ice thickness were conducted and physical–mechanical properties and measurements of ice interaction with the ship's hull were determined. Air, snow and ice sampling was started within the framework of the overall 'Monitoring' program. Regular ice reconnaissance flights from the icebreaker were also made by means of MI-2 and MI-8 helicopters. Using a direct downlink to *Sibir'*, an areal ice cover survey was made en route using side-looking airborne radar (SLAR) aboard an IL-24 aircraft. Extensive hydrometeorological information and forecasts from the leading weather centers of the world were received, processed and interpreted for the scientific–operational support of the expedition. On 12 May, the icebreaker crossed the 84th parallel and entered an area of multi-year ice. When moving from the ice edge to this latitude, *Sibir'*'s speed was reduced from 18 to 9 knots. From 13 May onward, the time required for the icebreaker to

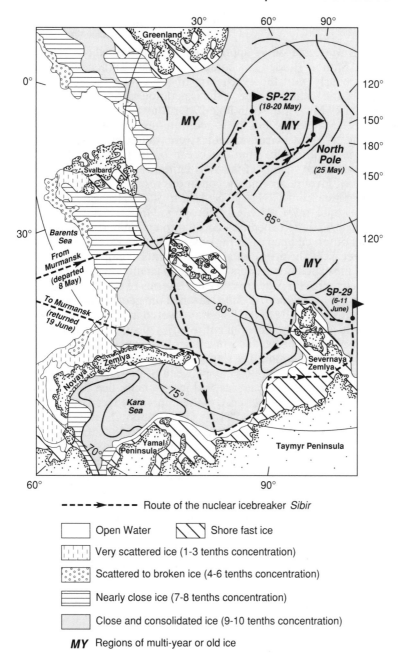

Figure 3.1 Route of the nuclear icebreaker *Sibir'* in the central Arctic basin between 8 May-19 June 1987.

make headway by ramming increased. By 17 May, the icebreaker reached 86°N.

On 18 May, the *Sibir'* approached the ice floe where North Pole-27 Drifting Station (under the command of Yu. Tikhonov) was situated. Simultaneously with the evacuation of the equipment, instruments and materials, the scientific teams of the expedition carried out a wide variety of work. On 19 May, the North Pole-27 Drifting Station was officially closed and, on 20 May, Stage I of the expedition was successfully completed.

During 21–3 May, scientific studies were conducted along the ship's track; soundings of all media from the ocean bottom to the ionosphere were carried out in the vicinity of the 87°N latitude as the *Sibir'* sailed eastward. By 23 May, favourable synoptic conditions resulted in ice divergence in the near-pole area from 87°N to 90°N, 42°E to 50°E. This was confirmed by ice reconnaissance from the MI-2 helicopter. On 22 May (2100 hours), the headquarters of the expedition decided to continue studies north to 88°N along an observed opening in the polar pack. The ice conditions which had been forecast by the operational team were then confirmed by satellite data. This led the expedition leaders to decide to attempt to reach the North Pole and, once there, for *Sibir'* to carry out a series of research studies.

On 25 May (1552 hours), *Sibir'* reached the geographic North Pole. The distance from 86°40'N to the Pole was covered in less than two days. In the immediate area of the Pole, an entire series of studies was carried out, the flag of the USSR hoisted and a meeting of the expedition participants held. On 26 May (0850 hours), the ship set sail again, heading southward along 50°E. By 27 May, ice conditions between 85°N and 87°N had worsened. Although zones of first-year ice and ice openings due to tides were used when available, the overall speed of the ship was reduced significantly when proceeding by ramming. On 29 May (1130 hours), the icebreaker departed from a zone of ice under pressure and reached 86°38'N. Overall, the return voyage from the Pole to the starting latitude thus required twice as much time as the voyage north to the Pole.

From there, the voyage proceeded southward to Franz Joseph Land along meridionally oriented zones of open ice in the area of 45-55°E. A research program was conducted en route. From Franz Josef Land, a course was laid to the north of the Zhelaniya Cape and toward Dikson Island. On 3 June, the icebreaker was positioned in the fast ice off the port of Dikson to take equipment and instruments on board for the North Pole-29 Drifting Station. Thus, Stage II of the expedition was completed. The original schedule of the expedition voyage, as calculated by V. Smirnov and Ye. Makarov at the AASRI one month prior to the expedition, was adhered to within an accuracy of one day.

On 4 June, having departed the port of Dikson, *Sibir'* set a course to the Laptev Sea through Vil'kitsky Strait. The ice navigation across the Kara Sea and to the boundary of the Laptev Sea was not difficult. Eastward to Vil'kitsky Strait, *Sibir'* navigated in a flaw polynya 20–30 miles wide and then in fast ice, where a lead (track) had been made earlier by the nuclear icebreakers *Arktika* and *Rossiya*, heading eastward with the cargo vessel *Kala*.

On 5 June (1130 hours), *Sibir'* entered close pack ice in the Laptev Sea with hummock concentration up to 30 percent. Specialists in the operational team recommended that the ice floe proposed for setting up the North Pole-29 Drifting Station (80°20′N, 113°23′E) be approached from the south, thereby avoiding an extensive zone of ice under pressure adjacent to the Severnaya Zemlya. The exit would be to the north along 113–115°E. On 6 June, V. Lukin, head of the North Pole-29 Drifting Station, chose a suitable ice floe for the station after observations from a MI-8 helicopter. A radiobeacon was set up on this two-year-old ice floe, whose dimensions were 700 by 900 meters with a thickness of 2.5–3.0 meters. From 6–9 June, the icebreaker moved to the location of the ice floe through heavily hummocked ice.

On 9 June (1457 hours), at 80°21′7″N, 113°23′6″E cargo unloading began for the establishment of the North Pole-29 Drifting Station. The next day the new drifting station was officially opened. As recommended by the operational team, on 11 June the icebreaker departed the station area and headed for Arctic Cape (Severnaya Zemlya). Navigation was maintained in the zones of open ice. On 14 June (0400 hours), the icebreaker sailed round Arctic Cape and then to Sredny Island, navigating in a flaw polynya and in very open pack ice. The icebreaker then sailed through a polynya to the south to 70°10′N and, using the recommended course, proceeded to Zhelaniya Cape. On 16 June (1220 hours), *Sibir'* crossed the meridian of Zhelaniya Cape and headed to her homeport of Murmansk, mooring 3 days later. Thus, during this expedition *Sibir'* covered a total distance of 5,517 nautical miles, 4,916 nautical miles of which were in ice. A distance of 2,041 nautical miles, 37 percent of the entire route, was traversed north of the 80th parallel in the heaviest ice conditions of the central Arctic Basin.

General scheme of scientific–operational hydrometeorological support

Taking into account the unique character of the voyage, a special scientific–operational group headed by the author was established. The group consisted of highly qualified scientists and engineers experienced in the field of providing hydrometeorological support to ice navigation.

The activity of the group had several objectives:

1. deploying and maintaining aboard the icebreaker a complex of technical means for collecting and processing hydrometeorological data;
2. organizing and determining an optimum scheme for scientific–operational support and establishing an operational communications system with the regional weather centers; and
3. providing the expedition headquarters with all necessary actual and prognostic hydrometeorological information for operational control of the voyage.

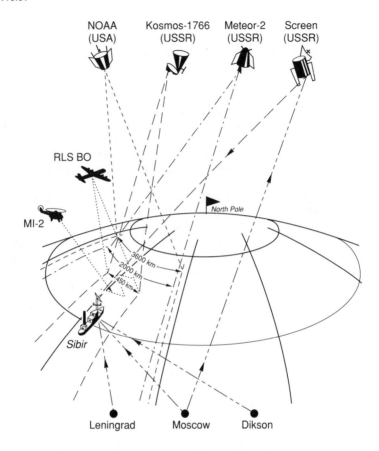

Figure 3.2 Sources of meteorological and sea ice information.

Weather and ice data were reported to the icebreaker in a wide range of spatial–temporal scales (see Figure 3.2). All incoming information was classed as either standard or specialized. The information referred to as standard was transmitted regularly by radio and TV communication channels from weather centers in the Soviet Union and other countries. Such information is of a review character and, as a rule, covers the entire Northern Hemisphere or extensive areas of marginal northern seas. In contrast, the specialized information is detailed hydrometeorological information. Indicating the specific conditions in the navigation area, it is received on request from the weather centers and through direct measurements by the onboard operational group.

To provide support for the voyage to the near-pole region, heavy aircraft were used. These aircraft were equipped with SLAR for sea/ice diagnostics and operational relay of images to the icebreaker. The general layout of the sources of actual ice information is shown in Figure 3.3. On the basis of the analysis of all incoming information as well as data collected directly on board the icebreaker, ice and weather forecasts were issued from one to seven days in advance, calculations of the time required for the progress of the icebreaker according to different factors were made and an optimum route was chosen. The criterion for the optimum route was time; the amount spent on certain sections of the route when *Sibir'* was moving in the general direction of the voyage track. This information was vital, since it enabled expedition headquarters to determine the route for the icebreaker.

During the planning stage, along with the hydrometeorological data, the scientific–operational group used the following prognostic information:

1. forecast of the surface-pressure-field distribution by uniform circulation periods for May;
2. forecast of the drift of North Pole-27 Drift Station in April–May;
3. forecasts of ice distribution by thickness in the Barents and Kara seas for the second half and the final ten days of May (Frolov 1981);
4. an experimental forecast of the ice drift and divergence in the Arctic Ocean by uniform circulation periods in May (Proshutinsky 1988); and
5. a specialized forecast of the time spent during a high-latitudinal voyage.

Forecasts were made for 2 to 3 months in advance. All proved to guide the operational group correctly.

Weather forecasts

Prognostic information was received by facsimile in the form of surface-pressure maps for 24 hours in advance, from radiocenters in Moscow, Dikson, and Hamburg and for 48 and 72 hours in advance from radiocenters in Moscow, Bracknell (UK) and Hamburg.

Also, biweekly forecasts for 8–10 days in advance were received from the Arctic and Antarctic Scientific Research Institute, and detailed daily forecasts of surface pressure fields and geopotential (H_{500}) over the Northern Hemisphere were received from the USSR Hydrometeorological Center.

A total of 524 weather maps were received from 8 May to 17 June. The largest portion of synoptic data (about 65 percent) was received from the Dikson Territorial Hydrometeorological Center. The AASRI 8–10 day forecasts were largely correct in informing the operational group about synoptic processes. A skill-score analysis of the short-range forecasts from Hamburg and Bracknell indicates that the location of synoptic formations in the near-pole area is less accurate than for temperate latitudes. The 6–7 day forecasts from the Hydrometeorological Center of the USSR predicted quite accurately the development of weather processes in the near-pole area during the first 3–4 days, and the data on the distribution of synoptic formations for 5–7 days in advance should be considered as climatic data. The verification score of these forecasts decreases during macrosynoptic changes over the hemisphere.

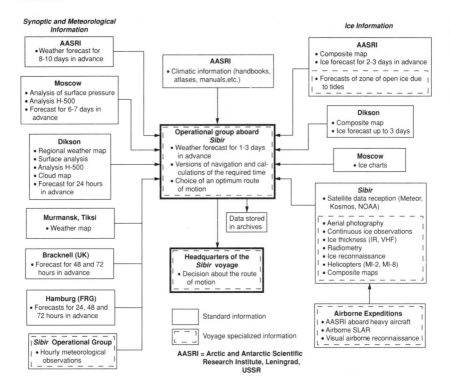

Figure 3.3 Flow diagram showing the various sources of standard and specialized information used by *Sibir*' s onboard operational and expedition headquarters' groups for route selection.

On the basis of a detailed analysis of all incoming data, the on-board operational group issued weather forecasts for 12, 24, 48 and 72 hours in advance all along the expedition's route. In total, 112 forecasts were issued. The skill-score of the weather forecasts for 48 and 72 hours in advance was 80 percent. The daily forecasts of visibility were not always successful. This can be attributed to the scarcity of information over the central Arctic and to insufficient satellite data.

Ice forecasts and navigation recommendations

The operational group received three-day advance information on open ice zones due to tides three times a week, by radio from AASRI. The most difficult decisions in choosing the route of the icebreaker arose when navigating north of 80°N. The high skill-score of the ice divergence forecasts in this area assisted in the selection of optimum-recommended routes of the *Sibir*'s advance. The forecasts of ice divergence due to tides also had a good skill-score, but it was not possible to make a quantitative estimation because of the difficulty in distinguishing openings in the ice induced by tides as opposed to winds. The forecasts from Dikson Island were correct in advising the operational group about the expected ice conditions in the seas.

On the basis of the analysis of all actual and prognostic meteorological and ice information, the operational group issued the ice forecasts-recommendations for up to 3 days in advance with a specification, if necessary, for each day. During the navigation in the central Arctic Basin, 24 forecasts-recommendations were developed. For navigational purposes, the main emphasis in the forecasts was placed on certain ice characteristics: location of open ice zones; and the duration and force of ice pressure along the route of the icebreaker *Sibir'*.

Special mention should be made of a successful forecast by the operational group on 18 May. This identified correctly 3 days in advance an expected zone of open ice by 21 May. It was this forecast, confirmed by a satellite image for 23 May, that was the basis for the decision to conduct studies at the point of the Geographical Pole, reached by the *Sibir'* on 25 May (see Figure 3.4). Despite a closure of the zone of open ice, further forecasts-recommendations enabled *Sibir'* to leave the Pole at an average speed of 3 knots.

On the whole, the forecasts-recommendations were quite successful. Their effectiveness is substantiated by the fact that for 70 percent of *Sibir's* navigation in predominately multi-year ice, the icebreaker was able to move at an average speed of 6 knots. The average skill-score of the ice forecasts-recommendations was about 80 percent.

Figure 3.4 Crew and scientists of *Sibir'* celebrate their successful transit to the geographical North Pole (Frolov).

Ivan Frolov

Hydrometeorological conditions during the voyage

The weather situation during *Sibir'* s operational period in the vicinity of the Pole was close to mean multi-year conditions. During May and the first half of June, the weather in the near-pole area was governed by the prevailing high-air-pressure area, while cyclonic activity was developing over the northern areas of Europe, western Siberia and also the Kara and Laptev seas. Decreased pressure over the arctic seas, and increased pressure in high latitudes contributed to prevailing northeasterly winds in the area of icebreaker navigation. The wind speed was normally 4–8 meters per second. When passing weakly pronounced fronts, wind speed was observed to increase to 10–11 meters per second. Increased cyclonic activity over the northern areas of western Siberia during the leg of the route from Dikson Island to Vil'kitsky Strait resulted in an intensification of the northeasterly winds on 3–4 June (up to 18 meters per second).

The expedition was accomplished during the transition period from winter to summer hydrometeorological conditions. In May, the ice cover was in the stage of its maximum development. As a result of the ice drift during the preceding period, by the end of May the boundary of the prevailing multi-year ice was 64–128 kilometers farther north in the region of the Spitsbergen ice extension. Ice export from the Arctic Basin through Fram Strait during the period from March to May decreased to 116,000 square kilometers (reduced from a norm of 197,000 square kilometers. The drift velocity of the North Pole-27 Drifting Station was lower than the mean monthly values for this area.

Although there was a positive anomaly in the sum of freezing degree-days, ice conditions in the Barents and Kara seas in May were close to normal. In the Laptev Sea, ice conditions were more severe due to the absence of ice export (1,000 square kilometers compared to a norm of 87,000 square kilometers). The Kara and Laptev seas were covered during the entire expedition by thick first-year ice. In the Taymyr Massif, persistent winds of unfavourable directions led to increased hummocking (up to 20 percent of the area) and to severe strains on the ice cover. In the zone of fronts, ice cakes and small ice cakes prevailed. On the whole, the ice cover had a polygonal structure. Melting was not observed north of 80°N. Only in the Kara and Laptev seas in early June were observed the first indications of ice decay (for example, the appearance of patches of wet snow and the initial disintegration in the ice breccia fields).

It should be noted that during the period of *Sibir*'s navigation in the central Arctic Ocean, leads, particularly their formation and persistence governed by atmospheric circulation, were of special importance. From 23–7 May, a vast zone of open ice (lead) in the ice cover developed, extending more than 600 miles in a meridional direction along 45°E. On 23–4 May, the development of a strong anticyclone over the Greenland Sea and rapid shifting of a deep cyclone to the north of the Barents and Kara seas resulted in a change in the overall ice field drift. This situation led to the formation of a drift divide and an associated opening in sea ice in a meridional direction.

According to the data of I.D. Karelin (Karelin 1985:86–93), who analyzed the structure of fractures in compact ice from 1979–82 satellite data, meridional fractures from Franz Josef Land across the Pole were observed in May of 1979, 1981 and 1982 but were not found in 1980, when the anticyclonic ice gyre in the North Atlantic was weakened and the development of a spring change was shifted in time to a later period. Analysis of satellite images for 1985 indicate that, during the period of 14–26 May, a meridionally–oriented zone of open ice (lead) was observed from Franz Josef Land across the Pole, almost extending to the Canadian Arctic islands. Similar zones of open ice formed in May of 1984 and 1986, but they were of a much lesser extent.

After conducting a series of planned experimental studies in the near-pole area on 27 May, *Sibir'* headed south to Franz Josef Land and then to Dikson Island. By that time the meridional zone of open ice had shifted westward and, on 28–31 May, the meridional zone of open ice had practically closed. On 30 May, *Sibir'* departed the zone of prevailing multi-year ice and the remainder of the expedition was completed within arctic seas. In the region of prevailing multi-year ice, progress of the icebreaker was maintained by selectively using zones of first-year ice.

Statistical analysis of visual observations of ice formations along the *Sibir'* route shows that prevailing floe dimensions did not exceed 100 meters (ice cakes were predominant) (see Table 3.1). This indicates that in the extended areas of open ice, in which the icebreaker was continuously moving, small and large ice cakes were the predominant form of ice. At the present time the formation process of these extensive zones of open ice within the polar ice cover has not been explained. However, analysis of atmospheric circulation and drift-field computations made during the 1987 expedition suggest that such zones form in regions with enhanced values of shear strain in the ice cover, mainly in zones with positive estimates of ice-drift-velocity divergence. It is the shear-strain values that appear to govern the fracturing of extensive ice breccia fields and the formation of zones of ice cakes.

On the basis of the results of airborne radar measurements, the distribution of the ice cover was analyzed by size and areas of multi-year ice breccia fields, for a 20–50 kilometer distance from *Sibir'*'s route along the leg from North Pole-27 Drifting Station to the North Pole. Radar images were processed to delineate the boundaries of ice formations and to determine their areas and horizontal size. The average of the maximum and minimum width of the ice breccia field was assumed to be the ice floe diameter. The scale of the survey allowed fields with horizontal dimensions more than 2 kilometers to be clearly distinguished. Also, the areas of the first-year ice with horizontal dimensions exceeding 500 kilometers were delineated and calculated. Statistical processing of radar data allowed the scientific–operational group to define the most characteristic measurement intervals for ice formations. In total, seven types were defined with characteristic ice floe diameters: less than 2 kilometers, from 2 to 5 kilometers, from 5 to 7.5 kilometers, from 7.5 to 10 kilometers, from 10 to 13.5 kilometers, from 13.5 to 20 kilometers, from 20 to 25 kilometers (see Table 3.1). The ice floe distribution by size from the airborne SLAR data (see Table 3.1) shows that within the navigation area, multi-year ice breccia fields with horizontal dimensions more than 2 kilometers in diameter were most prevalent. The quantity of ice floes of a smaller size did not exceed 38 percent.

Table 3.1 Size distribution of the ice from visual observations aboard the icebreaker and radar surveys from aircraft

Visual observations		Radar survey	
Ice floe diameter, m	Relative number, %	Ice floe diameter, km	Relative number, %
0 – 50	43	>2	38
50 – 100	36	2 – 5	18
100 – 250	7	5 – 7.5	16
250 – 500	5	7.5 – 10	12
500 – 1,000	4	10 – 13.5	7
1,000 – 1,500	3	13.5 – 20	5
1,500 – 2,000	2	20 – 25	4

Conclusion

The experience gained during the May–June 1987 voyage of the *Sibir'* to the North Pole convincingly proved the possibility of carrying out research expeditions aboard nuclear icebreakers in high latitudes during any time of year. The system of scientific–operational hydrometeorological information services played a decisive role in the successful fulfillment of the expedition and its goals.

The strategy of ice navigation proposed during the planning stage, which utilized global fractures in the ice cover as well as the tactic of moving through a system of openings in the multi-year ice massif, was fully justified. The diagnostic satellite and airborne radar ice data, as well as operational forecasts of the distribution of open ice and compacting zones in the ice cover, were also of special significance.

References

Frolov, I. Ye. 1981. 'Chislennaia model osenne-zimnih ledovyh iavlenii' [A numerical model of the autumn-winter ice phenomena]. *Trudy Aanii* 372:73-81.

Karelin, I. D. 1985. 'Issledovanie krupnomasshtabnyh potokov morskih l'dov po televizionnym snimkam s iskusstvennyh sputnikov zemli' [The studies of the large-scale flows of sea ice from television images of the Earth's satellites]. *J. Problemy Arktiki i Antarktiki* 60:86-93.

Proshutinsky, A. Yu. 1988. 'Modelirovanie sezonnyh kolebanii urovnia severnogo ledovitogo okeana' [Modelling of the level seasonal oscillations in the Arctic Ocean]. *J. Meteorologiia i Gidrologiia* 2:57-65.

Part II
Man and the natural setting

4

Sea ice distribution in the Soviet Arctic

Don Barnett

The history of the exploration and the development of the Soviet maritime Arctic has been shaped by the character and spatial distribution of the ever-present sea ice. This history spans the centuries: from the unsuccessful attempts of 16th-century explorers to find a northern sea route to the Orient to the successful voyages to the North Pole by modern Soviet nuclear icebreakers in 1977 and 1987. The ice conditions typical of the individual seas are discussed here, as well as the major environmental factors that determine physical distribution of the sea ice and the seasonal and year-to-year variations of the ice cover. The typical and extreme positions of the sea ice edge can be seen in Figure 4.1. A number of technical ice terms are used here which are defined in the internationally recognized *World Meteorological Organization Sea Ice Nomenclature* (WMO 1970) (see Table 4.1).

The Barents Sea

The Barents Sea lies on the western extremity of the Soviet Arctic. It is the only Eurasian arctic sea which is not totally ice-covered during the winter. This Sea experiences the greatest seasonal variation in ice extent. Approximately 90 percent of the area normally ice-covered at the winter maximum becomes ice free in summer. As in the Chukchi Sea on the eastern extremity of the Northern Sea Route, warm ocean currents from the south influence greatly sea ice behavior and extent. Major factors that determine

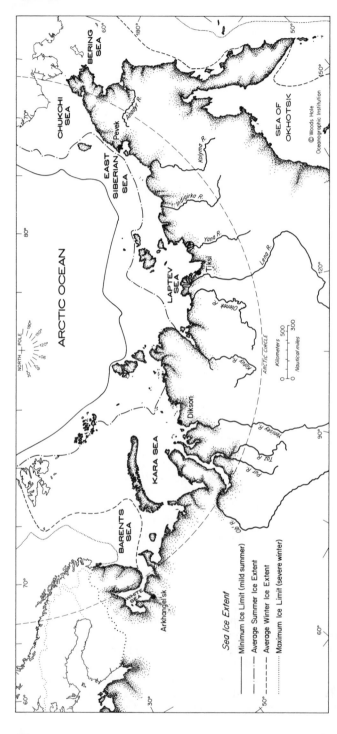

Figure 4.1 Average and extreme positions of sea ice extent throughout the Soviet maritime Arctic.

Table 4.1 Glossary of sea ice terminology

Area of weakness	A satellite-observed area in which either the ice concentration or the ice thickness is significantly less than that in the surrounding areas.
Drift ice	Term used in a wide sense to include any area of sea ice, other than fast ice, no matter what form it takes or how it is disposed.
Fast ice	Sea ice which forms and remains fast along the coast.
Flaw lead	A passageway between drift ice and fast ice which is navigable by surface vessels.
Ice edge	The demarcation at any given time between the open sea and sea ice of any kind, whether fast or drifting.
Ice free	No ice present.
Ice massif	A concentration of sea ice covering hundreds of square kilometers which is found in the same region every summer.
New ice	A general term for recently formed ice which includes frazil ice, grease ice, slush and shuga. These types of ice are composed of ice crystals which are only weakly frozen together (if at all).
Old ice	Sea ice which has survived at least one summer's melt.
Pack ice	High concentration of drift ice (generally 70 percent or more of the water surface covered by ice).
Polynya	Any non-linear-shaped opening enclosed in ice. Polynyas may be covered with new ice, nilas or young ice.
Ridge	A line or wall of broken ice forced up by pressure.
Young ice	Ice in the transition stage between new and first-year ice, 10–30 centimeters in thickness.

sea ice distribution in the Barents are the influx of warm Atlantic water; the general ocean circulation within the sea; the prevailing winds; several large island groups on the borders; and bathymetry.

The most influential factor in determining ice distribution within the sea is the North Cape Current, an extension of the Gulf Stream, that carries relatively warm Atlantic water into the sea from the southwest. The Current flows eastward in the southern Barents, then sends a branch northward along the east coast of Novaya Zemlya. The North Cape Current prevents ice formation in most of the southern Barents in normal winters and in the southwest Barents in even the most severe winters.

Ice distribution in the northwest Barents is strongly influenced by ocean circulation. Although the northeasterly winds that predominate in the northern Barents during winter and spring initially drive old ice and thicker first-year ice from the Arctic Ocean into the northern Barents between Svalbard and Franz Josef Land, it is the southwesterly flowing Bear Island Current that finally transports the ice farther south. As a result, old ice occasionally is observed as far south as Hopen and Bear Island during the late spring and early summer months (Vinje 1985). The ocean current is partly responsible for the broad ice tongue that typically extends southwestward to the vicinity of Bear Island during the winter.

From November through April, the southern Barents Sea normally is under the influence of southwesterly winds as a result of the seasonal deepening of the Icelandic low-pressure system. This maritime air provides an additional modifying effect that inhibits ice growth in the southern half of the sea. Winter air temperatures in the Barents Sea are the mildest of the Eurasian arctic seas. January averages range from about $-10°$ centigrade at southern coastal stations to $-15°$ at eastern and northern stations (Gorshkov 1980). Resultant first-year ice thicknesses are estimated to range from 50 to 100 centimeters in the south to 120 to 150 centimeters in the north. In occasional years, however, southeasterly winds dominate owing to an abnormal orientation of the Icelandic low- and the Siberian high-pressure systems. If this much colder continental flow persists for extended periods during the winter and early spring, ice conditions become exceptionally severe. Nearly 90 percent of the sea can become ice covered in these unusual winters compared to approximately 70 percent in a normal winter and less than 50 percent in mild winters.

The island groups of Novaya Zemlya, Franz Josef Land and Svalbard strongly influence ice distribution patterns within the Barents Sea by limiting interaction of its ice and water masses with those of bordering ice-covered seas. In addition, the islands interact with prevailing winds to create lee side weaknesses in the ice cover. The most dramatic and dependable of these occurs adjacent to the Franz Josef Land archipelago, affecting both winter ice conditions and the spring and summer melt pattern. Throughout the winter, a nearly permanent area of weakness exists along the southwest to northwest perimeter of the archipelago. Under the influence of persistent easterly winds, ice is driven offshore and, owing to refreezing, it is rapidly replaced by young and new ice. This polynya frequently extends more than 100 kilometers offshore of the outer islands. Examples of other commonly occurring lee-side polynyas can be observed off Northeast Land, Kong Karls Land, Kvitoya and Novaya Zemlya.

While all the major island groups in the sea contain glaciers that calve occasional icebergs, those on Franz Josef Land and Northeast Land produce the most. In occasional years, heavy concentrations of these icebergs have been observed in the Bear Island Current between Hopen and Bear Island. Many of these ground in the Spitsbergen Bank area. In rare years icebergs have been observed as far south as the mainland (Dobrovol'skiy and Zalogin

1981). They are found more normally in areas near their source and generally are small.

The Barents is one of the deeper seas of the Eurasian Arctic. Variations in bathymetry are important in the formation and distribution of sea ice in several areas. There are two areas of particular interest. The first is a group of relatively shallow areas (150–200 meters deep) that lie between 74° and 76°N and between 35° and 40°E. After early to mid-January, outbreaks of colder air from the north cause new ice formation over these shoals. This formation often appears as a circular area isolated from the main pack to the north. With continued cold airflow, the main pack expands southward to include the ice over the shoal and is evident as a southerly bulge of the ice edge (see Figure 4.2A). The second area is the southerly extension of the ice edge toward Bear Island. It is caused, partly, by drifting ice in the southerly flowing current east of Svalbard, but here also bathymetry has an effect. It is probable that, initially, most of this ice is new and young ice frozen in place. This results when relatively cold water mixes over the Spitsbergen Bank and then freezes. In some places it is less than 60 meters deep.

In late spring, winds throughout the Barents Sea become northeasterly. This transfers the Franz Josef Land polynya from its winter position on the western perimeter to the south and southwest of the archipelago and sets the stage for the typical seasonal melt pattern. With warming temperatures, the polynya ceases to refreeze and then widens (see Figure 4.3A) until it meets the retreating outer ice edge in the central Barents in midsummer, forming tongues. Because of the old ice in the colder arctic currents to the west and east of this polynya, melt here is much slower. Retreat of the ice edge in the tongues reaches only to 78°–79°N in normal years.

The White Sea

The White Sea is the smallest sea of the Soviet Arctic and the only sea that always becomes ice free during summer. Freeze-up normally begins in early November in the less saline waters of the river estuaries. New ice commonly appears first in the Mezen River mouth, then soon builds at the mouth of the Severnaya Dvina, Onega, and Kandalaksha rivers. Growth proceeds slowly until mid-December acceleration. The entire sea and most of its entrance becomes ice covered by 1 January (see Figure 4.4). The ice is predominately drift ice. The exception is a narrow band of fast ice which forms in the southern bays and along most of the western shoreline. Influenced by winter air temperatures of −10–15° centigrade (Gorshkov 1980), this fast ice grows to 50–70 centimeters in normal winters and exceeds 100 centimeters in severe winters. The thickness of the drift ice averages 35–50 centimeters but can exceed 100 centimeters during severe winters. Under the influence of currents and predominately southerly winds, some drift ice is released into the Barents Sea. This persistent movement, combined with the strong tides of the White Sea, often causes openings and weaknesses to occur. The most severe conditions develop when northerly winds compact ice against the southern coasts. Seasonal improvement in ice conditions becomes

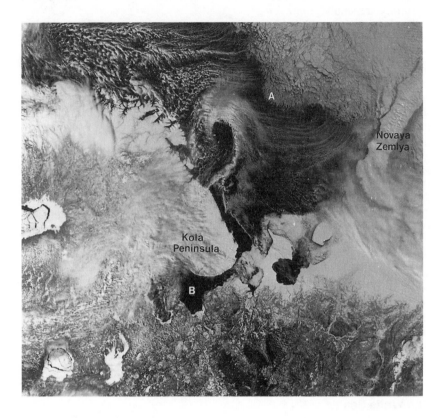

Figure 4.2A-B Outbreaks of cold air from the north can cause new ice formation over shallow areas in the Barents. Continued cold airflow causes the main pack to expand southward over shoal areas like those labelled A, which is evident as a southerly bulge of the ice edge. Area B shows evidence of seasonal improvement in ice conditions in the White Sea. Advanced Very High Resolution Radiometer (AVHRR) image from National Oceanic and Atmospheric Administration satellite NOAA 9: 15 April 1986.

noticeable in mid-April as average air temperatures rise above freezing and the wind-generated weaknesses along the southern shores cease to refreeze (see Figure 4.2B). By mid-May, the only remaining ice is found in the White Sea entrance east of 40°E and in Kandalakskaya Bay west of 30°E. The last ice floes usually persist until about 1 June in the entrance and vicinity but in severe years can persist into late June.

Figure 4.3 Nearly the entire White Sea and most of its entrance becomes ice covered by 1 January (AVHRR image from NOAA 7: 12 January 1982).

The Kara Sea

Continental air masses influence the remaining Soviet arctic seas and expose them to extremely cold winter temperatures. January air temperatures in the Kara Sea range from −15–20° centigrade in the southwest to −25–30° in the east and north (Gorshkov 1980). Beyond the obvious influence of these temperatures, sea ice characteristics are determined primarily by geography: the nearly landlocked location of the sea, winds, river runoff and the shallow coastal waters.

The islands of Novaya Zemlya prevent the warm extensions of the Gulf Stream that influence the Barents Sea from significantly affecting the Kara Sea. There is also little interchange between the Kara and the Laptev seas

53

due to the blocking action of the Severnaya Zemlya archipelago. Consequently, with the continent guarding the southern boundary of the sea, only the northern opening to the Arctic Ocean allows appreciable interaction between the Kara and its neighboring seas.

Fast ice forms along almost all coastlines in the Kara Sea. It is generally narrow except in the eastern Kara where it may extend up to 150–200 kilometers seaward. From mid-November until June, the only significant areas of weakness occur along this fast-ice boundary (see Figure 4.3B). Prevailing southerly winds constantly push drifting ice northward from the immobile fast ice. This drift ice is quickly replaced by polynyas of newly formed young and new ice. This continuous process through the winter results in the thinnest ice normally being found at the fast-ice boundary, with thicknesses increasing farther seaward. Based on normal air temperatures, ice thicknesses outside of these polynyas range from about 120 centimeters in the southwest to 2 meters in the northeast.

The mainland coast lies at 70°N at the western entrance of the Kara Sea but increases to more than 77°N at the eastern extremity in Proliv Vilkitskogo (the northernmost point of the Eurasian mainland). This latitudinal imbalance contributes to a significant difference in summer air temperature between the east and west sectors. July averages range from about 5° centigrade in the southwest to 0 – 2° in the northeast (Gorshkov 1980). This temperature range, combined with a large difference in river runoff, makes it convenient to treat the sectors as distinctly separate seas during the summer. Seasonal breakup throughout the entire sea begins in late June. Initially, the weaknesses adjacent to the fast ice cease to refreeze and begin to melt in the warmer June air (see Figure 4.3B). These open-water areas last only a few weeks, however, until the fast ice begins breakup and drifts seaward into the leads.

Kara Sea rivers are responsible for more than half of the total runoff into the Eurasian arctic seas (Dobrovol'skiy and Zalogin 1981). The warmer waters of the clearing rivers in the western Kara, chiefly the Yenisey and the Ob', accelerate melt initially in their estuaries, followed by a spreading arc farther seaward. When the seasonal ice minimum is reached by mid-September, the entire Sea south of 75°N is normally ice free — in sharp contrast to the severe ice conditions encountered by 16th-century navigators searching for a northern route to the Orient who usually halted near Proliv Karskiye Vorota at the southwest entrance to the sea. In extremely mild summers, part of the sea may become ice free as far north as 80° to 82°N. A southerly flowing counter-current along the east coast of Novaya Zemlya is an exception to the general south to north ice drift in the Kara. In unusually cool summers, ice fed by this current into the vicinity of the north entrance to Proliv Karskiye Vorota fails to melt completely. In those summers, ice may be present in all but the Yenisey and Ob' estuaries and the central portion of the southwest Kara.

In the eastern sector, with its colder temperatures and meager river runoff, melt is considerably less dramatic. Nearly half of the total area retains some ice through normal summers (see Figure 4.1). Year-to-year variation is great, however, ranging from near zero percent ice cover to near

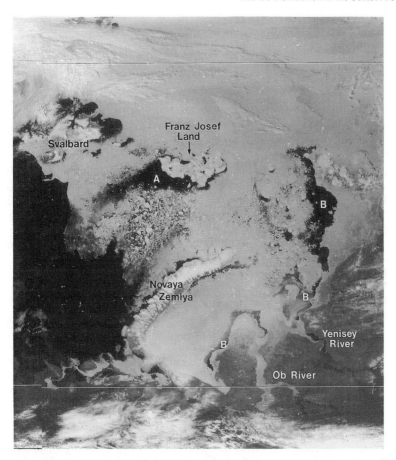

Figure 4.4A-B With warming temperatures, the Franz Josef Land polynya (area A) ceases to refreeze and then widens. By June, weaknesses in the fast ice boundary develop along the coastline areas of the eastern Kara Sea, as shown in B (AVHRR image from NOAA 5: 29 June 1978).

80 percent (NOCD 1986a). Summer winds in this sector are variable with little dominance from any direction. In some years, periods of westerly winds compact ice into the western approach of Proliv Vilkitskogo (the gateway to the Laptev Sea) which undoubtedly makes navigation difficult.

In September, freeze-up in the Kara begins with the appearance of new ice in the colder waters of the north. Freeze-up in the south starts in early October where breakup began, in the less saline waters of the estuaries. Rapid freeze-up of the remainder of the Sea east of 70°E follows. Waters of the southwest extremity are more resistant to rapid freezing. In average years, an open-water area remains from Proliv Karskiye Vorota to 180–275 kilometers northeastward as late as the first days of November. This open water disappears as early as late October in severe years but persists into the last half of December in extremely mild years.

Donald Barnett

The Laptev Sea

Distribution of sea ice within the Laptev Sea is determined by cold winter temperatures, southerly winter winds, ocean currents, river runoff and an extraordinarily wide continental shelf.

Due to its broad continental shelf, half of the total area of the Laptev is less than 50 meters deep. In fact, south of 76°N, the depth does not exceed 25 meters (Dobrovol'skiy and Zalogin 1981). Consequently, from early January until the beginning of breakup in June and July, the eastern Laptev and western East Siberian Sea experience the widest expanse of fast ice found in the world. Fast ice begins to form in mid-October in the fresher water of the river estuaries and expands to cover most of the continental shelf up to 500 kilometers from the mainland. The thickness of the fast ice commonly reaches 2 meters and grows to 2.5 meters in severe years owing to cold winter air temperatures. January temperatures average about −30 degrees centigrade (Gorshkov 1980). Southerly winter winds also influence sea ice distribution by persistently pushing drift ice northward from the fast ice boundary. Thus, before the moderating temperatures of late May there is a constant refreezing of newly opened water at that boundary. This new ice is then removed northward, resulting in a nearly permanent flaw lead or area of weakness that can reach 100 kilometers or greater in width. It is usually removed before reaching more than 15–30 centimeters in thickness, making the leads easy to distinguish on satellite imagery (see Figure 4.5A). Because the fast ice edge changes little in position or appearance during the winter, these areas of weakness are not only important sea-ice distribution features but also aid sea-ice experts in geographic recognition and analysis of satellite imagery.

Sea ice movement is influenced by ocean currents that flow from east to west and then turn northwest along the northern border of the Sea. In all but the extreme western Laptev, ice continues its northward drift under southerly winds, becomes trapped in the northerly setting current and is transported poleward by the Trans-Polar Drift Stream. This continuous removal of the thickest ice, and its replacement by new ice, limits the amount of old ice found in the Sea and contributes to a more extensive summer melt. In the west, along the coasts of Severnaya Zemlya and the Taymyr peninsula, ice drift is opposite to that elsewhere in the Sea. Along these coasts ice is carried southward by the weak East Taymyr Current (Sukhovey 1986) near to the mouth of the Khatanga River. This ice forms the Taymyr Massif which contains the only significant concentrations of old ice found in the southern Laptev. Much of this thicker old ice persists through the summer and often contributes to unfavorable navigation conditions.

From June to September, the relatively warm water discharge from a number of Siberian rivers accelerates ice melt. Water temperatures reach 10–14° centigrade at the river mouths. The largest of these rivers is the Lena which accounts for over 70 percent of the fresh water flowing into the sea (Dobrovol'skiy and Zalogin 1981). Other significant rivers are the Khatanga, Yana, Olenek, and the Anabar. In normal years, weakness in the sea ice begins to appear offshore of the Lena River delta by mid-June (see Figure 4.5B). By July, a nearly ice-free area extends seaward of the delta to about 75°N. Expansion of this ice-free area continues until mid-September. At that time most of the sea south of 77°N is ice free except for the areas west of about 117°E where ice usually persists south to 74–75°N in the East Taymyr coastal flow. It is the ice carried south by this current that can present the most serious obstacle to summer transit of the Laptev. Although winds are generally light and variable during summer, any extended period of strong easterly winds can compact the thick ice of the Taymyr Massif into the eastern approach of Proliv Vilkitskogo. It was this situation that was partly responsible for the disastrous finale to the 1937 shipping season. A

Figure 4.5A-B Area A indicates a nearly permanent flaw lead or area of weakness in the Laptev Sea partially caused by southerly winter winds and their influence on drift ice. These leads can achieve widths of 100 kilometers or more and are very easy to distinguish on satellite imagery. By mid-June, in normal years, offshore areas of the Lena River delta (area B) display areas of weakness. Vertical lines denote satellite data loss (AVHRR image from NOAA 6: 11 June 1985).

reported 20 Soviet ships (including seven icebreakers) were trapped and forced to winter at sea in the Laptev (Guzhenko 1983).

The East Siberian Sea

Ice distribution in the East Siberian Sea is determined primarily by cold winter and cool summer air temperatures, a wide continental shelf, winds, a weak river runoff and ocean surface currents. None of these factors favor a significant summer melt. As a result, the East Siberian experiences the least summer melt of any of the Soviet arctic seas. Normally, over 50 percent of the Sea still has at least a partial ice cover at the height of the melt season (see Figure 4.1).

The East Siberian Sea is the shallowest of the Soviet arctic seas. A wide continental shelf allows formation of an expanse of fast ice that extends 250–500 kilometers from the mainland coast. Air temperatures indicate that the fast ice attains thicknesses up to 170–200 centimeters in normal winters. Southerly winds prevail during the winter, carrying cold continental air and lowering average air temperatures to near $-30°$ centigrade (Gorshkov 1980). As in the Laptev Sea, these winds combine with fast ice over the continental shelf to create the only areas of weakness found during winter. Although less consistent than in the Laptev Sea, drifting ice periodically is pushed northward from the fast ice, resulting in polynyas of refrozen young and new ice.

During the short summer, prevailing winds turn northerly to keep air temperatures cool. Average air temperatures, which rise only several degrees above freezing, inhibit melting more effectively in the East Siberian Sea than similar temperatures in the Laptev and northern Kara seas. This is primarily due to the absence of any significant countering force. The influence of river runoff, for example, is comparatively weak. Total runoff is only about 20 percent of that in the Kara Sea and 35 percent of that in the Laptev Sea (Dobrovol'skiy and Zalogin 1981). Initial melt does occur in the estuaries of the Indigirka and Kolyma rivers as a direct result of seasonal runoff, but usually the influence is locally confined.

Ocean currents in the sea are generally weak, favoring ice input rather than removal. These currents are responsible primarily for a broad tongue of ice called the Ayon Ice Massif that projects from the Arctic Ocean toward the Siberian coast in the vicinity of 165°–170°E. The Massif carries large amounts of old ice and is very resistant to summer melt. Intrusions from the Massif which are caused by periods of strong northerly winds and the prevailing ocean currents frequently extend into the coastal shipping lanes. Seasonal freeze-up of the sea begins in September at the northern ice edge and along the rapidly cooling mainland coast. Freeze-up is complete by mid-October.

The Chukchi Sea

The Chukchi Sea experiences a wide seasonal variation in total ice extent (see Figure 4.1). Summer ice melt in the Chukchi is extensive, exceeding that in all other Eurasian arctic seas except the Barents. Like the North Cape Current in the Barents Sea, a relatively warm surface current flowing from the Bering Sea in the south greatly affects ice distribution in the Chukchi. Here, however, the effect of the current is confined to the summer months and a large part of the Chukchi, including the western coastal shipping lanes, is barely affected by it. Other forces that contribute to shape the characteristic ice conditions in the Chukchi Sea are bathymetry, winds, ocean currents, air temperatures and Wrangel Island.

Average January air temperatures in the Soviet Chukchi range from −20° centigrade in the east to −25–30° in the west (Gorshkov 1980). This would indicate a normal east-to-west ice thickness range of about 130 centimeters – 180 centimeters at the winter maximum. The Chukchi lacks the wide continental shelf found in the Laptev and East Siberian seas. Consequently, only a narrow band of fast ice (10 – 15 kilometers) forms along the mainland coast and around Wrangel Island. Although the remaining ice is mobile pack ice, few weaknesses occur during the winter. An exception is a polynya of young and new ice usually present in the lee of Wrangel Island. This lee-side polynya may be up to 50 – 100 kilometers wide during periods of stronger winds.

Thick old ice is fed into the Sea throughout the year by an ocean current that flows south from the Arctic Ocean west of Wrangel Island. This current then flows southeast through Proliv Longa. During winter, prevailing northerly winds compact this drifting ice against the Siberian coast to create extensive pressure ridging. These factors make the Chukchi Sea potentially the most difficult section of the Northern Sea Route during the navigation season. The Chukchi, combined with the difficult ice conditions in the eastern East Siberian Sea, provides the major impediment to year-round navigation of the Northern Sea Route. The degree of difficulty in passage depends on the predominant wind direction. Normally, the persistent northerly onshore winds of winter begin to ease in intensity by late April and reverse to offshore by June or July. Under the influence of this normal wind flow, a narrow lead develops along the length of the mainland by mid spring that later widens to provide a navigable lead through the shipping season (see Figure 4.6). In some years, Proliv Longa becomes nearly ice free. In other years, however, extended periods of northeast winds can close the lead and exert severe onshore pressure to make navigation exceedingly difficult. In the 1983 shipping season, for example, one Soviet ship was crushed and sunk and damage was incurred by as many as 30 of the possible 50 or more other ships (Armstrong 1984:173–82) that were temporarily trapped by late season onshore pressure.

Midsummer air temperatures which range on average from 2° centigrade in the north to 5° centigrade in the south (Gorshkov 1980) contribute to initial melt in the areas near the Bering Strait. It is the seasonal warm current flowing northward through the Strait, however, which causes the greatest

Donald Barnett

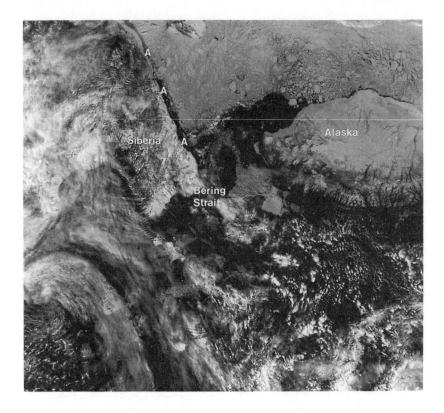

Figure 4.6A Wind direction is a crucial determinant of prevailing ice conditions in the Chukchi Sea. Area A shows how offshore winds can precipitate development of a narrow, navigable lead along the Siberian coastline (AVHRR image from NOAA 9: 31 May 1986).

melt. Eighty percent of the Chukchi Sea is cleared of ice by mid-September. The effects of the current generally are directed north and northeast of the Strait and occasionally northwest toward Wrangel Island. Bathymetry influences the shape of the Chukchi ice edge east of Wrangel Island by directing this northward flowing current through underwater canyons. As a result, northward ice-free intrusions into the ice pack are frequently evident during the summer over these canyons. Seasonal freeze-up is strongly retarded by the warm Bering Sea water. Although initial new ice usually occurs in late September or early October in the west and north extremities, freeze-up of the last open-water north of the Bering Strait normally is not complete before mid to late November.

Conclusion

A comparison of the winter and summer sea ice cover in the Soviet arctic seas (see Table 4.2) shows that, despite regional and seasonal variation, the ice cover is ever present. Results presented in this table were calculated from data presented in tables from *Sea Ice Climatic Atlas, Arctic East and Arctic West* (NOCD 1986a; NOCD 1986b). Geographic limits of the seas as used in the atlases included the fringes of the southern Arctic Ocean. Therefore, the open-water percentages shown are slightly lower than if strict geographic boundaries had been used. Nevertheless, the percentages of ice cover for the Kara, Laptev and East Siberian seas are striking, considering these numbers are for the summer minimum. This data has clear implications for the potential extension of the navigation season along the northeastern region of the Soviet Arctic.

Table 4.2 Comparison of the winter and summer sea ice cover in Soviet Arctic seas

Region	Summer Ice Cover Relative to the Winter Maximum Extent[1] (% of area)	Average Date of the Summer Minimum
Barents Sea	10	15 September
Kara Sea West[2]	25	24 September
Kara Sea East[3]	48	14 September
Laptev Sea	47	17 September
East Siberian Sea	57	13 September
Chukchi Sea	20	12 September

[1] % of the area of the winter maximum ice cover that remains partially ice covered at the summer minimum.

[2] Kara Sea west of 90°E.

[3] Kara Sea east of 90°E.

Sources: Dobrovol'skiy and Zalogin 1981; Gorshkov 1980.

Four centuries passed between the first serious attempts to transit the Northern Sea Route enroute to the Orient and the first one-season passage by the Soviet icebreaker *Sibiryakov* in 1932. Less than 50 years later, technological advances took man to the North Pole in surface ships, placing the dream of year-round transit of the Route on the doorstep of reality. But while it is probable that year-round navigation is now technically possible, these advances have still not made the venture economically practical. In fact, ship operations along the Northern Sea Route today remain primarily seasonal. For the immediate future, at least, successful marine transportation will continue to be significantly affected by the variable extent and distribution of sea ice along the Soviet North.

References

Armstrong, T.E. 1984. 'The Northern Sea Route, 1983.' *Polar Record* 22(137):173-182.

Dobrovol'skiy, A.D., and B.S. Zalogin. 1981. *Seas of the USSR*. Moscow. [Translated from Russian by the Foreign Broadcast Information Service, Washington, DC, 1982.]

Gorshkov, S.G. 1980. *World Ocean Atlas: Arctic Ocean*. Vol. 3. Pergamon Press.

Guzhenko, T.B. 1983. Interview with USSR Minister of the Maritime Fleet. *In*: *Izvestiya* 28 November.

Naval Oceanography Command Detachment (NOCD). 1986a. *Sea Ice Climatic Atlas: Arctic East*. Vol. 2. Asheville, NC NAVAIR 50-1C-541.

— 1986b. *Sea Ice Climatic Atlas: Arctic West*. Vol. 3. Asheville, NC NAVAIR 50-1C-542.

Sukhovey, V.F. 1986. *Seas of the World Oceans*. Leningrad. [Translated from Russian by the Foreign Broadcast Information Service, Washington, DC, 1987.]

Vinje, T. 1985. *The Physical Environment Western Barents Sea: Drift, Composition, Morphology and Distribution of the Sea Ice Fields in the Barents Sea*. Oslo, Norway:Norsk Polarinstitutt.

World Meteorological Organization (WMO). 1970. *WMO Sea Ice Nomenclature*. Geneva, Switzerland.

5

Environmental protection in the Soviet Arctic seas

Alexei Y. Roginko

The Arctic is one of the Soviet Union's largest geographical regions, where development is of prime state importance. The economic development of northern territories and arctic seas, provided for in the 'Basic Guidelines for the Economic and Social Development of the USSR in 1986–1990 and in the Period Up to the Year 2000', is based on rich energy and mineral resources.

Substantial reserves of oil, gas, coal, tin, precious metals and other minerals are concentrated in arctic territories and on the continental shelf of northern seas. The presence of such reserves inevitably leads to the intensive development of diversified industry, chiefly oil, gas and mining in the region. Rich natural resources and the presence of rivers, capable of supplying large cities and industry with pure water and cheap hydro-electric power, open up many prospects for economic development. At the same time, it is not intended simply to make these regions into a raw-materials adjunct to more developed regions of the country but to set forth their planned economic development for many decades to come.

In past years, a number of regional economic complexes, including the Kola, Noril'sk and Verkhnekolymsk complexes, have been developed in arctic territories. Examples of large prospective complexes, which are either in the stage of intensive development or in the initial stage of formation, include the East Siberian, Timan-Pechora and Yakut 'regional economic' complexes (Treshnikov and Rusanov 1985:22–8). Immense Siberian territories — which include the catchment areas of most Siberian rivers, the estuaries of the largest rivers and the coastal and shelf regions of arctic seas

— are being drawn into economic activity. This development process will inevitably be accompanied by increased anthropogenic loads on the marine environment of arctic seas and should call for monitoring of pollution of these waters and of the snow and ice cover.

Environmental research and monitoring

In the Soviet Union, stations and posts of the All-State Observation and Monitoring Network have been performing year-round monitoring of natural water pollution in the Arctic Ocean since the end of the 1960s. These monitoring stations are situated on rivers, estuarine shores and islands in the seas of the arctic zone. Apart from this, annual scientific research institute expeditions monitor the open-water environment of arctic seas during both summer and winter periods (Rusanov 1985:201–7).

This research has made it possible to:

1. establish the principal sources and entry paths of pollutants into Arctic seas;
2. assess the background levels of water and ice-cover pollution of Arctic waters; and
3. amass extensive data on the seas' physical and hydrochemical characteristics which determine the state of the aquatic habitat.

The study of ecosystems confined to northern seas, however, is still fragmentary and unsystematic. This, so far, makes it impossible to provide a complete characterization of the natural complexes of arctic seas and to bring to light the most essential links between elements of animate and inorganic nature: links that promote the existence and stability of arctic marine ecosystems (Korotkevich and Rusanov 1985:22–7).

Scientific studies carried out in recent years reveal that differences in the composition and volume of pollutants entering arctic seas, the conditions of their spread throughout arctic ocean waters, the transformation rate and the degree of their impact on ecosystems are the result of a complex of regional physical and geographical factors. These factors include differences in climatic conditions, water exchange with adjacent oceans and runoff volume. Thus, the inflow of Atlantic waters carries the bulk of pollutants entering the waters of arctic seas. These pollutants are mostly petroleum products originating from North Sea oil fields and the polluted surface waters of the north Atlantic Ocean. Microbiological investigations carried out in the Norwegian Sea in 1984 show that in regions where oil-contaminated waters from the Atlantic Ocean and North Sea flow to arctic seas, changes are occurring already in the composition of the microflora. Studies show an increase in the number of species and in the biomass of the microbial population that use anthropogenic hydrocarbons as a food source. It is still difficult to predict the impact on humans from this process because many species of oil-oxidizing bacteria are potential carriers of pathogenic properties (Korotkevich and Rusanov 1985:22–7). Two factors, cold arctic waters in the northern regions and continental waters in the southern regions, principally determine the physical and chemical characteristics of the environment and composition of ecosystems of arctic seas of the Siberian shelf — the Kara, Laptev and East Siberian seas. The waters of these seas, especially in their central and northern regions, are some of the world's most pristine. This makes it possible to use them as reference areas in a global system of monitoring possible changes in the state of the natural environment under the influence of man's economic activity.

As for the Chukchi Sea, the water exchange with the Bering Sea determines to a large extent the basic characteristics of its water mass and composition of marine life. At the same time, in summer, the northern part of the Chukchi Sea, and in winter, its central regions are under the predominant influence of arctic waters flowing from the direction of the Beaufort Sea, where during the past decade marine oil and gas recovery have been actively pursued. This could influence the level of water and sea-ice pollution, where in recent years an observed increase attests to surface water pollution in some regions of the Chukchi Sea (Korotkevich and Rusanov 1985:22–7).

Overall, the Barents and Chukchi seas are distinguished for their high levels of anthropogenic pollution; comparatively, the Laptev, Kara, and East Siberian seas are comparatively much less polluted (Danyushevskaya and Greben' 1982:142–3).

Recent studies show that the content of pollutants such as detergents and pesticides in the majority of arctic waters, including the estuaries of Siberian rivers, is not high, being within the error limits of the analytical methods and showing no tendency for increase. This can be explained by the fact that virtually all the continental drainage discharged into arctic seas (including river drainage) is formed on sparsely populated and agriculturally unexploited regions of tundra and forest tundra (Rusanov 1985:201–7). Moreover, loads of suspended solids and detergents in the arctic water basins are now twice as low as in 1980. Oil and oil product loads also have decreased considerably (Consultative Meeting, Soviet Delegation 1989b).

The Barents Sea stands out with respect to pollution through the presence of chlorinated hydrocarbons. As is known, the Arctic Ocean is a discharge zone for adjacent seas and the Atlantic Ocean. Residual concentrations of chlorinated hydrocarbons were found everywhere during organ and tissue analyses of several marine species in the Barents Sea. The levels of their accumulation in the overwhelming majority of cases, however, were well below international (recommended by the World Health Organization) and national maximum permissible norms. Nevertheless, as a number of researchers have noted, the possibility remains for an increased accumulation of these substances by organisms of higher trophic levels (Savinova 1985:102–3; Matishov et al. 1986:13–16).

Alexei Y. Roginko

Hydrocarbon pollution

Hydrocarbons, primarily oil and oil products, are potentially the most dangerous contaminants of arctic seas. Overall, the content of dissolved petroleum hydrocarbons in arctic seas near the Soviet coast does not, as a rule, exceed maximum permissible concentrations (0.05 milligrams per liter) (Izmailov 1982:103–4). The methods used to determine hydrocarbons in natural waters are incapable of differentiating between hydrocarbons of anthropogenic or biogenic origin. The latter predominantly include hydrocarbons (oils and fats) that are the products of zooplankton and phytoplankton activity which are found throughout arctic seas. These biogenic hydrocarbons form surface films covering vast areas of sea water. Recent estimates of petroleum hydrocarbons in arctic sea waters might not correspond to actual contamination. These estimates should take into account the important contribution of biogenic hydrocarbons (Rusanov 1985:201–7). The foci of their increased concentration are local in nature and are mainly confined to oil transportation routes, to estuaries of large rivers (in the basins where oil exploration or development is being carried out), to the busiest areas of maritime shipping and to areas where ships congregate (Rusanov 1985:201–7). Sometimes oil pollution in arctic seas is the result of exploratory work. For a number of years, deep wells drilled through the rock mass of the Vavilov ice dome (October Revolution Island) were repeatedly filled with diesel fuel and kerosene, which ended up in the periglacial zone and partially in the sea (Govorukha 1986:24–30).

The high-latitude position of the Arctic Ocean creates a unique setting for ecosystems in its waters. These conditions include low water temperatures, the presence of an ice cover throughout most of the year and sharp contrasts in the distribution of solar radiation during polar days and nights. Severe climatic conditions, which create a 'rigorous' setting, also determine the specific features of arctic ecosystems — short food chains, species scarcity, composition related to other oceans and pronounced fluctuations in the production of organic matter.

Life under these 'rigorous' arctic conditions is extreme, and so only a small amount of pollution represents a greater danger for the arctic ecosystem owing to the slower rates of physicochemical, chemical and biochemical processes determining the self-cleansing capacity of the natural environment (Rusanov 1985:201–7; Treshnikov and Rusanov 1985:22–8). Experimental observations by Soviet scientists in the Arctic show that the composition of petroleum products in water or ice varies intensely with factors such as evaporation, diffusion, biological utilization, photo-oxidation and ionization under the effect of direct solar radiation (Izmailov 1982:103–4). Evaporation processes play an important role in the removal of hydrocarbons from surface water and ice. Hydrocarbon-oxidizing microorganisms are encountered throughout the coastal and open waters of the central Arctic Basin; however, their numbers are extremely small, and biodegradation does not play a significant role in the purifying processes. Temperature is the chief factor limiting microbial oxidation of hydrocarbons (Il'inskii et al. 1986:171–3).

Apart from their direct toxic effects on aquatic organisms, the penetration of contaminants, primarily petroleum products, into water or the snow and ice cover brings about marked changes in the structure of ice, its physical and chemical properties, and can entail a host of ecological consequences. By disrupting the heat, moisture and gas exchange processes of water and ice with the atmosphere, the films of petroleum products slow down seawater evaporation by about 50 percent and the ice growth rate by a factor of 1.3–1.9. Oil films also decrease the albedo of snow and ice by 10–35 percent, which, by increasing their temperature, causes them to melt more rapidly. In spring and summer, snow melts in polluted areas 5–10 times faster than in unpolluted areas (Izmailov 1986:76–9; Izmailov and Simonov 1986:117–20).

Studies by Soviet scientists indicate that under conditions of continuous and large-scale oil pollution of areas near the edge of seas and ice masses, increased melting can cause ice edges to shift northward. This in turn can affect changes in the balance of heat and moisture exchange between the sea and the atmosphere; it can also bring about changes in the intensity and the course of cyclones and thereby affect the climate of vast geographical regions.

It is also very possible that increased seawater evaporation (as a result of the increase of its ice-free area) leads to an increased flow of moisture (snow) to the continent and to regions of human life and activity. If oil spills in arctic seas are infrequent, then their effect on physical processes will not be so long-lasting, as was once thought. These effects will have impacts varying from several days to 1-2 years, thanks to the processes of natural purification during the spring and summer months. It should be stressed, however, that the effect of oil films on the fauna and flora of arctic seas will be negative in any event and, in some cases, fatal (Izmailov 1986:76–9).

Oil pollution impact of arctic seas can lead to:

1. the disruption of many natural food chains in the ecosystems of the Arctic Ocean continental shelf;
2. the formation of vacant ecological niches;
3. the reduction in the bioproductivity of ecosystems; and
4. the change in the structure of populations of benthic and planktonic species.

Petroleum products significantly affect the structural and functional characteristics of phytoplankton by reducing initial production rates 4-8 times even under maximum possible concentrations, not to mention the mass mortality of aquatic species at large concentrations (Matishov *et al.* 1986:13–16). Moreover, the larvae of crustaceans when contaminated with oil are much more vulnerable in the Arctic than in the lower latitudes. Therefore, seawater pollution under such conditions can lead to the mass mortality of benthic invertebrates and to a reduction in the number of amphipoda in plankton (Govorukha 1986:24–30).

A disruption in the temperature stability of the surface layer, which occurs during the deterioration of the ice cover, can quickly lead to the complete local extinction of stenothermic species; this would have serious consequences for the Arctic Ocean's entire ecosystem. However, the increase in anthropogenic loads on arctic seas will be most distinctly manifested in the alteration of their gas conditions and primarily through a reduction of dissolved oxygen content. Such a reduction is especially dangerous because most fish species in arctic waters are commercially important whitefish and salmon, which require high levels of oxygen concentration (Rusanov 1985:201–7).

In speaking of ecological studies of arctic marine pollution, it should be mentioned that the ocean's snow and ice cover has a high sorption capacity with respect to many polluting substances. Therefore, it can be a factor contributing, on the one hand, to the purification of specific regions of the ocean from polluting agents entering the water, and on the other, to the transport of these substances far from the sources of entry.

The general circulation pattern of surface water and ice in the Arctic Ocean is such that from the chief and most likely pollution source areas (shelves and coasts of Alaska, Canada, and Barents Sea) the path of polluting substances will transect virtually the entire Arctic Basin (Treshnikov and Baranov 1972). Because the decay rate of most pollutants at low temperatures is minimal, their entry from ice to water will occur all along the path of their drift across the ocean. Therefore, not one arctic state can consider itself insured against the consequences of such pollution, even though the pollution source may be situated thousands of miles away from its shores. Moreover, apart from Arctic Basin pollution, contaminated ice also can pose a potential threat to the ecological balance of the North Atlantic, where the main mass of drift ice from the Arctic Ocean flows (Rusanov 1985:201–7).

Thus, any pollution of the arctic aquatic environment may have much more prolonged effects on the entire ecosystem than in the lower latitudes and can lead to serious disturbances of the ecological balance of vast areas.

The expansion of economic activity in the north, in particular the onset of a new stage in the development of the oil and gas reserves of the arctic continental shelf, the construction of tidal power stations, dams and dikes (which cut off gulfs) and the construction and development of ports, calls for careful scientific study and the introduction of a new environmental conservation strategy. Such a strategy needs to take into account the distinctive vulnerability of the arctic sea environment.

Although, from an engineering standpoint, the designs of water control structures may be worked out thoroughly, the assessment of their ecological impact is often delayed. Both the principles and methodology for environmental impact assessment of economic projects have yet to be fully developed with respect to the Arctic (Korotkevich and Rusanov 1985:22–7). It is important that scientific knowledge leads the pace of economic development, and in this connection it is necessary to monitor constantly the state of the natural environment.

Such monitoring has assumed special importance in connection with the oil and gas exploration work, which has begun already on the shelf of the Barents Sea, as well as in the development of offshore oil-fields. In the

Barents, small yet continuous seepage of oil and industrial waste is unavoidable, and there is the danger of accidental leaks of oil and gas.

Protection of groundwater is one of the biggest problems in shallow offshore drilling, particularly the possibility of artificial groundwater discharge in the sea during the exposure of the water table or penetration of seawater into the water table. The chance of uncovering gas hydrate deposits increases with the depth of drilling. This can cause gas to penetrate into the benthic zone and can generate substantial pollution, especially if the foundation of the gas hydrate deposits is made up of hydrogen sulfide (Ivanov *et al*. 1985:94–5).

At present, specialists from the Murmansk Marine Biological Institute and the Nature Conservation Laboratory of the Kola Branch of the USSR Academy of Sciences are carrying out a survey of the background level of seawater contamination by petroleum products, phenols and other polluting substances. Hydrobiological monitoring has been established and benthic communities have been selected for biological monitoring. A preliminary assessment has been made of the natural processes of purifying water from petroleum products through microorganismal activity; a collection has been established of the most active strains of oil-oxidizing bacteria. In relation to this problem, an experimental study is planned on the influence of drilling fluids, cuttings and oil on the ontogenesis of several commercial fish species. Quick tests are being developed to assess toxicity, and maximum permissible concentrations are being specified for chemical drilling agents on the basis of physiological criteria for aquatic organisms (Matishov *et al*. 1986:13–16).

The control of oil pollution and accidental oil spills is a problem that has become urgent with regard to increased drilling for oil and gas on the Barents Sea shelf. The main contributors to the biological breakdown of oil are hydrocarbon-oxidizing microorganisms, which are capable of using oil as their only source of organic matter and energy. Their activity can increase when they are attached to various types of mineral and organic particles, as well as to carriers that are nonsoluble in water.

Researchers at the Nature Conservation Laboratory of the Kola Branch of the USSR Academy of Sciences selected modified sorbents based on vermiculite from the Kovdor deposit (a layered aluminosilicate mineral formed as a result of the weathering of micaceous magnesium–iron ore) to be such a carrier. When thermally treated, this mineral swells and increases over 20 times in volume. The formed material possesses high porosity, a large unit surface, substantial oil capacity and good buoyancy (Krasnikova and Mesyats 1986:178–80). After regeneration by thermal treatment, this sorbent can be used no less than 10 times; each subsequent regeneration not only failed to decrease its effectiveness, but to some degree (sixfold use) increased its oil capacity. The selected sorbent's future use is governed by the substantial raw-materials base of the Kovdor vermiculite deposit, its relatively low cost and sufficiently simple fabrication. During studies, the degree of water surface purification by the vermiculite sorbent after repeated regeneration was 99.7 percent at a petroleum product–sorbent ratio of 4:1 (Mesyats and Kirillova 1986:181–3). The results of experiments conducted in Kola Bay point to the effectiveness of this sorbent in controlling oil pollution of seawater and to the possibility of using this method on an industrial scale during accidental oil spills (Mesyats and Kirillova 1986:181–3).

The necessity of pursuing special arctic ecological research arises also where economic activity in arctic seas has led to the biological isolation of river mouths, marine inlets and estuaries (when blocked by the dams and dikes of tidal power stations). The erection of these structures can lead to ecological disturbances of varying severity depending on the degree of reducted water exchange with the sea. In extreme cases, the mass mortality of aquatic organisms (primarily littoral) is possible, in addition to the irreplaceable loss of virtually all the biological resources of the blocked basin. The spawning areas of Atlantic salmon have already decreased in number owing to the regulation of the rivers flowing to the Barents and White seas (Matishov et al. 1986:13–16).

The emergent environmental situation in maritime regions adjacent to the northern coast of the USSR and the increased fragility of arctic ecosystems dictate the need to expand research into the natural complexes of arctic regions. A series of socioeconomic, organizational and legal measures must be aimed at putting an end to all forms of activity that negatively affect the ecology of the Arctic and that undermine the base for future economic development (Treshnikov and Rusanov 1985:22–8).

Natural reserves

Most Soviet scientists engaged in research on arctic environmental protection consider the most effective form of nature-conservancy measures for this zone to be the creation of reserves, sanctuaries and other protected areas (Vekhov 1984:91–7; Uspenskii et al. 1986:7–18). All forms of economic activity and recreation would be prohibited or severely restricted within these areas. The existing network of such protected areas, which would include arctic islands and waters, is still very small (see Figure 5.1). The network includes: Kandalaksha Reserve in Murmansk Province (58,000 hectares, established in 1932) which has several small islands in the Barents Sea and waters in the Kandalaksha Inlet (White Sea); and Wrangel Island Reserve (796,000 hectares, established in 1976) which includes Herald Island (Uspenskii and Feigin 1986:18–24). The goal of the Kandalaksha Reserve is to protect and to study the flora and fauna of sea islands, maritime reaches of the mainland and the ecosystem of the continental shelf of the Barents and White seas. It is populated by 30 mammal species, including the grey seal (a rare species), 208 species of birds, including the common eider, colonies of sea birds and gulls and rare species such as the white-tailed eagle and the gyrfalcon. The goal of the Wrangel Island Reserve is to preserve and study the animal population of the arctic islands. It is populated by 11 mammal species and over 100 bird species. The reserve boasts the largest polar bear breeding area in the Arctic, one of the largest walrus breeding

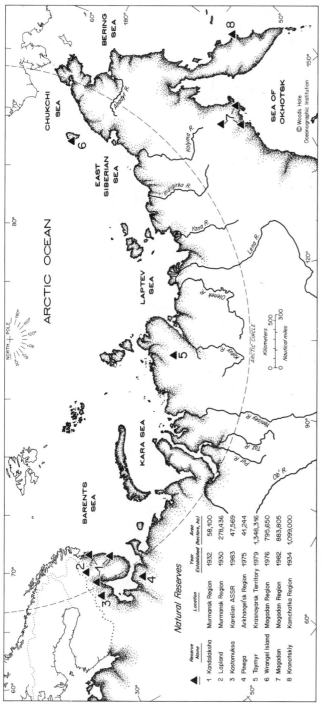

Figure 5.1 Current natural reserves in the Soviet maritime Arctic and Subarctic.

grounds in the world and the only colonial snow goose nesting site in the USSR. Interestingly, a herd of ox has also been introduced.

Existing protected areas in the Arctic are not representative with respect to arctic ecosystems and aquatic species as a whole. The area of waters included within them is not great and comprises only several percent of the total protected area (Vekhov 1984:91–7). Meanwhile, the vital necessity of expanding the network of such protected territories and waters in the Arctic, considering the many features of the actual complex, is extremely great. The considerable experience gathered both in the Soviet Union and abroad in organizing nature-conservancy reserves cannot be applied fully in the higher latitudes, first and foremost because of specific features of the natural environment (Uspenskii et al. 1986:7–18).

The most important features of arctic ecosystems from the standpoint of creating protected areas reside in the unbreakable unity of land and sea elements, comprising a single ecosystem. As one moves further into the high-latitude Arctic and as environmental conditions become more extreme, greater area is needed to ensure that ecosystems function in a natural fashion.

According to several Soviet authors, the required territorial minimum for the creation in the Arctic of nature-conservancy reserves is 0.5–1 million hectares (Uspenskii et al. 1986:7–18; Shtil'mark 1979:183–9). The practice of creating protected territories and waters corroborates these calculations. The Taymyr reserve (established in 1979), the first state reserve in the continental Soviet Arctic, encompasses over 1.8 million hectares. Islands in the Arctic Ocean comprise approximately 26 percent of the Ocean's area, which is much higher than that of the Pacific and Atlantic oceans (2.2 and 1.2 percent respectively) (Kryuchkov 1987:147–8). Another special feature of the region requiring careful consideration is the dispersal of animals in areas that are isolated and distant from each other: walrus breeding grounds, dens of female bears and rookeries. The measures for their protection must be very drastic because once these breeding areas are destroyed, they may not be restored. When threatened, animals that are uniformly and widely distributed will recover more quickly in any given area (Kryuchkov 1987:147–8). In addition, the fauna of the Arctic Ocean, including benthic organisms, display a high degree of endemism.

Many Soviet experts believe that nature-conservancy reserves in the high-latitude Arctic are required most urgently for most arctic islands, the wild and still self-regulating systems of which are being subjected to damage (Kryuchkov 1987:147–8; Uspenskii et al. 1986:7–18; Treshnikov and Rusanov 1985:22–8). At the same time, the ecological integrity and value of island reserves in the Arctic Ocean cannot be ensured without including sufficiently large bodies of water where protected animals, inhabitants of rookeries, walruses and polar bears feed (Kryuchkov 1987:147–8; Uspenskii 1983:16–17).

It is proposed to establish reserves separately on Novosibirskie and Severnaya Zemlya islands which, in the geologic past, apparently formed part of the Eurasian continent. This ancient continent extended northwards hundreds of kilometers beyond today's continent. A reserve and several sanctuaries also are needed on Novaya Zemlya Island with its immense rookeries and glaciers. The question has long been raised as to whether to establish a reserve on Vaygach Island for the protection of geese, swan and eider nesting grounds, polar bears, polar foxes and walruses (Kryuchkov 1987:147–8).

The ecological uniqueness and key position in the circumpolar region of the high-latitude Arctic, which impacts on ecosystems far beyond its boundaries, dictate a need to create a protection zone in the region of the Franz Josef Land archipelago in the far west of the Soviet Arctic. The system of sea currents and the continual presence of polynyas contribute to a close association of land and sea components of the ecosystems' complex. The Arctic Ocean is rich in polynyas and pools of open water in ice, where areas of pure water are quite often encountered even in winter. Over 80 percent of island surfaces are covered by glaciers, which contain approximately 1.5 million cubic kilometers of pure ice which is very valuable in itself.

Thirty-seven species of birds, over 60 rookeries and the largest nesting grounds of ivory gulls (entered in the USSR Red Book) in the USSR are found within the boundaries of the Franz Josef Land archipelago. Also concentrated here is a large number of rare animal species entered in world and Soviet Red Books (Greenland right whale, Atlantic walrus, and polar bear). Only in this region of the USSR can one encounter the narwhal, an arctic dolphin.

On the islands of Franz Josef Land, there are many historic memorials, associated with the names of such illustrious arctic explorers as F. Nansen, G. Sedov and many others. Within the confines of the proposed protected zone in the region of the archipelago, it is planned to include land and sea areas with varying forms of protection — from strictly-controlled areas to territories with reserve management — where permission would be given for economic and other activity that would not disrupt the normal operation of the natural complex. The hypothetical area of the reserve is approximately 4.2 million hectares, of which land, air holes and ice-covered waters would comprise 1 million, 1 million and 2 million hectares, respectively. It is proposed to establish sanctuaries on islands of the archipelago that are currently experiencing the greatest effects of economic and other activity: Zemlya Aleksandry Island (approximately 100,000 hectares), Graham Bell Island (approximately 170,000 hectares) and Rudolf Island (over 40,000 hectares) (Kryuchkov 1987:147–8; Uspenskii 1983:16–17; Uspenskii et al. 1986:7–18).

Apart from islands and adjacent waters, the system of protected natural territories in arctic sea must also include polynyas. These include such polynyas as the Cheshskaya, Pechora, Novozemel'skaya, Amderma, Yamal, Ob'-Yenisey as well as polynyas combined into the Great Siberian region (Vostochno-Severozemel'skaya Taimyr, Lena, Novosibirsk and others). These areas of open water are always rich in fish, sea mammals, polar bears and even polar foxes and birds. Some ecologists feel that these areas must be declared maritime sanctuaries (Kryuchkov 1987:147–8).

Naturally, reserves cannot be extended to include all arctic territories and waters (including a part of the arctic coast) already settled by man or the continental shelf of the arctic seas where mineral mining holds much promise. Furthermore, along the Soviet Arctic coast runs the Northern Sea Route, the principal shipping lane not only for the arctic regions but also for the vast and fast-developing regions of Siberia.

Measures to protect the environment in this zone must proceed from the need to achieve a reasonable balance between the population and the utilization of resources, the improvement of the quality of non-renewable resources and the maximum renewal of depleted resources, and preserving an environment that is both healthy and pleasing in esthetic and cultural senses (Treshnikov and Rusanov 1985:22–8).

Environmental protection measures

A number of important environmental protection measures have been implemented in the Soviet Arctic over the past few years. Treatment facilities have been and are being built in a number of ports. The overwhelming majority of operating ships have been equipped with collecting tanks for oil product waste and oil separation devices; and new control devices have been introduced (Korotkevich *et al.* 1985:3–9). The Hydrographic Enterprise of the USSR Ministry of Merchant Marine, under the general supervision of the Northern Sea Route Administration, conducts measures to control oil pollution from vessels in the Soviet Arctic. Its functions include vessel inspection, regular patrol flights over the Northern Sea Route and control over the port authorities' implementation of marine pollution prevention regulations. The 10-year operation experience of this service has proved its usefulness; during the past five years the number of antipollution rules and norm violations found per vessel inspected has decreased by a factor of two. During the same period the number of oil spills detected from the air has diminished three times (Ditz *et al.* 1988:37). A number of legal measures have been adopted to preserve individual components of the natural environment of the Far North, such as the animal kingdom, forests at the northern limit of their growth and deer pastures (Shcherban' 1985).

The decree of the Presidium of the USSR Supreme Soviet (see Appendix 1) entitled 'Improving the Protection of Nature in the Regions of the Far North and in the Sea Areas Adjacent to the Northern Coastline of the USSR declared a legal system governing the harmony between society and nature in the Arctic (Presidium, 1984:863). Today this document is the fundamental standard act regulating questions of nature preservation in the North. By optimizing nature management in this region, this legal act is aimed at preserving and studying the natural complexes of the Arctic and at the same time, guaranteeing the best living conditions for the inhabitants, the protection of the people's health and the utmost satisfaction of their domestic and cultural needs.

The decree contains a number of provisions that have not been included previously in Soviet nature conservation acts. Thus Article 2 of the decree emphasizes that in order to preserve and restore the ecosystems of the

Arctic, to elaborate scientific bases for nature preservation in these regions and to preserve the diversity of plants and animals and their habitat, a system of reserves and sanctuaries is created in regions of the Far North and in maritime regions adjacent to the country's northern coast. The reserves and sanctuaries include mainland and island areas, as well as seafloor and water areas, which may or may not be covered by ice. Ship navigation within the sea boundaries of reserves and sanctuaries and their protected zones may be permitted only along special corridors, while the movement of other transportation means along the ice surface in such regions is possible only via certain routes fixed by Soviet legislative bodies (Article 4).

Furthermore, in an effort to guarantee shipping safety and to control pollution of the marine environment, the decree provides for the introduction of special ship navigation regulations in ice-covered areas of arctic sea waters (Article 3). In these regulations, which are in full conformity with the provisions of Article 234 of the United Nations Law of the Sea Convention, provision is made for the placement of more stringent requirements upon the design and equipment of ships, the manning and qualification of their crews, the prohibition of navigation without pilotage, the establishment of periods and regions closed to navigation and other measures providing for navigation safety and protection of the sea environment against pollution. In the opinions of the prominent Soviet arctic research scientists A.F. Treshnikov and V.P. Rusanov, environmental protection could, in particular, include: drafting regulations for nonstop navigation of convoys and large-capacity solo ships while accounting for environmental requirements; limiting the operation and wintering of ships in ports and bays along the arctic coast in the absence of or noncompliance with standards of purifying bilge and ballast waters, and waste collection; and completing regulations for the destruction of ships sailing in arctic waters in the event of an emergency situation that might lead to large-scale loss of polluting substances (Treshnikov and Rusanov 1985:22–8).

On the basis of nature protection requirements for the Arctic, the decree provides for special regulations of air flights as they relate to the direction and width of air corridors and lines, flight altitude and to regions temporarily closed to air traffic (Article 5). It specifies that the reconstruction and use of any facilities and structures on land or in the sea can be permitted only on condition that the controlling government makes a favorable conclusion that the use is ecologically sound and protects the environment (Article 6). In accordance with a decision of the CPSU Central Committee and the USSR Council of Ministers, entitled 'On the Radical Restructuring of Nature Preservation in the USSR', the USSR State Committee for the Preservation of Nature, established in 1988, implements environmental impact assessments of economic projects (CPSU Central Committee 1988).

Exploration, mining, construction and other work in arctic regions, as well as the use of mechanized transportation in the tundra and forest tundra are all strictly regulated from an ecological standpoint (Article 7). Scientific and expeditionary activity that is incompatible with environmental protection requirements of the Far North and Arctic Sea is prohibited

(Article 10). Extremely important concerning the especially vulnerable environment of arctic seas are those provisions that prohibit the disposal in arctic waters of untreated sewage, refuse, materials and objects. As for the burial of such waste and materials within the confines of these sea regions, this may be done only with the permission and under the supervision of Soviet legislative bodies (Article 11). Tourism in the Arctic (tourist seasons), use of individual territories and waters and forms of transportation also may be restricted (Article 13). The decree provides for the establishment of special restrictions on the procurement of wild animals, birds and other animals (Article 12).

Persons found guilty of violating the decree's provisions will bear both administrative and criminal responsibility in compliance with existing legislation. Administrative penalties in the form of fines up to 10,000 rubles may be imposed on those guilty of such offenses as violation of ship navigation regulations and pollution of arctic waters. If the violations cause substantial damage to the natural environment of regions adjacent to the northern coast of the USSR, or produce other serious consequences, then fines of up to 100,000 rubles will be imposed on the guilty parties. In individual cases, as an additional penalty, the ship used by the violator may be seized (Article 14). It must be emphasized here that the use of measures of administrative influence does not free violators from reparation of the damages inflicted by them on natural resources (Article 16).

This decree was under preparation for a number of years. The commissions considered the draft for environmental protection and the rational utilization of natural resources. The commissions sought legislative proposals from both chambers of the USSR Supreme Soviet. Taking part in its discussion were ministries and departments, many collectives from Soviet scientific research establishments, the USSR Academy of Sciences and Soviet and Party bodies from northern regions. On the basis of their suggestions, many of the decree's provisions were strengthened, and a number of new clauses were introduced into the decree (Shcherban' 1985).

Work is proceeding currently in accordance with the decree on solidifying existing provisions of Soviet Union nature conservation and other legislation. Of greater importance, however, will be the practical observance and implementation of the provisions and their realization in practice. In this respect, it must be emphasized that the observance of legal standards for the conservation of nature in the Arctic must be largely aimed at averting possible disruptions in the environmental balance.

As A.F. Treshnikov and V.P. Rusanov have noted correctly, the system of civil liability in combination with reparation of damages may not be effective for arctic regions. It should be kept in mind that no material compensations can replace species that have fallen out of the ecological chain. A vacated ecological niche cannot be occupied by another species in view of the severe living conditions, for which species require a very long period of adaptation (Treshnikov and Rusanov 1985:22–8).

International cooperation

In a unique region of the world such as the Arctic, the interdependence and fragility of today's globe is especially felt. It is not by chance, therefore, that problems of environmental security in the north, first raised in President Gorbachev's Murmansk speech of October 1987 (Gorbachev 1987), are given important consideration in current Soviet initiatives toward creation of a comprehensive system of international peace and security. A certain amount of cooperative experience has been learned already by northern states in the area of environmental protection. The Soviet Union cooperates on a bilateral basis on northern problems with Canada, Norway, Finland and the United States.

Nevertheless, there is a vital need to create a comprehensive regional system of environmental cooperation in which, along with the eight arctic rim nations (including Finland, Sweden and Iceland), other countries having active scientific programs in the Arctic or contributing to the pollution of the area could participate. This need is dictated by several factors. First, the international exchange of information accumulated by each of these nations in the area of polar environmental protection and the development and use of ecologically safe technologies for their development will help to eliminate the duplication of costly research and developmental work. Second, the combination of efforts by arctic nations will help to improve shipping safety markedly in the Arctic and reduce the pollution of northern waters by ships. Third, the organization of such a system of cooperation will help demonstrate to all members of the international community the sincere interest of nations in the region to maintain the favorable state of arctic ecosystems, which exert a global influence on climate and other world-wide conditions. Finally, it would be difficult to overestimate the contribution of such an initiative on the part of northern countries toward developing and strengthening a cooperative atmosphere in the Arctic and toward establishing a true zone of peaceful and fruitful cooperation in Northern Europe.

One acceptable way for interested countries to pool their efforts would be to implement an Arctic Plan of Action. This model would foster cooperation among the 7 Baltic nations within the framework of the Helsinki Convention on the Protection of the Marine Environment of the Baltic Sea Region. An analogous plan could be drawn up or implemented in 11 maritime regions of the world within the framework of the Ocean and Coastal Areas Program under the auspices of the United Nations Environmental Program (UNEP). Similar proposals regarding the organization of a cooperative system in arctic environmental protection have been suggested in articles by several Western scientists (Hardeis 1987:285–98; Lamson 1987:3–15; Lamson and VanderZwagg 1987:49–99). It should be noted that the complex nature of the action plan makes it possible to conduct, within its framework, diverse joint activities aimed at protecting and preserving both the arctic maritime environment and the coastal tundra and forest tundra regions.

An integral part of such a plan might be a regional agreement on the security of shipping and the protection of the maritime environment from pollution by ships. Within its framework, provision might be made for requirements (coordinated between nations in the region and taking into account the interest of noncoastal states) on the design and equipment of ships, the composition of crews aboard ships navigating the ice-covered waters of 200-mile economic zones and for sufficiently rigid standards — up to a complete prohibition — relating to the discharge of pollutants from ships. In this connection, arctic nations might also give some thought to approaching the International Maritime Organization (IMO) with the question of re-examining annexes to the MARPOL — 73/78 international convention. Such a re-examination would add the Arctic Ocean and adjacent waters to the group of 'special regions' where more rigid requirements have been established on the discharge of any pollutants from ships. Apart from this, a regional agreement might include obligations of coastal states regarding:

1. the cooperation and mutual assistance in situations connected with accidental pollution of the sea;
2. the cooperation in training and retraining of arctic ship crews and in the joint design, construction and testing of such ships;
3. the exchange of meteorological information; and
4. the joint use in the Arctic of space systems for navigation, communications, search and rescue and remote sounding of natural resources.

Aside from measures to avert pollution by ships and to guarantee safety of shipping, integral parts of an Arctic Plan also might include:

1. joint, basic maritime scientific research;
2. cooperation in the environmental impact assessment of economic activity in the Arctic (for example, the study of the effects of industrial pollution and hydrotechnical projects on the arctic climate and on global weather conditions);
3. measures to avert pollution of northern waters as a result of dumping of wastes (or, possibly, the complete prohibition of the latter);
4. exploration and development of mineral resources on the continental shelf;
5. cooperation in the establishment of reserves and protected areas;
6. protection of rare and endangered species
7. development of ecologically sound land-use methods in the Arctic; and
8. restoration of damaged landscapes.

An Arctic Action Plan might also take fully into account the rights and concerns of arctic native peoples (including protection of the marine and other resources upon which they depend) and might provide for their active involvement (for example, through the Inuit Circumpolar Conference) at least at the policy-making and implementation stages. It should not be ruled out that arctic states might try to find ways of jointly resolving such a difficult international legal problem as the elaboration of principles and procedures for assuming responsibility for transborder damages inflicted on the arctic environment.

The first steps toward the elaboration of such an environmental cooperative regime for the Arctic have already been taken. As the follow-up to the Murmansk program, in January 1989 the Finnish government took the initiative in proposing a conference of the 8 arctic and Nordic nations on environmental protection of the arctic areas with the aim of concluding an agreement on joint actions to protect the arctic environment. According to the initial design, the framework commitment could lay the groundwork for at least 4 protocols: to limit transboundary marine and air pollution; to protect wildlife; and to exclude radioactive wastes from the region (MacKenzie 1989:29). In September 1989, the first Consultative Meeting on the Protection of the Arctic Environment was held in Rovaniemi, Finland, where it was agreed to prepare (by joint efforts) a series of reports on the state of the environment in the area, to start the elaboration of an arctic sustainable development strategy and to compile and analyze the list of existing international instruments on the subject (Consultative Meeting, *Final Report* 1989a). Creation of an international environmental program for the Arctic thus has moved from the theoretical into the practical realm.

Of course, there are obstacles to the development of such a form of regional cooperation. Admittedly, the greatest restraining role here is apt to be played by the military and by strategic considerations and the many interests of the nations in question. At the same time, we should not be unaware of the immense potential that regional environmental cooperation possesses in terms of strengthening confidence in international relations. Today, the successful resolution of urgent questions of security in the Arctic, including environmental security, is a distinct possibility. What is required above all else is the political will of interested countries. The Soviet Union for its part, as M.S. Gorbachev declared in Murmansk, attaches special importance to such cooperation and is ready to make its contribution to the organization of an integrated plan for protecting the northern environment.

References

CPSU Central Committee and USSR Council of Ministers. 1988. 'O korennoy perestroike dela okhrany prirody v strane' [On the radical restructuring of nature preservation in the USSR]. *Pravda* 17 January:1.

Consultative Meeting on the Protection of the Arctic Environment. 1989a. *Final Report of the Consultative Meeting*. Rovaniemi, Finland, 20-26 September.

— 1989b. 'Zayavlenjye Sovetskoy delegatsii' [Statement of the Soviet Delegation]. Rovaniemi, Finland, 20-26 September.

Danyushevskaya, A.I., and A.E. Greben'. 1982. 'Geokhimicheskaya otsenka tekhnogennoy zagryaznennosti donnykh osadkov Arkticheskogo shel'fa' [Geochemical assessment of technogenic pollution of clastic deposits of the Arctic shelf]. *In*: *Shel'fy: problemy prirodopol'zovaniya i okhrany okruzhayuschey sredy, Tezisy dokladov IV Vsesoyuznoy konferentsii* [Shelfs: Problems of Nature

Management and Environmental Protection, Abstracts of Papers of the 4th All-Union Conference]:142-43. Vladivostok.

Ditz, Yu., G. Doronin and G. Khalyavitski. 1988. 'Zagryazneniyu Arkiti – prochnyi zaslon' [Solid barrier to Arctic pollution]. *Morskoy flot*, 2:37.

Gorbachev, M.S. 1987. 'Rech na torzhestvennom zasedanii, posvyasshchennom vrucheniyu gorodu Murmansku ordena Lenina i medali 'Zolotaya Zvezda' [Speech at a ceremonial gathering dedicated to the presentation of the Order of Lenin and Gold Star medal to the city of Murmansk]. *Pravda*, 2 October. (see Appendix I)

Govorukha, L.S. 1986. 'Antropogennyi faktor v razvitii osnovnykh asrkticheskikh ekosistem' [The anthropogenic factor in the development of basic Arctic ecosystems]. *In*: *Prirodnyje kompleksy Arkitiki i vosprosy ikh okhrnay* [Natural Complexes of the Arctic and Their Preservation]:24-30. Leningrad.

Harders, J.E. 1987. 'In quest of an Arctic legal regime: Marine regionalism—a concept of international law evaluated.' *Marine Policy* 11(4):285-298.

Il'inskii, V.V., V.V. Izmailov, and T.V. Koronelli. 1986. 'Metodicheskiya osnovy i glavnyje rezultaty izucheniya roli fiziko-khimicheskikh i biologicheskikh faktorov v ochishcenii arkticheskikh vod i l'dov ot neftyanykh uglevodorodov' [Methodical fundamentals and principal results of the study of the role of physico-chemical and biological factors in the purification of Arctic waters and ice from petroleum hydrocarbons]. *In*: *Ekologiya i biologicheskaya produktivnost' Barentseva morya*, Tezisy dokladov Vsesoyuznoy konferentsii [Ecology and Biological Productivity of the Barents Sea, Abstracts of Papers of an All-Union Conference]:171-73. Murmansk.

Ivanov, V.L., A.S. Khomichuk, A.N. Rogovtsev, and V.A. Sokolov. 1985. 'Osnovy ratsionalnogo osvoyeniya i razrabotki mineral'no-syryevykh resursov severnykh regionov' [Fundamentals of the rational development and exploitation of mineral resources of northern regions]. *In*: *Geograficheskiye problemy izucheniya i osvoyeniya arkticheskikh morey*, Tezisy dokladov II Vesoyuznoy konferentsii po geografii i kartografirovaniyu okeana [Geographic Problems of the Study and Development of Arctic Oceans, Abstracts of Papers of the 2nd All-Union Conference on Geography and Ocean Mapping]:94-95. Leningrad.

Izmailov, V.V. 1982. 'Protsessy yestestvennogo ochishcheniya poverkhnosti Severnogo Ledovitogo okeana' [Processes of natural purification of the surface of the Arctic Ocean]. *In*: *II Vsesoyuznyi syezd okeanologov*, Tezisy dokladov [2nd All-Union Congress of Oceanologists, Abstracts of Papers]:(4) 103-104. Sevastopol'.

— 1986. 'Vozmozhnyje ekologicheskiye posledstviya neftyanogo zagryazneniya ledyanogo pokrova polyaynykh basseynov' [Possible ecological effects of oil pollution of the ice cover of polar basins]. *In*: *Metodologiyaprognozirovaniya zagryazneniya okeana i morey*, Tezisy dokladov Vsesoyuznogo nauchnogo seminara [Methodology of Forecasting Ocean and Sea Pollution, Abstracts of Papers of an All-Union Scientific Seminar]:76-79. Moscow.

Izmailov, V.V., and I.M. Simonov. 1986. 'Al'bedo i teplovoy balans snezhnoledyanykh poverkhnostey v Arktike v usloviyakh neftyanykh zagryaznenity' [The albedo and heat balance of snow-ice surfaces in the Arctic under conditions of oil pollution]. *In*: *Prirodnyje kompleksy Arktiki j voprosy ikhokhrany* [Natural Complexes of the Arctic and Their Preservation]:117-20. Leningrad.

Korotkevich, E.S. and V.P. Rusanov. 1985. 'Geograficheskiye aspekty ekologicheskogo monitoringa prirodnoy sredy arkticheskikh morey' [Geographical aspects of ecological monitoring of the natural environment of

Arctic seas]. *In*: *Geograficheskiye problemy izucheniya i osvoyeniya arkticheskikh morey*, Tezisy dokladov II Vesoyuznoy konferentsii po geografii i kartografirovaniyu okeana [Geographic Problems of the Study and Development of Arctic Seas, Abstracts of Papers of the 2nd All-Union Conference on Geography and Ocean Mapping]:22-27. Leningrad.

Korotkevich, E.S., E.S. Slevich, and A.A. Panchenko. 1985. 'Nekotoryje geograficheskiye problemy izucheniya i osvoyeniya arkticheskikh morey' [Some geographic problems in the study and development of Arctic seas]. *In*: *Geograficheskiye problemy izucheniya i osvoyeniya arkticheskikh morey*, Tezisy dokladov II Vesoyuznoy konferentsii po geografii i kartografirovaniyu okeana [Geographic Problems of the Study and Development of Arctic Seas, Abstracts of Papers of the 2nd All-Union Conference on Geography and Ocean Mapping]:3-9. Leningrad.

Krasnikova, T.I. and S.P. Mesyats. 1986. 'Sovmestnoye deystviye sorbenta na osnove vermikulita barentsevomorskikh shtammov nefteokislyayushchikh bakteriy' [Joint action of a sorbent based on vermiculite and Barents Sea strains of oil-oxidizing bacteria in an experiment]. *In*: *Ekologiya i bilogicheskaya produktivnost Barentseya morya*, Tezisy dokladov Vsesoyuznoy konferentsii [Ecology and Biological Productivity of the Barents Sea, Abstracts of Papers of an All-Union Conference]:178-80. Murmansk.

Kryuchkov, V.V. 1987. *Sever na grani tysyacheletiy* [The North on the Brink of the Millennia], 147-48. Moscow: Mysl' Publishers.

Lamson, C. 1987. 'Arctic shipping, marine safety and environmental protection.' *Marine Policy* 11(1):3-15.

Lamson, C. and D. VanderZwagg. 1987. 'Arctic waters: Needs and options for Canadian-American cooperation.' *Ocean Development and International Law* 18(1):49-99.

MacKenzie, D. 1989. 'Environmental issues surface at the summit of the world.' *New Scientist* 121(1653):29.

Matishov, G.G., V.S. Petrov, T.N. Savinova, V.N. Semenov, and N.G. Teplinskaya. 1986 'Ekologicheskiye problemy orhraney ahivoy prirody arkticheskikh morey' [Ecological problems of nature preservation in the northern seas]. *In*: *Ekologiya i biologicheskaya produktivnost' Barentseva morya*, Tezisy dokladov Vsesoyuznoy konferetsii [Ecology and Biological Productivity of the Barents Sea, Abstracts of Papers of an All-Union Conference]:13-16. Murmansk.

Mesyats, S.P. and L.A. Kirillova. 1986. 'Ispol'zovaniye prirodnykh sorbentov dlya udaleniya nefti s poverkhnosti severnykh morey' [Use of natural sorbents for skimming oil from the surface of northern seas]. *In*: *Ekologiya i biologicheskaya produktivnost' Barentseva morya*, Tezisy dokladov Vsesoyuznoy konferentsii [Ecology and Biological Productivity of the Barents Sea, Abstracts of Papers of an All-Union Conference]:181-83. Murmansk.

Presidium of the USSR Supreme Soviet. 1984. 'Ob usilenii okhrany prirody v rayonakh kraynego Severa i morskikh rayonakh, prilegayushchikh k severnomu poberezhyu SSSR' [Improving the Protection of Nature in the Regions of the Far North and in the Sea Areas Adjacent to the Northern Coast of the USSR]. *In*: *Vedomosti Verkhovnogo Soveta SSSR* [Record of the USSR Supreme Soviet]:48:863.

Rusanov, V.P. 1985. 'Sostoyaniye morskoy sredy v basseyne i ekologicheskiye posledstiya yee zagryazneniya' [State of the maritime environment in the basin and the ecological effects of its pollution]. *In*: *Severnyj Ledovityj i Yuzhnyj okeany (Geografiya Mirovogo okeana)* [Arctic and Southern Oceans (Geography of the World Ocean)]:201-7. Leningrad.

Savinova, T.V. 1985. 'Uroven' zagryazneniya khlorirovannymi uglevodorodami nekotorykh promyslovykh organizmov Norvezhskogo i zapadnoy chasti Barentseva morey' [Level of pollution by chlorinated hydrocarbons of several commercial organisms from the Norwegian Sea and the western part of the Barents Sea]. *In: Geograficheskiye problemy izucheniya i osvoyeniya arkticheskikh morey*, Tezisy dokladov II Vesoyuznoy konferentsii po geografii i kartografirovaniyu okeana [Geographic Problems of the Study and Development of Arctic Seas, Abstracts of Papers of the 2nd All-Union Conference on Geography and Ocean Mapping]:102-103. Leningrad.

Shcherban', V. 1985. 'Okhranyaya prirodnuyu dredu Severa' [Protecting the environment of the Far North]. *Izvestiya*, 5 March.

Shtil'mark, F.R. 1979. 'Proektirovaniye i organizatsiya zapovednikov' [The design and organization of reserves]. *In: Opyt raboty i zadachi zapovednjkov v SSSR* [Experience and Tasks of Reserves in the USSR]: 183-89. Moscow.

Treshnikov, A.F. and G.I. Baranov. 1972. *Struktura tsirkulyatsii vod Arkticheskogo basseina* [Structure of Water Circulation in the Arctic Basin]. Leningrad: Gidrometeoizdat.

Treshnikov, A.F. and V.P. Rusanov. 1985. 'Pravovyje problemy okhrany okruzhayushchey sredy polyarnykh territoriy' [Legal problems of environmental protection of Arctic territories]. *In: Problemy Biosfery. Informatsionnyje materialy* [Problems of the Biosphere. Informative Material]:(5)22-28. Moscow.

Uspenskii, S.M. 1983. 'Arkticheskiye zapovedniki: Kakimi im byt'?' [Arctic reserves. What are they like?]. *In: Okhota i Okhotnich'e Khozyaystvo* [Hunting and Game-Keeping]:(8)16-17.

Uspenskii, S.M. and Yu. M. Feigin. 1986. 'Okhranyayemyje prirodnyje territorii Severa' [Protected natural areas of the North]. *In: Prirodnyje kompleksy Arktiki j voprosy ikh okhrany* [Natural Complexes of the Arctic and Their Preservation]:18-24. Leningrad.

Uspenskii, S.M., L.S. Govorukha, S.E. Belikov, and V.I. Bulavintsev. 1986. 'Zapovednyje zony v rayone Zemli Frantsa-Iosifa' [Reserve zones in the region of Franz Josef Land]. *In: Prirodnyje komplesksy Arktiki i voprosy ikh okhrany* [Natural Complexes of the Arctic and Their Preservation]:7-18. Leningrad.

Vekhov, N.V. 1984. 'Okhranyayemyje territorii evropeiskogo sektora Arktiki i Subarktiki i okhrana vodnykh ekosistem v regione' [Protected territories of the European sector of the Arctic and Subarctic and the preservation of water ecosystems in the region]. *In: Issledovaniya v oblasti zapovednogo dela* [Research on Reserves]:91-97. Moscow.

6

The Arctic in the Russian identity

Franklyn Griffiths

The Arctic is an oceanic region surrounded by the territory of states whose populations live predominantly to the south and have little direct experience of the area. Obvious features of the arctic physical environment make any large-scale human undertaking there considerably more difficult and costly than in areas to the south. Nevertheless, the Soviet Union—a far-flung multinational state which enjoys a subtropical climate in parts of central Asia and the Caucasus—has moved forward with an array of arctic ventures that in their scale, persistence and consequences dwarf those of any other state.

The Soviets have built large cities and have engaged in vigorous exploitation of the onshore and increasingly the offshore natural resources of their portion of the circumpolar North. As of 1980, some 9 million people lived in the Soviet North, roughly 75 percent of whom were gathered in urban communities (Slavin 1982:21–22). Moreover, the Soviets have established a formidable naval presence on the Kola peninsula. They have sought military–strategic advantage from the under-ice operation of nuclear-powered ballistic-missile submarines and have built positions of naval strength centered on Kamchatka and the Sea of Okhotsk. Formidable maritime, air and more recently rail and pipeline transportation systems have been installed to service communities in the high North, to move arctic resources southward and to further the east–west economic and strategic integration of the USSR. Arctic scientific research has also burgeoned in the Soviet Union and, since 1958, an environmental awareness has emerged.

Soviet readiness to contemplate arctic engineering feats on an unprecedented scale was evident in long-standing projects that would redirect waters of the Ob' and Upper Pechora rivers from the Arctic to the south. But the decision in August 1986 to shelve these projects attests to the growing strength of Soviet environmentalism. Furthermore, while from the outside, Soviet central authorities long appeared to have had some success in sustaining the cultures and the option of a renewable resources way of life for their northern aboriginal peoples, under conditions of *glasnost'*, the sorry truth of environmental, cultural and social deprivation has emerged (Pik and Prokhorov 1988). Finally, as of Mikhail Gorbachev's pathbreaking address of 1 October 1987 in Murmansk, the Soviet Union has come out in favor of comprehensive international cooperation in the Circumpolar North (Gorbachev 1987:27-42). In so doing, it has initiated a transformation in circumpolar international relations and as of 1990 remains by far the most advanced of the arctic states in seeking multilateral solutions to the region's problems (Gorbachev 1987). Whatever our judgement on the details of Soviet activity in the Arctic, in the ensemble they can only be called outstanding.

The Soviet Arctic, it should be noted, falls entirely within the Russian republic, which alone faces the Arctic Ocean. Although non-Russians clearly have a hand in determining the thrust of Soviet policies at home and abroad, Russians remain the politically dominant nationality in the USSR and in the determination of Soviet Arctic policies. How then have the Russian people and its leadership managed to venture so much in such an inhospitable physical setting?

Hypothesis

Of the many variables that might be considered in accounting for Russia's arctic performance, this chapter focuses on the cultural dimension. Cultural factors, it is suggested, lie at the base of Soviet action in the Arctic.

The Arctic has spectacular natural beauty, majesty, vastness and a capacity to uplift and lend greatness to a people. As such, it may attract and draw them forward. But the remorseless working of its awesome and astonishingly powerful natural forces is also likely to repel, to evoke caution and even unwillingness to act. Regional peoples may thus in some measure view the Arctic as 'sublime' in the original sense of the word (Griffiths 1987:265–8; Loomis 1977). In the case of Canada, for example, notions of the arctic sublime are intimately connected to Canadians' conceptions of themselves as a people with a destiny all their own. As a result, whenever arctic policy issues are considered in Canada, the national identity and nationalism sooner or later come into play. So also do the conflicting forces of attraction and repulsion.

Outwardly, the Russian record in the Arctic has not been one of caution and self-deterrence. On the contrary, the Russian people would seem to identify with the Arctic in ways that predispose them to act vigorously and to produce great effects there. But if Russia has not been moved by notions of the arctic sublime, her record of venturing may still owe something to nationalism and to more subtle attachments that spring from a long-standing assimilation of the region to the Russian national identity. Historically, Russian nationalism has been a constrained force in the Soviet Union (Dunlop 1983:278–9). Accordingly, national identity may be the more appropriate concept in considering the effect of culturally based predispositions on Russia's arctic behavior. Here, national identity is taken to mean a sense of commonality or oneness that serves to integrate a people, to distinguish it from others and to provide a framework for collective action. There is, however, no generally accepted understanding of the relationship between national identity and public policy. Indeed, most analysts shy away from such concepts as national identity or 'national character' in the explanation of political action. And yet we all know that national customs, perceptions and behavioral predispositions cannot be ignored.

In the Russian case, the emergence of a national identity is attributable to three main forces: Orthodox Christianity; the experience of dealing with foreigners, especially Westerners and Western ideas; and the landscape itself. Our primary concern here is with the predisposing effects of national identity on the interaction of Russians with their immediate landscape and its related arctic environs. Russian land is a northern land, centered on the *Chernozem'e* (black earth) and to a lesser degree the *Nechernozem'e* (nonblack earth) areas to the east and north of Europe. By the 11th century or earlier, Russia's reach had extended to the shores of the White Sea. In the formative period of Mongol rule, key elements of a nascent Russian civilization were formed in the *Nechernozem'e,* as seen in the accomplishments of Novgorod, Vladimir, Suzdal, Ryazan and Yaroslavl which were then assimilated to the culture of Muscovy. Many other lands, also northern for the most part, entered the Russian domain, but a northern heartland and the ages-old experience of living in it exerted a powerful influence on the shared sense of what it is to be a Russian. Forests, lakes, rivers and snow-covered and icy expanses all acquired collective meaning for a people in whose mind the image and a love of the land came to loom unusually large.

Russians have many attributes as a people. Their identity is heterogeneous, confined neither to northernness nor derived solely from the land. But ultimately, Russians must be regarded as a northern people. They have powerful historical and cultural attachments to a northern landscape that has been a primordial force in shaping their customs and traditions. Indeed, the Russian identity may be understood not only in terms of shared self-awareness, but as a 'man–milieu' relationship that gives meaning to life. Russians removed from the native land, as in emigration, are likely to experience a profound feeling of deprivation.

Russians, it follows, may be predisposed to northern activities in which they are able to express themselves as a people. They are less constrained than others by perceptions of climatic severity, higher operating costs and greater uncertainty in the selection of means for northern activity. By extension, therefore, it could be that Russians are more favorably disposed toward undertakings in arctic regions, even if at some remove from their northern homelands.

Accordingly, it is the hypothesis of this chapter that the Soviet Union has ventured much in the Arctic quite simply because Russians are in their element there. This hypothesis must be tested against the view that Soviet Arctic activities have resulted primarily from the regime's economic development imperatives and organizational capabilities (Armstrong 1952:173). Specifically, we must consider whether and to what extent Soviet activity in the Arctic has depended upon predispositions that stem from the Russian sense of national identity and from ancient Russian attachments to a northern landscape. In seeking evidence of Russian predispositions that favor arctic ventures, Soviet (and to a lesser extent) Tsarist behavior is reviewed and analysed from economic, strategic, domestic-political, environmental and cultural perspectives.

Northern identifications

In the world literature there is no universally accepted definition of the Arctic. Various criteria are employed to delimit the region, among them the 10°C isotherm for the warmest month, the northernmost reach of the tree line for land areas or occasionally even the Arctic Circle.

Russian specialist conceptions of the Arctic are of interest here. Indeed, to help get a bearing on the Arctic it is useful to cite the definition offered in the *Great Soviet Encyclopedia,* which describes the Arctic as 'the northern polar region of the planet including the mainland extremities of Eurasia and North America, almost all of the Arctic Ocean (except the eastern and southern Norwegian Sea) with all of its islands (except the adjacent islands of Norway) and also adjacent parts of the Atlantic and Pacific oceans,' all of which is delimited primarily by isotherms of 10°C on land and 5°C at sea (*Bol'shaya* 1970:200–1). But this is a technical definition. Our prime concern is with the thoughts and feelings of a people who more probably view the Arctic as a condition than as a distinct geographical area.

Words used by Russians to identify what they see when they look northwards are varied and suggestive. As shown in Table 6.1, there are two vectors in the Russian orientation to things northern—one that runs straight over land, sea and ice toward the Pole and beyond and another that bears northeast and primarily over land to the furthest extremity of Eurasia. Russians would seem not to have a predominant orientation to the Arctic, especially to the Arctic as a maritime region. The Russian way of looking northwards is dualistic. An arctic orientation is present, but it is offset and possibly outweighed by the appeal of near-northern and northeastern lands. Furthermore, the arctic vector may be derivative, stemming from Russian thinking about northern lands. Were this impression to be confirmed by interviews in Soviet Russia or by surveys of Russian public opinion, it would support the hypothesis that culturally based predispositions which further Russian arctic performance arise more from attachments to the *North* than from a clear and compelling identification with the *Arctic* as such. To eliminate possible confusion, in this chapter the term 'Arctic' is hereafter employed in reference to offshore areas and activities; 'North' is employed to connote terrestrial equivalents.

Table 6.1 Russian words that describe the North

Terms used by Russians to identify what they see when they look northwards:

Sever	North
Russkii Sever	Russian North
Pripolyar'e	near North
Zapolyar'e	high North
Podarktika	subarctic
Arktika	Arctic
Severnyi Polyarnyi krug	Arctic Circle
Severnyi Ledovityi okean	Arctic Ocean
Tsentral'naya Arktika	central Arctic
Severnyi polyus	North Pole

Terms that refer to northern terrestrial spaces:

Evropeiskii Sever	European North
Severno-vostok	Northeast
Sibir	Siberia
Blizhnyi Sever	near North
Dal'nyi Sever	far North
Krainyi Sever	extreme North
Aziaticheskii Sever	Asiatic North

Economic Propensities

In the Soviet era, Russian interest in northern and arctic areas has been focused above all on the exploitation of nonrenewable and renewable natural resources. Though the breadth of this interest within the general population cannot be assessed, official practice and informed comment indicate very high levels of commitment to northern economic development. The governing objective of the Soviet Russians has been the *osvoenie* of the North as a land area reaching north and east from the *Chernozem'e*. *Osvoenie* is frequently translated as 'assimilation' or simply 'development,' but it can also be rendered as 'appropriation' or 'mastery.'

The desire to master the North and appropriate its resources reaches far into Russia's past. Indeed, M.V. Lomonosov (1712–65), born a fisherman's son in Archangel'sk, sponsor of arctic naval explorations and the country's first great man of science, is quoted even today for the prediction that, 'Russia's might will grow with Siberia and the Northern Ocean.' Soviet Russians have, in fact, acted like conquering invaders and, with some major exceptions, have taken pride in their assault on the North. S.V. Slavin, dean of Soviet northern economists, speaks approvingly of the 'offensive against the North,' and states with evident satisfaction that 'man creates ever new and ever more perfect means of subduing cruel Nature' (Slavin 1972:7; Slavin 1982).

While the North has been long associated with visions of Russian national wealth and greatness, it is only since the establishment of a multinational Soviet state in 1917 that effective ways have been found to exploit Russia's northern resources. And yet, in 1917 Russian national interests, to say nothing of Russian nationalism, were submerged in a new 'internationalist' political order and had to be expressed for the most part in indirect and covert ways. The process of *osvoenie* was set in motion under Lenin, (Shumilov 1974:3–26), but came into its own in the 1930s with the initiation of the Soviet industrialization program and five-year economic planning. The marching and sailing orders were given by Stalin, who is credited with asserting that 'the Arctic and our northern regions have colossal wealth. We must create a Soviet organization which can in the shortest period include this wealth in the general resources of our socialist structure' (Armstrong 1952:37). The ensuing record is a spectacular history of campaigning acquisition, some would say 'materialism' (Taracouzio 1938:41), that continues today.

The Soviet advance into northern and arctic areas has been accomplished by heavy reliance on megaprojects employing southern-based technologies and techniques. Adaptations to the demands of a novel and unforgiving environment have been required, but the essence of the Soviet northern economic effort has been the projection of southern ways and means onto a northern setting. Indeed, as a consequence of the Soviet drive to industrialize the area, the North is being 'denorthified' as development transforms 'far-northern' into 'near-northern' areas (Slavin 1982:13–14; Hamelin 1979).

In their eagerness to overrun the North and to suppress natural resistance there, Soviet Russians reveal a propensity to approach the region not as a northern people whose relationship to the land is symbiotic but as outsiders bent on gain. Their underlying predispositions have been those of the conqueror or treasure-hunter contemplating his future prospects: material gain, power, vindication. Soviet Industrialization has served not only to 'denorthify' the North but possibly to 'denorthify' the Russian people. Accordingly, the hypothesis that Soviet activity in the Arctic owes much to cultural factors and to predispositions associated with a desire to express a northern national identity is open to question.

Three major problems — labor resources, transportation infrastructure and economic subsidies — had to be solved for the Soviet assault on the North to succeed. How these problems were handled reveals much about Soviet Russian predispositions toward northern and arctic activity. On the first, labor resources, Soviet commentators until recently were notably silent when it came to the period between the First Five-Year Plan and the mid-1950s.

During the Stalin era, millions were sent to cruel death in northern forced-labour camps. Without this vast involuntary workforce, it is difficult to imagine how the offensive in the North could have gained its initial momentum or how the face of entire regions could have been transformed through the establishment of a succession of new territorial production complexes. Though all manner of inducements are now extended to attract manpower to northern industrial sites, the harsh fact remains that slave labor built the first of them. Indeed, if one asks Soviet *émigrés* to state what comes freely to mind when the word 'Arctic' is mentioned, they will reply, *inter alia*, 'forced labor camps' and 'exile'.

The point here is not so much that extraordinary ruthlessness marked the beginning of the *osvoenie* of the North, but that coercion and then inducements have been needed to bring the average Russian to the area. As a people, Russians have aversions to the Arctic and North as a place to live and work. Northern resources provide them with varied benefits, but the record of Soviet northern labor policy demonstrates that they are not predisposed to support arctic ventures if personal relocation is required. On this count, the hypothesis that the Soviet performance in the region owes much to the enabling predispositions of Russians is again called into question.

Second, transportation systems had to be put in place and continuously expanded to meet the growing needs of northern resource exploitation. The development of shipping, rail, pipeline and air transportation networks has been marked by the massive application of southern-based technology and administrative procedures in an effort to overwhelm all natural obstacles. Indeed, to Soviet Russians these efforts can be readily viewed as heroic, especially where the unrivalled feats of Northern Sea Route construction are concerned.

Formally established in 1932 after some years of vigorous preparatory work, Glavsevmorput (the Directorate of the Northern Sea Route) soon acquired a grant of authority that made it all but a separate republic, reaching from Kola to Kamchatka, within the Russian republic. In support of its arctic marine transportation mandate, Glavsevmorput was given control of everything from arctic scientific research to native affairs in the seas and islands off the European coasts of the country and in the entire area north of 62°N and east of the White Sea. Subsequently reduced in its powers and then incorporated as an administration of the Ministry of Merchant Fleet, Glavsevmorput retains operational responsibility for a vital and growing volume of bulk transportation along the full reach of Russia's northern shores. Formidable impediments to navigation have gradually been overcome with the development of the world's largest fleet of icebreakers and icebreaking bulk carriers to the point where year-round shipping is now contemplated.

Arctic marine disasters, bold rescues and demonstrations of ability to prevail in the midst of adversity all serve to endow Northern Sea Route activities with undoubted public appeal. Russians may not wish to live in the Arctic, but they are likely to derive vicarious satisfaction and a sense of common achievement from the spectacle of arctic marine operations and other precedent-setting attainments of Soviet northern development. In turn, responsiveness to the appeal of collective adventure in the Arctic could predispose Russians to accept and support undertakings there. Promotion of a spirit of collective achievement and pride in Soviet northern ventures has certainly been an objective of the regime since 1917.

In meeting labor, transportation and other requirements for northern economic development, Soviet central authorities have also been obliged to pour vast amounts of capital into ventures that cannot have been profitable in their own right. (Soviet oil and natural gas extraction is an exception.) The imposing cost of northern industrial facilities, transportation and social infrastructure has been absorbed as an overhead item in the long-term integrated economic development of the USSR. Shipping in ice-covered waters, for example, was reported in 1982 to have been 2–2.5 times more expensive than in open waters (Slavin 1982:48–9). During the period 1982–7, the net cost of arctic shipping itself is said to have risen by 14 percent (Zaika and Batskikh 1987:14). If the profitability of individual northern and arctic undertakings had been a Soviet priority, today the North would exhibit an altogether different pattern of economic development.

In sum, Soviet economic activity has been a derivative of larger interests which favor an extractive and instrumental approach to the region. Especially in terms of preferred means, the Soviet Russian predisposition to act in the Arctic would seem to owe little to an inherent sense of attachment to the area.

Strategic requirements

When Russians look northward with strategic considerations in mind, they think of themselves not so much as conquerors but as defenders in an arctic setting that extends far outward from their northern shores. Perceived external threats fall into two broad categories, military challenges and risks of informal penetration. The prime concerns that have animated Russians are those of security and sovereignty. Here sovereignty means not only the right to exclusive jurisdiction within internationally recognized frontiers, but also the capacity to regulate the use of Russian and Soviet space for Russian and Soviet purposes.

The theme of Russian attitudes toward security in the Arctic and North is a vast one. In this century alone it evokes the experience of the Russo–Japanese War, two World Wars, foreign military intervention after 1917, the need for air defenses against the US strategic bomber force and sea — as well as air-launched cruise missiles. Even more important may be the recent requirement to counter the forward deployment of US nuclear-powered attack submarines into arctic waters — itself prompted in part by new departures in the Soviet ability to position strategic ballistic missile submarines in the area. These and other developments have brought Soviet Russia to value the Arctic as a superior staging area for naval forces in the northwest and Far East, as a perennial physical barrier to land attack from the north and as a route for resupply of the Far East in the event of war. Though Gorbachev has now attached new significance to the Arctic in Soviet diplomacy, the underlying strategic assessment of the region remains quite traditional (Gorbachev 1987:27–42).

The overall pattern of Russian military behavior in the Arctic has been typical of a continental power bent on strengthening and projecting political influence outwards from only one among several border areas. Neither in Tsarist nor in Soviet times has the Arctic been viewed as the prime theatre of military operations. Certainly it has been recognized as a maritime area in which naval forces figure prominently. But the Soviet Union and, before it, Tsarist Russia have been continental states with military practices dominated by the army and its preoccupation with variants of the European land battle extending now to possible intercontinental artillery exchanges with nuclear-tipped missiles. Though political leaders and military officers view arctic strategic matters with utmost gravity, there is no evidence to suggest that the Arctic has been accorded an outstanding role in the conception and pursuit of Russian and Soviet security. As to the formidable Soviet naval presence in the Arctic, given the difficulty of egress from the Baltic and Black seas and the conducive effects of the Gulf Stream on navigation westward from the Kola Peninsula, where else but in the northwestern and far eastern parts of the country could naval strength be concentrated? But a strategic imperative to defend in the Arctic *per se* is hard to find.

Still more telling is the fact that arctic and northern appeals and symbols have not stood out in the perennial effort of Tsarist and Soviet authorities to generate patriotism, military preparedness or public support for the defense priorities of the regime. *Morskoi Sbornik*, the main journal of the Tsarist and Soviet navy, has paid no special attention to the Arctic, though images and references have become somewhat more frequent in the 1980s. Similarly, when Gorbachev appeared in Murmansk early in October 1987, he made a number of innovative proposals for international arctic cooperation, but aside from citing the wartime sacrifices of Murmansk itself he said nothing about the significance of the Arctic or the North in the life of the Soviet or Russian people (Gorbachev 1987).

Soviet Russians do, of course, take pride in their northern military history (Minaev *et al.* 1987; Arsen'ev 1985:63–5; *Patriot Severa*, 1985). Some may also prefer vigilance against Western military activity in the region (Guzarov 1987). But if cultural, historical and ideological factors predispose Russians to a degree of resentment and hostility to Western activity in the Arctic, the fact remains that anti-Western and more particularly anti-imperialist themes have been commonplace in Soviet military comment and, except where World War II and the foreign military intervention of 1918–20 is concerned, do not seem to have any special arctic significance.

As is the case with Soviet economic development, in basic Soviet security policy the Arctic is a derivative concern. There has been neither sound military reason nor good political cause for Soviet leaders to skew defense considerations toward the Arctic, or to draw on any popular attachments to the Arctic in marshalling support for defense. The situation is, however, somewhat different for Soviet Russian interests in arctic sovereignty, if only because the maintenance of exclusive jurisdiction is heavily dependent upon the evolution of practice *in situ*.

Apprehension over Western penetration of Russia's North harks back at least to the 17th century, when Tsar Mikhail Fedorovich prohibited foreign trading into the Kara sea (Butler 1978:43). The Western presence, primarily British and Norwegian, was renewed and grew in the 19th century to the point of arousing resentment among Russian entrepreneurs (Armstrong 1952:16; Slavin 1982:51–6). Even for Lenin, the North under Tsarist rule was 'an external market for England, not being an internal market for Russia' (quoted in Shumilov 1974:4). In looking back on that period, Soviet commentators have continued to see foreign activity in the North on a scale that threatened the country's 'independence and sovereignty' (Slavin 1982:52–4). After 1917 and the new Soviet determination to release Russia's productive forces through a self-sufficient socialist program of economic development, foreigners continued to fish, engage in whaling and sealing, to trade, conduct scientific research, explore, commit acts of 'vandalism' (Aktivist 1932:18–42) and to seek and claim new islands in waters off Soviet northern shores. Indeed, American whaling and on-shore trading activities in the Chukchi Sea and westward continued into the 1930s (Butler 1978:50–3; Slavin 1982:60; Slavin 1972:26).

Whereas direct military challenges had not figured prominently in Russia's arctic history, long before 1917 and into the early decades of the Soviet era, Russians had reason to be concerned over the erosion of northern sovereignty and political control. Under the old order, however, the prevailing attitude, with important exceptions, had been one of permissiveness in regard to Western penetration and indifference to northern exploration and economic development ventures. Under the new order these attitudes towards sovereignty and independence were rejected, and new predispositions were brought to bear on the Arctic. These predispositions took clear shape in the interwar years and proved to be very durable.

The Soviet regime moved with increasing vigor to assert its presence in northern lands and adjacent waters. Simultaneously, pre-existing anti-Western sentiment among Russians was compounded by the experience of foreign intervention in the North, by the mounting xenophobia of the Stalin years and by the prevalence of an increasingly dogmatic variant of Marxian ideology within the Soviet Union.

Meanwhile, the situation in the Arctic was changing as the pace of exploration and scientific activity quickened throughout the circumpolar North. Though there was no arctic military threat in sight, Russia under Soviet rule was impelled to come to terms with the region as a maritime area in which significant state interests were at stake. By the mid-1930s, external and internal variables had combined to produce a new stance toward low-intensity challenges in the area. It was strongly anti-Western and anti-imperialist, and called not only for the exclusion of foreigners from Soviet arctic lands and islands but also for the projection of a Soviet sphere or 'sector' of exclusive political control outwards into the Arctic Ocean (Taracouzio 1935; Taracouzio 1938:320–66; Butler 1978:71–7).

One manifestation of the new predisposition to exclude and ward off foreigners is particularly revealing. It concerns the naming of the Arctic Ocean. 'Arctic' is a Western term derived from the Greek *arktos*, or bear, in reference to the constellation Ursa Major. Tsarist and Soviet mapmakers and writers had been in disarray on the question of what to call the waters to the north, referring variously to 'Arctic Ocean' (1873, 1893, 1898), 'Arctic Sea' (1932), 'Ice-covered Ocean' (1914, 1935), 'Northern Ice-covered Ocean' (1914, 1932), 'Northern Polar Sea' (1930), and 'Polar Sea' (1932). Several of these references come from a single presentation of 1932 which is said to have been authored by no less than the legal adviser to the Commissariat for Foreign Affairs (Aktivist 1932:19; Butler 1978:155). On 27 June 1935, the All-Union Central Executive Committee, precursor of the Supreme Soviet, decreed, *inter alia*, that the term 'Arctic' would no longer be used to refer to the waters in question, which henceforth were to go only by the name 'Northern Ice-covered Ocean' (*Severnyi Ledovityi okean*') (Taracouzio 1938:377–80). The significance of a single act should not be overstated, but when viewed in context the decision of the Central Executive Committee reveals a variety of political and cultural meanings.

Faced with a choice, Soviet authorities opted for a native Russian and not a Western expression, and for 'North' as distinct from 'Arctic.' In declining to endorse generally accepted international usage, they would seem to have expressed an underlying determination not only to deny access by Westerners to Soviet land and offshore areas, but to deny the thought in Soviet Russia of shared access to a high-seas area denoted by a single generally accepted name. The Arctic Ocean was instead to be viewed as a high-seas area over most of which Soviet Russia exercised exclusive political control and over the remainder of which Soviet rights of access under international law would be unconstrained. The decision in favor of 'Northern Ice-covered Ocean' may thus be read to reflect a predisposition to fend foreigners away from Soviet northern lands shielded by a maritime political 'sector' that projected Soviet influence seaward without compromising freedom of action elsewhere in the region.

There is a Russian nationalist subtext to the decision of June 1935. By that date, Russian national symbols and appeals had begun to receive a degree of legitimacy in the Soviet Union as the gathering threat of a new world war increased the regime's need for public support. The selection of a Russian and not a foreign name for the Arctic Ocean thus reflected not only the new Soviet exclusiveness in dealing with Western activity in the region but also traditional Russian values and aversions to the West. Similarly, in opting for 'North,' Soviet decision-makers expressed a traditional Russian propensity to regard the Arctic not as a region in its own right, but as an extension of northern terrestrial spaces and interests.

The complex of attitudes that was manifested in the mid-1930s proved highly resistant to change but ultimately must be regarded as transitional. Soviet Russians found it necessary to resist multilateral arrangements that might bring Westerners into their part of the circumpolar North on terms not readily dictated by the Soviet interest. At the same time, they moved forward with scientific, coastal shipping and then naval activity into a maritime area that previously had not counted for much. As they succeeded in constructing a position of strength, the imperative to exclude foreigners and to avoid international cooperation waned, but very slowly. Only today, with Gorbachev's proposals for multilateral arctic military, scientific, environmental, resource development and other cooperation is Soviet Russia unquestionably prepared to move beyond its long-standing commitment to exclusiveness and unilateralism in arctic affairs.

Issues relating to sovereignty and political control in the Arctic have remained largely the preserve of officials and specialists. As is the case with defense, arctic sovereignty has not been a major theme in public discourse. Nor have arctic sovereignty or related political questions been discussed at length in leadership statements or speeches. There is no sense that low-intensity challenges in the Arctic present a signal threat to the heritage and future of Russians as a people. Where security and sovereignty are concerned, Russian identifications with the Arctic are not so much intrinsic and specific but derivative and generic.

Evoked attachments

Given the scope and duration of Soviet northern and arctic activity, consideration should be given to whether the momentum of the Soviet effort might have generated new public and elite-level identifications with the area. Evidence here is necessarily indirect. It is derived from a reading of official propaganda and specialist commentary and from an understanding of elite-level activity in other arctic countries.

Two themes stand out in Soviet propaganda and detailed comment on northern and arctic affairs since 1917: the break with the Tsarist past; and the celebration of Soviet accomplishments on their own merits. Preferring to draw sharp distinctions between Tsarist and later performance, Soviet writers at times resorted to ridicule in attempting to make the point that the North is now in good hands:

> As is well known, on the note of the Archangel merchant and industrialist, M.K.Sidorov, which was entitled 'On means of wresting the North of Russia from its impoverished state' and proffered to the Tsar in 1867, the ignorant Court General N.V. Zinoviev, remarked: 'Since the North is continuously covered by ice and grain cannot be grown there and any thought of industry is unthinkable, then in my opinion and that of my friends it is necessary to remove the people from the North to internal areas of the state and as for you, jump to it and turn around and explain what kind of Gulf Stream there can be in the North when such a thing cannot be' [Shumilov 1974:4].

Similarly, where rapacity, quarrelling and 'unorganized exploitation of the riches of polar waters and lands,' were attributed to Western imperialism in the 1930s, events in the Soviet North were depicted as proceeding in accordance with the overall economic plan of a Soviet Union content with its 'part' of the region (Aktivist 1932:18).

Soviet commentators writing in 1987 speak of 'heroism' and 'glorious feats' in the North (Minaev et al. 1987). The tone is not that different from Stalin's message of congratulation to the crew of the icebreaker Sibiryakov in 1932, after its precedent-setting trip through the Northern Sea Route in a single season: 'There are no fortresses which Bolshevik daring and organization are not able to storm' (Armstrong 1952:152). Similarly, a retired Admiral, commenting in 1987 on the first attainment of the North Pole by a Soviet nuclear submarine in 1962, describes the voyage as 'a triumph of our scientific-technical thought, of the fatherland's ship construction,' but notes that at the time the press emphasized the attainment of the Pole (Morskoi Sbornik 1987:60-1). Consider, too, the statement of fact that betrayed the wish of an arctic science administrator in 1935: 'In no other country does arctic research gain such popularity and profound sympathy of the popular masses as it does in the Soviet Union' (Samoilovich 1935:57).

Persistent Soviet efforts to gain credit from and to popularize northern and arctic achievements, coupled with the capacity of arctic exploits to stir the imagination, could well have worked upon mass attitudes to produce dispositions increasingly favorable to arctic undertakings and to the Arctic itself.

Similar processes may also have occurred at the elite level. What I am thinking of here is an informal community of elite arctic operators and enthusiasts whose interaction creates a supportive political and institutional environment for arctic ventures. Analogous communities are certainly a factor in the behavior of other ice states. Though there is no direct evidence as yet of elite-level Russian attachments to the Arctic or North that impel them to move vigorously on issues other than economic development, a culture of influentials conducive to arctic and northern activism may turn out to be a factor in Soviet Russia's regional presence. Nevertheless, in the absence of a mass base, the influence of an elite culture and community will be constrained unless its cause becomes identified with the larger concerns of society and the state. When we turn to Soviet environmental affairs, a Russian mass base comes into sight.

Russian environmentalism

In considering environmental and then cultural predispositions toward northern and arctic activity, we move directly into the interior of the Russian imagination. It is difficult and perhaps even improper to treat environmental and cultural factors in contemporary Russian thought under separate headings. Nevertheless, how do Russians relate to the northern and arctic physical setting when it is viewed through an environmental optic?

In 1958, when the first steps were taken to locate an enterprise for the production of rayon cord and later kraft paper and turpentine on the shore of Lake Baikal, environmentalism was born in the Soviet Union (Gustafson 1981:39–51). Opposition to the scheme gathered quickly in Siberia, and by the early 1960s the issue had surfaced in the central press. The Baikal project subsequently gained critical attention from within the Soviet leadership. At the Twenty-third Party Congress in 1966, the eminent Russian writer Mikhail Sholokhov stated that 'our descendants will not forgive us if we do not preserve this glorious lake, this sacred Baikal' (Gustafson 1981:41). By the mid-1960s, protest movements had also formed in opposition to hydroelectric projects that threatened to flood substantial areas of European Russia and Siberia. These ventures were cancelled or postponed through the combined effort of technical specialists, writers, political leaders and an aroused public opinion. Moreover, mass opinion became increasingly organized with the formation of the All-Russian Society for the Preservation of Nature, which by the early 1970s was said to have gained a membership of 19 million (Dunlop 1983:87). Meanwhile, officialdom was preparing far more spectacular ventures. Geared to the agricultural and industrial requirements of the USSR's European and central Asian areas, these vast civil engineering schemes envisaged the redirection of Russian and Siberian rivers southward to regions in need of water. But vigorous protest again led to cancellation in August 1986 (Zalygin 1987:3–18). Now there is news of widespread and effective resistance throughout the USSR to the construction of nuclear power stations in the wake of the Chernobyl disaster.

If anyone, the leader of the Russian environmental movement is Sergei Zalygin, a land reclamation engineer, acclaimed novelist and editor of the prestigious Soviet literary journal, *Novyi mir'*. Zalygin is not opposed to industrial development or to the notion of economic growth. His stand is consistent with economic development of the Arctic and North. However, his views reject decisively the *osvoenie* mentality and its readiness to wage war on Nature in pursuit of non-renewable and renewable resources. Zalygin insists that Nature not be viewed as standing apart from humanity, and that man–milieu relationships should be understood as an integral and mutually supportive whole in which mankind acts as respectful steward and in turn gains sustenance and meaning essential to life (quoted in Darst 1988:248).

Another figure whose views must be taken into account is Valentin Rasputin. Widely regarded as one of Russia's leading contemporary writers and a man with an immense personal following, Rasputin is passionately critical not only of environmental depredation but of heedless industrialization and, by implication, much of the Russian experience under Soviet rule. A Siberian who lives in Irkutsk, Rasputin is deeply attached to a Russian way of life that derives from and is sustained by an ancient landscape. He sees the destruction of Russia in the ransacking of his beloved Siberia. He also sees the salvation of Russia in the preservation of a Siberian natural environment that would not exclude economic development 'within reasonable limits' (Rasputin 1983:107). For Rasputin, Russia can be saved from the onslaught of soul-destroying industrialism and consumerist modernity only if she is true to herself in loving and preserving a native land that lends authentic meaning to human existence.

But the Arctic as such has not figured greatly in the hopes and fears of Russian environmentalists. Considering the major forests, open lands, rivers and lakes whose fate has moved Russian environmentalists to action, *northern* areas have, in effect, been at the center of their attention: Siberia, the Komi Autonomous Republic, the Nechernozem'e region, the Vologda area in particular; lakes Baikal, Kubena, Lacha, Onega, Vozhe; and the Andrush Yenisey, Irtysh, Kama, Ob', Pechora, Sukhona and upper Volga rivers. References to the *Arctic* have, however, been virtually absent except in regard to the potential downstream consequences of river diversion schemes. Nor, for that matter, have Russians been inclined to refer specifically to the North as an area that must be saved.

If environmental practice is any guide, Russians have yet to articulate a common awareness that they are a northern people. They have no doubt been constrained from attributing prime significance to the North by the fact that the Soviet environmental movement is an All-Union affair which embraces many areas and nationalities in addition to Russian lands and the Russian people. Variation in the experience and needs of Russian northern inhabitants from Vologda to eastern Siberia may also inhibit the expression of a common northern understanding. More broadly, under the effects of urbanization and industrialization, Russians living in the *Chernozem'e* heartland and particularly in Moscow could have been 'denorthified' in that they now are less prepared to think of themselves as northerners.

Russians are nevertheless powerfully inclined to reject the effects of *Soviet* economic performance on their well-being and future as a people. As Russian environmentalism has gained strength over the past 30 years, it has run counter to and served to disable large-scale Soviet economic undertakings in the North. Here the Russian identity has worked against, and not for, Soviet aims. Official decisions on Baikal, hydroelectric projects, river diversion and nuclear power moreover demonstrate that awareness of environmental requirements now is established in the Soviet, and therefore in the Russian political elite. And yet the fact remains that while Russians display a visceral attachment to their northern and Siberian spaces in challenging established Soviet economic practice, they decline to name the North itself as an area of singular environmental concern.

The hypothesis that the Soviet record in the Arctic owes much to enabling Russian identification with a northern landscape is clearly running into heavy weather. But before we take stock, let us go a step further and explicitly address the cultural dimensions of Russian northernness. Here our concern shifts from northern and arctic physical areas *per se*, to the role of abstract ideas about the North in Russian nationalism.

Ideas of the North

Russian nationalism and its re-emergence in the Soviet era are exceedingly complex phenomena. In the 1930s and wartime years Russian national feeling was evoked and controlled by the regime for purposes of mobilization and support. In the postwar era, it arose spontaneously 'from below,' and now permeates a regime nominally committed to the eradication of all nationalist and chauvinist sentiment (Dunlop 1983:278–9). First stirrings occurred in the field of literature during the 1950s, as Russian authors rediscovered the countryside and began to celebrate the aesthetic and moral qualities of a traditional way of life gravely damaged by collectivization and industrialization. By the 1970s, 'village prose' had become a major force in Russian writing. Its leading lights have been

Valentin Rasputin, the late Fyodor Abramov and Vasilii Belov, all three northerners with great appeal to the Russian literary audience. (Abramov wrote from and about the Arkhangel'sk area; Belov lives in and writes about the Vologda region.) Their work and that of many other writers of this genre stands today as a continuing reproach to the party and state for their destruction of Russian ways.

Concurrent with the environmental movement, the awakening Russian interest in traditional cultural values was institutionalized with the formation of a mass organization. Established in 1965 by decree of the RSFSR Council of Ministers, the All-Russian Society for the Preservation of Historical and Cultural Monuments (VOOPIiK) had gained some 12 million members by 1977. Active in the protection of old Russian architectural sites, especially churches, and in the prosecution of Russian environmental causes, VOOPIiK has drawn substantial support from Russian Orthodox believers who are estimated to number some 50 million (Dunlop 1983:41,73). Large numbers of visits have been organized to religious and cultural sites including those of the Arkhangel'sk and Vologda regions.

But though the evolution of broad-based public support for the affirmation of Russian cultural values, northern values included, is readily discernible in the fields of literature and architectural conservation, it is far more difficult to assess the growth of nationalist feeling within the apparatus of the Soviet party and state or even the underground before *glasnost'* gave groups like the ultra-nationalist Pamyat' a freer rein. It is, however, clear that by the late 1960s Russian chauvinist and anti-Soviet opinion had risen, with official approval, from the underground to the pages of *Molodaya gvardiya,* the Komsomol journal. Articles appeared there deploring Western influences in Russian and Soviet life and championing a 'single stream' view of Russian history according to which the prime moving force in the country's development is the nation and not the evolution of class forces within it (Dunlop 1983:218–21). Analogous views continue to be found in Russian commentaries on arctic affairs that, by implication, challenge Soviet triumphalism and the significance of 1917 by praising Tsarist achievements in polar exploration and scientific research (Galenko 1978). Not without pride is it noted that at one time Russia's writ in the Arctic reached from Kola to within 250 kilometers of the Mackenzie River (Pasetskii 1974:23).

Ideas about the North are also seen in the thinking of two leading but rather different nationalists, Aleksandr Solzhenitsyn and Valentin Rasputin. Several months before his exile in 1974, Solzhenitsyn sent off a 'Letter to the Soviet Leaders' which later circulated in *samizdat* as an influential contribution to the literature of Russian regeneration. His point was that Russia's leaders should cast aside their ruinous Western ideology of perpetual progress and external expansion in favor of a program of Russian national renewal centered on the Northeast:

> For half a century we have busied ourselves with world revolution, extending our influence over Eastern Europe and over other continents; with the reform of agriculture according to ideological principles; with the annihilation of the

landowning classes; with the eradication of Christian religion and morality; with the useless show of the space race; with arming ourselves and others whenever they want it; with everything and anything, in fact, but developing and tending our country's chief asset, the Northeast. Our people are not going to live in space, or in Southeast Asia, or Latin America: it is Siberia and the North that are our hope and our reservoir [Solzhenitsyn 1974:35–36].

In Solzhenitsyn's view, the way out for a Russia faced with economic ruin, spiritual decay and a befouled earth was 'for the state to switch its attention away from distant countries—even away from Europe and the south of our country—and to make the Northeast the center of national activity and settlement and a focus for the aspirations of young people' (Solzhenitsyn 1974:40).

Solzhenitsyn views the Northeast as a Russian nationalist and as an outsider, albeit with experience of the area in prison camp and exile. He wrote in programmatic fashion from Moscow and from a position of thorough-going rejection of the Soviet order. Rasputin, on the other hand, conceives of the same area as a Siberian as well as a Russian nationalist. For Solzhenitsyn, the Northeast is an awaiting land. It lies ready to receive a devastated but still viable Russian way of life. For Rasputin, Siberia is a powerfully creative landscape which itself shapes the character of the people who come there and yields something new.

Rasputin's Siberia is as much an idea as a place. He likens it to a bell, sounded long ago, whose echoing peal gives rise to conceptions of 'something vaguely mighty and impending', of 'trust and hope', of the 'anxious step of man on the far land', of 'relief', 'renewal', and indeed 'salvation' or *spasenie* (Rasputin 1983:106–7). In thinking of Siberia, the Russian outsider imagines a 'vast, severe, and rich' place which 'intimidates' and 'frightens' in the immensity of its spaces, in the extremity of its cold and inhospitability to man. As such, it prompts feelings of 'melancholy and anxiety' (Rasputin 1983:107, 124). And yet, the outsider who ventures in is excited and amazed by its glorious spaces and rare beauty, and communicates this back to Russia proper, whose idea of Siberia has all along been influenced by hearsay (Rasputin 1983:124–6). Splendid rivers, stunning lakes, astonishing mountains all bring 'delight' (Rasputin 1983:125). On seeing Baikal for the first time, the traveller almost dies at the beauty of the sight. In the Altai, mountains rise to heights that are measured not from sea level but from the level of human perception. Siberia uplifts the human spirit. It 'attracts', as well as repels, the outsider (Rasputin 1983:125). In a word, it is sublime.

As with Solzhenitsyn, Rasputin's idea of North is one of *spasenie* or national salvation. Russians, he pleads, must respect and not ruin this priceless natural setting which is akin to an entire new planet itself. Indeed, they could begin a new life by settling Siberia, which, in his view, is able to sustain far more people than it currently holds if kept unspoiled. But while Solzhenitsyn and Rasputin both see *spasenie* in the 'Northeast' or Siberia, Rasputin's evaluation stands out in its articulation of a latent and possibly widespread Russian identification with the sublime. Whether the sense of sublimity is extended from Siberia to the Arctic cannot be determined on the basis of current available evidence. Nevertheless, there is little reason to doubt Rasputin where Russian conceptions of Siberia are concerned.

As occurs with Canadians when they look to the Arctic, fear and favor mingle in varying proportion as Russians contemplate their Siberian vastness. And as with Canadians, the unvoiced notion of the sublime may not only divide the Russian imagination but import dualism to Russian actions. Accordingly, it may be necessary not so much to reject as to reconstruct the hypothesis that has governed this chapter. But before attempting to do so, we should briefly consider the policy implications of what we have uncovered.

A northern strategy?

As with virtually everything else in the Soviet Union of today, the evolution of environmental and cultural issues makes it clear that Soviet Russia has entered upon a period of profound soul-searching and transformation. Democratization, the disintegration of the Communist Party of the Soviet Union, the unbinding of Eastern Europe and now possibly the unwilling minority nations as presaged by Solzhenitsyn in 1974, the value of the Soviet industrialization effort to date — these are only some of the critical issues that have now been opened in the process of *perestroika*. Moreover, while much attention is being given in the West to minority national secession from the Soviet Union, the fundamental reality would seem to be that Russia herself is seceding from the Soviet order whether the leadership likes it or not. For his part, Gorbachev has assumed a position of unqualified commitment to Soviet and not Russian or other nationalist solutions for the many problems of the USSR. 'Soviet patriotism is the greatest of our values,' he has said. 'Any manifestations of nationalism and chauvinism are incomparable with it' (Gorbachev 1988).

But the door has long been ajar for Russian national sentiment. If environmental and cultural questions are any indication, Gorbachev and his colleagues in the leadership have already come to accept important elements of the Russian nationalist critique of the Soviet record. A principal issue before Gorbachev now is how to deal with the growing force of Russian nationalism without either attempting to suppress it or allowing it to supplant the Soviet order.

The question the leader surely faces is what variants of Russian national opinion have mass appeal but are relatively benign. The only answer can be the moderate tendencies of cultural and environmental nationalism represented by Zalygin, Rasputin and others even including Solzhenitsyn. The ensuing requirement for Gorbachev and his advisors would be to ensure that reformist Russian nationalism fully pre-empted the appeal of violently anti-Soviet and pathological alternatives. This need could be met by elaborating and acting upon a new national mission for Russia that had merit in its own right. To the extent that such a mission proved genuinely popular, it would draw support away from extreme nationalist groups like Pamyat which presumably will remain active under conditions of *glasnost'*.

What do Zalygin, Rasputin and Solzhenitsyn have in common as spokesmen for Russia's national aspiration? Despite their differences, among them a shared cultural and environmental interest in Siberia and the Russian North stands out. The details of how this interest might be converted into a program that allowed Russians to realize their identity as a Soviet people need not concern us here. But the thrust of the solution is already clear. It centers on a freer and more meaningful way of life in a natural environment that substantiates the singular identity of the Russian people. In Siberia, Russia could embark on a course of decentralized, high-tech, small-is-beautiful, sustainable economic development not dissimilar to that recommended in the recent report of the Brundtland Commission. In 'Siberia and the Northern Ocean' Russia's might would lie primarily in the example she set for the rest of the world in dealing with the twin problems of environment and development on a planet with limited carrying capacity.

Gorbachev would need to overcome major obstacles in settling on a northern strategy of *spasenie* that featured the creation of a new Russia in Siberia. Foremost would be the long-standing aversion of Russians to living there. Other impediments could be cited, such as the need for extensive foreign economic participation. Yet a 'salvationist' but modern Siberian mission for the people of Russia could meet the twin needs of containing Russian nationalism and moving a post-industrial Soviet Russia to a position of world leadership in the next century. Already Gorbachev is endeavoring to incorporate Russian nationalism into the process of Soviet reform and not merely by changing long-established Soviet policy on matters such as arctic cooperation. In selecting his first cabinet, Gorbachev has chosen Valentin Rasputin to be one of the inner circle (Keller 1990). It would not be surprising if, before long, he soon began to speak about a new Soviet future in Siberia and the Far East.

Conclusion

Now we know why analysts of public policy veer away from explanations based on cultural variables like national character and national identity: they are hard to handle and take us only so far when considered in isolation. Nevertheless, in attempting to account for the Soviet Union's arctic performance in terms of the predisposing effects of Russia's identification with a northern landscape, we have found that cultural factors do have force. We have also come some of the way to an understanding of the sources of Soviet activity in the region.

The hypothesis was that the Soviet Union has displayed great initiative and wrought great effects in the Arctic because the dominant nationality, the Russians, are a northern people who identify positively with a northern setting, feel themselves to be in their element there and by extension are favorably disposed to arctic undertakings despite the difficulty and cost of operations in this part of the world. The proposition here is that the dependent variable—Soviet arctic behavior—is to be explained not so much by reference to independent variables such as international threats or internal demands for economic development, but by intervening cultural variables which have oriented the Soviet Union to the Arctic when all along it could have acted in other, less forbidding domains. There are several assumptions here that need to be clarified, modified or dismissed.

To begin with, the dependent variable is not well stated in terms that stress the magnitude of the Soviet arctic effort. The Soviet Union or more exactly the Soviet regime has indeed undertaken and followed through on vast projects in the Arctic. It has also set the pace in arctic international relations. But the scale and scope of Soviet activity turn out to be less significant than its quality.

Two basic tendencies are to be observed in Soviet arctic behavior since 1917. (The distinction here is derived in part from the discussion of environmentalism in Darst, 1988.) On the one hand, we have what may be termed a developmentalist tendency as seen in the program of *osvoenie* in the exploitation of advantages offered by the Arctic for purposes of strategic defense, and in a posture of exclusiveness towards other arctic countries. Running counter to Soviet developmentalism is a preservationist tendency as expressed primarily in the regime's environmental decisions and its new openness to arctic international cooperation. Preservationism has come to the fore since Stalin's death in 1953, and most emphatically since Gorbachev's ascent to the leadership in 1985. The dependent variable or behavior to be explained is not an undifferentiated and continuous Soviet performance in the region, but change in the correlation between developmentalism and preservationism in Soviet arctic activity.

Independent variables provide some of the explanation first for the long predominance of developmentalism, and then for the emergence of a correlation that has increasingly favored preservationism.

Why did the Soviets embark upon and then persist in a program of arctic and northern development when Russia under the Tsars had failed to do so despite numerous private attempts? Altered class relations and the new capacity for centrally directed action account for much of the answer. Slavin notes that old Russia lacked the ability to act in the Northeast because the export of cheap Siberian wheat would have undercut the regime by challenging powerful landed interests in European parts of the empire (Slavin 1972:5; 1982:52–7). Such impediments vanished with the advent of the new order. As Armstrong pointed out long ago, Soviet advances in the Arctic flowed from the nature of the Soviet system (Armstrong 1952:173). Once the decision was taken to exploit the terrestrial wealth of the region, a centrally planned and controlled economy had the ability to get the job done with lavish use of manpower and other resources. But why did the Soviets choose to go north? The Marxian ideology of progress and material plenty obviously had something to do with it. But there was nothing inevitable about the effects of ideology. After all, Soviet decision-makers could have ignored the Arctic as their predecessors had done.

Ultimately, national security requirements and the ensuing need to do far better than the Tsars in building military and autonomous industrial strength would seem to have driven the Soviet regime into the Arctic. Speaking in

1931, Stalin stated the underlying necessity in words that reflected a 'single stream' view of Russian and Soviet history:

> Those who fall behind get beaten. But we do not want to be beaten. No, we refuse to be beaten! One feature of the history of old Russia was the continual beatings she suffered for falling behind, for her backwardness. She was beaten by the Mongol Khans. She was beaten by the Turkish Beys. She was beaten by the Swedish Lords. She was beaten by the Polish and Lithuanian gentry. She was beaten by the British and French capitalists. She was beaten by the Japanese barons. All beat her — for her backwardness; for military backwardness; for cultural backwardness; for political backwardness; for industrial backwardness ... Such is the jungle law of capitalism. You are backward, you are weak — therefore you are wrong; hence you can be beaten and enslaved. You are mighty — therefore you are right; hence we must be wary of you. That is why we must no longer lag behind [Stalin 1931:38-9].

Industrialization and the creation of new means to exploit the 'colossal wealth' of arctic and northern regions were to contribute to the might that Lomonosov had aspired to generations earlier. The same applied in due course to Soviet military uses of the Arctic.

In both the economic and the military domains, external situational variables gave rise to overarching strategic imperatives which shaped Soviet policy across the board. Developmentalism in a high northern and arctic setting may therefore be viewed as the local expression of a systemic tendency to mobilize all resources at all costs.

The independent variables that prompted the rise of Soviet arctic preservationism were those that brought on *perestroika* in all its aspects. Here, too, Soviet regional behavior has been the product of larger forces at work within and upon the Soviet system.

Though the Soviet order after Stalin's death remained unchanged in many respects, it was altered to permit the freer expression of contrasting views on social and economic affairs. Even as northern and arctic developmentalism intensified after 1953, Russian nationalism experienced a rebirth and open debate on environmental protection and economic reform became commonplace. Meanwhile, Soviet society and the economy were evolving under the effects of industrialization, urbanization, education and increased exposure to international communication. The command system of economic and social development, which slighted all outcomes except gross values for production and strength, was itself becoming counterproductive. And then, at some point in the 1970s following the attainment of strategic nuclear parity with the United States, it became clear that the historic mission of avoiding a beating at the hands of foreigners had very largely been accomplished. The structures and practices of developmentalism, increasingly viewed as anachronistic, were thus deprived of a key legitimating purpose. Subsequently, the descent of the Soviet Union towards economic crisis and chronic backwardness became sufficiently steep to bring forth, once again, a leader fully determined to transform the old order.

The result since 1985 has been substantial change in the correlation of developmentalism and preservationism as the latter began to influence

Soviet arctic policies directly. Evidence of change is to be had in the river diversion decision of August 1986, the commitment of October 1987 to arctic international cooperation, the formation in the spring of 1989 of a new State Commission on Arctic Affairs in order to eliminate the abuses of developmentalism, the deferral and curtailment of new arctic resource megaprojects and growth in the ability of the aboriginal peoples of the Soviet Arctic to affect central decisions bearing directly on their circumstances and way of life.

This much allowed, it might be concluded without further ado, that Soviet Arctic behavior including change in the correlation of developmentalist and preservationist tendencies is adequately explained by reference to independent international and domestic variables alone. And yet, while we have in effect done away with our original hypothesis in redefining the dependent variable, we have also produced evidence to suggest that deep-seated Russian beliefs and feelings have conditioned the assessment of cost, benefit and uncertainty in Soviet arctic operations. Patterned aversions and attachments have influenced the commitment of resources, the selection of ways and means and the evaluation of consequences. They have biased decisions on what to undertake in the first place. We should therefore consider whether Russian cultural factors have mediated the force of independent variables in the determination of Soviet conduct. Indeed, might it be that intervening Russian predispositions have structured the dominant developmentalist and preservationist tendencies of the Soviet system?

Russian identifications with the Arctic and the North more generally have been neither uniform nor solely positive and enabling. Russians, we have seen, are loath to live in a northern setting, whether it be the Russian North, the Northeast, Siberia or the Arctic. They have derived vicarious satisfaction from arctic and northern exploits, but have otherwise preferred to view the area from a safe distance and to send the convicted there. Siberia and the Arctic are widely viewed as dangerous and melancholy places, a scene for heroism in the face of brute natural forces that must be overcome and subdued. They are also a repository of wealth and might that Russians have dreamt of for ages. The dream here has little or nothing to do with the Arctic or North as such. It is to prevail in competition primarily with the West and on Western terms by exploiting the advantages of science, technology and natural resources. There is nothing symbiotic or caring in such an orientation to Russia's northern spaces. Nor is there any sense of being in one's element here. On the contrary, the mentality is that of the outsider who must summon the will to *osvoenie* or mastery in forbidding circumstances.

And yet Russians do identify with the North, if not equally with the Arctic, in ways suggested by the original hypothesis. The predisposition and desires here are those of *spasenie* or salvation. Northern lands, lakes and rivers are to be saved from destruction not only for their intrinsic value but for the meanings essential to human existence that come from harmonious man–milieu interaction. Further, in a Siberia and Northeast governed by principles of sustainable development, Russians envisage an opportunity to nurture a native way of life that has suffered greatly at the hands of the Soviet regime. Russians, it is believed, can truly be in their element in a northern setting. Russians moved by a salvationist identification with the North and Arctic will therefore assert in conversation that Lomonosov's dictum was not a prediction but a curse. And yet an enabling identification with Russia's northern lands does not so far extend in equal measure to the Arctic. For example, in referring to the arctic shoreline of Siberia, a leading salvationist prefers to speak of 'these vast and wretched spaces' (Rasputin 1983:113).

It seems appropriate to conclude that Soviet arctic developmentalism and the will to *osvoenie* are as much in the Russian tradition as Soviet preservationism and the desire for *spasenie*. We may further suggest that the historic conflict between *osvoenie* and *spasenie* in the Russian imagination has served as a dichotomous intervening variable by predisposing Soviet arctic behavior as it responds to autonomous situational forces. The dependent variable as we have defined it — the correlation of developmentalist and preservationist tendencies in the arctic conduct of the regime — does conform to the dichotomy between *osvoenie* and *spasenie*. It is hard to believe that the correspondence here is fortuitous. Nor can we readily accept the thought that the dependent variable has been formed and maintained without reference to a Russian milieu. The evidence obliges us to conclude that the culture and traditions of the dominant nationality have indeed shaped the arctic behavior of the Soviet Union, but it also reminds us that intervening variables, while influencing conduct, are themselves subject to influence.

In striving to avoid a beating at the hands of foreigners, Soviet Russians administered a tremendous beating not only to Russian lands but to Russian ways of life originally derived from a northern landscape. Consequently, awareness of the arctic and northern areas, and of the benefits to be had from them, is now highly explicit when the region is viewed through the modernizing and Westernizing optic of *osvoenie* . After all, it was in the Soviet era that the Arctic and North began to figure actively in the Russian consciousness. The case for *spasenie*, on the other hand, slights the Arctic, has yet to cite the North as such and dwells upon Siberia and the Northeast where industrialism is less advanced and habitation easier. Moreover, as stimulated by the appeals of the Soviet state to the spirit of collective adventure, evoked attachments to the Arctic and North would seem to have reinforced *osvoenie* at the expense of *spasenie* in the predispositions of Russian society.

Russians and Russian lands have thus in some measure been 'denorthified' under Soviet rule. In the same measure, Russians have been de-russified. And yet *osvoenie* and old-style developmentalism have ultimately proved unworkable. Preservationism and the corresponding urge to *spasenie* have appreciated at the eleventh hour. They now begin to offer an alternative framework for collective action in the Arctic by the Russian people. Having suffered but survived the Soviet experience, the ancient Russian desire to achieve a saving relationship to modernity will survive and prosper in the Arctic in the years ahead. It deserves to prosper.

References

Aktivist ou A. 1932. 'Imperializm na Polyarnom Severe i interesy SSSR' [Imperialism in the Polar North and the interests of the USSR]. *Byulleten' Arkticheskogo Instituta*:1-2, 18-42.

Armstrong, T. 1952. *The Northern Sea Route: Soviet Exploitation of the North East Passage*, 16, 37, 152-73. Cambridge: Cambridge University Press.

Arsen'ev, V. 1985. 'Geroi Arktiki' [A hero of the Arctic]. *Morskoi sbornik* 11:63-65.

Bol'shaya sovetskaya entsiklopedia [Great Soviet Encyclopedia]. 1970. Vol. 2, 200-1. Moscow: Izd-vo 'Sovetskaya entsiklopedia'.

Butler, W. E. 1978. *Northeast Arctic Passage*, 43-77. Alphen aan den Rijn:Sijthoff and Nordhoff.

Darst, R.G. 1988. 'Environmentalism in the USSR: The opposition to the river diversion projects.' *Soviet Economy* 3:223-52.

Dunlop, J. B. 1983. *The Faces of Contemporary Russian Nationalism* 41, 73, 218-79. Princeton: Princeton University Press.

Galenko, V.I. 1978. *Kurs — Sever* [Course — North]. Murmansk: Murmanskoe knizhnoe izd-vo.

Gorbachev, M.S. 1988. Quoted in *The New York Times* 19 February.

— 1987. 'Rech' tovarishcha Gorbacheva M.S' [Speech of Comrade M.S. Gorbachev]. *Izvestia* 2 October. [Translation available through Foreign Broadcast Information Service, *Daily Report: Soviet Union*, 2 October 1987:27-42.] (see Appendix I)

Griffiths, F. 1987. 'Beyond the arctic sublime.' *In : Politics of the Northwest Passage*, ed. F. Griffiths, 265-68. Kingston and Montreal: McGill-Queen's University Press.

Gustafson, T. 1981. *Reform in Soviet Politics: Lessons of Recent Policies on Land and Water*, 39-51. Cambridge: Cambridge University Press.

Guzarov, D. 1987. 'Nadezhnyi flang rodiny' [Reliable flank of the motherland]. *Literaturnaya gazeta* 7 October.

Hamelin, L-E. 1979. *Canadian Nordicity*. [Translated by W. Barr]. Montreal:Harvest House.

Keller, B. 1990. 'Gorbachev picks a new cabinet: Old allies and a few hard-liners.' *The New York Times*, 25 March 1990.

Loomis, C.L. 1977. 'The arctic sublime.' *In: Nature and the Victorian Imagination*, eds. U.C. Knoepflmacher and J.B. Tennyson, 95-112. Berkeley: University of California Press.

Minaev, A., et al. 1987. 'Idti vpered po puti peremen' [Forward along the path of change]. *Pravda* 2 October.

Morskoi sbornik. 1987. 'K polyarnoi vershine planete' [To the planet's polar summit]. 7:60-61.

Pasetskii, V.M. 1974. *Arkticheskie putishestviya Rossiyan* [The Arctic Voyages of Russians]. Moscow: 'Mysl'.

Patriot Severa. 1985. [Patriot of the North]. Arkhangel'sk: Severo-zapadnoe knizhnoe Izd-vo.

Pik, A., and B. Prokhorov. 1988. 'Bol'shie problemy malykh narodov' [The big problems of the small peoples]. *Kommunist* 16:76-83.

Rasputin, V. 1983. 'Sibir' bez romantiki' [Siberia without romantics]. *Sibir* 5:106-28.

Samoilovich, R.L. 1935. 'Nauchno-issledovatel'skaya Deyatel'nost' vsesoyuznogo Arkticheskogo Instituta' [Scientific activity of the All-Union Arctic Institute]. *In : Byulleten' Arkticheskogo Instituta*:3-4, 56-61.

Shumilov, M.I. 1974. 'V.I. Lenin o promyshlennom osvoenii prirodnykh bogatstv

Evropeiskogo Severa' [V.I. Lenin on the industrial development of the natural resources of the European North]. *In : Voprosy istorii Evropeiskogo Severa* [Problems in the History of the European North], 3-26. Petrozavodsk: MINVUZ RSFSR.

Slavin, S.V. 1972. *The Soviet North: Present Developments and Prospects*, 7, 26. Moscow: Progress Publishers.

— 1982. *Osvoenie Severa Sovetskogo Soyuza* [The Northern Development of the Soviet Union]. Second edition, 13-60. Moscow: Nauka.

Solzhenitsyn, A.L. 1974. *Letter to the Soviet Leaders*, 35-40. New York: Harper and Row.

Stalin, I.V. 1931. 'O zadachakh khozyajstvennikov' [On the tasks of economic managers]. *In*: I.V. Stalin, 1955. *Sochineniya* [Works]. Vol. 13, 29-42.

Taracouzio, T.A. 1935. *The Soviets in International Law*. New York: Macmillan.

— 1938. *Soviets in the Arctic*, 41, 320-80. New York: Macmillan.

Zaika, B., and Yu. Batskikh. 1987. 'Problemy gruzoperevozok v Arktike' [Problems of bulk carriers in the Arctic]. *Morskoy flot* 5:14.

Zalygin, S. 1987. 'Povorot:uroki odnoi diskussii' [Turnabout: Lessons of one discussion]. *Novyi Mir* 1:3-18.

7

Oil and gas resources in the offshore Soviet Arctic

James W. Clarke

The geology of the Soviet Arctic indicates three main offshore oil and gas basins for potential development: Barents Sea, Kara Sea and Northeast Siberia Arctic Shelf. This chapter describes the stratigraphic section of rock strata for each of these basins and additionally provides an understanding of where source beds, reservoir rocks and seals are present. As shown by stratigraphic section, the thickness of sediment indicates the depth of burial and the consequent maturation of resources. Understanding the structural configuration of these sedimentary rocks (described herein) also indicates where oil and gas may have accumulated.

In order for oil and gas pools to form and to be preserved as commercially recoverable deposits, a number of conditions must be met. First, organic matter must be deposited to form a source bed. Assessing the oil and gas potential of a region requires, among other factors, an understanding of where source beds are present in the stratigraphic column and how deeply they have been buried. For oil to form, this source bed must be buried at least 1,000 meters so that the higher temperature at that depth may 'cook' the organic matter, thereby producing oil. The source beds are then said to be in a temperature zone called the oil 'window'. At depths of 4,000-5,000 meters the temperatures are too hot for oil generation, and only gas is formed; the source beds are then said to be in the thermal gas window. Meanwhile, gas has been evolving from the source beds since their initial deposition: first as biogenic gas formed by bacterial activity, then as thermal gas along with oil within the oil window, and finally, gas alone formed in the thermal gas window. Maturation or catagenesis refers to these processes of oil and gas generation.

Once oil and gas form, they must migrate from their source bed into a reservoir rock, which is generally a porous sandstone, porous and fractured limestone or dolomite. An impermeable material such as clay or salt seals this reservoir rock from above. The rock must also be in some sort of closed structural configuration, like an inverted saucer or trap, which is enough of a physical barrier to prevent the escape of the oil and gas out of the sides.

Barents Sea

The subsurface geology of the Barents Sea has been compiled on the basis of offshore seismic surveys and observations made on its peripheral islands and coastal areas (Gramberg and Pogrebitskiy 1984). A regional seismic refracting interface divides the sedimentary section into an upper clastic assemblage and a lower predominantly carbonate assemblage. This interface is in the Lower Permian part of the stratigraphic section (see Figure 7.1).

Geologic Age			Age (million years)	Thickness (meters)	Type of Sedimentary Rock	
CENOZOIC	Quaternary		2	20-100	All types from gravel to mud	Upper Assemblage
	Neogene		23	0-3000	Sand-clay varieties	
	Paleogene		67			
MESOZOIC	Cretaceous		144	0-1000	Sand-silt varieties; volcanic rocks in north	
	Jurassic		208	250-1000	Clay and sand varieties	
	Triassic		245	600-4000	Sand-clay varieties; some basalt	
PALEOZOIC	Permian	Upper		400-2500	Sandstones	Lower Assemblage
		Lower	286	1000-2000	Carbonate rocks	
	Carboniferous		360			
	Devonian	Upper			Clastic-carbonate rocks	
		Middle				
		Lower				
PROTEROZOIC	Basement					

Figure 7.1 Geologic time scale.

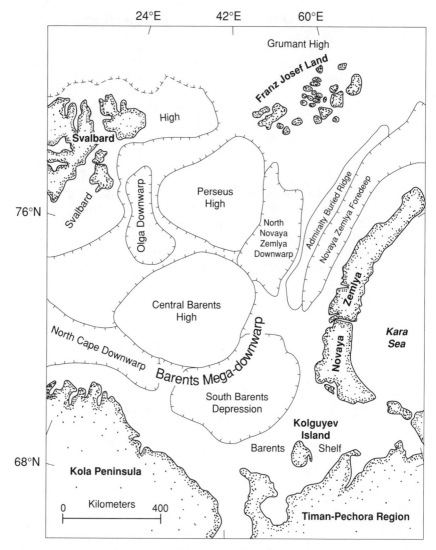

Figure 7.2 Subsurface marine geology of the Barents Sea and surrounding region (adapted from Gramberg and Pogrebitskiy 1984).

Stratigraphy

Quaternary sediments

The top of the Quaternary is commonly recorded somewhat lower than the physical surface of the seafloor; it is at the interface between liquid and semi-liquid bottom mud and the more consolidated sediment. The base of

110

the Quaternary coincides with a seismic reflecting horizon. Thicknesses of these deposits range in general from 20–100 meters, and they consist of all types from gravel to mud (see Figure 7.1).

Neogene and Paleogene sediments

Below the Quaternary deposits is a unit of sediments that ranges in thickness from about 1 kilometer in the North Cape downwarp to about 0.4–1.0 kilometers in the South Barents depression (see Figure 7.2). These sediments appear to be sand-clay material.

Cretaceous rocks

These rocks occur over a wide area of the Barents Sea. Seismic reflecting horizons bound them at both top and bottom. Depth to the top of the Cretaceous system measured down from the seafloor ranges from a few hundred meters on the southern Barents shelf to 1.8 kilometers in the deepest troughs; this unit, however, is absent on the Central Barents high. Velocity characteristics of the Cretaceous period are fairly uniform at 2.0–2.3 kilometers per second throughout the entire area of their occurrence.

Sand-silt varieties compose the Cretaceous rocks over most of the basin; volcanic rocks, however, are present in the north and on Franz Josef Land. Prograding deltas that were deposited during the Early Cretaceous are host to giant oil fields in West Siberia. Similar deltaic deposits may be present to the west of Novaya Zemlya and to the south of Franz Josef Land (Ulmisek 1985). The thickness of this system is generally 400—700 meters, reaching 1,000 meters in places.

Jurassic rocks

Within the Middle Jurassic section is a very good seismic marker, which separates overlying argillaceous rocks from underlying sandstones. The seismic velocity within the lower sandstone unit is 0.5–0.72 kilometers per second greater than in the upper rock unit.

Depth to the top of the Jurassic ranges from a few hundred meters on the highs to 2–2.5 kilometers in the troughs. A maximum depth of 3 kilometers has been found in the South Barents depression.

The upper part of the Jurassic consists of homogeneous marine clays, some of which are bituminous and appear to correlate with the Bazhenov bituminous shale of West Siberia (Ulmisek 1985). The Bazhenov shale is the source rock for the rich oil fields of West Siberia. The thickness of these marine clays ranges from 250–1,000 meters, the thickest being recorded in the South Barents depression.

Triassic rocks

Reflecting horizons are present near the top and at the base of this section. Depths to the base of the Triassic range from 0.5–1.5 kilometers on the Barents shelf to 6–8 kilometers in the deepest parts of the South Barents depression.

Variations in velocity for these sediments suggest variations in composition. Clayey varieties predominate in the north, whereas sandy

111

types are more common in the south. Basaltic volcanic rocks appear to be common in the Lower Triassic. The thickness of the Triassic section averages 600–800 meters on the Barents shelf and increases to 3.5–4.0 kilometers in the South Barents depression, Novaya Zemlya foredeep and other structural lows.

Permian rocks

Several reflecting horizons are recorded in the Permian section, two of which are good markers. The first marker is set at the base of the Upper Permian clastic unit, and the second marker is at the base of the system. The upper marker is traced for several hundred kilometers from the south shore of the Barents Sea northward where it plunges from a depth of a few hundred meters on the south to 10–12 kilometers on the north. On the Central Barents high the Permian sediments are at 3–4 kilometers' depth.

Three lithologic units are recognized in the Permian section: an upper clastic unit, mentioned above, which onshore is largely continental sandstone; a middle marine carbonate–clastic unit; and a lower carbonate unit. The upper clastic unit is the lowest part of the upper clastic assemblage. Thickness of these clastic deposits is generally 400–700 meters, decreasing to 100–200 meters on the highs and increasing to 2–2.5 kilometers in the South Barents depression. The middle and lower lithologic units of the Permian are in the lower, predominantly carbonate assemblage (see Figure 7.1).

Carbonate subassemblage

This part of the sedimentary rock consists of high-velocity carbonates of Late Devonian, Carboniferous and Early Permian age; some evaporites and volcanics are also present. Their thickness is rather uniform at 1–2 kilometers with no tendency to increase in the structural lows. This section consists of clastic sedimentary rocks in the western and northern parts of the Barents Sea.

Clastic-carbonate subassemblage

These rocks extend from the base of the carbonate subassemblage to the surface of the basement. They are at great depth, their base being at 12–14 kilometers in the South Barents depression. Consequently, little is known about them other than that they appear to be clastics and carbonates. If the Domanik calcareous shale, the source rock for the Timan–Pechora and Volga–Ural oil and gas provinces to the south, should be present in the Barents Sea, it would be in this subassemblage.

Structure

The Barents Sea region is known structurally as the Barents–Kara platform and includes the offshore structures shown in Figure 7.2 as well as the North Kara basin, which is shown in Figure 7.4. A reference horizon for describing the structure of the Barents Sea region is the reflecting horizon at the base of the upper clastic assemblage in the Lower Permian.

The Barents mega-downwarp is a feature that extends a distance of 1,200 kilometers from Norway to Franz Josef Land and consists of the North Cape downwarp, South Barents depression and North Novaya Zemlya downwarp. Structural saddles separate the different sections (see Figure 7.2). The thickness of the upper clastic assemblage is 5–6 kilometers in the North Cape downwarp, 10–12 kilometers in the South Barents depression and 9–10 kilometers in the North Novaya Zemlya downwarp. Thicknesses are generally 2–3 kilometers less on the intervening saddles. Magnetic anomalies on the intervening saddles suggest the presence of structures that could contain oil and gas pools. The sediments within the downwarps appear to be quite undisturbed; no significant structures are present except in the North Cape downwarp where salt domes have been recorded. Some of these rise nearly to the surface from depths of 4.5–5.5 kilometers (Verba 1984).

Central Barents high

A thinning of the upper clastic assemblage by 1.5 kilometers characterizes this uplift; the seafloor topography also expresses it. Magnetic surveys indicate an abundance of structures on this high which are controlled by faulting in the rocks below the upper clastic assemblage.

The Central Barents high and to its north, the Perseus high, form a single large arch, which bounds the Barents mega-downwarp on the west. The Olga downwarp separates it on the west from the Svalbard high.

Novaya Zemlya foredeep

Sediments 6–8 kilometers thick fill this depression. The Admiralty buried ridge flanks this structural feature on the west where the section thins.

Petroleum geology

The onshore geology of the productive Timan–Pechora and West Siberian petroleum provinces guides the synthesis of the petroleum geology of the Barents Sea. The potential for the Barents Sea combines elements of the productive Paleozoic rocks of the Timan–Pechora as well as elements of the productive Mesozoic rocks of West Siberia.

By comparison, the principal source beds in the onshore Timan–Pechora oil–gas province are the Upper Devonian Domanik calcareous shales, which contain 5–10 percent organic matter and more. They are also the principal source beds for the oil-rich Ural–Volga province to the south. The distribution of this Domanik shale within the Barents Sea is unknown. During the time of deposition of the Domanik shale, northern Europe and central and northern North America were juxtaposed; this was long before the tectonic opening of the Atlantic Ocean. The Chattanooga Shale of central North America is similar in composition and age to the Domanik shale, suggesting widespread distribution of this rock type. Consequently, the Domanik may well be present over large parts of the Barents Sea and would be a good source rock where it has not been eroded or buried too deeply for oil generation. On Svalbard, the age equivalent of the Domanik shale is continental clastic rock, which has no oil- or gas-generating potential.

The Triassic section is also good source rock for the Barents Sea region. Deep-water, organic-rich black shales are predicted over much of the western part of the region, grading eastward into shallow-water, near-shore clastics. The oil and gas potential of the Barents Sea region depends heavily on the presence of these Triassic source beds, which appear to be restricted to the Norwegian sector of the sea.

Black shales of Late Jurassic age are probably the most organic-rich shales of the Barents Sea region. The 'hot' shales of the North Sea and the Bazhenov shales of West Siberia, both of Late Jurassic age, are the source rocks for those two regions. The Upper Jurassic black shales are probably present over much of the Barents Sea region and would be good source beds where buried deeply enough for oil formation. The problem, however, is that in most places they have not reached the level of maturation necessary for oil generation (Ulmishek 1985).

By analogy with the Timan–Pechora and Volga–Ural petroleum provinces, the Devonian clastic rocks and Carboniferous and Lower Permian carbonate rocks of the Barents Sea probably contain important reservoirs and seals. Uplift of the Ural orogenic belt in the Late Permian and Triassic periods resulted in deposition of broad aprons of sand in the Barents Sea region. Transgressive seas deposited thick sands and clays. The resulting sandstones are good reservoirs, and the clays are good seals. Additional sandstones (reservoir rocks) were deposited during the Jurassic and clays (seals) during the latest Jurassic time. These Upper Jurassic clays were deposited in a deep and extensive sea, which was then filled by prograding sands during the Cretaceous period. The resulting Cretaceous sandstones would serve as reservoirs for any petroleum generated by the underlying Upper Jurassic clays (shale).

The distribution of small-scale structures generally mimics the distribution of large-scale structures (highs or structural ridges; downwarps, depressions or foredeeps). The large high-closure structural highs of the Barents Sea suggest strongly that abundant smaller structures capable of trapping petroleum will be found.

Several oil and gas discoveries have now been made in the Barents Sea (see Figure 7.3). Two large oil fields are present on Kolguyev Island. Peschanoozer field was the first discovered; it extends offshore. One of the first wells drilled here tested oil and gas at 10 intervals in the Triassic section. Oil was recovered in this well at 1,095 barrels per day and gas at 11.3 million cubic feet per day. Thirteen wells were in production in 1987. To the northwest of Peschanoozer field is Kolguyev oil field. Two additional oil discoveries were announced in September 1989, one about 130 kilometers north of Kolguyev Island and another (Admiralty) about 130 kilometers west of Novaya Zemlya, apparently on the Admiralty buried ridge. Additional oil discoveries are Prirazlom and Severo-Gulyaev in the southeastern part of the Barents Sea.

Pomor, Murmansk, Severo-Kildin and Shtockmanov gas fields have also

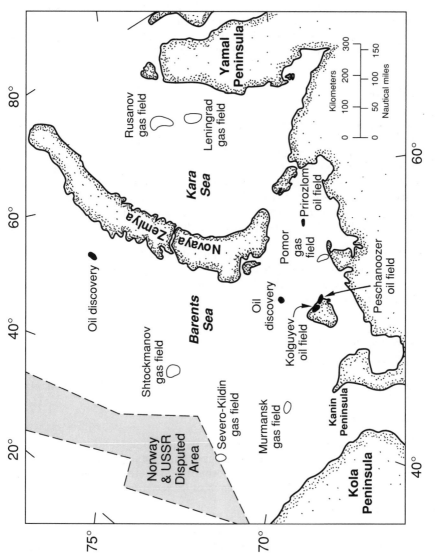

Figure 7.3 Recent oil and gas discoveries in the Barents and Kara seas.

been discovered (see Figure 7.3). Of these, Shtockmanov reportedly carries about 100 trillion cubic feet of gas in Jurassic reservoirs.

It is likely that the offshore resource potential of the Barents Sea will probably be mostly gas. This is because the Upper Jurassic shale, which is the principal oil source bed, was probably never buried deeply enough to enter the oil window in most of the region. Further, the thickness of the sedimentary rocks is so great that the lower part of the section is in the thermal gas window, and gas from these deep-occurring rocks has probably driven most of any earlier formed oil out of the traps.

Kara Sea

Two major structures are juxtaposed against one another beneath the waters of the Kara Sea: the Barents–Kara platform on the north and the West Siberian platform on the south. These major structures are separated from one another by a buried ridge, which connects the northern tip of Novaya Zemlya with the southwestern part of the Taymyr peninsula. This buried ridge is called the North Siberian sill. Its existence has recently been confirmed by seismic surveys (Gramberg and Pogrebitskiy 1984). The geology to the north of this sill is quite different from that to the south (see Figure 7.4).

Water depths in the Kara Sea are generally less than 100 meters except to the west near Novaya Zemlya where they are deeper. Only the South Kara basin is discussed here; the North Kara basin, being part of the Barents–Kara platform, was reviewed earlier.

Stratigraphy

Quaternary sediments

At the top of the section in the South Kara basin are glacial-marine deposits 100–200 meters thick.

Paleogene deposits

Beneath the thin Quaternary sediments are shales and sandstones of Oliogocene, Eocene and Paleocene ages. Their total thickness is estimated at 0.7–1.0 kilometers. Uplift of perhaps 500 meters at the end of the Paleogene resulted in erosion of much of these sediments.

Cretaceous sediments

During the Late Cretaceous (Turonian time), a wide marine transgression resulted in deposition of 300–600 meters of marine clays. These are plastic and commonly are deformed into diapirs. It is these clays that seal the giant gas pools to the south in West Siberia. Middle Cretaceous alluvial and deltaic sandstones, 800–1000 meters thick, are directly beneath the Turonian clay seals. These contain the gas pools onshore. The Lower Cretaceous also consists largely of sandstones, which were deposited as

116

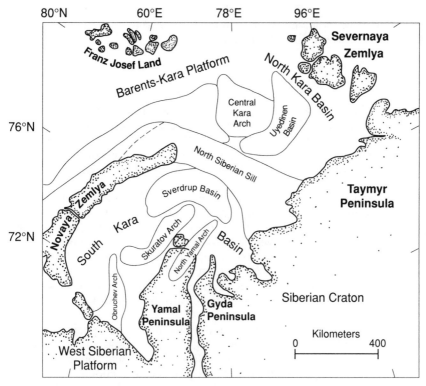

Figure 7.4 Subsurface marine geology of the Kara Sea (adapted from Gramberg and Pogrebitskiy 1984).

deltas, gradually filling a vast, deep-water basin initiated in Late Jurassic time. This interval is 1,200–1,400 meters thick and contains the rich oil deposits in central West Siberia.

Jurassic sediments

This part of the section appears to be almost 2 kilometers thick; it consists of sandstones and shales. At its top is the rich oil-source Bazhenov Formation, the main source of the oil to the south in West Siberia.

Beneath the Jurassic rocks are thick, presumably marine shales and siltstones of Triassic age.

Structure

The southern part of the South Kara basin is structurally a continuation of the north-trending structures of the West Siberian platform, which is exposed onshore to the south. In the northern part of this basin, however, these north-trending structures give way to transverse highs and lows that

117

parallel the Novaya Zemlya–North Siberian sill trend. The thickness of post-Paleozoic sedimentary rocks in the lows is up to 6 kilometers, and on the highs it is as little as 1 kilometer.

Petroleum Geology

When projected northward, the geology of the onshore areas of the West Siberian petroleum province indicate an excellent potential for oil and gas discoveries in the Kara Sea. The area to the west of the Yamal peninsula should contain large gas deposits, an extension of the gas-rich region of the peninsula. Farther north, oil pools may be associated with the North Siberian sill.

Sources beds of the Jurassic shales and sandstones below the Bazhenov Formation probably carry humic organic matter, which tends to generate gas rather than oil. The Bazhenov at the top of the Jurassic section carries sapropelic organic matter, which tends to generate oil. Source beds similar to the Bazhenov rocks are also in the Lower Cretaceous. The Middle Cretaceous sedimentary rocks contain much coal-like material, which generates gas. Finally, the Upper Cretaceous Turonian marine clays are a source for gas, which will have migrated downward into Middle Cretaceous sandstones.

By analogy with the West Siberian petroleum province, good sandstone reservoir rocks should be present in both the Jurassic and Cretaceous sections. The Bazhenov Formation will act as the seal for the Jurassic reservoirs and the Turonian clays for the Cretaceous section.

The tectonic movements within the basement rocks that formed the domal highs of the West Siberian platform have been regional and will have affected the entire area of the Kara Sea, resulting in extensive development of structural arches, which are excellent traps to store oil or gas. The buried ridge of the North Siberian sill is a very large additional trap.

With all variables pointing to rich, potential resources, two gas discoveries have been made in the Kara Sea as of early 1990 (see Figure 7.3). These are the Rusanov and Leningrad fields. The Rusanov is said to be larger than the Shtockmanov field in the Barents Seas, which is estimated to have 100 trillion cubic feet of gas.

Potentially, the fields of the southern Kara Sea will be largely gas, unless the seals on the traps have been broken by faulting, thereby releasing sufficient gas to leave residual oil in the trap. To the north, the oil-generating Bazhenov Formation may have supplied oil to traps on the flanks and crest of the North Siberian sill. Any oil pools that formed in this region may have been subsequently destroyed by gas migrating up the regional dip of the Mesozoic strata toward the crest of this buried ridge. If such destruction has taken place, then this region will also only have gas fields.

Northeast Siberia Arctic Shelf

Nine basins are recognized in the northeast offshore region of Siberia; these lie within the Laptev, East Siberian and Chukchi seas, which cover the large shelf area between the Asiatic continent and the Arctic Ocean (see Figure 7.5). The South Laptev and Novosibirsk basins are filled with Paleozoic and Mesozoic rocks; the other basins are filled with Cretaceous and Tertiary sediments. The region has had little study, just a few gravity and aeromagnetic surveys. Water depth on the shelf is less than 200 meters everywhere and commonly less than 100 meters over large areas. A review of the known stratigraphy of several basins provides the basis for initial projections of resource development for the shelf.

South Laptev basin

The lower part of the section is composed of Upper Proterozoic through Devonian sediments 3–5 kilometers thick. Overlying are Carboniferous and Permian deposits, the latter containing source beds. The section is completed by Mesozoic and Cenozoic sediments for a total sedimentary thickness of up to 10 kilometers.

Novosibirsk basin

This basin contains several kilometers of Paleozoic sediments, overlain by Triassic, Jurassic, and Cretaceous rocks. The Triassic section contains source beds, and coal beds are present in the Cretaceous.

Cloud-like plumes that rise out of the water next to Bennett Island on the northeast margin of this basin may be the result of escaping methane from the breakdown of gas hydrates in Cretaceous and Paleozoic rocks (Clarke *et al*. 1986).

Hope basin, Soviet area

About 4 kilometers of Tertiary sediments rest on a folded Mesozoic basement. Source beds are coal-bearing clastics and are clearly gas-prone.

East Siberian Sea–Chukchi Sea basin

This is the most favorable region of the northeast Siberian offshore for potential resources. The section consists of Cretaceous and Tertiary coal-bearing sediments. The Chukchi Sea part of the basin on the east appears to have good source beds—organic, rich clay-like deposits. In the part of the East Siberian Sea on the west of the basin the only source beds are coal-bearing clastic sediments.

For the Chukchi Sea area, undiscovered recoverable oil is assessed at 1.5 billion barrels and gas at 18 trillion cubic feet. For the East Siberian Sea portion, these assessments are 2 billion barrels for oil and 40 trillion cubic feet for gas (Ulmisek 1984).

Little is known about the other basins of the Northeast Siberia Arctic Shelf. They are likely to contain significant thicknesses of Cretaceous coal-bearing sedimentary rocks and consequently gas pools will predominate rather than oil.

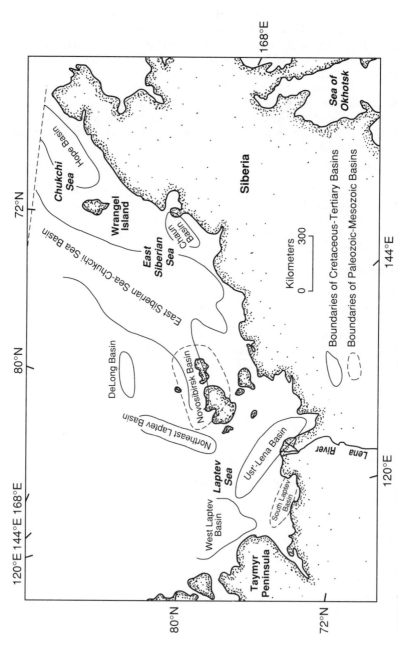

Figure 7.5 Subsurface marine geology of the Laptev, East Siberian and Chukchi seas. Although nine basins have been found under the offshore arctic shelf regions of northeast Siberia, this region has not been surveyed extensively (adapted from Ulmishek 1984).

Conclusion

The Soviet Union is well positioned with respect to gas reserves and prospects for new discoveries. New gas discoveries in the Barents and Kara seas over a 3-year period, 1987–9, probably approach 14.2 million cubic meters and exploration is still in early stages. Production of this gas will be achieved with great difficulty, however, and may have to be delayed until new market forces come into play. Transport in the liquid phase or conversion to a liquid fuel are very costly processes, and such endeavors are subject to being rendered uneconomic by drops in energy prices on the world market. On the other hand, the development of these gas deposits by the Soviets as a joint venture with Western companies might successfully bring these resources onto the world market as just one more additional component of an industry that is already perhaps the most international in the world economy.

The situation with respect to oil is very different from that of gas. The Soviets must find an additional 4 billion barrels of oil each year to maintain their present reserves-to-production ratio. Discovery of 20 billion barrels of offshore oil in the Soviet Arctic region would extend the life of their oil industry only 5 years, and this oil would be won at great expense. Further, the offshore Arctic region appears to be strongly prone to gas deposits. Several oil deposits, however, have already been found in the Barents Sea. The 2 oil fields on Kolguyev Island appear to be large and in a part of the stratigraphic section (Triassic-age rocks) that is different from the section hosting the nearest onshore oil fields to the south. The thickness of the sedimentary rocks increases considerably to the north of Kolguyev Island, and consequently it would not be much of a surprise if large oil deposits were discovered on any of the structural highs or in the downwarps and depressions of the Barents Sea region.

In the Kara Sea, gas is expected in the southern part, but oil deposits may be present on the flanks and crest of the North Siberian sill. The Northeast Siberia Arctic Shelf should contain mostly gas, except the South Laptev and Hope basin where some oil may be found.

Gas resources seemingly now predominate over oil in offshore basins of the Barents Sea, Kara Sea and Northeast Siberia Shelf. Discovery of very significant amounts of gas and oil can be expected in the Barents and Kara seas. These deposits may not be produced, however, until well into the 21st century.

References

Clarke, J.W., P. St. Amand, and M. Matson. 1986. 'Possible cause of plumes from Bennett Island, Soviet Far Arctic.' *American Association of Petroleum Geologists Bulletin* 70(5):574.

Gramberg, I.S., and Yu.Ye. Pogrebitskiy. 1984. 'Geologicheskoye stroyeniye SSSR i zakonomer-nosti razmeshcheniya poleznykh iskopayemykh' [Geology of the USSR and regularities in the distribution of natural resources]. *In: Morya Sovetskoy Arktiki*, t. 9 [Seas of the Soviet Arctic, vol. 9.] Leningrad: Nedra.

James W. Clarke

Ulmisek, G. 1984. *The Geology and Petroleum Resources of Basins in the Asian Arctic and Offshore East Greenland*. Argonne National Laboratory, ANL/EES-TM-247 (Available through NTIS, Springfield, VA 22161).

— 1985. *Geology and Petroleum Resources of the Barents-Northern Kara Shelf in Light of New Geological Data*. Argonne National Laboratory, ANL/EES-TM-XXX (Available through NTIS, Springfield, VA 22161).

Verba, V.V. 1984. 'Sravnitel' naya geologo-geofizicheskaya kharakteristika Barentsevomorskogo i Severomorskogo osadochnykh solenosnykh basseynov' [Comparative geological-geophysical characteristics of the Barents Sea and North Sea salt basins]. *In: Neftegazonosnost' mirovogo okeana* Leningrad: PGO Sermorgeologiya.

Part III
Challenges of marine and river transport

8

Technical developments and the future of Soviet Arctic marine transportation

Lawson W. Brigham

Modern marine operations along the Northern Sea Route (NSR) represent a remarkable achievement as well as a huge capital investment by the Soviet Union. Technological advancement, adaptation and technology transfer have all played leading roles in the development of the diverse arctic fleet that is the central element making possible an expansion of NSR operations. During the past 40 years the increased level of support for this national enterprise has spawned a broad range of significant technical and operational accomplishments. Most noteworthy of these, perhaps, is that the Soviet Union has gradually gained effective marine access along its entire, remote arctic coastline. Ship convoys have been led during various seasons to all the major ports in the Soviet maritime Arctic and to each of the major Siberian rivers which eventually penetrate into the heart of the USSR. Driven by a desire to develop Siberia's vast resources and forced by geography to seek innovative solutions using advanced technology, the USSR has succeeded in building a formidable arctic marine transportation system. Now this complex and expensive system is being challenged to function more efficiently and effectively. The long-term hope is that the NSR can become more economically viable.

The objectives of this chapter are threefold. The first is briefly to review the technical development of modern Soviet icebreakers and icebreaking cargo ships. A second purpose is to explore various operational accomplishments of recent years and relate these to the potential for expansion of the navigation season along the NSR. Finally, the chapter speculates on the prospects for the future of Soviet maritime transportation in the Arctic Ocean.

Evolution of modern Soviet icebreakers

In order to develop feasible and commercially viable marine transportation in the Arctic Ocean, the Soviet Union has had to acquire an extraordinary fleet of state-of-the-art polar ships. During the past 4 decades the largest Soviet polar icebreakers have evolved along two parallel technological (design) paths: one Soviet, the other Finnish (see Figure 8.1). Since the 1950s Soviet designers and shipbuilders primarily concentrated on the design and construction of a fleet of nuclear-powered polar icebreakers. Concurrently, the Finnish shipbuilder Wartsila built a series of conventionally powered (diesel-electric) polar icebreakers. There has been significant collaboration between both Soviet and Finnish design teams, particularly in the early years with the *Moskva* class ships. In fact, technical specifications for that class were developed and models were tested in the ice tank at the Arctic and Antarctic Scientific Research Institute (Maksutov 1981:18), prior to the completion of a final design by Wartsila. As indicated in Figure 8.1, the 2, long-term development efforts (comprising Finnish shipbuilding technology and Soviet nuclear ship technology) merged in the late 1980s with the design and construction of 2 shallow-draft, nuclear icebreakers of the *Taymyr* class.

The 1959 commissioning of the Soviet-built *Lenin*, the first nuclear-powered surface ship, ushered in a new era of polar icebreaker technology. Steam produced by *Lenin*'s nuclear reactors drove turbines and generators, which in turn powered electric motors on 3 propeller shafts. *Lenin*'s unlimited endurance and high power (44,000 shaft horsepower, 32,300 kilowatts) were precisely the capabilities required for extending Soviet arctic operations. Although beset with early technical problems, *Lenin* proved to be a good test platform for nuclear propulsion of future arctic ships. *Lenin*'s icebreaking capability (an estimated ability to break approximately 1.5-meter level ice continuously at 3 knots) was operationally tested during winter operations in the Kara Sea. Several pioneering voyages, with *Lenin* escorting ice-strengthened cargo carriers, paved the way for year-round navigation from Murmansk to Dudinka on the Yenisey River.

Lenin had clearly demonstrated the tremendous advantage of nuclear power for extended high-latitude operations. During the early 1970s the Soviet Union conceived and began a long-term building program for a new generation of nuclear icebreakers. The new ships' designers were primarily concerned with improving icebreaking capability and performance, as well as enhancing nuclear power plant reliability. The resulting vessels, *Arktika* (1975) and *Sibir'* (1977), were huge polar ships (23,460 tons full displacement) with power plants generating 75,000 shaft horsepower (55,200 kilowatts) from 2 pressurized water reactors. Their wide beam

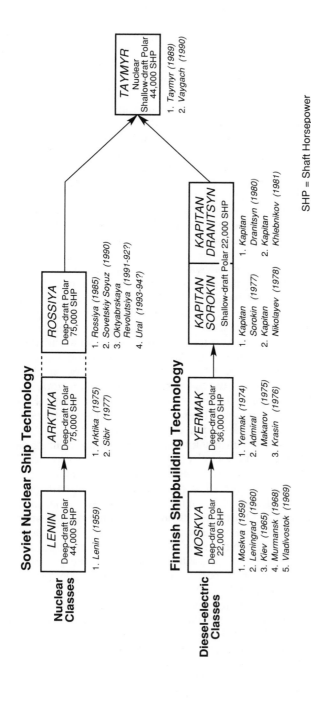

Figure 8.1 Flow diagram representing the technical and design evolution of Soviet polar icebreakers, from 1959 to the present.

Soviet Nuclear Ship Technology

Nuclear Classes

LENIN
Deep-draft Polar
44,000 SHP

1. Lenin (1959)

ARKTIKA
Deep-draft Polar
75,000 SHP

1. Arktika (1975)
2. Sibir (1977)

ROSSIYA
Deep-draft Polar
75,000 SHP

1. Rossiya (1985)
2. Sovetskiy Soyuz (1990)
3. Oktyabrskaya Revolutsiya (1991-92?)
4. Ural (1993-94?)

TAYMYR
Nuclear
Shallow-draft Polar
44,000 SHP

1. Taymyr (1989)
2. Vaygach (1990)

Finnish Shipbuilding Technology

Diesel-electric Classes

MOSKVA
Deep-draft Polar
22,000 SHP

1. Moskva (1959)
2. Leningrad (1960)
3. Kiev (1965)
4. Murmansk (1968)
5. Vladivostok (1969)

YERMAK
Deep-draft Polar
36,000 SHP

1. Yermak (1974)
2. Admiral Makarov (1975)
3. Krasin (1976)

KAPITAN SOROKIN
Shallow-draft Polar 22,000 SHP

1. Kapitan Sorokin (1977)
2. Kapitan Nikolayev (1978)

KAPITAN DRANITSYN

1. Kapitan Dranitsyn (1980)
2. Kapitan Khlebnikov (1981)

SHP = Shaft Horsepower

127

(28 meters on the waterline) and large physical size made them particularly effective when escorting convoys.

The *Arktika* class ships are currently the largest and most powerful polar icebreakers in operation. Owing to their extraordinary icebreaking capabilities, immediate improvements were felt in NSR operations upon their introduction to the arctic fleet. Convoying speeds were reported to be more than double the earlier 3 to 4 knot speeds (Dem'yanchenko and Livshits 1984:1). These ships were the most important elements in extending the navigation season in several sectors of the Soviet maritime Arctic. Three high-latitude voyages also demonstrated the *Arktika* class ships' reliability and capability in the most severe arctic ice conditions. The North Pole voyage in August 1977 by *Arktika* and a spring 1978 crossing of the NSR north of the Soviet island groups by *Sibir'* escorting the cargo ship *Kapitan Myshevskiy* gained international attention (Brigham 1985:132) (see Figure 1.1 for the routes of these 2 voyages). The May to June 1987 scientific voyage in the central Arctic Ocean and to the North Pole by *Sibir'* also displayed the endurance and operational flexibility of these remarkable icebreakers (see Chapter 3).

A third ship in the class, *Rossiya*, was added in 1985. Although the major physical characteristics remained unchanged, a number of internal improvements were made. Changes in the Rules of the USSR Register and several new international conventions also required that new equipment be installed. A unique system for heating the hull plating along the ice belt (to melt accumulations of snow) and ice-deflecting nozzles around the wing propellers were added to improve *Rossiya*'s icebreaking performance (Dem'yanchenko and Livshits 1984:1). Three new ships of the class scheduled for completion in the next few years — *Sovetskiy Soyuz*, *Oktyabrskaya Revolutisiya* and *Ural* — will surely incorporate the latest technological advances available. Thus, by the mid-1990s 6 *Arktika* class nuclear icebreakers will be operational along the NSR.

Since the late 1950s the Finnish shipbuilder Wartsila has built 12 diesel–electric polar icebreakers for the USSR (see Figure 8.1). Each of these ships ranks among the largest and most capable polar icebreakers in the world. The *Moskva* (5 ships), *Yermak* (3 ships) and *Kapitan Sorokin* (4 ships) classes, ranging from 122 to 135 meters in length, were designed for icebreaking along the Northern Sea Route in regions of first-year and multi-year ice. The *Moskva* class was relatively deep draft (10.5 meters) and was designed with considerable power (22,000 shaft horsepower, 16,200 kilowatts) distributed among 3 propellers (one half of the power to the center shaft with one-quarter power to each of the side propellers) (Maksutov 1981:18). From 1974 to 1976 3 larger ships of the *Yermak* class were built, each with 36,000 shaft horsepower (26,500 kilowatts). They have remained the most powerful diesel–electric polar icebreakers currently in operation in the world. As a trial, the lead ship, *Yermak*, was fitted with an air hull lubrication system, an auxiliary device which forces large volumes of air along the hull to reduce the friction of sea ice and snow cover and thereby improve icebreaking performance (Maksutov 1981:19).

The deep drafts of the nuclear and largest conventionally powered polar icebreakers proved to be a severe restriction for operations along the deltas and mouths of the key Siberian rivers. If the navigation season was to be extended throughout the winter in the Kara Sea, it was necessary to have icebreakers escort cargo carriers into the shallow reaches of the coast. Therefore, Wartsila's designers were tasked in the mid-1970s with developing a class of shallow-draft polar ships. Four *Kapitan Sorokin* icebreakers with drafts of only 8.5 meters were commissioned from 1977 to 1981. Significantly, their power level was maintained at 22,000 shaft horsepower, identical to the earlier *Moskva* class. These ships have proved highly effective at escorting ships in the Ob' and Yenisey river mouths and along the entire shallow Soviet Arctic coast. Their hull air lubrication systems have been particularly effective when navigating in regions of thick snow cover.

In April 1988 a new, shallow-draft polar icebreaker named *Taymyr* was delivered to the Soviet Union by Wartsila's Helsinki shipyard. A single nuclear reactor was installed at the Baltic Shipyard in Leningrad and the ship was ready for service along the NSR in 1989. A second ship of the class, *Vaygach*, will also complete construction phases in Finland and the USSR and should be operational in 1990. The design of this class in many respects represents the apex in the development process for the Soviet polar icebreaker fleet. Coupled in its design are Wartsila's advances in shallow-draft design (features incorporated in the *Kapitan Sorokin* class, see Figure 8.2) with nuclear propulsion developed in the Soviet Union (using the

Figure 8.2 *The Kapitan Khlebnikov,* one of four shallow-draft *Kapitan Sorokin* class Soviet icebreakers now in service (Tass from Sovfoto).

experience gained with *Lenin* and *Arktika* class ships). A draft of only 8 meters was attained which compares very favorably with the average 11-meter draft for a majority of the largest Soviet polar icebreakers. Both ships will also be capable of operating in arctic coastal waters where there is only 0.8 meters of water beneath their keels (Wartsila 1988). The power plant of 44,000 shaft horsepower (32,500 kilowatts) should provide a capability of continuously breaking 1.8 meters of level ice at a 2-knot speed.

Taymyr and *Vaygach* will employ a variety of modern technology developed in the Soviet Union, Finland and the Federal Republic of Germany (see Figure 8.3). Wartsila's hull air-lubrication system and a low-friction hull coating have been incorporated to improve icebreaking performance. Ship external systems have all been designed to endure air temperatures as low as $-50°$ centigrade. The main propulsion plant represents an unusual mix of components — a Soviet pressurized water reactor, Soviet steam turbines, West German main generators, and 3 alternating-current propeller motors of Finnish design (Wartsila 1988). These revolutionary motors were first installed aboard the new Finnish Baltic icebreaker *Otso*. Thus, the *Taymyr* class represents a unique merging of technologies and the most technically advanced ships in the Soviet polar fleet.

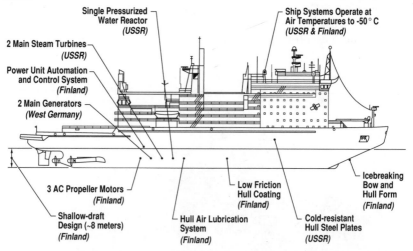

Figure 8.3 *Taymyr* class shallow draft nuclear icebreaker, including relevant ship systems with their country of origin.

Polar icebreakers, defined as those larger ships capable of operating in multi-year ice, are clearly the mainstay of the Soviet arctic fleet. However, a variety of USSR organizations operate a significant number of smaller polar ships, all of which have been specially designed as icebreakers. They conduct a wide range of missions, including ship escort, along the Soviet maritime Arctic, on Siberian rivers, and in coastal regions such as the Baltic, Bering Sea and Sea of Okhotsk. Most can operate with effectiveness in first-year ice less than 1.0 meter thick. Sixty-one of these specialized

Table 8.1 Soviet icebreaker and icebreaking freighter acquisitions, 1959 – 1989[1]

Number of ships	Function/duties	Class name (no. in class)	Years completed	Length (meters)	Propulsion[2] & shaft horsepower		Country built
21	Polar icebreaking (Escort)	*Lenin* (1)	1959	134	N	44,000	USSR
		Moskva (5)	1959–69	122	DE	22,000	Finland
		Arktika (4, 2 building)	1975–present	150	N	75,000	USSR
		Yermak (3)	1974–6	136	DE	36,000	Finland
		Kapitan Sorokin (4)	1977–81	132	DE	22,000	Finland
		Taymyr (1, 1 building)	1986–present	150	N	44,000	Finland & USSR
18	Subarctic Icebreaking (Escort)	*Dobrynya Nikitich* (15)	1960–71	68	DE	5,400	USSR
		Mudyug (3)[3]	1982–3	89	GD	10,000	Finland
9	Naval Service (Coastal/port escort)	*Dobrynya Nikitich* (7)	1960–71	68	DE	5,400	USSR
		Ivan Susanin (2)	1974–81	68	DE	5,400	USSR
6	KGB Maritime Border Guard (Coastal Patrol)	*Ivan Susanin* (6)	1974–81	68	DE	5,400	USSR
4	Polar Research	*Vladimir Kavrayskiy* (1)	1973	68	DE	5,400	USSR
		Otto Schmidt (1)	1979	68	DE	5,400	USSR
		Mikhail Somov (1)	1975	133	DE	7,200	USSR
		Akademik Fedorov (1)	1987	141	DE	16,100	Finland
14	River Icebreaking (Escort)	*Kapitan Chechkin* (6)	1977–8	78	DE	4,490	Finland
		Kapitan Yevdokimov (8)	1983–6	77	DE	5,170	Finland
3	Harbor Icebreaking	*Kapitan Izmaylov* (3)	1976	56	DE	3,400	Finland
7	Salvage Operations	*Stroptivy* (7)	1979–83	73	DE	7,600	Finland
40	Icebreaking Freighter	*Noril'sk* (19)	1982–7	174	GD	21,000	Finland
		Aleksey Kosygin (3)	1983–7	263	GD	33,580	USSR
		Sevmorpui (1)	1989	260	N	40,000	USSR
		Vitus Bering (3)	1986–9	160	DE	12,470	USSR
		Amguema (14)[4]	1962–72	133	DE	7,200	USSR
122	Total						

[1] Data assembled from Soviet and Finnish technical publications and other Western sources. Only major icebreaking freighters are included. A significant number of ice strengthened cargo ships navigate the Northern Sea Route usually in convoy with icebreakers.
[2] Propulsion: N=nulcear, DE=diesel-electric, GD=geared-diesel; 1 horsepower equals .7457 kilowatt.
[3] Mudyug fitted with a new icebreaking bow by Thyssen Nordseewerke (Federal Republic of Germany) in 1986.
[4] Estimated number; class one of the earliest icebreaking freighter designs.

icebreakers — including subarctic, naval, research, harbor, salvage and river types — were built in Finland and the USSR during 1959 to 1989 (see Table 8.1). Collectively, these ships represent a remarkable diversity of icebreaking capabilities; they provide the Soviet Union with an important ability to navigate in all of its surrounding arctic and subarctic seas.

It should not be surprising that many of these smaller icebreakers utilize advanced technology for navigation and operations. Most unique in these respects are the 2 shallow-draft river classes, *Kapitan Chechkin* and *Kapitan Yevdokimov*, whose 3.3- and 2.5-meter drafts allow them to break ice and escort barges (and other small vessels) along the shallow Siberian rivers. *Kapitan Chechkin* class icebreakers have been reported to move continuously through level ice 0.75 – 0.80 meters thick (Tronin *et al.* 1984:257). Another recent class, consisting of 3 *Mudyug* subarctic ships, is also unique in that it is the first Soviet icebreaker class to use a geared-diesel propulsion plant with controllable pitch propellers. These examples serve to emphasize that advanced design techniques and technological innovation have played leading roles in the Finnish effort to provide specialized icebreakers to the USSR. All of the classes have proven to be suitably adapted to their unique and often harsh operating environments.

Evolution of modern Soviet icebreaking cargo ships

The modern technical development of specialized cargo ships for operation along the NSR began in the 1950s. Prior to this time, particularly during the Second World War, small timber carriers and other strengthened ice class freighters made up the majority of the arctic cargo fleet (Chubakov *et al.* 1982:25). Five *Lena* class ice strengthened ships built 1954-57, the Amguema class carriers (noted in Table 8.1) and other ice strengthened ships from Finnish and East German yards were added to the Soviet polar fleet. However, many of these ships were either too small or under-powered for the extended navigation season made possible by the introduction of the highly capable polar icebreaker fleet. As a result, a program was initiated to develop a fleet of freighters with larger cargo capacities and enhanced icebreaking capabilities.

Designers of Soviet arctic cargo ships face a broad range of technical and environmental challenges. Arctic freighters must now be capable of navigating in convoy through ice with thicknesses of at least 2 meters. If designed with enough shaft horsepower and an appropriate icebreaking hull form, a freighter will be expected to operate independent of polar icebreakers. Limited port facilities and the remoteness of many regions in the Soviet Arctic may dictate a requirement to unload on fast ice. To overcome the problem of shallow depths, barges or lighters might be sent from an offshore transport. The lack of fueling ports make refueling from icebreakers or tankers necessary; nuclear power becomes attractive, just as it was for *Lenin*, *Arktika* and *Taymyr* class nuclear polar icebreakers. Draft limitations and the effects of extremely low temperatures on handling equipment also present unique constraints to the designers of these polar transports.

One of the most versatile and successful icebreaking cargo ship classes added to the Soviet polar fleet in recent years has been the *Noril'sk* or SA-15 class. Nineteen were delivered by Finland's Valmet and Wartsila shipyards during 1982-87, the last 5 vessels incorporating many improvements (including hull strengthening in specific areas) developed following a review of the earlier ships' performances. The 174-meter *Noril'sk* ships, capable of maintaining continuous progress through ice one meter thick, are able to operate independent of icebreaker assistance during many periods of the NSR navigation season. The SA-15s have, on occasion, assisted other arctic cargo ships (acting as an icebreaker) and they performed well during the fall of 1983 when severe ice conditions in the Chukchi Sea trapped a large Soviet convoy. They have also made a number of successful eastbound transits of the NSR during the month of June, early for the normal navigation season. In 1985, 3 SA-15s completed late season voyages (October to December) from Vancouver, British Columbia to Arkhangel'sk during which they were escorted periodically by polar icebreakers (Burkov and Arikaynen 1986:44).

Many of the special technical features of the *SA-15* class are shown in Figure 8.4. Noteworthy are the systems related to improving ship performance in the ice; identical features are usually found only aboard specially-built icebreakers. The SA-15's configuration also allows for unloading on ice, at a pier, and by use of embarked air cushion vehicles. These multi-purpose carriers of 15,000 deadweight tons are designed for a variety of cargo including containers, trailers, other vehicles, refrigerated cargo, bulk ore, grain and coal. In many respects the *Noril'sk* class ships are exceptional icebreakers in their own right and they serve as advanced prototypes for future arctic icebreaking freighters.

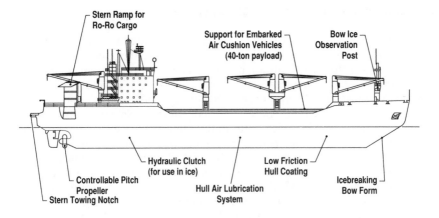

Figure 8.4 Noril'sk class (SA-15) icebreaking cargo carrier showing relevant ship systems.

During the 1980s, Soviet shipyards constructed 4 advanced LASH (lighter-aboard-ship) vessels for arctic operations. Three ships of the *Aleksey Kosygin* class are diesel-powered, while the fourth, *Sevmorput*, is nuclear. The motivation behind building icebreaking barge carriers was to reduce transshipment problems at arctic coastal sites lacking adequate port facilities. Lighters (barges) and tug trains work inshore along the shallow deltas and estuaries of the Siberian rivers with the deeper draft carriers standing offshore. Each of the LASH ships, among the largest in the entire Soviet merchant marine, is huge as evidenced by the data presented in Table 8.1. *Sevmorput* represents an unusual merging of barge carrier technology with nuclear propulsion — an incorporation of the innovative features of a nuclear icebreaker with those of a LASH transport. *Sevmorput* is designed to carry 74 barges or more than 1,300 shipping containers and can move continuously through 1.0 meter thick ice (Brigham 1985:132). While there were potentially great benefits from adapting LASH technology to arctic operations, early use of these ships have shown them at times to be difficult to operate (independent of icebreaker escort) and perhaps not nearly as viable economically as had been envisioned (see Chapter 12).

Continuing a trend in the diversification in the arctic cargo fleet, in the late 1980s Soviet shipbuilders completed a new and unusual class of icebreaking freighters, the *Vitus Bering* or SA-10 class. The ships were designed as multi-purpose supply vessels and are shallow draft (9.0 meters compared to 10.5 meters for the *SA-15* class). They employ embarked helicopters for rapid offloading of all cargo holds. Diesel-electric powered and with a displacement of 10,800 deadweight tons, they represent an intermediate size arctic cargo vessel. Intended for supplying remote outposts and drifting ice stations, the *Vitus Bering* class is yet another innovative adaptation of modern marine technology to the rigors of NSR operations.

Environment and the ice navigation season

Navigation along the NSR depends in part on the seasonal meteorological conditions and the distribution of sea ice. As indicated in Chapter 4, the ice conditions on the broad continental shelves of the region are a complex mixture of fast ice, first-year ice and multi-year ice from the polar pack. Figure 8.5 illustrates 9 major ice massifs (or regional 'clusters' of ice) found along the Soviet maritime Arctic. For many decades Soviet ice forecasters have observed these large ice fields in the same regions each summer. The overall movement and ice concentration of each massif influence summer ship traffic patterns along the NSR. The Taymyrskiy, Ayonskiy and Vrangelevskiy massifs are the most important obstacles to ship traffic along the NSR (Arikaynen 1987:216). Each contains significant concentrations of multi-year ice and frequently heavily hummocked ice is present.

A number of pioneering voyages have demonstrated the potential for extension of the navigation season on the NSR. In the early 1970s several experimental winter voyages were conducted where icebreakers led convoys of cargo ships across the Barents and Kara seas. These successes led to the

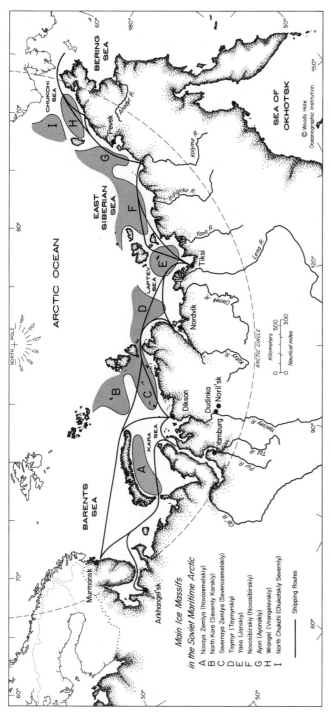

Figure 8.5 Main ice massifs of the Soviet maritime Arctic.

Main Ice Massifs
in the Soviet Maritime Arctic

A Novaya Zemlya (Novozemelskiy)
B North Kara (Severnly Karskiy)
C Severnaya Zemlya (Severozemelskiy)
D Taymyr (Taymyrskiy)
E Yana (Janskiy)
F Novosibirskiy (Novosibirskiy)
G Ayon (Ayonskiy)
H Wrangel (Vrangelevskiy)
I North Chukchi (Chukotskiy Severnly)

——— Shipping Routes

135

attainment during the 1978-79 season of a nearly year-round navigation season on the route between Murmansk and Dudinka. The feasibility of navigating the entire length of the NSR early in the season has been successfully tested on two occasions. During May and June 1971, the polar icebreakers *Lenin* and *Vladivostok* forged a high-latitude passage across the NSR. However, no freighters were escorted. In a celebrated operation (see Figure 1.1), *Sibir'* and the cargo ship *Kapitan Myshevskiy* navigated the NSR north of the Soviet island groups in May and June 1978 (Brigham 1988:22).

Although each of these experimental voyages yielded significant knowledge about winter navigation, as of 1990, neither convoys nor routine polar icebreaker transits are undertaken during the winter east of Severnaya Zemlya. On occasion, early voyages into the Chukchi Sea have been conducted by polar icebreakers to resupply remote sites, but the ships normally do not venture west of Wrangel Island. Clearly, any limitations to navigation are due to the extreme ice conditions that exist in the Laptev and East Siberian seas during the October to May 'winter' ice season. While it is technically possible to extend the navigation season to perhaps 7 months in the eastern seas (using the full capability of the nuclear fleet), the need has not yet been clearly identified nor the costs justified.

Prospects for the future

During the past 6 decades the Soviet Union has invested heavily in the overall development of the Northern Sea Route. Particularly costly have been the huge fleet of polar ships and the extensive infrastructure of port facilities, communications and navigation systems. These are long-term, capital investments that demand full utilization to make the system economically viable despite the burden of their large operational costs. There is also little doubt arctic shipping is highly expensive relative to other sectors of the Soviet Merchant Marine — a situation which will be quite difficult to mitigate in the future. What follows is a brief review of several critical problems, constraints and opportunities that may potentially influence the future directions of Soviet Arctic marine transportation.

The current restructuring of the Soviet economic system provides the most difficult challenge to the continued and perhaps expanded operation of the Northern Sea Route. For how long and with how much funding will the system continue to be subsidized by the Ministry of Merchant Marine? Since 1 January 1988 most organizations in the USSR, including the various shipping companies, were to be established on a 'cost-accounting' basis (Armstrong 1988:131). Developing an equitable, cost-accounting or cost-sharing program so that arctic shipping might become self-financing will be a monumental task. Such an extraordinarily expensive marine operation (with huge attendant overhead costs) will be very difficult to transform in the short term. In addition, competition for a share of smaller allocations of national funds to the Ministry of Merchant Marine will make the situation particularly difficult for arctic shipping companies. This comes at a time when larger budgets may be necessary for fleet additions and equipment improvements.

Further use of the Northern Sea Route by foreign shippers may be one way to generate hard currency from Soviet arctic marine transportation. Foreign shipping companies might charter Soviet polar ships for single, through-passages or for longer, possibly seasonal periods. The *SA-15* icebreaking cargo ship *Tiksi* made just such a voyage along the NSR in August and September 1989. Chartered to a foreign shipper, *Tiksi* carried cargo from Hamburg to Osaka (Butler 1990:174). Another alternative would be for Western merchant ships to transit the NSR (in convoy or individually) under escort by Soviet icebreakers. Currently, however, there are few foreign merchantmen with adequate ice-strengthening capable of safely navigating in convoy through the Soviet maritime Arctic. A third plausible option might be to transfer various cargoes to Soviet icebreaking ships waiting at both ends of the NSR — possibly in Alaskan ports and in Murmansk. This might be a workable system provided the cost of this specialized Soviet service is attractive and the navigation season can be extended, particularly in the Laptev and East Siberian seas. The *Noril'sk* class ships (*SA-15* carriers) would be the most likely choice for such a joint venture with Western shippers (see Figure 8.4).

Owing to the present economic state of the USSR, large capital expenditures for the Soviet polar fleet would appear to be seriously constrained. However, a number of icebreakers and icebreaking cargo-ship classes (built in the 1950s and 1960s) will be reaching the end of their respective service lives during the 1990s. Any replacement strategies may be compelled to consider a somewhat smaller, yet more capable arctic fleet for the future. One indication of this is a trend toward increasing icebreaking capability through the continued addition of nuclear icebreakers of the *Rossiya* class. The shallow-draft nuclear icebreakers *Taymyr* and *Vaygach* are also very significant and highly capable additions that will operate several decades into the next century. Moreover, new technological developments will likely be applied to replacement icebreaking cargo carriers. The experience of operating the *SA-15* ships should be influential in the determination of the appropriate size, power and type of future Soviet polar cargo vessels. In many respects the buildup of more capable Soviet polar icebreakers may force a comparable investment in more capable cargo ships that may be escorted (if only along the most difficult stretches of the NSR) or sail independently a majority of the time. Larger and better carriers may, in turn, require a substantial investment in the improvement of arctic port facilities. Thus, formidable financial challenges exist with regard to the appropriate distribution of capital costs for both a ship replacement program and for improvement of the large NSR infrastructure.

Future prospects for maintaining the nearly year-round navigation season to Dudinka appear promising. Major icebreaker support in this region has been available for more than a decade. Icebreaking on the Ob' and Yenisey rivers will, in fact, be improved with the operation of *Taymyr* and *Vaygach*. However, extensive use of large icebreakers on this segment of the NSR, particularly during February through May, is obviously costly and contributes negatively to the overall economic performance of the system. Improvement in the economic situation may come from a strategy of having improved icebreaking cargo ships sail independently (without icebreaker support) for as long into a given navigation season as feasible.

High-latitude voyages (north of the island groups and in the central Arctic Ocean) have been shown to be technically feasible (see Figure 1.1). Yet a future convoy on such a route would face difficult operational challenges. Any such trans-Arctic route will probably not become economically viable until well into the next century (if ever). Extension of the navigation season in the Laptev and East Siberian seas will be possible, but the current economic development of the region may not yet require such an advance. Also, sea transportation will face increasing competition from the Siberian river fleet, particularly to ports along the Lena river. Nevertheless, the eastern sector of the NSR could witness an extension in the navigation season, if for example SA-15 carriers were to move Western cargoes (roundtrips between the Pacific and Europe) in late fall and early summer.

There can be little doubt arctic marine transportation has been of national economic importance since the NSR has been substantially linked to the overall early development of the Siberian Arctic. However, new competition for the NSR may come from current and future improvements to the Siberian rail system. New railways to Yamburg, Yakutsk and perhaps to Noril'sk may provide stiff competition to sea transportation. A recent estimate noted the cost of freight deliveries by rail to Noril'sk at 5 to 6 times lower than using a mixed transportation route (rail and sea) from the ports of Arkhangel'sk and Murmansk (Arikaynen 1988:41). Further developments in road and air transportation throughout the region may provide additional competition. Thus, it is very risky accurately to forecast levels of marine traffic and any potential extensions of the navigation season even for the decade of the 1990s.

References

Armstrong, T.E. 1988. 'The Northern Sea Route, 1987.' *Polar Record* 24(149).
Arikaynen, A.I. 1987. 'Ice conditions in the Soviet Arctic: trends of multi-year variations.' Proceedings of the Ninth International Conference on Port and Ocean Engineering Under Arctic Conditions, Fairbanks, 17-22 August 1987.
— 1988. 'The problem of year-round navigation along the Northern Sea Route.' Proceedings of the IAHR (International Association for Hydraulic Research) Ice Symposium, Sapporo, Japan.
Brigham, L.W. 1985. 'New developments in Soviet nuclear Arctic ships.' *US Naval Institute Proceedings* 111(12).
— 1988. 'Soviet Arctic marine transportation.' *Northern Perspectives*, Canadian Arctic Resources Committee 16(4).
Burkov, G., and A. Arikaynen. 1986. ' *Tiksi* forsiruet l'dy' [*Tiksi* overcomes the ice]. *Morskoy flot*, The Journal of the USSR Ministry of Merchant Marine, No. 6.
Butler, W.E. 1990. 'Joint ventures in the Soviet Arctic.' *Marine Policy*, March.
Chubakov, A., A. Arikaynen and M. Shevelev. 1982. 'Severnyi Morshoi Put':

proshloe i nastoyashchee' [The Northern Sea Route: past and present]. *Morskoy flot*, The Journal of the USSR Ministry of Merchant Marine, No. 12.

Dem'yanchenko, V. and S. Livshits. 1984. 'Atomnyi ledokl *Rossiya*' [The nuclear icebreaker *Rossiya*]. *Sudostroenie*, The Journal of the USSR Ministry of Shipbuilding, No. 8.

Maksutov, D.D. 1981. 'Sovetskoe ledokolostroenie. Ego sostoyanie i perspektivy' [Soviet icebreaker construction. Its present position and future prospects]. *The Transactions of the Arctic and Antarctic Scientific Research Institute*, Vol. 376.

Tronin, V., V. Malinovsky and Yu. Sandakov. 1984. 'Problems of river shipping in ice-bound conditions.' Proceedings of the IAHR (International Association for Hydraulic Research) Ice Symposium, Hamburg, FRG, Vol. III.

Wartsila Marine. 1988. Press Release 5 April 1988. 'Nuclear-powered icebreaker *Taymyr*.'

9

Management of the Northern Sea Route: stages and problems of development

A. I. Arikaynen

The Northern Sea Route, a national transport line in the Soviet maritime Arctic, is of great national economic significance. This is particularly true for the development of the Soviet arctic region — a remote, unique, and at times inaccessible area (Arikaynen 1984:2). The efficient running of the Northern Sea Route (NSR), as a complex economic, scientific and highly technological system, depends on a number of important factors (see Figure 9.1). Along with a scientifically determined rational structure and makeup of the fleet, ports and supporting facilities (Arikaynen 1987:78–9; Arikaynen 1988:99–103), a very significant role belongs to improvement of the management organization and of the economic mechanisms. This chapter provides an overview of some of the most basic problems facing management of the NSR.

Starting a Northern Sea Route agency

The special economic and strategic importance of the arctic sea line to the nation caused the Soviet government to issue a decree in 1932 to establish a Chief Northern Sea Route Agency (CANSR) reporting to the Council of People's Commissars of the USSR. From the very start, the assumption that arctic navigation should not be effected as ordinary transport operations guided its activity as a government entity that required joint efforts from various professionals — mariners, hydrographers, scientists, pilots and signalmen.

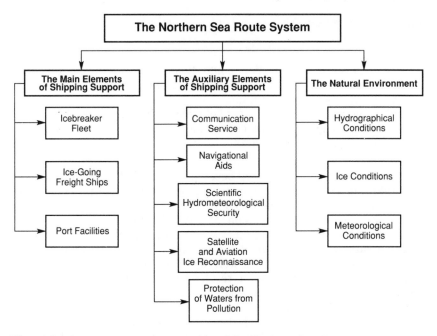

Figure 9.1 A management systems view of the Northern Sea Route.

On the whole, the CANSR system fulfilled a critical need: concentration of the main forces in the same agency ensured prompt operational decision in case of unexpected change in the ice conditions. It was a period of rigid directive command, and a government resolution had to approve the program for each arctic navigation season. All the contributors to the transportation process had no other choice but to fulfill unconditionally their responsibilities under the arctic transportation plan which was the main criterion of the CANSR's performance. In the 1930s and 1940s, economic efficiency of arctic sea transportation was hardly ever discussed because it was a period when cargo ships navigated in the form of expeditions.

As a result of a series of transformations that started in 1953 (Arikaynen 1990) the CANSR found itself by the 1960s as a Chief Department under the USSR Ministry of Civil Aviation, whereas the hydrometeorological network, the arctic radio transmitting stations, and the Arctic and Antarctic Scientific Research Institute (AASRI) were transferred to the Hydroment Service of the USSR (now called Goscomhydromet or USSR State Committee for Hydrometeorology). In 1964, the CANSR was completely disbanded, while its functions with respect to sea navigation were given to the Department of Maritime Ice Operations of the Chief Authority on Navigation (CAN). As a result, the department, staffed by only seven people, was vested with broad and varied responsibilities in a region with complex navigation conditions.

Thus, a more powerful sea transport organization absorbed a weak business organization. The positive outcome of this reorganization consisted of the following:

1. The transport organization could finally get rid of the functions irrelevant to its line of activity: mining and geological work, polar medicine, trade and agriculture.
2. The complex relationships were eliminated between the CANSR and shipping companies when concerned with the lease of vessels for a period of arctic navigation.

The latter arrangements required docking the ships before commencement and following termination of arctic navigation. Numerous disputes that were difficult to settle accompanied each of the dockings.

At the same time, elimination of CANSR resulted in 2 significant problems: first, the transfer to other agencies of scientific, operational and aviation support functions vitally important to arctic navigation led to a situation where these functions were dissolved ultimately in the general plans of those agencies. As a result, necessary decision-making was inhibited by interdepartmental friction. Second, the Ministry of Merchant Marine paid less attention to arctic navigation which is quite understandable. Fulfillment of the arctic transportation plan was the CANSR's main and only objective; whereas, the Ministry of Merchant Marine's interest in promoting development of the NSR was actually diminished by the fact that the share of arctic sea shipping in the total volume of the Ministry's transportation was quite insignificant. Expenditures on arctic navigation, however, considerably exceeded those for other sea shipping lines.

In this connection, upon disbanding the CANSR, there appeared a certain contradiction in the Ministry of Merchant Marine's interest in the arctic region. On the one hand, the final result of the Ministry's performance was evaluated as follows: the more cargo that was handled within a certain period of time, the better evaluation it would get (other conditions being equal). On the other hand, the economic and operational costs of arctic shipping, despite its relatively small volume, reflected unfavorably on the general accomplishments of the Ministry. This is especially true during navigation seasons with unusually severe ice conditions.

Developing the Northern Sea Route administration

Establishing the Administration of the Northern Sea Route (ANSR) in 1970 within the framework of the Ministry of Merchant Marine contributed to a concentration of effort towards developing viable arctic navigation. For the past 20 years, the ANSR's accomplishments have been substantial and have resulted in both improving the operational aspects of arctic navigation and the long-term development of navigation along the NSR. Arctic navigation plays a greater role in the USSR's national economy and has made the central ministerial staff give more serious attention to arctic shipping problems.

At the same time, one cannot help but note that in the last few years the weaknesses in the arctic navigation management system are increasingly discussed in the central press. In particular, the newspapers *Pravda*, *Izvestiya*, and *Trud* attributed the mishaps of the 1983 navigation in the eastern sector of the Soviet Arctic (approximately 50 ships stuck in very severe ice off the north coast of Chukotka had to be rescued by a fleet of icebreakers; one freighter was crushed and sank) to the inadequate organization of the arctic fleet management. Moreover, those publications, in one way or another, raised the question of whether it was reasonable to disband the CANSR under whose management there had been a successful collaboration of mariners, pilots, signalmen and scientists. Somewhat earlier, and well before the unfortunate events of the 1983 navigation, the newspaper *Vodnyy transport* carried an article by polar experts of the AASRI. They said that the 'time has come to overcome more resolutely the interdepartmental barriers and bring closer together the efforts of all the ministries and agencies concerned'.

Such suggestions were not accidental. Their explanation lay in the fact that the ANSR's functions had been considerably transformed and its influence on other organizations had diminished. The ANSR was intended to be a special, national, supradepartmental agency. It was due to this feature that the USSR Council of Ministers approved the ANSR procedures earlier. According to the procedures, the USSR Council of Ministers — not the Ministry of Merchant Marine — appointed the ANSR's top executive. This created conflict, however, because the Administration had been set up under the auspices of the Ministry of Merchant Marine. Thus, at the very outset, the ANSR's status was not very clear; and it became less ambiguous only in the process of the administration's activity.

The ANSR reported directly to the central staff of the Ministry of Merchant Marine and, in fact, became one more agency in its organizational structure. It represented primarily the interests of the Ministry of Merchant Marine and not the integrated national interests oriented towards the NSR system's development. As a result, other agencies such as Goscomhydromet and the Ministry of Civil Aviation instantly began to regard the ANSR as an organizational unit within the Ministry of Merchant Marine. Thus, the ANSR was not, in fact, an organization affiliated with, but was incorporated within the Ministry. What impact did this have? On the one hand, it meant that the Ministry of Merchant Marine monitored the pollution of arctic waters by seagoing vessels — creating a situation in which one and the same agency both caused and controlled pollution. On the other hand, the Ministry's relationships with the Goscomhydromet and the Ministry of Civil Aviation weakened; whereas, the interdepartmental barriers became more apparent.

At the same time, in recent years, the ANSR has incurred structural changes and reduction in personnel. When this agency was established, there were 35 people on the staff. In 1981, its strength was reduced to 16. When eventual reshuffling of the Ministry of Merchant Marine staff occurred, the ANSR's numbers were reduced to 9, of which 2 performed support and general functions. Thus, as ANSR's objectives increased over the years, staff size dwindled.

A fact that partly explains the transformation is that the majority of the ANSR's functions are of a controlling and coordinating nature. Its responsibility for fulfilling the plan of arctic freight transportation, the provision for safe navigation and the control and prevention of arctic waters' pollution, however, was not defined nor was its performance evaluated. In fact, the only criteria that existed to evaluate the ANSR's performance was a general verbal definition 'to control, agree, participate'. Many of the ANSR's accomplishments are to a great extent due to the personal merit of the Administration's top management and its experts, veterans of the Arctic, who are always enthusiastic about handling the urgent problems of arctic navigation. It is, however, not enough to be enthusiastic — one also needs people and time, but in recent years these two have been in short supply in the ANSR. It needs a staff with clearcut objective functions and criteria to evaluate their performance.

The fact that the previously mentioned elements are lacking in the medium and top levels of the arctic fleet management system accounted for the discussion in the central press as to the expedience of establishing a single think tank. It is important to note that a serious contradiction characterizes the ANSR's top level of management: responsibility for the economic aspect of the fleet's performance is not vested with those who are knowledgeable about the specifics of ice navigation. On the one hand, the ANSR is responsible for the technological aspects of the icebreaker fleet's work and on the other hand, it is not actually permitted to handle economic problems and issues.

Characterizing the lower level of management

Analysis shows that a totality of complex responsibilities of individual units for the outcome of their work characterizes the lower level of management (sea shipping companies — the headquarters of arctic sea operations). The main thing is that the management of the Murmansk and Far East shipping companies bears a narrowly functional character while effecting a substantial volume of transportation in the Arctic and disposing an operating icebreaker fleet. There is practically no central responsibility for the overall end results. On the whole, the essential feature of the lower level of the arctic fleet management is a lack of common economic interests on the part of the Far East, Murmansk and other shipping companies when they seek to meet the arctic transportation plan.

Defining the sea transportation plan

The distinctive feature of the NSR management is that fulfillment of a sea transportation plan depends heavily on the ice conditions in the arctic seas.

Therefore, when the transportation plan is formulated, it is submitted to the experts of the AASRI for correlation with their long-term ice and weather forecasts. Since only 80 percent of the forecasts prove to be correct, there is always a probability that within a certain sector of the NSR some forecast parameters may be wrong. In fact, each plan of arctic transportation is formulated for uncertain conditions prior to its implementation. Also, it should be taken into account that the percentage of the forecasts that prove to be correct have been calculated on the assumption that an admissible deviation of the actual ice conditions from the ones forecast will not exceed 0.8Σ (mean square deviation of ice conditions parameter from its average). For example, in certain cases even if the forecast is correct, the actual ice conditions may differ considerably from those predicted.

Figure 9.2 Polar icebreakers *Yermak* and *Kapitan Makarov* during the 1983 rescue of a convoy in the Chukchi Sea (Tass from Sovfoto).

In view of the above, and because more technologically advanced icebreakers and freighters (see Figure 9.2) are involved in ice navigation, the planning horizon of arctic sea operations for long-term ice and weather predictions was reduced with each decade. In the 1950s, the directive document stated that the AASRI's March ice forecast 'serves as a basis for all documents directing the implementation of the planned operations' and that it was 'extremely important'. In the 1960s, the new directive document emphasized that the NSR's navigational capacity calculation rested on the AASRI's March long-term forecast of the ice conditions for the first half of the navigation period and on the *mean* multi-year statistical data for the second half of the navigation period. In other words, in the 1960s, the document revealed that the mean multi-year statistical data on ice conditions could be used in planning arctic operations.

Currently, in conformity with the latest directive document, basic guidelines in arctic navigation are formulated 'on the basis of the mean ice conditions, with due respect to the long-term ice forecast issued by the AASRI in March'. Thus, the mean multi-year statistical data on ice conditions comes to the foreground; whereas, the long-term ice forecast retreats to the background despite the emphasized need for elaboration of alternative moves in case of more severe ice conditions.

At present, arctic sea operations are, in fact, planned on the basis of the mean multi-year statistical data on ice conditions or, at least, for dates close to those of the mean multi-year data. The latter can also be explained by the fact that the overwhelming majority of long-term ice forecasts do admit the possibility of anomalous ice conditions, although with an insignificant deviation from the mean multi-year figures. Taking into account that the probability of unfavorable ice conditions amounts to 20-30 percent, then the probability of the sea operations plan being pursued, while remaining consistent with the ice conditions programmed into it, amounts to 70-80 percent in each transportation sea line of the NSR.

It should be emphasized that with the existing mix of icebreaker and icebreaker–freighter fleets, the ice conditions in unfavorable summer periods cannot but handicap guaranteed fulfillment of the transportation plan itself (whereby the delivery of cargo is guaranteed in any ice conditions). The previously mentioned uncertainty in forecasting ice conditions for the coming navigation season may impact the operation and economic parameters of the freighter and icebreaker fleet's performance. That is why the traditional planning methods as they are, where past accomplishments serve as a basis for future directive figures, remain acceptable. The important fact is that each arctic navigation season differs from the preceding one owing to substantial changes in the ice conditions in navigable routes year in and year out.

Fulfilling the sea transportation plan

Owing to the variability of the ice conditions, sea transportation requires careful planning and perfect organization of arctic operations. Constraints include the tight periods of navigation, the capacities of base and arctic ports, the mix and capabilities of icebreakers and the number of vessels of various ice classes. The success of each navigation depends on the timely and comprehensive preparation of all the contributors whose participation is necessary for fulfillment of the transportation plan (see Figure 9.3).

Fulfillment of the arctic transportation plan depends on each unit of the arctic 'assembly line', beginning with packing the vegetables harvested on the farms into boxes and ending with unloading the motor vessels at an arctic port. There are still many unsolved problems in this process. Practical experience has shown that arctic transportation implies close relationship of all elements. In order to ensure a highly effective delivery of arctic cargoes, a

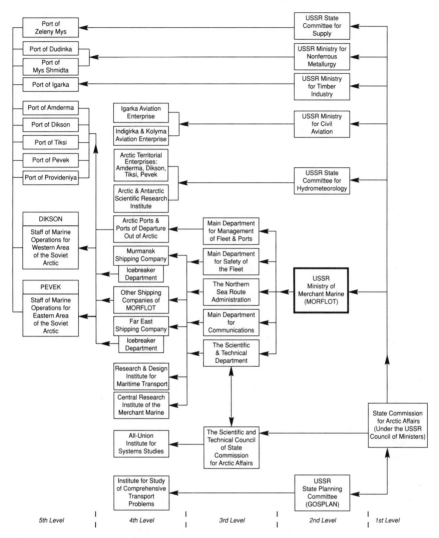

Figure 9.3 Organizational diagram of Soviet Arctic shipping and development.

plan should provide for a number of appropriate steps each year. The consignors should ship high-quality cargo in periods most favorable for the arctic transportation standards. Officers of the local organizations of the State Committee for Material Supply should ensure strict control of the terms and conditions of cargo shipments to the arctic destination points. They should group shipments into large lots and use containerization. Railwayment of all the nation's rail lines should give a 'green light' to all arctic cargoes. There should be a timely supply of freighters for loading. The dockers in the ports of departure should see to it that the loading is accomplished in conformity with all cargo handling requirements, and the ship's crews should rigidly control their work performance. If these tasks are assured, better guarantees can be given that the cargoes will be delivered to arctic ports safe and on time.

If one takes an integrated overview of the problem, fulfillment of the arctic transportation plan depends on the following existing conditions:

1. The timely delivery of arctic cargoes to the ports of departure in packets and containers, if possible.
2. The provision of freighters to the ports of departure as per schedule.
3. The loading of arctic vessels should be completed without delay in strict conformity with the existing requirements; to this end, it is necessary to effect rational registration of arctic cargo distribution at the ports of departure.
4. The observation of the navigation schedule by icebreakers.
5. The operational decisionmaking on the transfer of icebreakers from one arctic sector to another; and elimination of a parochial approach to the provision of icebreaker escorts for freighters of various shipping companies.
6. The regulation of the priority of freighter convoys along the NSR (with due account of the capacity of the destination ports) aimed at better organization of the provision of vessels.
7. The regular supply to the fleet of reliable information on the predicted and actual ice and weather conditions.

Thus, out of 7 tasks relating to the arctic transportation plan, 5 bear an intradepartmental character (they pertain to the Ministry of Merchant Marine). Only 2 (the first and the seventh) are interdepartmental; however, both are very basic. From this comes a key, first conclusion: the structure of the arctic fleet management needs improvement in order to be able quickly to tackle the previously mentioned tasks.

It would be wrong, however, to depend only on improvement of the management's organization structure. It is necessary to create an appropriate economic management mechanism that can stimulate fulfillment of the arctic transportation plan at a minimum cost instead of at any cost. Use of the traditional economic management mechanisms by the Ministry of Merchant Marine is not useful owing to the planning uncertainties — a lack of reliable and distinct data at the time of plan formulation on the ice conditions where the fleet will be operating. Hence, a second conclusion: it is necessary to elaborate an economic management mechanism providing for evaluation of the fleet's performance with due regard to the ice conditions during navigation.

Are the proposed tasks feasible? Analyses have shown real possibilities exist. They will not be considered here, as it is a large topic and deserves separate treatment in other publications. The time, however, must pass (into oblivion!) when the main criterion for the arctic fleet's performance evaluation is plan fulfillment at any cost. The fleet's higher technological capability allows for the system to make greater demands for improved economic performance. The time has come for a full payoff of what the state has invested into development of the Northern Sea Route system.

References

Arikaynen, A.I. 1984. *Transportnaia Arteriia Sovetskoi Arktiki* [Transport Artery of the Soviet Arctic]. Chapter 1. Moscow: Nauka Publishers.

— 1987. 'Narodnohoziaistvennye kriterii ocenki sravnite lnoi economicheskoi effektivnosti variantov ledokola razlichnoi moscnosti i tipov — Moskva' [National economic criteria of evaluating comparative economic efficiency of icebreakers of different models and capability — Moscow]. *In*: *Trudy Vnii Sistemnyh Issledovanii* [Collective Papers of the Institute for Systems Studies] 9:78-79.

— 1988. 'Obosnovanie struktury ledokolnogo flota s narodnohoziaistvennyh pozioii' [Substantiation of icebreaker fleet structure from national economic standpoint]. *In*: *Trudy Cniimfa* [Substantiation, Planning and Organization of Fleet Performance, Collected Papers of the Research Institute of Merchant Marine]:99-103.

— 1990. *Sudohodstvo vo ldah Arktiki* [Navigation in Arctic Ice — Moscow]. Leningrad: Transport Publishers.

10

Northern Sea Route operations in the 1986–7 season

Terence Armstrong

It is necessary to emphasize that any report of this kind, written by someone quite unconnected with the authorities responsible for running these operations, is severely limited as to source material. No official reports for each season's events are issued, so total reliance must be placed on journal, press and radio accounts. Journal articles are not frequent and generally appear a year or two after the events described. That is too late for this sort of account; so press and radio reports become the mainstay, and one does not need to emphasize the likely, indeed inevitable, shortcomings of such sources. An omission which is not necessarily quite so obvious, however, is the absence of virtually all information on naval activities in these waters.

Source references will not be given for every item of information. Important sources will be identified, but in general, the news items will have been taken from *Pravda*, *Vodnyy transport*, and the BBC's *Summary of World Broadcasts*, *Part I. USSR, passim*. Reports on earlier years' activities, based on similar sources, will be found in *Polar Record*, generally the May issue, and in the News Notes section of *Polar Geography and Geology*.

The term 'Northern Sea Route' in current Soviet usage refers to the sea lanes joining European and Far Eastern ports of the USSR by a northabout route and connecting both with Siberian rivers. The most important and most difficult part of this route is the stretch traversing the fringe seas of the Arctic Ocean — Barents, Kara, Laptev, East Siberian, and Chukchi — and it is this part of it, between the eastern Barents Sea and Bering Strait, that I am concerned with here. The timespan is from early 1986 to early 1987.

Since the operation is now year-round in one part of the route, it is necessary to choose, more or less arbitrarily, a dividing line between seasons, and this can be the moment of least traffic which occurs in February.

Ships and ports

Icebreakers

Not all the icebreakers possessed by the USSR are deployed in the Arctic, for which some, indeed, are not designed. In 1986, 18 polar icebreakers (that is, with more than 10,000 shaft horsepower) and 4 smaller ones were mentioned as operating in the Arctic Ocean. The 4 largest were nuclear-powered: *Lenin*; *Leonid Brezhnev*; *Sibir'*; *Rossiya*. The last 3 of these are 75,000 shaft horsepower — the most powerful icebreakers afloat. Four new nuclears are under construction: 2 in the *Rossiya* class, to be called *Leonid Brezhnev* (while the existing *Leonid Brezhnev* reverts to her old name *Arktika*) and *Oktyabrskaya Revolyutsiya* (since writing the above, *Leonid Brezhnev* has become unusable for political reasons, and the new ship is to be called *Sovetskiy Soyuz*); and 2 in a new shallow-draught class of 52,000 shaft horsepower to be called *Taymyr* and *Vaygach*. One of 3 so-called subarctic icebreakers, *Mudyug*, had a newly designed bow fitted by Thyssen Nordseewerke of Emden, Federal Republic of Germany. There was

Figure 10.1 The nuclear-powered Soviet LASH (Lighter-Aboard-Ship) vessel *Sevmorput'*, capable of passage through arctic ice conditions (Tass from Sovfoto).

also brief mention of plans for 150,000 shaft horsepower icebreakers (that is, twice as powerful as the most powerful ships in existence) by N.A. Volkov, an established sea ice expert, who stated they were 'being designed' (Volkov 1986:63). These are ships which might be capable of going anywhere in any season in ice-filled waters. A later report states that the decision to 'start planning and construction of a super-icebreaker has definitely been taken, after long discussion, and the ship may be expected to operate in the 1990s' (Serokurov 1987).

Ice-strengthened freighters

The most notable addition will be *Sevmorput'*, a nuclear LASH ship, 26,400 deadweight tonnes, 40,000 shaft horsepower, equivalent to Canadian Class 4, launched in February 1986 and planned for delivery in 1988 (see Figure 10.1). Other new classes of smaller dry-cargo freighters and tankers were mentioned. The total number of freighters approved for Arctic use (that is, classes ULA and UL) in 1981 was about 270 (*Registrovaya kniga* 1981), but half of these were tugs and other small craft. Even with subsequent additions of perhaps 40 ships, it is clear that many ships used in the Arctic are not officially approved for such use.

Other vessels

The idea of a polar-operating semi-submersible was again mentioned in the Western press in 1984, when patent information associated with the Soviet designer Pikul' was released, but there is no indication of intent to build. The idea has been discussed in the West also, but was not regarded as promising. There was also mention of 'cargo vessels that can travel under the ice' in an article by A.I. Arikaynen, a sea ice specialist (Arikaynen 1985:12-13). This is rarely mentioned in the USSR, where depth limitations were believed to be too severe a constraint. The same article mentions 'new ways to clear ice from routes, including thermal and mechanical methods', but no details are given.

Ports

Use of SA-15 icebreaking cargo ships has increased loading and unloading rates at Pevek by a factor of eight. But deeper draft berths are required at Dudinka, where, at present, standard ore-carriers (*Dmitriy Donskoy* class) have to be underloaded by 10 percent.

Operations

Kara Sea

The main traffic route remains the Murmansk–Dudinka link, along which ships carry general cargo to Noril'sk and return with nickel ore. Year-round navigation on this sector has been achieved (if we do not count an interval of some weeks during spring break-up), and 1986 was the eighth year of this. Heavy ice during February–March obliged some convoys to go round the northern end of Novaya Zemlya, and 5 icebreakers were operating in the Kara Sea. The last winter convoy (that is before break-up) left Dudinka for the west on 23 May. The summer season started in mid-June, and the first ships into the timber port of Igarka (farther upstream) arrived on 22 June. Icebreaker escort dropped to 3, but winter caused the allocation of 2 more, and it again became necessary to transit Novaya Zemlya from the north.

The volume of traffic for this navigation season was, as usual, not reported. However, the number of voyages into Dudinka must have run into the hundreds. Timber exports from Igarka were said to average 800,000 tonnes a year in the early 1980s (Slavin and Stoyanov 1985:74) which could imply 100–200 voyages. In both cases — ore and timber — there was comparatively little outbound freight.

While these Yenisey traffic volumes continue to be the largest, the oil and gas industry on the lower Ob' has greatly increased traffic to that river system. Traffic starts each year with voyages to the west coast of Yamal in mid-April using the fast ice as a quay. Then it moves into the Ob' estuary, serving both Novyy Port on the west shore and Yamburg in the east. Almost all the freight is pipe for a gas pipeline. In 1986 the Yamal traffic was to lift 100,000 tonnes; the Ob' estuary 400,000 tonnes. Included in the ships used were bulk carriers of 50,000 deadweight tonnes, larger than most ships operating along the Northern Sea Route. It should be added that a much larger volume of freight, 4 million tonnes, reached Yamal by way of the river system. The seaborne traffic lasted from about June until late November, using the icebreakers servicing the Yenisey route. Among the freight reaching Yamburg were pre-fabricated buildings, made in Finland, for a settlement planned to house 9,000 people. None of this traffic had any back-haul.

Laptev Sea

The first convoy, from the west, reached Tiksi, at the mouth of the Lena, on 4 July. The season here lasted until 18 October. The Lena river fleet, which operates a number of sea-river ships, was due to move 2.25 million tonnes northwards from the railhead at Osetrovo. This was reported as completed, but at the end of the season 100,000 tonnes were still awaiting dispatch. A 'sharp increase' in freight arriving by sea was planned, but whether it transpired or not is not known.

East Siberian and Chukchi Seas

The plan here was to open communications with Pevek by a convoy from the west due to arrive on the very early date of 28 May. However, *Rossiya* and the SA-15 *Monchegorsk*, which composed the convoy, had a difficult passage from Murmansk, meeting heavy ice in the East Siberian Sea. They reached Pevek on 4 June — itself remarkably early. Meanwhile the first convoy from the east had arrived on 27 May, one month earlier than usual and without nuclear icebreaker escort. Other ports in the east opened later: Mys Shmidta on 19 June; the Kolyma in early July. The season ended in late October, and the last ship departed the Chukchi Sea on 1 November.

Transits

The whole route was thus accessible from mid-July until mid- or late October, with icebreakers stationed at the difficult points. But few transits were mentioned. There was no repetition of the so-called 'polar experiment' of 1984 and 1985, whereby grain ships went to Vancouver and back by the northern route. There were only 3 specifically mentioned transits: a returning Antarctic ship sailed in July by way of the Baltic and the Northern Sea Route to her base at Vladivostok; and 2 freighters made a similar west to east traverse in October, bound for Vancouver, but without mention of a northabout return trip. The usual convoys of river ships going to their assigned work stations included some which were heading for the Amur — and this would imply traversing the whole route. However, Gorbachev's speech at Vladivostok on 28 July included the sentence, 'It is necessary to speed up measures to increase the economic benefit of through traffic on the Northern Sea Route' (Gorbachev 1987). It is not clear just what that may mean, but it is evidence that further attention is being given to the route at the centre.

Perestroika and Glasnost

It was to be expected that there would be examples of Gorbachev's new broom at work in the Northern Sea Route complex. Since 1986 several actions have attracted attention in the Soviet press.

In August 1986, the Minister of the Merchant Fleet, T.B. Guzhenko, within whose department all non-military operations on the Route fall, was sacked as a result of the disaster involving passenger ships in the Black Sea. His record in arctic operations, as it has appeared to outsiders, had been quite good, and he had been one of the principal figures in the first-ever voyage of a surface ship to the North Pole in 1977. But this was clearly irrelevant in view of the Black Sea disaster.

The head of one of the administrations of the Ministry — the Northeast Administration of the Merchant Fleet, abbreviated in Soviet usage to SVUMF — was sacked in December for corrupt practices. It was reported that financial abuses at this Administration, which is based at Tiksi, were at such a level that there was no money in the bank to pay the wages. The press article describing this situation (Simkin 1986) ended with an editorial postscript, 'Prosecutor please note'. This seems to imply that there was more to investigate than had yet been discovered.

Another organizational failure was noted by the vice-chairman of the Council of Ministers of Yakutskaya ASSR (Yevdokimov 1986). He wrote that in the Lena River fleet, incentives had been rearranged in such a way that it was hardly an exaggeration to say that the best course of action for the managers to follow was to do nothing. By so doing, they would most fully meet the requirement of saving fuel and of minimizing damage to the fleet.

Encouragement of more socially responsible attitudes was apparent in the call by *Pravda* (Chertkov 1986) to condemn the thoughtless destruction of historical monuments in the Arctic. Buildings used by early explorers were evidently often vandalized or simply pulled down — a problem in many parts of the world.

There were two long articles in *Vodnyy transport* (Vinogradov *et al.* 1986) on the rarely ventilated subject of morale of ships' crews. The longer operating season has led to longer spells at sea for individual crew members — up to 9 months. The strain imposed by this could, it was urged, be reduced by greater attention to work conditions, food, clothing and noise levels. Ships' captains may not normally be experienced with the breadth of these problems. It is perhaps significant that an advertisement for positions in northern maritime work offered a permanent job for a sociologist at the port of Anadyr'. Some of the people employed in the north, another article observed, are attracted only by the extra money provided by the so-called 'northern increments'. Such people were said to be 'wringing money out of the climate'.

Ice conditions

Conditions were expected to be worse than in 1985, but on the whole they were not. In March and April of that year the southwest Kara Sea was blocked — not unusual, but this time ships were there. Similarly with the western part of the East Siberian Sea in May. The worst area was the northwest Laptev Sea during July–August. Up to 5 icebreakers were deployed there, escorting 7 freighters, and a timber ship was severely damaged. The Ayon ice cluster in the eastern East Siberian Sea moved shorewards in August 1985 and caused 3 to 4 icebreakers to attend, but no serious problems were reported. However, the long-term outlook remains rather bad, the situation being expected to deteriorate over the next decade (Arikaynen and Burkov 1985:37; Berezovikov 1986:17).

Improvement was made in navigational aids and ice reporting services during the 1986–7 season. The Satellite Kosmos 1500 transmits ice

Figure 10.2 Three Soviet icebreakers escort a cargo ship through difficult ice conditions.

information, and Kosmos 1766 is said to have further improvements, including an ice thickness determination capability. If effective, this last factor would represent a considerable breakthrough in sea ice reporting techniques.

Conclusion

The 1986–7 season saw no major dramatic happenings, but there seems to have been a steady advance in freight movement. My best estimate, based on 1985 Soviet press comment, would be that there were on the order of 600 freight voyages, lifting 6 million tonnes. This estimate is based on items of information relating to earlier years: in 1985 it was stated that 'each year up to 400 ships sail in the ice of the Northern Sea Route'; and in 1984 that the Murmansk shipping agency (*parokhodstvo*) deployed 255 ships and organized 419 voyages, implying that 2 ships out of 3 made a second voyage during the season. The surmised total of 600 would presuppose an input by the Far Eastern Shipping Company (FESCO) (the other major operator) of 110 ships, which could be about right. The tonnage lifted is arrived at by averaging deadweight tonnage at 10,000. An effort on this scale can only be achieved by extensive use of ships not designed for the Arctic — hence the building program. The massive treatment, and the stated objective of year-round navigation over the whole route in the 1990s, indicate determination to press on despite probably worsening natural conditions (see Figure 10.2). The national importance of the route was expressed strongly in the rubric to Volkov's article in *Priroda* already mentioned: 'The Northern Sea Route has become a continuously functioning transport route, without which the development of the economy of our country is unthinkable.' The first part of that sentence is not really true, but the second indicates the strength of informed belief in the route's economic potential.

References

Arikaynen, A.I. 1985. *Soviet Weekly* 21 December:12-13.
Arikaynen, A.I. and G. Burkov. 1985. 'Ukhudshayutsya li ledovyye usloviya v Arktike' [Are ice conditions in the Arctic getting worse?]. *Morskoy flot* 6:37.
Berezovikov, L. 1986. 'Soviet Arctic navigation in 1986-1990.' *Arctic News Record* 5.1:17.
Chertkov, V. 1986. 'Arktika pomnit' [The Arctic will remember]. *Pravda* 14 October.
Gorbachev, M.S. 1987. Speech at Murmansk. FBIS-SOV-87-191. 2 October, 42. (see Appendix I)
Registrovaya kniga morskikh sudov SSSR, 1980–1981. 1981. [No place of publication available.]
Serokurov, S. 1987. 'Rabota v Arktike' [Work in the Arctic]. *Vodnyy transport*, 26 May.
Simkin, G. 1986. 'Gipnoz 'blagopoluchnoy' statistiki' [The hypnosis of 'favorable' statistics]. *Vodnyy transport* 9 December.
Slavin, S.V., and I.A. Stoyanov. 1985. 'Severnyy morskoy put' v narodnom khozyaystve SSSR' [The Northern Sea Route in the economy of the USSR]. *Letopis' Severa* 11:74.
Vinogradov, S., T. Onkina, and T. Sömonova. 1986. 'Moryak v Arktike' [The seaman in the Arctic]. *Vodnyy transport* 26 and 28 August.
Volkov, N.A. 1986. 'Kolumb Rossiyskiy mezhdu l'dami' [A Russian Columbus amidst the ice]. *Priroda* 9:63.
Yevdokimov, S. 1986. 'Pora obnovleniya' [Time to renew]. *Vodnyy transport* 12 August.

11

Technical aspects of ice navigation and port construction in Soviet Arctic

Gordon G. Watson

The Soviet mariner's mastery of seamanship has made navigation through the ice — once the stuff of heroes and legend — an almost routine activity today. Unfortunately, the techniques that have been developed through the years have not, as a rule, been documented. Nor is a search of Soviet patents very helpful; information on navigational design innovations is scant. There is simply no way systematically to research and document the field.

A few articles that exist on ice navigation are reviewed here. They have been gleaned from 2 journals: *Morskoy flot* and *Sudostroyenie*. The first, *Morskoy Flot*, is the Soviet merchant marine monthly where mariners, and particularly ice mariners, exchange ideas about the techniques they have tried and found useful. *Sudostroyenie* is the journal of the USSR Ministry of Shipbuilding.

The material discussed here does not constitute a representational selection; it is only a small piece of the body of knowledge that has accumulated through the years. It is unlikely that the West will ever know entirely what has become standard practice on the Northern Sea Route. Mariners on icy decks in the bone-chilling winds of the Arctic Ocean have undoubtedly had to show much more ingenuity coping with real situations than will ever be revealed in journals and papers.

The ice convoy

The Northern Sea Route, the shortest passage from the Atlantic to the Pacific, stretches approximately 3,800 nautical miles from the port of Murmansk to the Bering Strait. Travelling this route in convoy is challenging and often dangerous. One convoy captain at a meeting to discuss procedures said, 'Being at sea is risky; being at sea in ice is twice the risk; being at sea in ice in convoy with an icebreaker is three times the risk' (Arikaynen and Chubakov 1987:130–84).

In the ice convoy, ships typically proceed in single file astern of the icebreaker, each feeling its way past the freshly broken ice slabs that litter the channel. These sharp-edged, half-submerged obstacles are hard to see even in good visibility, and collision with a large slab at too high a speed can badly damage a cargo vessel's light hull plating.

The ship immediately astern of the icebreaker has the easiest passage since it can travel through the channel before most of the floes have floated back into the track. In relatively level ice the broken floes can become lodged beneath the ice edges leaving the channel less cluttered. The propeller wash of a passing ship, however, can sweep some of these ice pieces back into the channel, making travel more hazardous for ships farther back in line. Meanwhile, as the ice field continues to drift, the channel narrows. If the last ship in the line drops too far astern, it may become gripped by the ice as in a vise. If the ship is unable to break free, it must radio the icebreaker for assistance. In response, the icebreaker will stop the convoy, double back and maneuver around the seized ship to break the surrounding ice. When the ship is free, the icebreaker resumes the lead. By the time the convoy is ready to move again, the ice may have closed in around every ship in the line and all traces of the channel may have disappeared.

Travel is slow and despite vastly improved ships, aerial reconnaissance by ship-borne helicopters and the ice patrol, meteorological reports and satellite photographs of leads through the ice, it is still not always possible to predict the time of arrival of a convoy in harbor. Naturally, the lack of a scheduled arrival time has repercussions, not only for the port which cannot plan its work efficiently, but also for other enterprises dependent on regular service. Plants and mineral complexes, for example, cannot maintain a steady rate of production when service is unreliable. Consequently, erratic service disrupts the supply of essential goods and the distribution of exports from these operations.

As we have seen, even under optimum conditions, travel in the ice convoy is unpredictable; harsher ice conditions cause even more delays. When the ice compresses under the influence of the wind, the freshly cut channel starts to close in as soon as the icebreaker passes. The commander of the convoy attempts to keep his ships close and maintain a high speed to create a wider and clearer channel. High speed is particularly important because at speeds above 6 knots, the icebreaker is less influenced by the lateral pressure of the ice and can cut a straighter channel making it easier to follow (Arikaynen and Chubakov 1987). Also, high speeds enable the commander to maintain

Gordon G. Watson

headway when the ships come into areas of thickening ice. If the convoy can maintain headway through these areas of hummocked ice, there is less risk that one ship, slowed down in the thicker ice, will be rammed by a ship following it.

But there is a disparity between the capability of Soviet icebreakers and the ships they are required to escort. The largest Soviet polar icebreakers that work the Route are relatively new ships with the power and hull strength to travel at high speed through the ice. They cannot use it, however, without outdistancing themselves from the convoy and letting the ships in the line, proceeding at low speed to avoid hull damage, fall further astern into an ever worsening situation.

Ships travelling in convoy must also maintain a safe stopping distance from each other in case one ship suddenly loses headway. When this occurs the stopped ship must begin running astern. Ships with direct diesel drive attempting this maneuver, however, must first stop their engines and then restart them in reverse. These are massive engines and reversing some of them can take a full minute. During this time the ship following maintains headway, while the path to the stern of the stopped ship ahead continues to close. If it is travelling in continuous ice hemmed in by the edges of the channel, it cannot turn to avoid a collision. Even large vessels, like the *Dmitrii Donskoi* bulk carriers and the *Samotlor* tankers, relatively new ships built in the mid-1970s, are slow to reverse engines and lack the requisite power to maintain the optimum distance astern of a nuclear icebreaker (Sledzyuk 1983:44–5). Many other vessels still in arctic service, the *Amguema*, *Volgoles*, *Belomorskles*, *Vytegrales* and *Pioner* classes, are not only underpowered but old. Their hulls are worn by long service in the ice.

Rules for the conduct of ice convoys were established in 1932, when the Council of National Commissars passed a resolution setting up the Directorate of the Northern Sea Route. Glavsevmorputi, as it was then known, was entrusted with the task of extending 'the Northern Sea Route from the White Sea to the Bering Strait; to service it, maintain it and assure the safety of navigation along it'. The Directorate gave the convoy commander authority to dictate the convoy's speed and the distance to be kept by every ship in the group (Arikaynen and Chubakov 1987:130–84).

Every captain is required to accept the commander's ruling in all matters concerning the conduct of the convoy. When the ice conditions and the visibility in the convoy change, it is the commander who radios changes of speed and distances to the captains. According to the rules the convoy commander is discharged from all responsibility for damage, however sustained, by any ship in the convoy. If circumstances permit, a captain may discuss orders with the commander, but the individual captains retain full responsibility for damage suffered by their own ships, whether the cause be impact with the ice or with the ship ahead. The problems of the ice convoy clearly have a personal dimension as well as a technical one.

In 1960, the Ministry of Merchant Shipping responded to a proposal by the Arctic and Antarctic Scientific Research Institute in Leningrad that the relationship of convoy commander to the captains be systematically studied.

The outcome of this work was the preparation and issue of documents known as 'ice passports' (Maksytov and Popov 1981:26–33).

The ice passport

Between 1973 and 1976 an ice passport was issued to nearly every cargo vessel in arctic service. Its purpose was to provide a basis for rational discussion of ship speeds and intership distances between the captains of cargo vessels and icebreakers. This document contained:

1. A list of the ships for which passports were prepared with data about ship type, year of construction and port of registry.
2. General characteristics of the ship and a table of its ice qualities including the USSR Register ice category, key dimensions, coefficients and peculiarities of its hull form, ice reinforcement, characteristics of the power plant, propellers and rudders (their ice protection) etc.
3. Diagrams for determining the safe speed during unaccompanied passage through the ice. These concerned the types of ice cover through which the ship could make passage without the aid of an icebreaker. Included were coastal ice belts, large, vast and very extensive fields of relatively thin ice with little snow cover, as well as naturally formed brash ice in the absence of compression.
4. Diagrams for determining safety parameters when in convoy with an icebreaker. These were intended for the regulation of safe speeds and minimum safe intership distances. Diagrams were provided for relatively level, continuous ice (the coastal belt, vast and very extensive fields) of various thicknesses as well as drifting ice fields with different degrees of cover. It was assumed that the width of the channel cut by the icebreaker would be greater than the beam of the escorted ship.
5. Diagrams for evaluating the benefit to the ship of making passage in convoy with arctic icebreakers and the selection of power-plant-running conditions. The safe towing speed (with regard to the ability of the icebreaker) was indicated for most ice conditions. Each diagram included the loaded and ballasted condition of the ship.
6. Recommendations to the shiphandler, including special instructions for passage through ice formations, that were not illustrated in the diagrams.

Figure 11.1 shows the ice passport of the *Volgoles*, recommending safe distance (cables) from the ship ahead for different convoy speeds (knots) in continuous ice cover of various thicknesses (meters). These curves show how ships in convoy are able to close one another in thicker ice. The lower curve is for open water. The diagram was prepared assuming the shaft is brought to a stop from full-ahead revolutions and with no running astern. The distances recommended should therefore be considered very safe.

Ice passports were issued to ships of the following classes: *Volgoles* (1960), *Amguema* (1962), *Belomorskles* (1962), *Vytegrales* (1964), *Pioner*

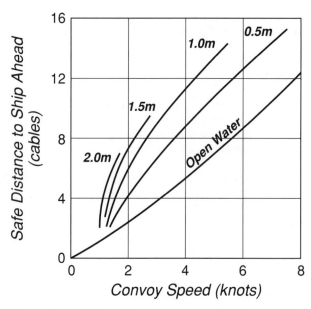

Figure 11.1 Ice passport of the arctic cargo carrier *Volgoles* (one cable equals 608 feet or approximately 185 meters).

(1968), *Pioner Moskvy*(1973), *Samotlor* (1975) and *Dmitrii Donskoy* (1977). The first 5 classes are weak-hulled dry-cargo and wood carriers, all below 9,000 deadweight tons. These are now being replaced by newer ships with better built hulls. The *Samotlor* class tankers and *Dmitrii Donskoy* dry cargoes are large displacement vessels (17,200 and 19,590 deadweight tons, respectively). They have been criticized as unsuitable for convoying by nuclear icebreakers owing to their low powers and the long stopping distances (up to a nautical mile) imposed by their direct-drive diesel propulsion. Chief Engineer A. Sledzuk, of the nuclear icebreaker *Sibir'* maintained that these large ships were under-powered for working the ice. Sledzuk claimed that nuclear steam turbine propulsion was the only viable way of providing the power that was needed. In 1982, the *Noril'sk* entered service, the first of 19 very capable universal dry cargo vessels known as the SA-15s. These ships, of 14,700 deadweight tons, have powers of 13.85 million watts (compared with the *Dmitrii Donskoys'* 8.25 million watts) as well as controllable pitch propellers for rapid reversing in convoy. The *Sevmorput*, an arctic barge carrier displacing 61,000 tons, has been commissioned and has a nuclear plant producing 29.4 million watts of power.

Ships built later than those listed above have not been issued passports. It seems these documents were only a temporary measure intended for the protection of the weaker-hulled and lower-powered ships to which they were issued.

Convoying in echelon

The ice convoy, which usually consists of 3 or 4 ships astern of the icebreaker, can waste time and fuel in difficult ice conditions. President Gorbachev has stated that arctic navigation must become more cost effective. An alternative to the single-line convoy already decribed has been proposed by Professor Leskov of the Higher School of Marine Engineering, Leningrad (Leskov 1987:30–1).

Leskov considered the case of a convoy travelling in continuous cover under compression with the last ship in the line hindered by the progressive narrowing of the channel. He investigated the advantages that would be gained if an icebreaker could cut a channel wider than its beam ('beam' here meaning greatest waterline breadth). This is not a new idea: on the inland waterways icebreakers do this routinely with the aid of ice-cutting attachments.

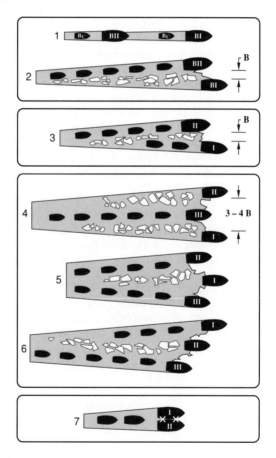

Figure 11.2 Seven examples of icebreaker convoy formations (adapted from Leskov 1987).

Leskov concluded that an icebreaker's effectiveness (defined as the number of ships it can convoy in single-line formation) can be quantified in terms of 2 ratios:

1. The ratio of the beam of the ships in the line to the beam of the icebreaker (the beam ratio).
2. The ratio of the initial width of the channel to the beam of the icebreaker (the width ratio).

In practice, an increase in initial channel width can be obtained effectively by 2 icebreakers working together. In Figure 11.2, Formations 2 and 3, 2 icebreakers (each alone able to convoy one ship through a narrowing channel) are shown working together in 2 possible echelon formations. Stationed a beam distance apart they are shown convoying first five, and then six ships — an increase in effectiveness of three. Leskov points out that the first of these formations is not new; it is currently resorted to under difficult ice conditions. As the figure shows, in a crosswind the second icebreaker would take station to windward of the first, so that the ice floes would drift out of the path of the following ships. In an emergency, he claims, a ship could avoid ramming the one ahead by turning into the trail of broken ice. Because it is so effective, Leskov proposes this formation be adopted under all conditions. Formations for 3 icebreakers and 2 icebreakers secured abreast are also shown (see Formations 4, 5, 6 and 7).

The formations proposed by Leskov present evident advantages over the traditional method: ships lined up for escort by one icebreaker, which takes the lead; a second icebreaker attached to the convoy if conditions are difficult. Convoys that are more ice-capable would be faster, more fuel efficient and better able to keep to scheduled times of arrival. If echelon towing were adopted, there would be fewer, but larger, convoys. Arctic ports, in their present capacity, however, would be unable to handle the increased traffic because they are not equipped to turn around ships in large numbers. The cargo-handling capacity of the ports is already reduced in the winter because their equipment is not designed for work in extreme cold. At Dudinka, for example, the permitted working load of the cranes has to be reduced at $-50°$ centigrade (Kurnosov 1987:18–22). The technical development of many Soviet arctic ports (Novyy Port, Dudinka, Dikson, Khatanga, Tiksi, Pevek) generally lags behind that of the ships they handle, particularly the capable SA-15 icebreaking cargo ships.

The short tow

The conditions under which ships transit channels that have been cut into rivers and estuaries are different from those encountered at sea. Ice in estuaries and rivers is landlocked and immobile; when a channel is cut the sides are not likely to close in again. Once broken at the start of the season, the same channel tends to be recut and reused many times over; where the fairway is narrow and bounded by shallows, the channel has to remain in the same place. The same agglomeration is thus successively rebroken and refrozen, and the channel eventually becomes filled with brash ice to a greater depth than the cover on each side. A slurry of brash ice 2.0 metres deep, as in the Yenisey estuary, offers a high resistance to a ship's hull. By slowing a ship's headway, the brash ice prevents ramming and makes it relatively safe for one ship to follow close astern of another.

In the technique of the 'short tow', the distance between ships can be reduced to 50 metres. The presence of deep brash ice in the channel enables ships to be towed rapidly and relatively safely into and out of port. Figure 11.3 represents the short tow arrangement between an icebreaker and a ship being towed.

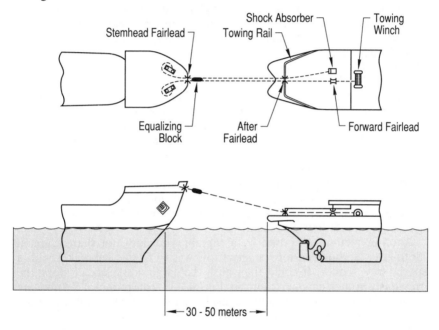

Figure 11.3 Schematic of short tow technique (adapted from Plotnikov 1986).

The need to reduce time and save fuel in the convoying of large bulk carriers up the 300-nautical-mile stretch of the Yenisey river to the port of Dudinka led to the development of the 'short tow' technique (Plotnikov 1986:37–8). In 1986, this method of towing, which had been reserved for difficult conditions, became the standard method for convoying all large displacement ships by the polar icebreakers *Kapitan Sorokin* and *Kapitan Nikolayev*. Although it is a very economical towing method, the opinions of Soviet mariners, based on its safety, seem to be mixed.

Typically, in a short-tow operation one icebreaker goes ahead to break the refrozen channel while the second takes the bulk carrier in tow. Captain Plotnikov, who developed the short-tow technique, claims that at a distance of 30 – 50 metres the towed ship's tendency to yaw can be controlled well enough to prevent its sides scraping the edges. A speed of, at least, 6 knots is maintained and the cargo vessel turns its propellers to keep the towline tension between 20 and 40 tonnes; revolutions are changed on the icebreaker's orders as necessary. At 6 knots the icebreaker relies on its high inertia and a freshly reworked channel to guarantee its continuing headway. At this speed the cargo vessel depends on the high resistance of the brash ice to ensure that it will lose headway quickly enough to avoid ramming if tension is lost.

Before this technique was introduced two icebreakers needed 7 days to cut new channels (where this was possible) and convoy one large-tonnage bulk carrier, untowed, along the 300-nautical-mile stretch. Under short tow one of these ships can be brought through in only 2 to 3 days — a threefold savings in time. The progress of the non-stop tow is considerable: covering this distance in this time means that an overall speed between 4 and 6.25 knots is maintained.

Captain Plotnikov admits that the short-tow method involves a higher degree of risk than the traditional one of free in-line convoying. However, he writes, 'nothing was ever gained for nothing. The captain looking for a quiet life will always find objections to its acceptance on the grounds of inadequate assurance of navigational safety' (Plotnikov 1986:37–8).

Captain Plotnikov developed this short tow technique in the Yenisey estuary because he was unable to bring ships through under 'close-coupled' tow, the technique that, at that time, was most often used under difficult conditions. The disparity in freeboard between the *Kapitan Sorokin* class icebreakers and bulk carriers such as the *Dmitrii Donskoy* and *Mikhail Strekalovskiy* makes it impossible to lodge the stems of these ships into their notches for a safe tow in tandem.

Another method proposed by a captain who does not share Captain Plotnikov's enthusiasm for the short tow was to fit the icebreaker with a special bow fender. It could then push the cargo vessel ahead along the previously broken channel (Smirnov 1987:42–3). This proposal did not gain favor in written discussion; it was considered premature to employ it under heavy ice conditions until strain-gauge measurements of the bow structure proved it was safe.

The tow in tandem — improved towing gear

One feature of most major Soviet icebreakers, the fendered stern notch, enables an icebreaker to accommodate a ship's stem under close-coupled tow. (The SA-15 icebreaking cargo vessels are also provided with notched sterns.) The technique of towing in tandem was not put to the test until the fall of 1983 in the East Siberian Sea when it was used to tow stranded cargo vessels from the grip of very heavy ice. During the course of the 1983 navigation season, however, the polar icebreaker *Admiral Makarov* broke 66 towing strops (Shatalin 1984). Because the tows lacked elasticity, they had to be pulled up very tight so that the working of the gear would not chafe and destroy the fenders. Towing strops that are tightened hard have little resilience and will break under surges of tension. Sometimes owing to the shortage of towing strops, ships had to be towed by their anchor chains. An attempt by the nuclear icebreaker *Arktika* to tow the tanker *Samotlor* in this manner ended when the chain links broke in brittle fracture in the exceptional cold (Shatalin 1984:24–5). There was an evident need to improve the towing gear of icebreakers.

Improved fender gear has been fitted to the *Arktika* class icebreakers. When towing in tandem, surges of movement are accommodated by compressing 2 pneumatic rubber cushions that are sandwiched between the flat surfaces of the ship's stern bulkhead and a loading frame. The rubber cushions and the loading frame are suspended from rollers and are free to move horizontally. The cargo vessel's stem is pulled by its 'whiskers', into snug contact with contoured rubber cushions in a tilting frame hinged to the loading frame.

On the icebreaker's stern deck the towing cable is rove through an equalizing block and then back to a hydraulic shock absorber located next to the towing winch. Before the tow is connected, 2 hydraulic cylinders are connected to accumulators that are loaded with compressed air. In this way the tow's stiffness can be preset to suit the ice conditions and the size of the ship to be towed. A pointer on the sheave trolley indicates the tension in the tow (Starshinov and Kuperman 1985:14–16).

The *Mudyug* conversion — Thyssen/Waas bow

The radically new bow form of the small West German icebreaker *Max Waldeck*, on trials in the Baltic Sea in 1981, quickly attracted Soviet interest. Captain Mikhailichenko, deputy head of the Northern Sea Route Administration, wrote in *Morskoy flot*: 'In 1982, phlegmatic Finnish pilots were astonished to see a toy icebreaker continuing to make headway through compressed ice in which other, more powerful, icebreakers couldn't move' (Mikhailichenko 1988:23–7). Between July and October 1986 a similar bow was fitted to the *Mudyug*, a Soviet subarctic icebreaker which had been delivered to the Soviet Union by Finland's Wartsila in 1982 (see Figure 11.4). During the conversion in the Thyssen Nordseewerke shipyard at Emden its overall length, icebreaking beam and draft were increased. Tonnage increased from 6,210 to 7,775 tons. The West German yard guaranteed that the conversion would increase *Mudyug*'s continuous icebreaking performance from 0.9 to 1.4 metres (at 1.0 knot). With reporters and specialists from the Federal Republic of Germany, Sweden, Finland, Norway and the United States on board, the converted *Mudyug* performed ice trials off Spitzbergen on 18 and 30 April 1987.

The Thyssen/Waas bow is designed to cut through ice with the least expenditure of effort. To achieve this, total length of ice fracture is kept to a minimum and, as a result, the slabs of ice tend to be relatively large and few. The bow works by grooving the ice and marking the channel edges with the 'ears', (the outward-flared runners, or cutting edges, in the bow's most forward and widest section). Some distance ahead of the ship two

Figure 11.4 Thyssen/Waas icebreaking bow outfitted on Soviet subarctic icebreaker *Mudyug*.

continuous cracks begin to appear along these lines of shear. Between the ears, the transverse bow sections form a concave vault; because there is no stem, the full icebreaking force of the ship is applied by the ears at the edges of the channel. A continuous swath of ice, the full width of the channel, is thereby cut downwards out of the cover in double shear. As the ship progresses, the bow sections further aft submerge the swath and bend it downwards until it snaps off into a succession of rectangular slabs. As the slabs move further aft, they are broken in two by a centerline knife. At this point the increasing slope of the hull section and the strong flow of water outward cause these half slabs to rise to the surface. They come to rest beneath the intact ice cover on each side of the ship.

The process is more nearly one of ice 'cutting' than of icebreaking. There is none of the chaotic and random cruising, breaking and smashing typical of a conventional icebreaking bow. Only one shear and two bending fractures are needed to form each half slab. Beyond these, there is little superfluous breakage to consume unnecessary propulsive power. The action generates little brash ice, and little or none passes through the propellers, leaving propulsive efficiency unimpaired. Because the bow is wider than the ship (by more than a metre to each side), the hull does not contact or rub the channel edges. It has been suggested that the Thyssen/Waas bow requires less than one-half the power consumed by a conventional icebreaking bow in ice of the same thickness. It is, above all, the promise of smaller power use and greater fuel savings that has attracted the Soviets to this bow.

In his article, Captain V. Mikhailichenko sees a future for the new bow, 'for minor and medium icebreakers operating in fast coastal ice in the gulfs and estuaries of arctic rivers'. After the design is improved to overcome problems of backing and working in compression, the concept may well be adopted in the construction or modernization of more powerful icebreakers and icebreaking cargo vessels. The next advantageous step would be the modernization of a *Kapitan Sorokin* class polar icebreaker for winter operation on the Yenisey river as well as a cargo vessel for the winter run to Dudinka (Mikhailichenko 1988:23–7).

If icebreakers working the Yenisey estuary are fitted with this bow, the technique of convoying to and from Dudinka will be forced to change. Because the Thyssen/Waas bow does not create brash ice in quantity, every time a channel refreezes a 'new' one will have to be cut. The short-tow technique, which depends on the accumulation of brash ice to retard a ship's headway when necessary, would not be safe, and this technique would become obsolete for the rapid transit of large bulk carriers. In the fast ice of the estuary, however, it is possible that one *Kapitan Sorokin* class icebreaker fitted with the Thyssen/Waas bow could convoy several ships at a time. Because the Thyssen/Waas bow cuts a wider channel, it will be less likely that long bulk carriers will get stuck at the bends where the channel changes direction. At the present time, the *Kapitan Sorokin* requires up to 3 hours to free the *Mikhail Strekalovskiy*, from this situation (Volosov 1985:11–24).

Although the bow seems particularly suited to work in the continuous fast ice of rivers and estuaries, it would also appear to offer advantages for operation in the converging channels of the sea routes. Because it engages the ice by its front-edge knives while the hull remains clear, the icebreaker is not likely to experience the transverse pressure felt by a conventional hull when opening a winding lead. In fact, its vastly improved performance in first-year ice may render convoying less dependent on finding suitable leads. Icebreakers with this bow should be able to cut straighter channels when working at the slow speeds that are dictated by the limited abilities of the ships in the convoys.

The icebreaking–clearing attachment

Cutting a straight-edged shipping channel with equipment specially designed to tuck the broken ice away beneath its edges was first attempted in the Soviet Union more than 40 years ago. A modern attachment, pushed by an icebreaker or pusher tug through the ice of the Volga River, is the result of 20 years of active development by a number of specialists, mostly at the Gorky Institute of Water Transportation Engineers and the Leningrad Institute of Water Transport. More than 20 patents for pushed and pulled attachments of all kinds have been taken out in the Soviet Union since 1971. That year the Russian Ministry of River Shipping began using the attachments to extend the navigating season by 2 to 3 weeks before the spring ice break-up (Mikhailichenko 1988:23–7).

Ballasted with water to the best trim and immersion for the ice conditions, these attachments are used routinely on the major ice-bound Soviet rivers, often by *Kapitan Chechkin* class river icebreakers. By 1985 they were being used as far west as the Dnieper river and one was even in use in the Arctic, on the lower Yenisey estuary. The latter attachment, an LLP 20 of Gorky Institute design, may well be the one delivered to Dudinka from Murmansk by the *Kapitan Voronin* in 1984. Pushing a river attachment ahead of it through the Kara Sea, this subarctic icebreaker was able to maintain 1.5 knots through 1.1-metre ice. Without it, the ship is capable of only 0.8 metres at this speed. This is thought to be the first use of an icebreaking/ clearing attachment in open arctic waters.

Although using attachments for cutting and cleaning shipping channels has long been routine, only recently have the difficulties in using them been resolved. A satisfactory connection with the pushing ship that is strong and flexible enough has been difficult to achieve. However, a coupling has now been devised that allows the attachment freedom to float and assume its natural working position. Also, it can be adapted readily to the rounded bows of different ships. Another problem has been the growth of 'ice beards' on the underside of the attachment, impairing its cutting performance. An effective ballast tank heating system that prevents such ice build-up, however, is now available.

The successful use of attachments on the river has led to the development of other novel icebreaking bows. The Thyssen/Waas technique of building an attachment into the bow structure of a ship provided an effective solution

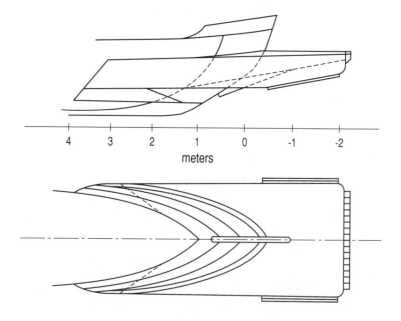

Figure 11.5 Soviet patent for an icebreaking/clearing extension (filed by B.V. Bogdanov).

to the long-standing coupling problem. This design also increased the attachment's cutting capability by adding the ship's weight to its own. These features are also apparent in patent SU 1062116 filed by B.V. Bogdanov for an 'Icebreaking-Clearing Extension for a Ship'. (See Figure 11.5). Filed in 1983, this patent is interesting for its many points of similarity with the Thyssen/Waas bow: a long overhanging arch-shaped vault; lateral ice knives at the forward edges more than a beam width apart; a centerline ice knife further aft where the hull sections became conventional. Bogdanov's design was clearly intended to operate like the Thyssen/Waas bow.

Berthing in the coastal ice belt

Berthing in the ice is a technique that has long been employed in the Antarctic and that has been increasingly employed in the Soviet maritime Arctic in the last ten years. It presents evident advantages over unloading at anchor onto barges, an operation which becomes difficult in even a slight swell. Working directly on the ice is the same as working at a jetty except that the ship uses its own cranes and unloads onto trucks or trailers. Where coastal waters are shallow relative to the draft it is the only effective method possible.

The success of this operation depends on selecting the most advantageous place to berth the ship. This requires an aerial reconnaissance of the area several days before the ship's arrival. If the plane is equipped with ice thickness measuring radar, as well as side-looking radar, to reveal hummocks and ridges, it is possible to construct a morphological map of the ice belt on which areas of flat ice suitable for berthing can be identified with confidence. The optimum place for berthing is found by studying this map in conjunction with a navigational chart showing the depth of water. Hydrologists take test drillings of the ice at the intended place of berthing. On the basis of site observations and calculations, they then determine the safe working load of the ice. The site is also examined for cracks, and the best routes across the ice for wheeled vehicles are chosen.

Depending on its ice-strength category a ship may, or may not, need the aid of an icebreaker to berth in the ice. Normally an icebreaker opens an approach channel from the edge of the sea ice. When approaching the intended berth the icebreaker must break the last 2 or 3 ship's lengths of ice under sternway in order to limit fragmentation of the jetty area. If the ship has the ice strength, it will enter the channel and take a run to ram itself fully into the ice. If not, it may be pushed into position by the icebreaker.

Cargo is discharged simultaneously from both sides of the ship. Even if there is too wide a gap to discharge from both sides at the time of arrival, it becomes possible in 2 to 3 days when the brash ice in the gap freezes. The ship, however, must not freeze into the ice during berthing. This can be avoided either by heating the trim or fuel tanks, affecting slight changes of trim periodically, or turning the propellers and moving the rudder from side to side. The change of draft due to discharging will also tend to prevent the ship from freezing into the berthing site. If freezing does occur, however, the entire jetty can be destroyed when the buoyancy of the ship finally breaks it out of the ice.

Building jetties on the permafrost

The port of Yamburg in the mouth of the Ob' river was opened in 1984. It was built to meet the construction and operational needs of the gas wells of the Yamal peninsula, from which natural gas now flows by pipeline to Western Europe. It is situated approximately 1 kilometer up a small river on the eastern side of the estuary. Opening the port required widening and dredging the river from a depth of less than a metre to over 4 metres for the access of river vessels and barges from ports on the rivers Omsk, Tobol'sk, Tyumeni and Surgut.

From 1981 onwards, repeated attempts were made to dredge the channel for the silt carried back and forth by the tides of the Ob'. The permafrost under the silt could not be penetrated by dredgers and had to be blown out of the dry river bed with dynamite in the winter. Over 1.2 million cubic metres of earth were removed to deepen and widen the channel from the Ob' river to Yamburg.

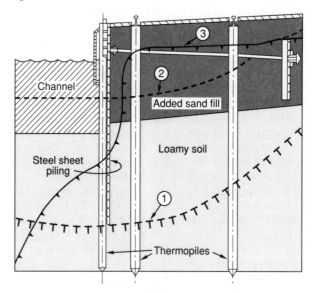

1. Upper limit of permafrost prior to jetty construction
2. Original location of channel bottom
3. Upper limit of permafrost after jetty construction

Figure 11.6 Example of a dry cargo jetty constructed in the coastal permafrost (adapted from Vinogradova 1986).

Building jetties on the permafrost presented a number of problems. A section of the port's dry cargo jetty, which illustrates the design solution adopted, is shown in Figure 11.6. A jetty 620 metres long was built for an unexpected transfer of 606,000 tonnes of general cargo and 106,000 tonnes of petroleum products (Vinogradova 1986:39–41).

The first line of Figure 11.6 represents the upper limit of the permafrost before the jetty was built. At that point it was relatively deep in the ground and depressed by the presence of water. The dock wall, which consisted of interlocking steel sheet piles, was driven down through the river bed as far as the permafrost. Land for the jetty was reclaimed by filling fine sand between the piling and the shore. In the course of the fill the tie rods and anchors of the dock wall support structure were installed. Holes were drilled for 3 rows of thermopiles: the first being placed just outside the sheet steel piling. Thermopiles were set up in these holes and driven several metres into the permafrost.

The loamy soil into which the steel sheet piling was driven had practically no strength in its unfrozen state and could never provide adequate support for a dock wall. The purpose of the thermopiles was to bring the surface of the permafrost up into the sand fill of the jetty.

The thermopiles against the steel sheet piling were pitched at 1.63 metres. The other 2 rows were situated to support the rails of the travelling crane. When the permafrost had risen through the loam of the river bed into the wet sand of the jetty, it consolidated the base of the sheet steel wall beneath the river bed and braced the anchors and tie rods that support its top. Line 2 indicates the surface of the permafrost in the completed jetty after the thermopiles had exerted their effect. The result was a dry cargo jetty capable of supporting 80 tonne cranes.

The thermopiles act as thermal syphons between the ground and the atmosphere. Each is essentially a hollow pipe, filled with diesel oil and sealed at both ends. A longitudinal baffle separates a warmer, less dense, stream of rising oil from a colder, denser, descending stream. A net transfer of heat is thereby effected from the ground to the atmosphere. Circulation is set up only in the winter, when air temperatures are lower than permafrost temperatures. In the summer, the upper ends of the piles are warmer than their lower ends and no circulation is promoted. The piles thus come into operation each winter to provide a one-way heat flow; they are entirely automatic and require no maintenance.

In addition to this dry cargo jetty, an experimental jetty was built at Yamburg for research into construction techniques employing locally available materials such as ice and river sand. The core material of this jetty is ice. It is protected on the water side by an outer facing of wooden planks, polyethylene sheeting and a layer of a sawdust/sand mixture. The top surface of the core is covered with a layer of sand on which slabs of reinforced concrete are placed. The weight of these slabs provides thermal insulation and serves to load the naturally buoyant ice down in the water.

Gordon G. Watson

Ice as a constructional material for jetties

Ice has been employed for many years in the Soviet Union to build jetties and dams. It has also been used to construct barriers to protect ships and port structures from the waterborne avalanche of ice that scours the banks of the rivers Ob', Yenisey, Dudinka, Lena, Khatanga, Bodaibo, Yana, Indigirka and Kolyme every spring when the thaw comes.

Using the technique recommended by the Water Transport Scientific Research Institute, the ice structure is raised from the frozen river bed in the dry season by freezing successive layers of ice (Gosman and Kutikov 1987:44). Each layer is 2–3 centimeters thick and is applied by a water spray regulated so that ice crystals form in the jet. Time is allowed between each spraying for the layers to harden. A barrier of snow or planking 20 – 30 centimeters high around the structure prevents loss of water during this process. Thermal insulation is provided by prefrozen blocks of wet sawdust, 80 centimeters thick, which are incorporated into the sides of the structure as it rises. These blocks also serve to isolate the core from the river water. In this manner, enough cold is stored within the ice core during its construction to hold the temperature in the contact zone with the river bed down to −1 or −2° centigrade until the end of the summer.

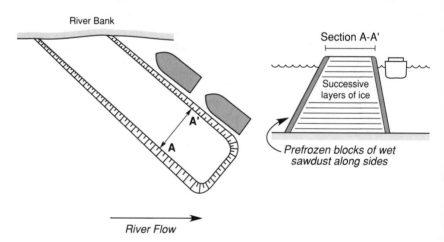

Figure 11.7 Example of a temporary jetty in ice (adapted from Gosmar and Kutikov 1987).

Figure 11.7 illustrates a dam constructed to protect vessels from damage by ice during the spring break-up. The dam at the port of Dudinka proves that such a construction is both permanent and effective.

A jetty in ice, with a load-bearing capacity only slightly inferior to one in concrete, can support mobile cargo-working equipment. The jetties are constructed during the winter, when the rivers are at their lowest levels and hard frozen. The permafrost in the river bed, the foundation for the structure, is relatively easy to expose. It has been demonstrated that during the five months of the winter a team of four men with a 60-centimetres-per-metre-per-hour pump can erect a jetty 8 metres high, 40 metres wide and 50 metres long.

Ice jetties are also built on the sea coast. The one built at Cape Schmidt in the Chukchi Sea in 1986 (by reputation the most difficult port for a ship to negotiate in the eastern Arctic) is claimed to be the first. In 1987, the *Igarka* and *Pioner Rossi* berthed at this jetty with supplies. Until its construction, ships were unloaded at anchor with the aid of barges (*Vodnyy transport*, 1987).

The future

The Soviet Union is the only country in the world with a permanent plan to develop shipping of bulk cargoes systematically, by sea and by river, above the Arctic Circle. Fifty years of experience has been gained by the Soviets, their due reward for an immense investment of human effort. Design techniques for building port structures in the Soviet Arctic are based largely on Soviet experience and research. Technical innovation, however, in the design of ships for the ice results from the work of specialists in Europe, the United States and Canada as well as the USSR. Our Soviet counterparts in this field are much more aware of the work done in the West than we are of their problems and achievements.

Yet, there is no difficulty (other than linguistic) in keeping up-to-date with their technical progress; Soviet technical journals are available by subscription like any other national journals. In them, it is clear to see how widely read Soviet specialists are by the number of non-Soviet sources cited in the bibliographies of their articles. But the flow of information and ideas is one-way, and this is not to our advantage.

Our technical press informs us of topical events like the launching of a new nuclear icebreaker or a technical breakthrough like the Thyssen/Waas bow. But we tend to regard these events as happening a long way away, too remote to be relevant to the particular problems waiting to be dealt with on our own desks. So while scientists and many other professionals go to Moscow to attend conferences and have discussions with their Soviet counterparts, engineers and naval architects stay put, driven by a slavish determination to solve their own problems by their own unaided efforts.

Speaking in Murmansk on 1 October 1987, Mikhail Gorbachev said, 'The shortest route by sea from Europe to the Far East, to the Pacific, lies via the Arctic. I believe that, depending on how things will progress with the normalization of international relations, we could open the Northern Sea Route to foreign ships providing them with our icebreaker escort' (Gorbachev 1987).

The prospect that ships with Western cargoes will one day be sailing through the Arctic, instead of the Suez Canal, would seem to be one good reason for opening a dialogue with the Soviets on ice navigation technology. With instability in the Middle East, shipping companies may not be able to count on the Suez Canal in the future. Despite the ice, the Northern Sea Route may be safer as well as shorter.

References

Arikaynen, A.I., and K.N. Chubakov. 1987. 'Azbukha ledovogo plavaniya' [The A to Z of ice navigation]. *Transport*: 130-184.

Gorbachev, M.S. 1987. Speech at Murmansk, FBIS-SOV-87-101. 2 October, 42. (see Appendix I)

Gosman, V., and I. Kutikov. 1987. 'Vremennye prichaly iz l'da' [Temporary jetties in ice]. *Rechnoy transport* 2:44.

Kurnosov, M. 1987. 'Budet li liniei Dudinskoe napravlenie?' [Will we ever have scheduled sailings to Dudinka?]. *Morskoy flot* 12:18-22.

Leskov, M. 1987. 'Izmenit' taktiku ledovykh provodok' [Change the tactics of ice convoying]. *Morskoy flot* 2:30-31.

Maksytov, D.D., and Yu. N. Popov. 1981. 'Opyt razrabotki i vnedreniya ledovykh pasportov' [Experience with the development and introduction of ice passports]. *Transactions of the Arctic and Antarctic Scientific Research Institute* 376:26-33.

Mikhailichenko, Captain V. 1988. 'Ne tol'ko moshchnost'' [Not by power alone]. *Morskoy flot* 1:23-27.

Plotnikov, Captain K. 1986. 'Risk minimal'nyi, vygoda ochevidnaya' [For a minimal risk, an obvious advantage]. *Morskoy flot* 12:37-38.

Shatalin, N. 1984. 'Iz opyta arktiki - 83' [From the experience of the Arctic, 1983]. *Morskoy flot* 10:24-25.

Sledzyuk, A. 1983. 'Energeticheskie ustanovki dlya ledokolov' [Power plants for icebreakers]. *Morskoy flot* 5:44-45.

Smirnov, Captain A. 1987. 'Buksirovat' ili tolkat'?' [To tow or to push?]. *Morskoy flot* 12:42-43.

Starshinov, V.A., and A.M. Kuperman. 1985. 'Buksirnoe ustrositvo arkticheskikh ledokolov' [A towing connection for arctic icebreakers]. *Sudostroyenie* 1:14-16.

Vinogradova, N. 1986. 'Port v zapolyar'ye' [An arctic port]. *Rechnoy transport* 4:39-41.

Vodnyy transport. 1987. 11 July.

Volosov, M.I. 1985. 'Rezhimy raboty glavnogo dvigatelya sudov tip *Mikhail Strekalovskii* vo l'dakh' [Operating conditions of the main engines of the *Mikhail Strekalovskii* class ships in ice]. Transactions of the Central Scientific Research Institute of the USSR Merchant Marine Ministry. *In: Sudovye energeticheskie ustanovki i elektrooborudovanie [Ships' Power Plants and Electrical Equipment]*: 11-24.

12

The Siberian river as a transport system

Robert N. North

The Soviet maritime Arctic, the focus of this volume, can scarcely be held to include Siberian rivers. Nevertheless, there are excellent reasons for examining their role in northern transportation. First, river transport offers a direct alternative to sea transport in many parts of the Arctic. Second, the area of overlap is growing and is likely to continue growing. Third, where there is overlap, river transport usually takes much more traffic than sea transport. Rivers account for 65 percent of waterborne freight in Siberia as a whole, and 92 percent to points beyond the Arctic Circle (Zachesov 1986:13). And fourth, Soviet sources uniformly state that where both alternatives exist, river transport is normally much cheaper. Estimates for different routes range from 20 to 60 percent.

With this situation in mind, the chapter will look in turn at 4 aspects of the Siberian river system:

1. those physical characteristics of the system which affect its ability to provide transportation in the north;
2. the tasks facing transport in Siberia, and the role currently played by river transport;
3. the present extent of functional overlap between river and sea transport; and
4. prospective relationships between the 2 modes.

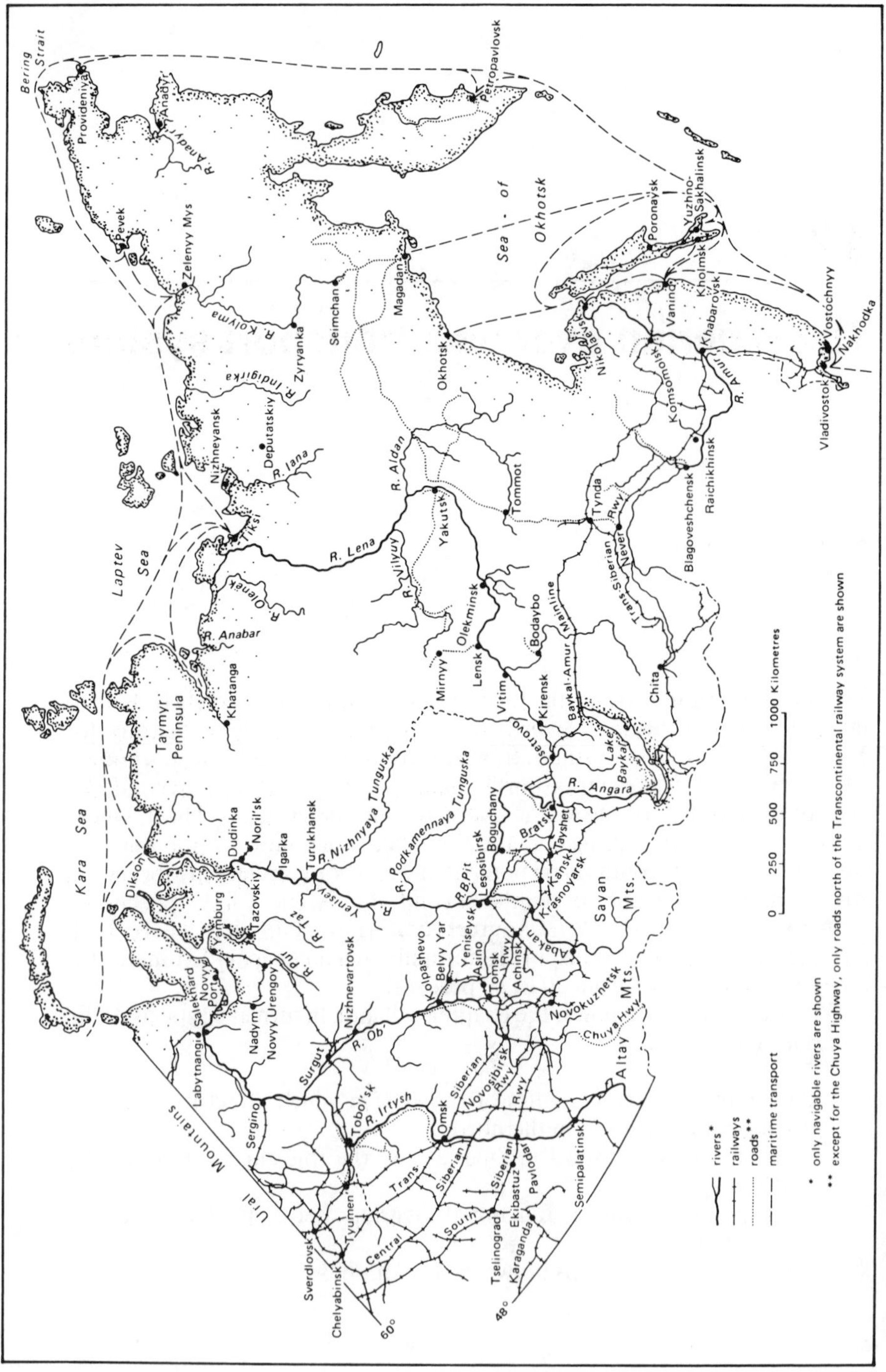

Figure 10.1 The Siberian transport network

Physical characteristics of the Siberian river system

Siberia, including the Soviet Far East, is furnished with an impressive length of navigable waterways — 4 times the length of railways and 11 times that of highways (see Figure 12.1). One third of the navigable length lies within the Arctic circle (Zachesov 1986:13). However, it is not really valid to refer to 'the Siberian river system' as far as transport is concerned. There are 4 major and several minor basins and they function separately. A few, mainly east of the Taymyr peninsula, are linked in summer by river–sea vessels (river vessels certified for limited use at sea) using arctic coastal waters, but there are no water connections farther south. At the end of the 19th century the Ket'-Kas canal linked the Ob' and Yenisey basins, but it was technically inadequate and fell into disuse shortly after construction. The situation contrasts markedly with that west of the Urals, where shipping can exit from the Volga to the Baltic, White, Caspian and Black seas.

In addition to their mutual isolation, the major Siberian river basins differ considerably in physical characteristics, transport functions and even vessel designs. On one physical characteristic, however, generalizations can be made: the length of the navigation season.

In Siberia the length of the navigation season is subject to 2 major influences, namely ice and low water. The ice free season at arctic river mouths west of the Taymyr peninsula averages 120 days (see Table 12.1); east of the peninsula averages range from 76 to 93 days. In both cases, variations can be expected of 20 days on either side of the mean. Soviet studies suggest that the ice-free period has declined during the past quarter century, particularly in the east. In the south, where the major rivers are crossed by east–west railways, the mean ice-free season ranges from 160 to 180 days. The exception is the Lena river, with an average of 129 days at Osetrovo.

Low water occurs in summer after the spring run-off. It particularly affects the area east of the Yenisey river, where much of the land is underlain by permafrost, and melting snow cannot seep into the ground to even out stream flow. But sparse precipitation means that the problem occurs farther west too, notably along the Irtysh river, and it affects small rivers everywhere. Many, even in the south where the ice-free season is well over 160 days, have a normal navigation season of only 30 days. (This assumes that navigation is possible with a depth of 0.6 meters.) In a dry year the navigation season may be less than 10 days.

Unpredictability, and a short season even in average years, are the worst problems faced by river transport as it tries to maintain its status *vis-à-vis* other modes. Even limited area coverage is a minor inconvenience by comparison.

The Ob'-irtysh system

The main river system of the West Siberian Plain has gradients averaging well under 1 in 5000. Consequent problems include meanders, which add

Table 12.1 Soviet eastern rivers: navigation

	Ob'Irtysh	Yenisey	Lena/ Northeast	Amur
Navigable, all basin (kilometers incl. with guaranteed depths)	28,500 15,000	16,500 10,800	26,200 10,100[1]	8,700 5,200
Depths guaranteed, (meters)	2.5–3.0 (main channels)	1.0 (upper reaches)	1.0–3.0 (overall range)	0.85–1.5 (side channels)
	1.4–2.0 (major side channels)	7.0 (below Igarka)	2.0–2.2 (Osetrovo to mouth of Vitim)	
	1.0–2.0 (other rivers)		2.6–2.9 (Vitim-Lena Delta)	
Navigable, specific rivers (kilometers)	3,650 (Ob') 3,784 (Irtysh)	3,487 (Yenisey)	4,125 (Lena)	2,824 (Amur)
		1,779 (Angara)	1,665 (Kolyma)	
			872 (Yana)	
Navigation season (days)	100–140 (Gulf)	av. 181 (mouth of Angara)	av. 129 (Osetrovo)	av. 186 (Komsomol'sk Khabarovsk)
	190–200 (center and south)	av. 127 (Igarka)	av. 91 (Lena Delta)	av. 178 (below Blago- veshchensk)
		av. 173 (Baykal)	av. 76 (Nizhneyansk)	
			125–93 (middle and lower Kolyma)	

[1] Includes navigable sections of rivers controlled by the RSFSR Ministry of River Fleet (21,300 km). Some northeastern rivers are controlled by USSR Ministry of the Merchant Marine.

Source: Tonyayev 1977

greatly to the length of journey, and shifting sandbanks. Guaranteed depths vary between 2.5 and 3.0 meters on main channels but may be as little as 1.4 meters on side channels to major towns such as Tyumen' and Tomsk (see

Table 12.1). Upstream the main channel itself is shallow. For example, the stretch between Biysk and Barnaul on the Ob' river is only now being deepened to 1.5 meters (Orlovich 1986:39). These figures compare with 3.5 – 4.0 meters on main channels west of the Urals. Another problem is that the Gulf of Ob' is very shallow, especially close to shore. Transshipment between river and ocean-going vessels takes place at roadsteads using floating cranes. Apart from the expense and inconvenience, work is often interrupted when conditions become too rough for the river vessels. On the positive side, the West Siberian Plain has a huge network of minor rivers, which can be used by shallow-draft vessels to give very good area coverage.

The Yenisey system

The Yenisey itself is mainly a lowland river, though there are difficult rapids above the mouth of the Angara. On the other hand, most of the right-bank tributaries are mountain rivers originating in regions underlain by permafrost. Spring run-off is fast and heavy, and it causes extreme fluctuations in depth on the main river. The Yenisey may rise 15 – 20 meters at Igarka (Tonyayev 1977), and at Dudinka the port is normally evacuated for two weeks or more to avoid ice and flood damage. After spring run-off most of the right-bank tributaries are unnavigable because too little water covers their rapids. An exception is the Angara, which is being transformed into a string of deep lakes separated by dams and hydro-electric stations: Irkutsk; Bratsk; Ust'-Ilimsk; and most recently Boguchany. Unfortunately, when the dams were built river traffic was forecast to remain below 6 million tons per annum, the lower limit for incorporating locks. The forecasts now seem to have been too low, but a potential long-distance east–west route has been lost (Vol'fson 1986:41). The Yenisey itself, on the other hand, does have a boat-lift at the big Krasnoyarsk dam.

The Yenisey has one distinct advantage over the Ob'. Adequate depths for ocean-going ships reach south about the same distance in both cases, but the Yenisey is no longer a gulf by then and has an accessible port at Igarka, 600 kilometers upstream. Depths range from 7.0 meters there to 18 to 30 meters downstream.

The Lena basin and the Northeast

Most of the Northeast is underlain by permafrost and has low precipitation. Problems of rapid spring run-off and summer low water are therefore especially acute. On the upper Lena the railway transshipment port of Osetrovo is badly affected. There is supposed to be a guaranteed depth of 2.2 meters from Osetrovo to the mouth of the Vitim, and 2.6–2.9 meters thereafter, but even constant dredging does not always suffice. In 1985, a particularly bad year, depths at Osetrovo fell to 1.6–1.8 meters. Tommot, scheduled to have rail capabilities within five years, is an auxiliary port on the Aldan with depths supposedly maintained at 1.3–1.4 meters that have at times fallen to below 1 meter. Both rivers are being deepened a little, but substantial improvement would require dams and locks (Orlovich 1986:38; Vorob'yev 1986:42). The Lena and other Northeastern rivers also have shallow water downstream, caused by deltas or rivermouth bars. An exception is the Khatanga, where small seagoing vessels can penetrate upstream. The Lena delta cannot even be crossed by loaded river–sea vessels. Transshipment takes place at Tiksi which means that river vessels have to cross an open bay with uncertain weather. The situation is now improving with the recent purchase from Finland of ice-capable dredgers. The Yana bar has been dredged to give a reliable depth of 1.8 meters, and work is expected to begin shortly on the Indigirka river. The ultimate aim is to eliminate transshipment and the movement of river-only vessels in exposed coastal conditions (Nikol'skiy *et al.* 1975; Lena United Steamship Co. 1989).

The problem of ice, naturally, is at its worst in the Northeast. Rivers freeze to a depth of 2.5 – 3.0 meters, which means that smaller rivers freeze to the bottom. It also means that even the deeper rivers are too shallow to take icebreakers powerful enough to break winter ice.

The Amur basin

The Amur lies wholly outside the Arctic. Running through mountainous terrain with a cold monsoon climate, it suffers from severe spring floods but avoids the summer low-water problems of the northern rivers. Its value for navigation could be greatly enhanced by dams and locks. Plans to control the river in co-operation with China were shelved in the 1950s, but President Gorbachev has recently tried to revive interest as part of his overtures to China — admittedly with an eye to power generation and flood control more than navigation. At present, depths are 0.85–1.5 meters on tributaries and a little more on the Amur itself (see Table 12.1).

In sum, the rivers of Siberia comprise a very extensive network of navigable waterways, offering in many areas both long distances without breaks in navigation and remarkably good areal coverage. They are plagued by three major problems: a short ice-free season; water shortage in summer; and a failure to incorporate locks in several hydro-electric dams.

Tasks faced by Siberian transport, and the role of river transport

From the point of view of transport, Siberia and the Far East can be divided into two broad zones. The first is an east–west belt in the south, served primarily by the transcontinental railways. The second is a 'pioneering zone' in the north. Within the southern zone, rivers are a minor mode of transport and in effect provide north–south feeders for the east–west railways. They move such low-value bulk goods as sand, gravel and wood into the railway towns for local use and, in the case of wood, export from Siberia. The Amur fits the general pattern in that it carries mainly short-distance bulk traffic.

However, it also parallels the Trans-Siberian Railway where the latter is overloaded and not electrified, so it carries some coal over long distances.

In the northern pioneering zone, river transport fills a much more important role. Indeed in most areas it is the leading form of transport. Some generalizations can be made before the principal river basins are examined separately.

The northern economy depends on resource extraction, mainly for export from the region. Some resources (building materials, coal, and wood, for example) are produced for the local market, but the population is small. There are fewer than 2 million people in the whole of the northeast, and about another 2 million in the rest of northern Siberia. Therefore, the two main functions of transport are to move supplies into the region and resources out. For general traffic there is a common sequence of modal use as traffic grows. The first stage combines river transport from the railway towns in the south, or from the arctic coast, with rudimentary roads. In many areas the latter are primarily winter roads. In the second stage a sparse network of all-weather roads is added. This has occurred more in the northeast than the northwest, where muskeg is prevalent and the building of permanent roads extremely expensive. Experiments there have concentrated on preserving winter roads through the summer by insulation. The third stage is to build railways, which immediately become the favored and principal mode if they have adequate capacity. Some writers claim that this is because tariffs are set below those of river transport, despite the fact that total river transport costs are lower (Kolesov 1982). Construction costs heavily favor the rivers. To build a kilometer of railway in northern Siberia (presumably the swampy regions of the northwest, since only there has there been recent experience) costs over 1 million roubles. An all-weather road costs 800,000–900,000 roubles, followed by 13,000–15,000 per annum for maintenance. A river costs on average 8,000 roubles per kilometer to bring into use, with maintenance costs of 4,000–5,000 per annum. To deepen one kilometer from 1.5 to 1.8 meters costs 1,500 roubles, and from 1.8 to 2.0 meters, 8,000 (Zachesov 1986:13). However, the advantage of railways is that they can operate year round and are therefore less subject to irregular work schedules and unpredictable delays. Nor do they cause their customers such high inventory costs.

The sequence described above applies to general freight. However, by far the biggest traffic flows in northern Siberia move by specialized transport. They consist of oil and natural gas moving out of the northwest by pipeline. The weight of oil alone is about 2.5 times that of the freight on all Siberian and Far Eastern rivers, and probably about 8 times the weight moved into the north of the West Siberian Plain by all forms of transport. At the other end of the scale, air transport accounts for most passenger travel but very little freight, although it does move valuable commodities such as gold and diamonds out of the north. Its role in construction projects is growing as a new generation of heavy-freight aircraft comes into use, able to operate from primitive northern airstrips.

Freight traffic flows in the principal river basins are shown on Figures 12.2, 12.3 and 12.4. All depict conditions in the early 1970s and are therefore dated. However, most changes are likely to be in volumes rather than basic patterns, and the source maps do not give volume scales anyway.

The Ob'-Irtysh system (see Figure 12.2)

Since oil and natural gas move out of northwestern Siberia almost entirely by pipeline, river transport has two main functions: to bring in supplies, mainly from Omsk, Tomsk and Novosibirsk, the railway towns in the south, and to move wood within and out of the region (see Table 12.2). Supplies are brought into the North also by a railway from Tyumen' to Surgut, Novyy Urengoy and, since mid-1986, the Yamburg gas field. However, the railway

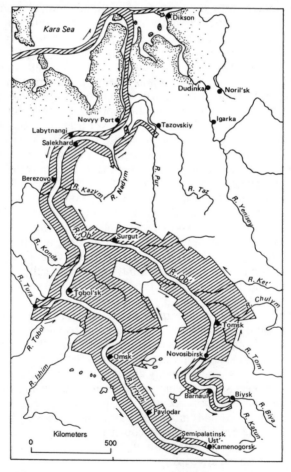

Figure 12.2 Principal freight flows in the Ob'-Irtysh Basin (adapted from Tonyayev 1977).

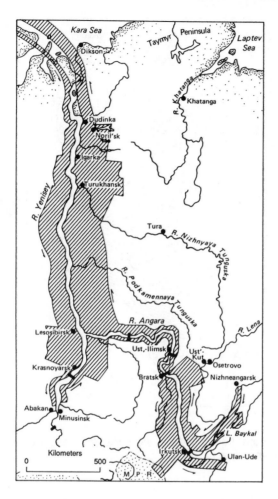

Figure 12.3 Principal freight flows in the Yenisey Basin (adapted from Tonyayev 1977).

lacks the capacity to move more than a third of the traffic for the North. River transport accounts for about 60 percent of movements into the oil and gas fields as a whole, and over 90 percent of those to the new northern gas fields (Zachesov 1986:13). In northwestern Siberia, heavyweight consists (barge trains) use the main channels, and small vessels distribute and collect freight along the network of minor rivers. The heavyweight consists range from 18,000 to 24,000 tons and occasionally 30,000 tons when moving downstream, although they may be underpowered at those weights by Western standards. Tons per tug-horsepower are 1.5–2.0 times North American, and 2.0–3.0 times West European levels (Ovchinnikov

185

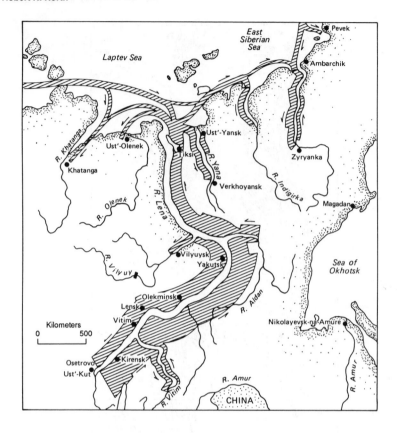

Figure 12.4 Principal freight flows in the Lena Basin and Northeastern USSR (adapted from Nikol'skiy *et al.* 1975).

1986:10). Bulk freights moving north include sand and gravel (3 million tons in 1985); metallurgical slag from the Kuznetsk basin, used for road construction (2.2 million tons in 1986); and petroleum products (Komolov 1986:10; Olenev 1987:28).

Small rivers are those with depths of 0.6–1.25 meters. Freight volumes on these have been rising much faster than those of river transport as a whole. In all of northern Siberia, small rivers now account for a quarter of all tons moved (Zachesov 1986:13). In western Siberia their tonnage is planned to grow three times as fast between 1986 and 1990 as total tonnage on the national system and over 1.5 times as fast as national small-river tonnage (Barakin 1986:13; *Rechnoy transport*, 1986a:2) . Small rivers have become especially useful as oil exploration has shifted from a few supergiant fields to many small ones for which the cost of permanent overland transport facilities would be excessive. River transport writers claim that operational costs are 8–11 percent those of road transport and 4.5–5.0 percent those of

Table 12.2 Soviet eastern rivers: traffic (million tons)

	1985	1986	1987 plan	1988 plan	1990 plan
Total loaded	100.5	159.4	161.5		176.2
Percent of RSFSR	21.1	29.2	29.3		
Deliveries to far north[1]	40.0			49.3[5]	
Ob'-Irtysh Basin					
Total loaded[2]		70.0+			
To oil and gas regions	11.5	19.8	18.8[3]		
including to Ob'-Taz Gulf	3.6				
of which, to Yamburg	1.4	2.2	2.2		4.8
Yenisey Basin					
Total loaded[2]		30.0+			
To far north	6.0				
Including Dudinka	3.6				
Lena Basin and Northeast					
Total loaded[2]		10.0+			
To north, from Osetrovo	3.6	4.8		4.0+	
including oil products	1.7	2.0	1.7		
General dry goods	2.0		2.3[4]	2.7[6]	
Amur Basin					
Total loaded[2]		20.0+			

[1] Per annum average, 1981–5.
[2] Totals loaded for individual basins add up to 29.4 million tons less than known 1986 total, so are probably all underestimates, especially Ob'-Irtysh. Total for Lena River in 1988 was probably 19.0–20.0 million tons, including 16.0 million carried by the Lena Steamship Co. (Lena Steamship Co. 1989).
[3] Actual: Olenev 1988:27.
[4] Actual the same as the plan: Olenev 1988:27.
[5] Gor'kov 1988:1. According to *Vodnyy transport*, 1988:1, over 51.0.
[6] Actual. Interview with Osetrovo port manager, June 1989.

Sources: *Narodnoye khozyaystvo RSFSR v 1985 godu: Statisticheskiy yezhegodnik* 1986:200; Olenev 1987:28–9; Vinogradova 1986b:4; *Rechnoy transport* 1986:6; 1987:2; Vinogradova 1986a:39; Olenev 1986:17.

air transport (Zachesov 1986:13). Railways are not an option for such small volumes.

Almost all deliveries to the North by river transport in the past have been from the railway towns in the south. As gas exploration and exploitation have moved to the Taz and Yamal peninsulas, however, the rivers have begun to receive freight from the railway at Labytnangi and from sea transport at roadsteads near Novyy Port and in the Taz Gulf near Cape Chugor. The principal freight delivered by sea has been large-diameter gas pipe from Western Europe and Japan. Transshipment began at Novyy Port in 1979 and in the Taz Gulf in 1985, and it reached 430,000 tons in 1987 (Olenev 1988:28; Kocherga and Purtov 1986:19).

The Yenisey system (see Figure 12.3)

The main natural resources in the Yenisey basin are the copper–nickel–platinum ores of Noril'sk in the north, and wood farther south (see Figure 12.3). Both move out largely by sea. The former move from the port of Dudinka to the Kola peninsula, in the amount of 4 – 5 million tons in recent years, while Igarka accounts for some 14 percent of Soviet wood exports. The principal function of river transport, therefore, is to deliver general supplies from the south, as it is in the Ob'-Irtysh basin. In the case of the Yenisey river there is no competition from railways, but some supplies for Noril'sk, including petroleum products and containerized cargo, come in by sea from the west (though river transport also delivered 212,000 tons of petroleum products in 1987) (Olenev 1988:28; Ivanov 1986:7). The 1987 total was 13,000 tons below target because insufficient supplies arrived at the river ports in the south for shipment north. River transport also delivers wood to Igarka from tributary rivers and from Lesosibirsk, carries sulphur south from Dudinka (200,000 tons in 1985) and supplies geological expeditions along the right-bank tributaries in the Central Siberian Plateau.

The last-named function can serve to illustrate both the general approach to using small rivers and the problems involved. The 3 small rivers most used are the Bol'shoy Pit, Podkamennaya Tunguska and Nizhnyaya Tunguska. Tonnage on the 3 together rose from 217,000 in 1976 to over 300,000 in 1985. The rivers are usable only during spring high water. The first to open, in mid-May, is the Bol'shoy Pit. Its maximum navigation season is about 15 days, so a convoy of 100 or more vessels is assembled at the mouth to await the opening. They include self-propelled vessels of up to 1,300 tons capacity and non-self-propelled barges of 300–800 tons, with a maximum draft of 1.6 meters. They proceed upstream as a caravan, most going to Bryanka, about 130 kilometers upstream, and must return to the mouth within the 15 days. In 1985, a bad year, the season was only 9 days, but 77,000 tons were delivered nevertheless.

Similar operations supply the 2 Tunguska rivers at the end of May, with about 100 vessels on the Nizhnyaya and 160 on the Podkamennaya. Vessels can be larger than on the Bol'shoy Pit, up to 5,000 tons capacity self-propelled and 3,000 tons non-self-propelled. They cannot be fully loaded but are used because craft purpose-built for small rivers are in short supply. In 1985 each river received about 126,000 tons of freight. Principal destinations are Tura, about 800 kilometers up the Nizhnyaya Tunguska, and Baykit and Vanavara, respectively 500 and 900 kilometers up the Podkamennaya Tunguska (Zachesov 1986:14).

The Lena Basin and the Northeast (see Figure 12.4)

The main regional exports are gold, diamonds and tin, which create only low-volume outbound traffic. The provision of supplies is therefore the main function of transport, and inbound traffic exceeds outbound in the ratio of about 6 to 1 by weight.

Several alternative routes can be used to supply the northeast. From the upstream rail-river port of Osetrovo on the Lena, or the nearby Ust'-Kut oil terminal, river vessels can operate to the seaport of Tiksi, near the Lena delta. Transshipment to seagoing vessels for the trip to the mouths of other rivers is followed by a second transshipment for travel upstream. This is the traditional procedure for deliveries from the south by river. Alternatively, river–sea vessels can now travel the whole route, operating below capacity at present but expected to approach capacity as rivermouth dredging becomes more effective. The same vessels can also distribute freight delivered to northern seaports by ocean-going vessels either from Murmansk and Arkhangel'sk in the west or from Vladivostok and neighboring ports on the Pacific coast. Formerly ocean-going vessels made deliveries to many of the river mouths, but in the exceptionally severe conditions of 1983, several became trapped in ice and one was lost. Since then transshipment has focused on the better-equipped ports of Tiksi and Pevek (Korshunov *et al.* 1987:33). One exception is the extreme northeast: the ports of Anadyr and Provideniya are supplied directly by sea, and river transport on the Anadyr is also operated by Ministry of the Merchant Marine. Finally, some parts of the northeast can be reached by all-weather road, either from Never and Berkakit in the south or from Magadan on the Pacific coast. The roads comprise the only year-round surface link to the outside world: Magadan has operated as a winter port since the early 1960s.

River transport authorities claim that the Lena route is by far the cheapest. It is stated to be 20 to 60 percent cheaper than the Northern Sea Route, depending on circumstances. For example, goods from central European USSR and the Urals to the River Yana cost 48–61 percent less to move by rail to Osetrovo and thence by river-sea vessel, than by rail to Murmansk or Arkhangel'sk and thence by sea and river vessel. Goods from East Siberia and the Soviet Far East to the River Kolyma cost respectively 35 and 20 percent less by the river route than by rail to the Far Eastern ports and thence by sea (Korshunov *et al.* 1987:33).

As might be expected from the costs cited, river transport has been said to account for 85 percent of the tons delivered to the Yakut ASSR and over 90 percent of the deliveries to the northeast (Zachesov 1986:13), though the 1986 plan targets suggested a slightly smaller share. It was intended to deliver 2,200,000 tons of dry goods to Yakutia by rail and river through Osetrovo, 1,750,000 tons of petroleum products by the same route through the Ust'-Kut oil terminal, 600,000 tons by sea and 250,000 tons by road through Berkakit. The main reason for using the road so heavily, and part of the reason for using the Northern Sea Route, was to relieve congestion at Osetrovo. In addition to the physical problems described earlier, and despite an expansion which made it the biggest river port in the eastern

USSR, Osetrovo suffered from congested railway lines and storage areas, poor coordination between railway and river transport and a labor shortage. Only in 1987, for the first time in recent years, did it manage to ship all the traffic offered. That performance is believed to have been repeated in 1988 and probably in 1989, a year of unusually high water levels (Olenev 1986:17; Olenev 1987:28; Osetrovo Port Manager, 1989).

Overlap of modal service areas

River and sea transport are involved in 2 main types of modal overlap. First, both river and ocean-going vessels can reach some of the same ports. On the one hand, ocean-going vessels can penetrate well inland on the Yenisey and the Gulf of Ob', and coasters can reach shorter distances inland on the Khatanga and, in favorable conditions, the Kolyma. On the other hand, river vessels, especially those in the river–sea category, can reach coastal ports. They serve the Ob' and Taz gulfs in northwestern Siberia and much of the northeast coast from the Lena. In 1985, when water levels on the Lena were unusually low, and passage downstream from Osetrovo was interrupted by smoke from forest fires, river–sea vessels even served the northeast coast by travelling along the Northern Sea Route from west of the Taymyr peninsula. They brought in 12,000 tons of oil and 38,000 tons of dry goods which implies 10–17 vessels or trips (Olenev 1986:17; Olenev 1987:28; Osetrovo Port Manager, 1989). However, they are not normally permitted to venture so far from safe harbors. For serving the northeast coast from the mouth of the Lena they have 4 particular advantages over deep-sea transport: the river and coastal navigation seasons open earlier than that for deep-sea shipping; the coastal navigation season is also longer; river–sea vessels can avoid river mouth transshipment more often than deep-sea vessels; and there are more places along the very shallow coast where they can offload onto the shore than is the case for deep-sea vessels.

Second, modal overlap also occurs where river vessels can serve the same regions from both seaports and railway transshipment points. Data cited earlier suggest that very few destinations can be served more cheaply by the former method from points of origin within the Soviet Union.

In recent years river–sea vessels have widened the range of coastal ports which can be served by river transport. Costs, as we have seen, favor river over sea transport. The experience of 1983, as we have also seen, led maritime authorities to abandon some destinations in the Northeast. In areas of direct sea–river overlap, therefore, the balance seems to have swung in favor of river transport. An exception is the movement of ores from Dudinka to the Kola peninsula. The route is far more direct by sea than by river and rail, and the sea route can be kept open all the year, except briefly during spring thaw on the Yenisey.

Despite the comparative costs quoted above, there was an increase from 1984 to 1988 in the amount of freight delivered to the north by sea, for further distribution by river or river–sea vessel. Growing deliveries of gas pipe to northwestern Siberia probably reflect the convenience and economy of direct shipment from foreign ports: pipe from within the Soviet Union still arrives by rail and river. Growing shipments of general cargo to the northeast, on the other hand, seem mainly to have reflected the inability or unwillingness of river transport to handle all the cargo offered at the railway ports in the south (Mikhaylov 1987:5).

There are several reasons for the rivers' failure to move more goods in addition to the physical problems described earlier. The first reason, according to river authorities, is inadequate investment. Siberian rivers are said to account for 40 percent of the revenues of the RSFSR Ministry of the River Fleet but only 8 percent of its investments. The high figure for revenues results partly from high pricing where there is little competition, especially in the Lena basin (Kolesov 1982). Lack of investment makes itself felt primarily in inadequate riverside facilities, the recent upgrading of the port of Osetrovo being apparently an exception. There is also a shortage of specialized shallow-draft vessels for small rivers, referred to above, which has led to the less efficient use of deep-draft vessels partly laden. Part of the inefficiency is in reducing the length of the navigation season (Gerasimov 1988:22-23; Barakin 1986:13; Zachesov 1986:13).

Figure 12.5 A portion of the 72 dockside gantry cranes at the Siberian river port of Osetrovo.

A second reason is shortage of labor, in Siberian river transport in general and at Osetrovo in particular (see Figure 12.5). The Lena Steamship Company, with a total payroll of 22,000, including 9,000 working on its ships, has to bring in 3,000 students and other temporary workers each summer. The port of Osetrovo, through investing heavily in housing, has recently managed to reduce its annual labor turnover from 23 to 12 percent

(Lozhnikova 1987:15; Olenev 1986:17; Lena United Steamship Co., 1989; Osetrovo Port Manager, 1989). In a society short of labor, river transport cannot easily compete.

A third reason for the river's failure to move more goods relates to containerization. By keeping freight in good condition, economizing on labor and speeding transshipment, containerization offers great advantages for transport in the North. In the last 4 years it has probably done more than anything else to relieve congestion at Osetrovo. Unfortunately, containerization has been a mixed blessing. Containers sent to the North frequently stay there to be used for storage. Currently about a third of those dispatched by river from Osetrovo — about 35,000 medium-sized containers — fail to return in the same year. At the end of the 1987 season the Lena Steamship Company owed the East Siberian Railway 63,400 containers. Suppliers of goods for the North consequently send freight in boxcars instead, and congestion returns to Osetrovo. The river authorities' most recent response has been to turn to non-returnable packaging. The port currently packages or puts into containers or onto pallets about 475,000 tons of general freight annually. Another drawback of containers is the expense of equipment for handling them. At a port like Osetrovo it soon pays for itself which is not the case at wharves on minor rivers navigable for a few days a year (Mikhaylov 1987:4–5; Olenev 1988:28).

A final reason concerns reluctance on the part of river transport authorities to give top priority to northern traffic. Short-distance movements of sand and gravel, the staple of river transport throughout the country, are very profitable, giving an average national return of 97.5 percent on a 50-kilometer run. By contrast general cargo, including that in containers, covers on average 60–70 percent of port handling costs. The use of small rivers creates similar problems. The national economy profits by their use, since average costs by road and air transport are respectively 9–12 and 20–22 times as high. But ton-kilometer costs on small rivers range from 3.6 to 5.0 times those on big rivers, so for river transport authorities it is expensive to divert resources from big-river transport. Their performance indices also suffer. Clearly this set of problems should be correctable by price reforms and administrative measures, and indeed the calculation of performance indices has been changed for the current Five-Year Plan (Pronin *et al.* 1987:2-3).

Prospective relations between river and sea transport

The balance of functions between river and sea transport is most evidently in a state of flux in the Lena basin and the Northeast. It was stated before that the share of sea transport in traffic to the Northeast rose from 1984 to 1988 (see Chapter 10). During that time measures were implemented and projected to raise the capacity of river transport, in the anticipation that they would enable it to recapture its share of a growing market. The measures included dredging northern river mouths, introducing more river–sea vessels and drawing up a plan to raise water levels at Osetrovo by building a dam below the port. The plan was drawn up by the river authorities, approved by the USSR Academy of Sciences and submitted to Gosplan. At the same time construction was announced of the railway from Berkakit to Tommot and Yakutsk, to be completed to the former by 1990 and the latter by 1995. Completion to Yakutsk would enable transshipment to take place at a port with more reliable water depths than at Osetrovo, and possibly reduce the role of river transport above Yakutsk (though only a small amount, since the river would still be cheaper), but it would enable river transport to reach the lower Lena and the northeast more quickly and reliably.

Despite all this, measures undertaken by Ministry of the Merchant Marine in the past few years suggest maintenance or even expansion of its role in northern supply. Ports are being improved and the fleet renewed. Multipurpose icebreaking freights of the *Noril'sk* and *Vitus Bering* classes, able to offload onto ice or by helicopter, are facilitating direct deliveries to many more coastal and offshore destinations. Icebreaking barge carriers of the *Aleksey Kosygin* and *Sevmorput* classes have been introduced in an effort to serve the northeastern rivers without transshipment delays despite rivermouth bars. In part, these investments reflect the inadequacy of investment in the past. Facilities at most northern ports are primitive, and the existing fleet is overaged and underequipped for operation in the north. They also reflect the need for deep-sea vessels to service explorations for, and eventually the exploitation of, offshore mineral resources. Logistical support for the military may also be a consideration, and so may the rapidity of growth in demand for general transport to the north, coupled with the fact that improvements to river transport will take several years. Even with all these considerations, however, the Ministry's plans have seemed very ambitious, at least up to 1988. They have even included talk of year-round navigation in the northeast by the end of the century, despite the fact that it could not be achieved with the present generation of icebreakers. They have 75,000 horsepower; Soviet sources suggest that 200,000 horsepower would be needed (see also Chapter 8).

In 1989, however, *perestroika* began to make an impact on the northeastern economy. In the first place traffic started to fall, as northern customers, forced to manage their own finances, became less prodigal in their ordering. In the second place, both customers and shippers began to pay closer attention to transport costs, with the result that traffic by sea fell more than that by river. In June 1989, the latter was expected to be some 130,000 tons short of target by the end of the season. Since the maritime total in 1988 was under a million tons anyway, the prospect of an even larger decrease became a matter of no little concern to the Northern Sea Route operators (Volkov 1987:47; Mikhaylov 1987:5; Orlovich 1986:38; Brown-Humes 1989; Lena United Steamship Co., 1989; Murmansk Shipping Co., 1989).

The new generation of deep-sea vessels seems unlikely to lower costs on the Northern Sea Route to levels competitive with river transport. In fact, arctic shipping costs have been rising — by 14 percent in the 11 Five-Year-Plan period alone. The *Noril'sk* class vessels have proved to be much less economical than expected, and the big icebreaking barge-carriers virtual white elephants (Zaika and Batskikh 1987:14-15; Lena United Steamship Co., 1989). They are deep draught and often have to anchor well offshore which makes for a dangerous passage to the coast or river mouth for their small barges. They are difficult to keep on station in rough weather which can delay or endanger the barge-handling process. And they were designed without consultation with the river transport authorities, so that their barges are incompatible with river transport equipment and indeed are too deep draught to cross some of the river bars. A typical complaint concerns a trip by the *Aleksey Kosygin* to Cape Schmidt in 1988. Far from being able to operate independently of icebreakers, it apparently required the assistance of 2 nuclear-powered and 3 diesel icebreakers, with the result that all other traffic in the region 'ground to a standstill for 7 days' (*Soviet Shipping*, 1989:7).

To add to the inherent problems of the new maritime technology, it appears that river transport could easily become even more competitive. River–sea transport costs could probably be lowered further by a shift from self-propelled freighters to integrated tug-barge combinations. The latter have been successful in reducing crew and machinery idle time in Western Europe and North America, and they should prove at least as useful in Soviet conditions, since long delays at ports are common. At the same time it should be pointed out that two of the principal measures intended to improve access to the northeast by river, namely the dam below Osetrovo and the railway to Yakutsk, are both meeting stiff opposition. The former is opposed by environmentalists and even some river transport specialists, the latter by the railways, who want no part of what they see as a money-losing proposition, and many Yakuts, who feel that too many southerners are encouraged to move to their republic as it is. Financing for the railway has been cut off 15 times so far (Basin 1989:1).

On balance, long-term prospects for sea transport do not look promising in those parts of the northeast which can be served by river transport. For the short term, the maritime authorities have switched the icebreaking barge-carriers to non-Arctic work, and the project for an icebreaker capable of keeping northeastern routes open all the year seems to have been shelved until at least the end of the century. In the longer term, a major shift in relative advantages is likely to come only if traffic volumes grow so much that all-year transport becomes essential. River transport cannot achieve year-round navigation in the northeast with present technology, but sea transport can, albeit at very high cost. It is primarily the cost of year-round navigation (though secondarily the relative lack of direct high-volume routes) which differentiates the northeast from northwestern Siberia. Even in the northwest, one suspects that the costs of keeping the Dudinka–Kola peninsula route open all year have contributed to the overall rise in arctic maritime transport costs, cited above.

This analysis has treated river and sea transport, and for that matter sea and rail transport, as competitive and even antagonistic modes. Such a characterization reasonably reflects the national situation. The various transport ministries have competed more than they have cooperated, despite official claims to have created a unified transport system.

Ministerial attitudes have been natural, given the type of performance indices by which they are judged, the sources from which they can draw lobbying power and the constant shortage of resources, which may prevent smooth intermodal co-operation except at some sacrifice to a ministry's internal operations. But in the North the various modes compete directly only to a limited extent, and some co-operation has always been necessary. Improved co-operation is likely to result from the Gorbachev administration's enhanced concern for efficiency. In particular, modular construction techniques are being adopted to save labor costs in the north. Modules can weigh several hundred tons, and their dimensions are too big for rail transport. Delivery most often requires close coordination of sea, river and overland (for example air-cushion) transport.

Conclusion

In the Soviet Arctic the future of sea transport is closely linked with that of river transport. West of the Taymyr peninsula, year-round navigation and favorably located freight origins and destinations have enhanced the role of sea transport. East of the peninsula, its role in the short and medium terms will depend on its ability to reach areas inaccessible to river transport, and, if the current decline in traffic for the northeast should prove to be temporary, on the capacity of river transport to move freight north from the railways. In the long term much may depend on the interplay of three factors: national resource policies; technological advances; and prestige. If the current national drive for economic efficiency is pursued to logical ends, some northern resource exploitation may be abandoned in favor of imports, or perhaps joint projects in developing countries. As far as technology is concerned, submarine freighters or semi-submersibles could shift the balance of advantages from river to sea transport. So too, less decisively but more immediately, could the adoption of techniques used by the Canadian icebreaking freighter, the *MV Arctic*. It uses navigational aids more sophisticated than those used on the *Noril'sk* class vessels, to locate ice-free channels and avoid having to force its way through ice or use the help of icebreakers to the extent that they do. Finally, it seems likely that arctic sea transport has been able to secure heavy investments partly because it carries more prestige and lobbying power than river transport. Will the drive for economic efficiency negate such considerations, or will the allocation of investments continue to reflect Soviet determination to be recognized internationally as master of the arctic seas?

References

Barakin, A. 1986. 'Bol'shiye problemy malykh rek' [Big problems on small rivers]. *Rechnoy transport* 9:13-14.

Basin, Ye. 1989. 'Perestroika — vremya deystviya' [Restructuring — a time of action]. *Pravda* 1 November:1-2.

Brown-Humes, C. 1989. 'Soviet shipping. Special report.' *Lloyd's List*. 13 September:6-17.

Gerasimov, B. 1988. 'Razvivat' tekhnicheskuyu bazu na malykh rekakh Sibiri' [Develop technical resources on the small rivers of Siberia]. *Rechnoy transport* 8:22-23.

Gor'kov, N. 1988. 'Navigatsiya nyneshnego goda' [This year's navigation]. *Vodnyy transport* 28 April:1.

Ivanov, V. 1986. 'Na linii Leningrad — Dudinka' [On the Leningrad — Dudinka run]. *Rechnoy transport* 10:7.

Kocherga, I., and R. Purtov. 1986. 'Osvaivayetsya novyy rayon perevalki trub' [Pipe transshipment is being developed in a new region]. *Rechnoy transport* 3:19.

Kolesov, L.I. 1982. *Mezhotraslevyye problemy razvitiya transportnoy sistemy Sibiri i Dal'nego Vostoka* [Interbranch problems of the development of the transport system of Siberia and the Far East]. Novosibirsk:Nauka.

Komolov, I. 1986. 'Po puti ratsionalizatsii perevozok, [Rationalising freight shipments]. *Rechnoy transport* 10:10.

Korshunov, S., A. Kazakova, and Ye. Gagarina. 1987. 'Razvivat' Arkticheskiye perevozki' [To develop arctic shipments]. *Rechnoy transport* 3:33.

Lena United Steamship Company. 1989. personal interview, June.

Lozhnikova, L. 1987. 'Yedinstvo flota i berega' [Unity of the fleet and riverbank]. *Rechnoy transport* 1:14-16.

Mikhaylov, V. 1987. 'Zadacha slozhnaya i vazhnaya. O tom, kak uluchshit zavoz gruzov na krayniy Sever' [A complex and important task. How to improve the delivery of goods to the Far North]. *Rechnoy transport* 1:4-5.

Murmansk Shipping Company. 1989. personal interview, October.

Narodnoye khozyaystvo RSFSR v 1985 godu: Statisticheskiy yezhegodnik [Economy of the RSFSR in 1985. Statistical Annual]. 1986. Moscow:Finansy i Statistika.

Nikol'skiy, I.V., V.I. Tonyayev and V.G. Krasheninnikov. 1975. *Geografiya vodnogo transporta SSSR* [Geography of Water Transport of the USSR]. Moscow:Transport.

Olenev, P. 1986. 'Zalog uspekha — v slazhennoy rabote smezhnikov' [The guarantee of success is neighbors working together in harmony]. *Rechnoy transport* 3:17.

— 1987. 'Dostavka gruzov na Krayniy Sever' [Delivering freight to the Far North]. *Rechnoy transport* 4:28-29.

— 1988. 'Problemy zavoza gruzov na Krayniy Sever' [Problems of delivering freight to the Far North]. *Rechnoy transport* 4:27-28.

Orlovich, K. 1986. 'Perspektivy razvitiya' [Prospects for development]. *Rechnoy transport* 6:38-40.

Osetrovo Port Manager. 1989. personal interview, June.

Ovchinnikov, Ye. 1986. 'Bol'shegruznyye tolkayemyye sostavy' [Heavyweight pushed barge trains]. *Rechnoy transport* 3:10.

Pronin, V., S. P'yanykh, and V. Levitin. 1987. 'Pervyye itogi i uroki khozyaystvennoy perestroyki' [First results and lessons of economic restructuring]. *Rechnoy transport* 1:2-3.

Rechnoy transport. 1986a. 'Pyatiletka rechnikov Rossii' [Russian river-transport workers' Five-Year plan]. 10:2-3.

— 1986b. 'Shagi pyatiletki' [The Five-Year plan marches on]. 5:6.

— 1987. 'Pyatiletka: god vtoroy' [Five-Year plan: second year]. 2:2.

Soviet Shipping. 1989. 1:7.

Tonyayev, V.I. 1977. *Geografiya vnutrennikh vodnykh putey SSSR* [Geography of Inland Waterways of the USSR]. Moscow: Transport.

Vinogradova, N. 1986a. 'Port v Zapolyar'ye' [A port beyond the Arctic Circle]. *Rechnoy transport* 4:39.

— 1986b. 'Dlya promyslov Yamburga' [For the Yamburg drilling-sites]. *Rechnoy transport* 12:3-6.

Vodnyy transport. 1988. 'Nyneshnyaya vesna rechnikov' [This spring with the river transport workers]. 14 April:1.

Vol'fson, P. 1986. 'Soblyudat' interesy vsekh vodopol'zovateley' [Take account of the interests of all water users]. *Rechnoy transport* 10:41.

Volkov, V. 1987. 'Doroga v Yakutiyu' [Line to Yakutia]. *Zheleznodorozhnyy transport* 2:46-52.

Vorob'yev, Yu. 1986. 'Dlya sudokhodstva na Aldane' [For navigation on the Aldan]. *Rechnoy transport* 8:42.

Zachesov, B. 1986. 'Zadachi razvitiya perevozok na Kraynem Severe' [Tasks in the development of traffic in the Far North]. *Rechnoy transport* 3:13-14.

Zaika, B., and Yu. Batskikh. 1987. 'Problemy gruzoperevozok Arktike' [Freight shipment problems in the Arctic]. *Morskoy flot* 5:13-15.

Part IV
Legal and geopolitical perspectives

13

The geostrategic conditions of deterrence in the Barents Sea

Willy Østreng

Of the 4 Soviet Naval fleets, the Northern Fleet based on the Kola peninsula ranks second to none with regard to strategic retaliatory capability. This Fleet makes use of 66 percent of the Republic's total number of nuclear-ballistic-missile submarines (SSBNs) (42/63), 67 percent of its submarine-launched ballistic missiles (SLBMs) (624/928), 76 percent of its warheads (2,208/2,896) and 73 percent of the mega-tonnage disposed to each fleet (818/1,114) (Ries 1986:61–2, 64).

Great emphasis on anti-submarine warfare (ASW) is another characteristic feature of this Fleet. About 70 percent of the USSR's ASW Kresta-II cruisers and 75 percent of the ASW attack submarines, the *Alfa*, *Tango* and *Victor* classes, are all based on Kola. This is valid also for the ASW-aircraft carrier *Kiev* and the combatants of *Kirov*, *Udaloy* and *Krivak* classes. Of the *Alfa* submarines — the fastest and deepest diving of any attack submarine ever built — 100 percent are based in the North (see Figure 13.1).

Thus, by the mere fact of geography, the Barents Sea is bound to serve the *strategic* as well as *defensive* purposes of uppermost importance to the Soviet Union.

It is commonly believed in the West that the Northern Fleet has 4 distinct and partly integrated military objectives related specifically to the Barents Sea:

Figure 13.1 Soviet *Alfa* class nuclear attack submarine, the fastest and deepest diving sub ever built (U.S. Naval Institute).

1. the *Delta* and *Typhoon* class submarine are supposed to take station in these waters for strategic purposes;
2. ASW forces are supposed to protect the transit routes within the Barents Sea so that the SSBNs have safe access to any extended arctic station;
3. ASW forces are supposed to defend the station area from ASW attacks; and
4. ASW forces, among others, are supposed to protect and defend the highly concentrated bases on the Kola peninsula.

Objective 1 is primarily an *offensive* one, aiming at deterring any attacks on Soviet sites of interest, while objectives 2, 3 and 4 are *defensive*, aiming at preserving the survivability of the SSBNs to the fulfillment of objective 1. In this way the 4 objectives are both compatible and interdependent. If, however, we take a closer look at the military requirements under which each objective has to be taken care of in times of war, certain incompatibilities appear, making Western assumptions more questionable.

Military forces assigned the task of defending and protecting vital elements of war-fighting, such as the Kola bases, will not approve of any restrictions in their performance of the assignment. Restrictions increase the likelihood of failure. ASW forces play a dominant role in the defense of the Kola bases and the protection of the transit routes within the Barents Sea. These forces, however, usually have to impose operational restrictions in or near a SSBN-station area. Normally they are not given permission to attack submarine contacts in a station area designated 'own SSBNs', to avoid mistakes and hence attacks on one's own submarines. Thus, if the defensive and offensive tasks of the Northern Fleet are to be executed in the same waters, there is an inherent contradiction between the military requirements of these objectives: the execution of the defensive tasks will be to the detriment of the offensive ones, and vice versa.

The purpose of this chapter is to discuss these contradictions and how the Soviets may cope with them, in view of the natural and strategic challenges facing the Northern Fleet in these waters.

The Barents Sea as a SSBN station area

The Barents Sea is limited for the purposes of this chapter to the area south of straight lines drawn from the northern tip of Northeast Land via the southern tip of Franz Josef Land to the northern tip of Novaya Zemlya. It is limited by Novaya Zemlya in the east and the 500-meter contour line from the South Cape to the North Cape. The Barents Sea, based on these borders, is then 1,196,437 square kilometers in area. These limitations have

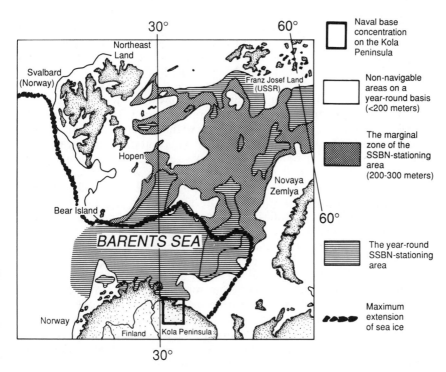

Figure 13.2 Potential year-round stationing area for Soviet submarines in the Barents Sea.

been introduced because this is the area in which the Norwegian Polar Institute has the most reliable data on depth measurements. A more correct definition might be to limit the Barents Sea either to the Egga-edge or to the continental shelf margin; the Barents Sea then would measure about 1,400,000 square kilometers. All percentages and calculations of area — ice depths, etc. — are based on our delimitation of the Barents Sea.

In 1981 the Pentagon, through its yearly publication *Soviet Military Power*, identified the Barents Sea (see Figure 13.2) as the one and only arctic station area (US Department of Defense, 1981:84–5). Three years later the same source expanded the area to include, apart from the Barents Sea, the East Greenland Sea and the area north of the Greenland–Iceland–United Kingdom (GIUK) gap (US Department of Defense, 1984:114–15). Simultaneously with this geographic expansion came another: American naval authorities in Washington acknowledged that the Soviet SSBNs show great interest in operating under the ice of the Arctic Ocean, particularly in the marginal ice zone (Polmar 1984:121–3). Thus, in the course of a few years the arctic station was enlarged by millions of square kilometers, making the Barents Sea a minor region. However, this growth increased, rather than decreased, the strategic significance of the Barents Sea in the minds of most Western naval analysts. Apart from being an assumed missile-launching area, these waters, by the mere fact of location, had become a transit link between the Kola bases and the extended station area. As such, the Barents Sea met more obligations in Soviet naval strategic planning than had any other part of the arctic station. This point becomes particularly important in view of US maritime strategy, which involves fighting the Soviet Navy in its own waters in the opening phase of a war.

The Barents Sea offers both advantages and disadvantages as a station area (see Figure 13.2). The advantages are obvious. First, the distance is short between home base and the operational area. In the early 1970s, Soviet SSBNs spent as much as two-thirds of their operational time at sea in transit between base and station, between Kola and the station area off the East Coast of the United States. Today, base and station are assumed to be virtually identical. Second, the station lies in an area where the Soviet Union has military control, both at sea and in the air. This provides the best conceivable protection for SSBNs. Because sonar range is drastically reduced to only a few nautical miles in shallow coastal waters, advancing Western SSNs will have great problems tracing Soviet SSBNs. In this connection it must be added that Soviet submarines operate under the same sonar conditions as the attacker. Soviet forces, therefore, will have great problems discovering and tracking down submerged attackers trying to sneak into the area. In this way Soviet counterattacks are rendered more difficult. What is publicly known from the integrated submarine tracking program, Operation Holystone, strongly suggests that US SSNs have for a long time been able to operate virtually undetected in the most protected Soviet waters, such as the harbor of Vladivostock and the mouth of the White Sea (Ball 1985-6:3–31). Occasionally, during this program, US submarines had minor collisions with their Soviet counterparts and '...in each case the Soviets appear to have been ignorant of the presence of the

USN SSNs, and unable, after the collision, to track the departing Western subs' (Ries 1986:61–2, 64). What these sub-surface intrusions and collisions suggest is that detection is complicated in shallow waters, both for defender and attacker. It is a fact, however, that it is easier to hide an SSBN than to find it; SSBNs are defensive in their self-protective role and will have to retreat to, and operate in, waters which give them protection. They can also lie quiet on the bottom and reduce their own engine and reactor noise. In this position they are almost impossible to find. The ice and ice edge can also complicate detection; in the transit area between the ice and open water there is a lot of noise in which an SSBN can 'hide' its self-generated noise (Østreng 1987). The noise conditions in the Barents Sea are also of great importance in this context. Fishing activity, oil and gas exploration, the local shipping trade, seismic research on land and in the sea, animal life in the sea — all create background noise which complicates detection by passive sonar (Bergesen *et al.* 1987).

This renders the Barents Sea a favorable and suitable station area. However, the Barents Sea is not without disadvantages. For instance, the United States will have longer warning time for missiles launched from the Barents Sea than from the area off the United States' East Coast. Moreover, ice and depth conditions represent serious impediments to SSBN operations in these waters.

Ice, depths and SSBNs

In the Barents Sea, winter conditions present the most severe challenges to SSBN navigation. From January until May as much as 56 percent of the Barents Sea is covered with ice, consisting of ice floes, ice ridges and icebergs (Vinje 1985). The biggest icebergs extend more than 100 meters down from the surface, while the largest ice floes may have keels approaching 50 meters of depth (Elverhoy and Solheim 1983). Since the Barents Sea has an average depth of just 230 meters, the submarine commanders are faced with 2 crucial questions:

1. What depth does the submarine need for optimal and safe maneuvers in a shallow coastal station area? and
2. How much room does it need to navigate between the ice and the bottom, both while in station and in transit from one area to another?

It is not possible to give an exact, universally valid depth in which a SSBN can maneuver in a station area. The depth depends on a series of local conditions to be evaluated in each individual case. This does not mean, however, that there is no rule of thumb. Based on their general experience, Norwegian submarine captains have found this depth to be around 200 meters (Berg 1984:11). Independent Canadian estimates generally confirm this suggestion, calculating the necessary depth to be around 180–190 meters (Critchley 1986).

If we take 200 meters as the depth necessary to maneuver SSBNs sufficiently for them to fulfill their functions in the station area, then about 33 percent of the Barents Sea (approximately 395,000 square kilometers) cannot be used for such purposes on a year-round basis. The space between the ice and the bottom will be too narrow. These areas can be found in the northwestern corner of the Barents Sea, from Northeast Land in the north and southward past Bear Island; depths here are less than 100 meters for a continuous stretch. Since this is where the greatest concentrations and most frequent occurrences of icebergs and pack ice are located, this area is unsuitable as a year-round station area; this is also the part of the Barents Sea in which one finds deep furrows in the sea bottom caused by icebergs in as much as 100 meters of depth. Nor does the area meet the requirements for operational depth in summer.

The other large area of the bottom where depths are less than 200 meters can be found in the east, along the coast of Novaya Zemlya. This leaves an area in the central Barents Sea of about 800,000 square kilometers which has depths between 200 and 500 meters. But this entire area does not meet the demands for full maneuverability; about 63 percent of the area (506,000 square kilometers) has depths between 200 and 300 meters. This implies that SSBNs have to face unfavorable operational conditions in large parts of these areas; between 30°E and 60°E longitude deep, protruding icebergs are not uncommon, posing safety problems in the winter.

In this context, the size of the submarines is important. Width, length and weight are stated in most of the sources which give information on Soviet submarines (as in US Department of Defense, 1981; 1984). The height from the keel to the highest point of the tower is, however, not to be found in these same sources. Both civilian and military Norwegian naval experts have been consulted but are unable to provide exact specifications. However, from pictures and drawings of the boat we have tried to calculate the height based on the figures for length and width. These approximate calculations indicate a height of between 25 and 30 meters. These calculations were later presented to the same experts, who found that they gave a realistic estimate. Therefore, the height of 28 meters has been chosen. Similarly, the height of the *Delta* class is estimated to be around 21 meters. *Delta* submarines are between 140 and 150 meters long, while the *Typhoons* (see Figure 13.3) measure 170 meters. That is to say, both are much longer than a soccer field (110 meters). The *Typhoon* is, in fact, as tall as a 10–12 storey building.

It is obvious that these large vessels need considerable space to maneuver, both in the horizontal and vertical plane. From the end of the 1950s, there have been reports of submarines that have sailed into hollows in the shelf without any outlet to the deep sea and have had difficulty getting out because of ice conditions above the ship — the so-called 'valley of death' problem. Similar seabed conditions can also be found in the area between Northeast Land and Franz Josef Land where there is also a high frequency of icebergs. Clearly, ice conditions can, in such cases, be a question of life or death. One does not take unnecessary risks in a station area. It is only with a depth of 300 meters or more that there is the necessary operational space between the ice and the bottom and, horizontally, between deeply protruding icebergs.

Figure 13.3 Soviet *Typhoon* class nuclear ballistic missile submarine (U.S. Naval Institute).

Only 25 percent of the Barents Sea (approximately 294,000 square kilometers) has depths of over 300 meters or more. The area under the ice meeting this depth requirement in winter is equivalent to about 163,000 square kilometers. This area is not contiguous but is made up of separate deep hollows connected with depths of 200 meters or more. This continuous stretch of 200 meters' depth may be termed the stationing area's *marginal operational zone*, that is, one can operate freely there in the summer but must impose limitations in the winter. The Northern Fleet, thus, cannot count on being able to use this area throughout the year on a complete and unlimited basis. The remaining 131,000 square kilometers, with sufficient depths under the ice and direct access from the ice-free area, are to be found in the southern and central part of the Barents Sea which is estimated at around 150,000 square kilometers. Depths here are 200 – 300 meters. The total extent of an all-year stationing area where maneuvers can be performed safely will be around 281,000 square kilometers. The question is: how many SSBNs can operate in this expanse of sea?

The problem of the size of each vessel's maneuver space is complex. It depends on many factors such as the natural characteristics of the region, the submarine's qualities, the range of weapons, sensor capacity etc. A highly competent submarine authority in Norway estimates that each vessel, at a minimum, will need an operational radius in the horizontal plane of 50 times 100 nautical miles – 100 times 100 nautical miles or approximately 17,000 – 34,000 square kilometers (Skarlo 1987). This will provide sufficient space for a total of 8 – 16 SSBNs. Today the Soviet Union has 26 modern SSBNs stationed in the North – 22 *Deltas* and 4 *Typhoons*. Theoretically, 30 to 60 percent of the SSBN fleet can find a station in the Barents Sea.

This kind of conclusion is only of theoretical interest. In reality the Soviet Union will neither be able nor wish to place so many submarines in such a limited sea area for many reasons. First of all, it should be noted that this calculation does not take into account the ocean space being occupied by civilian interest groups. For instance, extensive fishing for cod and haddock with longline and trawl goes on year-round in the fairway of the Northern Fleet. In recent years, incidents where submarines have been caught in trawls have occurred several times in the Barents Sea. In peacetime, a certain competition for available space can occur. This would hardly be the case in wartime when fishing would simply have to adjust to military requirements. Oil rigs, however, cannot be removed so easily in a war situation. They can be blown up, but this means risking serious blow-outs, which in turn might interfere with war operations. If left behind, oil rigs would occupy space in competition with battleships, both surface and subsurface. So far the presence of oil rigs has been restricted to the summer season, but in the immediate future the entire area between the Norwegian mainland and Bear Island is to be opened up for oil exploration (see Figure 13.4). This implies that a substantial part of the station area on the Norwegian side will be affected by activities that, in the long run, may lead to oil development. The Soviets seem equally determined to produce oil and gas on their part of the Barents shelf. So far they have drilled 20 wells, most of which are located in the eastern and southeastern part of the Barents Sea.

The petroleum activities going on at Murmansk High and Severo-Kildinskaya may already have caused problems to submarine operations (Bergesen *et al.* 1987). The same applies to the recent gigantic find of oil condensate at Shtokmanovskaya and for the 2 oil strikes made north of the island of Kolguyev, at 50 meters of depth, and north of Shtokmanovskaya oil at 300 meters of depth, close to the ice edge. Most rigs placed in the ice-free areas will contribute to the shrinking of the space available for SSBNs.

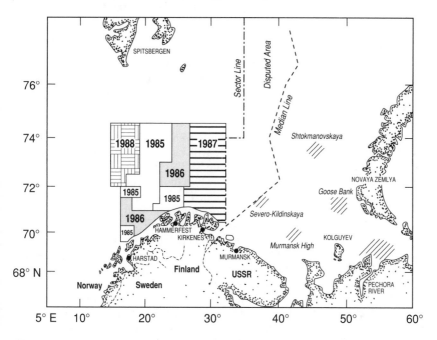

Figure 13.4 Norwegian hydrocarbon exploration areas in the Barents Sea.

Moreover, the calculation does not take account of the 95 Kola-based SSNs, which either need space for transit or for accomplishing their regional defense tasks of protecting the Kola bases and the internal transit routes. These regional tasks hold the highest priority and will be attended to both outside and inside the Barents Sea, but the zone of combat would comprise all waters necessary to secure success, including the station area and its marginal zone. The attackers will have to be fought where they are, not where the defender would like them to be. The safest area in which to operate, from the point of view of an attacking SSN assigned to bomb the Kola bases, would be the station area itself where Soviet ASW forces most probably have imposed operational restrictions. Thus, the only restrictions Soviet ASW forces will encounter are shore and harbor lines, not any invisible lines delineating a station area from the rest of the sea. If this reasoning proves incorrect, however, the mingling of Soviet SSBNs and

SSNs to these confined waters will create a 'strategic traffic jam' serving no other purpose than to cripple the combat potential of all the vessels.

The part of the SSBN fleet which lies in port is also of interest in this context. It must be assumed that some of these vessels can be readied relatively quickly if the need should arise; in a war situation one would wish to get them out and away from the main bases as swiftly as possible, to avoid being put out of the running in the opening phase of hostilities. Only an intact fleet can be used for the purposes ascribed to it by the former US Chief of Naval Operations, Admiral James D. Watkins: '[the Soviets] keep their [SSBN] forces under the ice...to keep them as a viable force which after a nuclear exchange [would become] a key bargaining tool' (Ulsamer 1983:89). The Soviet Union has 85 percent of this fleet in port at any given time. If this part of the fleet is to play the role assigned to it by Admiral Watkins, it must come free of the harbors, which will be high-priority bomb targets in the early phase of a war. The Barents Sea is the closest and most natural recipient for the SSBNs of the Northern Fleet. If this stationing area is already filled with SSBNs, and eventually SSNs in operation, there will be less operational space, and the result will be further traffic chaos. It is, therefore, reasonable to assume that the SSBNs in operation first of all will leave the Barents Sea and station themselves in the area north of the GIUK gap and under the ice in the Arctic Ocean. The Barents Sea is thus primarily to be considered *a crisis and reserve stationing area* for the port-based part of the SSBN fleet. This is not to say that the port-based SSBNs would prefer to stay in the Barents Sea after having escaped the base. The assumption is rather that if the port-based SSBNs have neither the time nor the possibility of exiting to other areas, and hostilities are on the verge of nuclear exchange, the Barents Sea may be the only option for missile launching. In situations leaving the Soviets with more than one option, the likelihood is that the SSBNs will exit, both to give room for the port-based SSBNs and to avoid a concentration of vessels that would give the enemy a possibility of concentrating ASW forces for a collective effort in a limited area.

On this basis, the most preferred station area for the new generations of Kola-based SSBNs would appear outside rather than inside the Barents Sea, both in times of peace, tension, crises and war. The primary SSBN assignment of the Barents Sea appears to be that of transit. This raises the question of what impact ice and depth conditions may have on strategic transits from base to the extended station area.

Transit conditions and possibilities in the Barents Sea

SSBNs need less space between the bottom and ice when in transit than when stationed. This was clearly shown in the period 1957–62, when the American Pacific and Atlantic Fleet carried out protracted operations under the ice in very shallow waters. In January 1960 — the year's worst ice conditions — the USS *Sargo* sailed in a submerged position through the shallow and ice-covered Bering Strait and into the Arctic Ocean; for 31 days it sailed a distance of 6,000 kilometers in the Bering Sea and the Chukchi

Sea, which has an average depth of 80 meters. In some places the boat was only 7 meters above the bottom to avoid top collision with the ice (Lyon 1963). Navigation with such small margins naturally assumes adapting the speed accordingly: the average speed of the *Sargo* was only 4 knots. If the speed is increased, the room for maneuver must also be increased.

From the American experience in this period, we can make a rough estimate of the absolute minimal depth that the *Delta* and the *Typhoon* need for transit trips. Clearance between seabed and keel normally should not be less than 10 meters; the height of a *Typhoon* from the keel to the highest point of the tower is estimated at about 28 meters; clearance between the submarine tower and the keel of surface vessels or ice ridges is estimated at about 15 meters and the keels of boats or of ice ridges, on average, protrude another 15 meters under the surface. In total, this results in a minimum depth of 68 meters. We can assume that the crew will find this minimum depth scarcely comfortable, if they have to navigate with such limited margins for a long time and especially if speed has to be increased. Preferred depth is hard to estimate, but we can safely add on about 30 meters so that a relatively comfortable transit depth for the large SSBNs is about 100 meters.

In this sum, no allowance has been made for icebergs. This is because SSBNs, for reasons discussed previously, need to avoid areas with a high frequency of icebergs and shallow regions. This means that SSBN transits in the shallow areas between Spitsbergen, Hopen and Bear Island would be very risky and are almost irresponsible in the period from January to May–June. The safest transit route on a year-round basis is between Bear

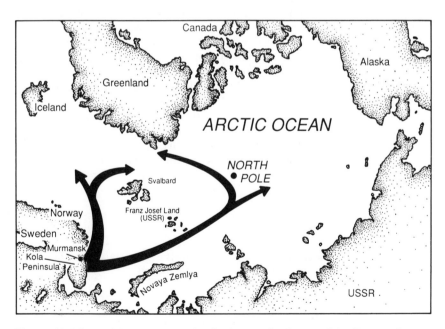

Figure 13.5 Potential transit routes by Soviet naval units out of the Barents Sea.

Island and northern Norway. From there on the vessels can choose between stationing in the Norwegian Sea or continuing northwards through the Fram Strait and into the Arctic Ocean. Similarly, the sailing depths from Kola and northeastward towards the outlet of the Arctic Ocean between Franz Josef Land and Novaya Zemlya offer sufficient transit depths. Even if the frequency of icebergs here can be great, depths are sufficient to ensure a sailing room of 100 meters. In the 1950s 3 approaches to the Arctic Ocean were described in the Soviet press: between Svalbard and Greenland; between Svalbard and Franz Josef Land; and between Franz Josef Land and Novaya Zemlya (see Figure 13.5) (Østreng 1978:139–41).

In the late 1950s and early 1960s, SSNs were so small that it was possible to transit between Svalbard and Franz Josef Land without too much risk. The smallest can probably still do so. However, it is very doubtful that large SSBNs can copy such voyages today on a regular basis. This is primarily due to the seabed being quite hilly so that a submarine must weave in and out of twisted valley formations, at the same time avoiding a high frequency of icebergs. In this area submarines can get caught between the ice and the valleys—the 'valley of death' problem.

The safe transit routes are thus between Bear Island and northern Norway and between Franz Josef Land and Novaya Zemlya (see Figure 13.5). These transit routes are vital for the Northern Fleet to protect in order to maintain its strategic deterrent effect.

In this context, the ice and depths contribute to channelling transits out of the Barents Sea, thus implying that the enemy can group and gather his ASW-forces and counter offensives around the outlets (that is in the northern reaches of the Norwegian Sea and on the edge of the Arctic Ocean). Similarly, the SSN-forces of the Northern Fleet will try to counter this gathering of force in the same area and will serve as 'gate-keepers' to the Barents Sea. To reduce the concentration of force at these gates, they will have to meet Western ASW-forces as far south in the Norwegian Sea and north in the Arctic Ocean as possible. In this way they will protect both the transit routes out of and within the Barents Sea by deployment in depth.

The conclusion to be drawn is that SSBN transits in the Barents Sea are feasible on a year-round basis. Ice and depth conditions, however, force the SSBNs to choose routes that are easy to identify and consequently leave the Soviets with the challenge of coping with enemy ASW counter-measures at the outlets.

Conclusion

The 2 reasons most frequently cited for the Soviets to station their submarines beneath the ice of the Arctic Ocean are:

1. the maritime strategy of the United States; and
2. US ASW tracking and destruction capability, specifically in the Barents Sea.

According to this school of thought, Soviet naval strategic analysis shows a US determination and intention to fight the Soviets in their most protected inner waters and, as a result of the lessons learned from Operation Holystone, shows US capabilities to do so through undetected submerged intrusions:

> For the VMF (Voyenno-Morskoj Flot or translated, Soviet Navy) the message is clearly that deployment of SSBNs to waters where the surface and airspace can be secured is not enough. They also have to go someplace where sophisticated Western ASW technology will have trouble tracking them. Such an area appears to exist in the Arctic under-ice waters, and it is significant that all modern Soviet SSBNs appear to be specially constructed for under-ice operations [Ries 1986:61–2, 64].

There are no reasons to doubt that these aspects of US war-fighting plans and capabilities add to a Soviet desire to practice a rear-deployment strategy for its SSBNs in the Arctic Ocean. Among other things, the entering-into-service in the early 1990s of the new US attack submarine, SSN-21, specifically designed for arctic conditions, might enhance US capabilities and fuel Soviet desires in this respect.

As of now, however, the case still seems to be that it is easier to hide than to find a SSBN in its self-protective role. Most experts tend to agree that the West has a long way to go before undetected SSN intrusions into shallow coastal waters, such as the Barents Sea, will equal potential SSBN destructions in such a war that the Soviets would need to fear for their retaliatory capability. The detection and tracking lessons learned in Norwegian and Swedish waters during the 1980s suggest instead that the state of ASW art in coastal areas is poorly developed and that no revolutionary breakthroughs are anticipated for the years to come. On these grounds, the most compelling reason to establish a Soviet SSBN station in the central Arctic Ocean is not to overcome the threats of US naval strategy and ASW capabilities in the Barents Sea but to resolve the inherent contradictions of military requirements between the assumed defensive and offensive objectives of the Northern Fleet in the confined waters of the Barents. This implies that the Barents Sea is primarily designated a defense zone where the Northern Fleet has been assigned the tasks of defending and protecting the Kola bases, the internal transit routes and the extended SSBN station. The offensive task of strategic deterrence is taken care of in the ice-covered waters of the Arctic Ocean and in the area north of the GIUK gap. These waters are large enough in aerial extension to host both SSBNs and SSNs without interference in their respective assigned missions. By this scheme of geographical separation between the 4 objectives, all assignments can be accomplished in an optimal manner.

References

Ball, D. 1985-86. 'Nuclear war at sea.' *International Security* 10(3):3-31.
Berg, J. 1984. *Noerbilde av Sovjets ubater* [Close-up Pictures of Soviet Submarines], 11. Oslo:Sem og Stenersen A/S.

Bergesen, H.O., A. Moe, and W. Østreng. 1987. *Soviet Oil and Security Interests in the Barents Sea*, Chapter 3. London: Francis Pinter.

Critchley, H. 1986. 'Canadian security policy in the Arctic. The context for the future.' (Mimeographed copy provided to the author.)

Elverhoy, A., and A. Solheim. 1983. 'The physical environment western Barents Sea. Sheet A: Surface sediment distribution.' *In: Norsk Polarinstitutt Skrifter* no. 179A, Oslo.

Lyon, W. 1963. 'The submarine and the Arctic Ocean.' *Polar Record* 11(75):699-705.

Østreng, W. 1978. *Polhavet i internasjonal politikk* [The Arctic Ocean in International Politics], 139-141. Lysaker:Fridtjof Nansen Institute Publication Series.

— 1987. *The Soviet Union in Arctic Waters. Security Implications for the Northern Flank of NATO*, Chapter 4, Occasional Paper No. 36. Honolulu:The Law of the Sea Institute, University of Hawaii.

Polmar, N. 1984. 'Sailing under the ice.' *US Naval Institute Proceedings* June:121-3.

Ries, T. 1986. *The Soviet Military Operational Command Structure and Its Application to Fenno Scandia*, 61-62, 64. Oslo:Norwegian Institute of International Affairs (NUPI).

Skarlo, R. 1987. Personal communication.

Ulsamer, E. 1983. 'Bobbing, weaving and fighting smart. The US Navy looks to new systems and to new concepts to maintain its maritime edge.' *Air Force Magazine* August:89.

US Department of Defense. 1981. *Soviet Military Power*, 84-85. Washington, DC: US Department of Defense.

— 1984. *Soviet Military Power*, 114-5. Washington, DC:US Department of Defense.

Vinje, T. 1985. 'The physical environment western Barents Sea. Sheet C: Sea ice distribution 1971-80.' *In: Norsk Polarinstitutt Skrifter* no. 179C,Oslo.

14

The legal regime of Soviet Arctic marine areas

William E. Butler

The legal regime of the waters north of the Soviet coastline between Norway and the Bering Strait has been consolidated and altered significantly since the Soviet government took the decision in late 1982 to sign the United Nations Convention on the Law of the Sea (1982 LOS) (United Nations, 1983). The consolidation takes the form chiefly of legislation giving effect to the 1982 LOS. The alterations reflect both changes or clarifications introduced into the Law of the Sea pursuant to the consensus reflected in the Convention and of certain interpretations and applications of the new Soviet legislation. As the largest maritime power to have signed it, Soviet views on the LOS Convention are now of the utmost consequence in its future development.

The principal changes introduced since 1982 in the legal regime of the waters lying northward of the Soviet Union are examined here. However, certain collateral developments potentially affecting the utilization of arctic sea lanes and the exploitation of arctic resources also should be noted. First is the continued use of the arctic waters by several countries to reach the North Pole via submarine and the increasing availability of Soviet polar airspace for international commercial aviation. Second is the enactment in January 1987 of new Soviet legislation authorizing the formation of equity joint enterprises and other production entities with 'capitalist countries' (Butler 1987a:215–60). Joint resource exploitation on the Soviet arctic continental shelf must be regarded as having considerable potential in this connection, as indeed could joint shipping and possibly fisheries ventures.

Third is the still speculative (but increasingly possible both politically and technologically) utilization of the Northeast Passage as an international shipping route between the Atlantic and Pacific Oceans. Fourth, as a region the Arctic has a profound influence on the world's climate and is itself ecologically fragile. Environmental protection and disturbance of the Arctic is necessarily an international concern. And finally, the Arctic is an important arena for marine and other scientific research, pure and applied, whose findings are of regional and international consequence.

Legislation on USSR state boundary at sea

The principal Soviet enactment implementing the LOS was adopted several days before the Convention was formally opened for signature. Entitled the 'Law on the State Boundary of the USSR', it was adopted by the USSR Supreme Soviet on 24 November 1982 (Butler 1983: *Vedomosti SSSR*, 1982) and entered into effect from 1 March 1983, replacing the 1960 Statute on the Protection of the State Boundary of the USSR. Inasmuch as the law determines the entire state frontiers of the Soviet Union, it applies in full to the arctic coastline.

State boundary

The Soviet state boundary in the Arctic is the line and perpendicular surface passing along that line which determines the territorial limits of the USSR on land, waters, subsoil and in the airspace. The precise coordinates are fixed by the highest legislative and governmental agencies of the USSR and in international treaties concluded with foreign states by the USSR. Unless otherwise established by treaty, the sea boundary runs along the outer limits of the territorial waters (territorial sea) of the USSR; on land along the characteristic relief points and lines or clearly visible reference points; and on navigable rivers, water reservoirs or bridges as designated by details of Soviet legislation not relevant here.

Territorial waters

The 1982 LOS accepted that states may fix the breadth of their territorial waters at up to 12 nautical miles. This view, so long advocated in Soviet doctrine and, since 1960, in state practice, was consolidated in the 1982 Law on the USSR State Boundary (Article 5). The key issue has been from what point the territorial waters are to be measured. Since 10 June 1971, Soviet legislation has made provision for three possibilities: from the lowest ebb tide line both on the mainland and on islands which belong to the USSR; from straight baselines joining appropriate points, the geographic coordinates of which are to be confirmed in the procedure established by the USSR Council of Ministers; from points established by international treaties of the USSR or, in the absence of treaties, in accordance with generally recognized principles and norms of international law. So far as the public record discloses, straight baselines were not fixed generally along Soviet coasts even after the enabling legislation was approved (Butler 1971:750–2). Nevertheless, the legislation itself was yet another strong signal that the so-called 'sector theory' was not being asserted in Soviet Arctic expanses with respect to ice and water, a view further confirmed by a 1979 Soviet decree delimiting time-zone jurisdiction (Johnston 1982).

On 7 February 1984 the USSR Council of Ministers established the geographic coordinates for straight baselines along Soviet coasts of the Pacific Ocean, Sea of Japan, Sea of Okhotsk and the Bering Sea, and, on 15 January 1985, similar coordinates were established for the Baltic Sea, Black Sea and northern Arctic Ocean (see examples of straight baselines in Figure 14.1). Neither decree appeared in the official gazette, but both were

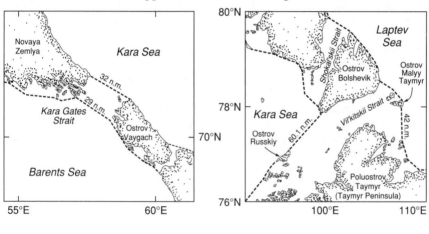

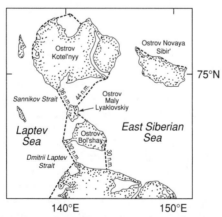

Figure 14.1 Straight baselines (in nautical miles, n.m.) across major straits in the Soviet Arctic (adapted from maps provided by John E. Cooper, Technical Adviser to Department of External Affairs, Ottawa).

summarized in *Izveshcheniia moreplavateliam* (both translated in Butler 1983). On the whole consistent with the 1982 LOS, the baselines reportedly have been the object of protest in certain instances, but the protests have not been published. The baselines enclose certain bodies of water previously asserted in doctrinal writings to be 'historic' (see below) but otherwise are confined chiefly to highly irregular and archipelagic portions of the Soviet coastline.

Internal waters

Soviet legislation establishes 5 categories of internal waters: sea waters on the landward side of straight baselines fixed in order to determine the breadth of the territorial waters of the USSR; waters of Soviet ports delimited by lines passing through the farthest points of hydro engineering and other port installations; the waters of bays, inlets, coves, and estuaries whose shores belong wholly to the USSR up to a straight line drawn from shore to shore in a place where, seaward, one or several passages are first formed, provided that the breadth of each closing line does not exceed 24 nautical miles; the waters of bays, inlets, coves and estuaries, and seas and straits historically belonging to the USSR; and waters of rivers, lakes and other waters whose shores belong to the USSR.

It is the fourth category that has been especially contentious with regard to the Soviet Arctic. A number of the straight baselines are intended to reinforce Soviet claims to the historic nature of certain bodies of water, notably the White Sea, the Cheshskaya Guba and the Vilkitskiy and Sannikov straits, among others (see examples of closing lines in Figure 14.2).

Innocent passage

Unless and until shipping technology develops to the point where the Northeast Passage can be traversed under the ice or through the icepack northwards of Soviet territorial waters in the Arctic, successful utilization of that Passage requires that vessels enjoy a right of innocent passage through the coastal seas and straits of the Soviet Union. The development of Soviet attitudes toward innocent passage has been treated extensively elsewhere (Butler 1987a:215–60; Butler 1989a; Butler 1989b). Notably the essential provisions of the 1982 LOS have been incorporated into Article 13 of the 1982 Law on the State Boundary of the USSR.

Innocent passage through the territorial waters of the USSR is to be for the purpose of traversing those waters without putting into internal waters of the USSR or for the purpose of passage into or departure from the internal waters and ports of the USSR, (in the latter case, of departure to the high seas). Foreign nonmilitary vessels enjoy the right of innocent passage in accordance with Soviet legislation and international treaties of the USSR and are, when effecting passage, to follow the ordinary navigational course

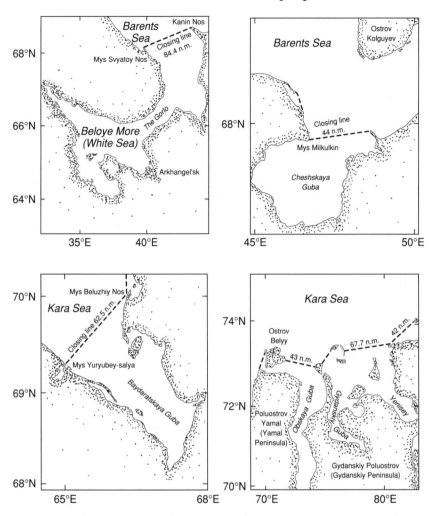

Figure 14.2 Examples of closing lines (in nautical miles, n.m.) across important bays in the Soviet Arctic (adapted from maps provided by John E. Cooper, Technical Adviser to Department of External Affairs, Ottawa).

or the course recommended by competent Soviet agencies, and where established, sea corridors or traffic separation schemes.

Foreign warships and all submarine means of transport, on the other hand, are to effect innocent passage through territorial waters in the procedure established by the USSR Council of Ministers which procedure is set out in a special set of Rules discussed below. All submarine vessels are to navigate on the surface and under their own flag. Foreign nonmilitary vessels may put into Soviet roadsteads and ports in the Arctic that have been listed in *Izveshcheniia moreplavateliam* provided that they observe the procedures for cargo and passenger operations, vessel communications with the shore, shore leave for crew and the like. Foreign warships, on the other hand, require the previous authorization of the Soviet government before putting into internal waters.

Both foreign nonmilitary vessels and warships are required, while in Soviet territorial or internal waters, to observe rules for radio communications, navigation, port, customs, sanitary and other relevant rules. In the event of forced entry, the nearest Soviet port must be notified at once. Any trade, research or survey activities by foreign vessels is prohibited in Soviet territorial or internal waters unless specifically authorized by competent Soviet agencies or by international treaties of the USSR. Selected areas where the navigation or sojourn of foreign vessels is prohibited may be established within the territorial or internal waters of the Soviet Union and announced in *Izveshcheniia moreplavateliam*.

Innocent passage of warships

As noted above, special 'Rules for Navigation and Sojourn of Foreign Warships in the Territorial Waters and Internal Waters and Ports of the USSR' were confirmed by the USSR Council of Ministers on 28 April 1983 (translated in Butler 1983), replacing the rules of 25 June 1960. The 1960 rules were at the heart of protests generated by 2 arctic voyages undertaken by 2 American icebreakers in 1965 and 1967. As Coast Guard vessels, the icebreakers were regarded under Soviet law as warships and were expected to obtain the previous authorization of the Soviet government before traversing the territorial or internal waters of the USSR.

Contrary to the view taken in the 1960 rules, those of 1983 proceed from the premise that foreign warships do enjoy a right of innocent passage on condition that the procedure for exercising that right is observed. In order to emphasize that view, the draftsmen of the 1983 Rules began not by defining innocent passage but by setting out certain procedural requirements: a foreign warship must fly its flag, submarines and other underwater vehicles must navigate on the surface, navigational and other rules must be observed, compulsory pilotage and icebreaker services must be used, areas barred to navigation must be avoided and a request from the coastal state's authorities to observe the rules must be complied with or the foreign warships may be asked to leave Soviet territory (Articles 1–7, 1983 Rules).

Articles 8–12 of the 1983 Rules incorporate key provisions of the 1982 LOS, sometimes verbatim and in certain instances introducing modifications that sharpen or reconceptualize the Convention text. Innocent passage in this formulation is conditional upon observance of the 1983 Rules, the laws and rules of the USSR relating to the regime of territorial waters and international treaties of the USSR (in other words, a 'right subject to ...'). A reconceptualization of innocent passage then follows. What the 1982 LOS (Article 18(1)) calls the 'Meaning of Passage' is described in the 1983 Rules (Article 9) as the 'Purposes of Innocent

Passage'. The essence of Article 18(1) is reproduced in Article 9 of the Rules with the omission of any reference to roadsteads. Next, the 1983 Rules develop the 'concept of innocent passage' (Article 10) by taking the first sentence of Article 19(1) of the Convention and combining it with the text of Article 18(2), thus bridging a distinction drawn in the Convention between the meaning of passage and the meaning of innocent passage. This enables the draftsmen of the 1983 Rules in Article 11 to treat as 'conditions of innocent passage' what those who prepared the 1982 Convention enumerated as activities considered to be prejudicial to the peace, good order or security of the coastal state.

Article 22 of the 1982 LOS allows a coastal state in the interests of navigational safety to require that foreign vessels use designated sea lanes or traffic separation schemes when exercising their right of innocent passage. When designating sea lanes or prescribing traffic separation schemes, the coastal state is obliged to have regard to the recommendations of the competent international organization, to any channels customarily used for international navigation, to the special characteristics of particular ships and channels and to the density of traffic. The 1983 Rules (Article 12) make reference in this connection only to innocent passage for the purpose of traversing the territorial sea of the USSR without entering Soviet internal waters or ports, in which case in 3 seas (the Baltic Sea, Sea of Okhotsk and Sea of Japan) the routes ordinarily used for international navigation are to be followed with observance of the prescribed traffic separation schemes.

For a foreign warship, the 1983 Rules, unlike the 1982 LOS, link innocent passage for the purpose of entering or departing from the internal waters or ports of the USSR with the requirements of prior authorization. Herein probably lies the reason for the reconceptualization of innocent passage in the 1983 Rules mentioned above. By shifting emphasis from the 'meaning' to the 'purposes' of passage, the second 'category' of passage defined in Article 18(1)(b) of the Convention — that is, to proceed to or from internal waters or call at a roadstead or port a facility outside internal waters — is, in fact, made wholly subject to the previous authorization process. This approach represents a significant departure from that of the Convention, and in substance amounts to a negation of the notion of innocent passage embodied in Article 18(1)(b).

To date, however, state practice under the 1983 Rules has developed in another controversial aspect. Perhaps influenced by an assertive American policy of 'showing the flag' through naval vessels traversing Soviet territorial waters in the Black Sea in a period when Soviet naval expenditures and capabilities show signs of retrenchment, several Soviet jurists developed a doctrinal gloss to the effect that coastal states may establish sea lanes and traffic separation schemes for passing vessels and confine the passage of foreign warships to such designated areas. Accordingly, under this view, there is no right of innocent passage for foreign warships in seas off the Soviet coast where sea lanes and traffic separation schemes have not been established. The entire Soviet Arctic coastline, according to this interpretation, would not be open to the innocent passage of foreign warships.

In the Black Sea affair of 13 March 1986, the presence of 2 American warships in Soviet territorial waters was formally protested by the Soviet government on the grounds that 'the innocent passage of foreign warships through the territorial waters of the USSR is permitted only in specially authorized coastal areas that have been announced by the Soviet government. In a word, there are no such areas in the Black Sea off the coast of the Soviet Union' (Lukashin 1986).

That interpretation, in my view, is not consistent with the 1982 LOS or with the 1983 Rules. The international legal system operates a presumption in favour of the innocent passage of foreign vessels wherever they wish in the territorial sea of the coastal State, subject to the rules of international law and coastal State legislation in conformity with international law. The 1982 LOS clarifies to an unprecedented degree the relationship between the vessel in passage and the interests of the coastal state in navigational safety, including the right of coastal states to declare certain areas of the seas closed to shipping or subject to the observance of certain courses or traffic systems. Article 12 of the 1983 Rules stipulates that in the Baltic Sea, Sea of Okhotsk and Sea of Japan foreign warships are to follow the ordinary navigation routes and certain designated traffic separation schemes. So long as those sea lanes and traffic separation schemes take account of subparagraphs (a) – (d) of Article 22(3) of the 1982 LOS, foreign ships are bound to use them. The text of Article 12 of the 1983 Rules is consistent with Article 22 of the 1982 LOS; however, the coastal state need impose such navigational requirements, according to Article 22, only 'where necessary'; their absence in no way implies that the right of innocent passage is not applicable. The right of innocent passage is not a 'gift' of the coastal state to passing vessels but a limitation of its sovereignty in the interests of international intercourse (Butler 1987b).

The 1986 events in the Black Sea led to a constructive dialogue between the United States and the Soviet Union regarding traditional uses of the oceans that culminated, on 23 September 1989, in the issuance of a Joint Statement containing a uniform interpretation of the rules of international law regulating innocent passage. The essence of the interpretation is as follows:

1. The rules of international law regulating innocent passage through the territorial sea are contained in the 1982 LOS, particularly Part II, Section 3.
2. All vessels, including warships, irrespective of their cargo, armament or type of engine enjoy in accordance with international law the right of innocent passage through the territorial sea for which neither prior notification nor authorization is required.
3. The enumeration of types of activity in Article 19(2) of the 1982 LOS which, if performed, renders passage not innocent is deemed to be exhaustive.
4. If a coastal state has doubts as to whether a specific passage is innocent through its territorial sea, it shall inform the vessel as to the reasons for

its doubt and afford the vessel an opportunity to explain its intentions or rectify its activities within a reasonably brief period.

5. Vessels exercising the right of innocent passage are to comply with all coastal state laws and regulations adopted in conformity with rules of international law contained in Articles 21–23 and 25 of the 1982 LOS. This includes laws and regulations requiring the use of sea lanes and traffic separation schemes where they have been prescribed for safety of navigation. Vessels enjoy the right of innocent passage in areas where sea lanes and traffic separation schemes have not been established.

6. Laws and regulations of a coastal state may not amount in practice to a deprivation or violation of the right of innocent passage as defined in Article 24 of the 1982 LOS.

7. If a warship engages in activity that violates coastal state rules and regulations or deprives a passage of its innocent character and does not rectify its behaviour after a request to do so, the coastal state may request the vessel to leave the territorial sea as laid down in Article 30 of the 1982 LOS. The warship is obliged to comply at once.

8. Without prejudice to the rights of the coastal state and the flag state of a vessel, all differences which may arise in connection with the individual passage of a vessel through the territorial sea are to be settled through diplomatic channels or other agreed means (Vestnik Ministerstva inostrannykh del SSSR, 1989:25; *International Legal Materials*, 1989).

How influential a Joint Statement by 2 powerful maritime nations, only one of them a signatory to the 1982 LOS, will be as an interpretation of that Convention must await the practices of other states which are parties to the 1982 LOS. Amendments to Soviet and American legislation respecting innocent passage will follow in any event.

As regards the Arctic, however, there remain unresolved issues. Most pertinent is the issue of innocent passage through waters landward of Soviet straight baselines or historic waters. Under the 1958 Geneva Convention on the Territorial Sea and Contiguous Zone, foreign vessels (Article 5(2)) retain a right of innocent passage through such waters; also see Article 8(2) of the 1982 LOS. Some Soviet jurists are of the view that in the Arctic this is not the case with respect to historic straits on the grounds that there has never been international navigation through them (Kolodkin and Volosov 1990). In this respect the Soviet position is said to be at one with Canadian attitudes towards the Northwest Passage.

Exclusive Economic Zone

During the deliberations of the United Nations Conference on the Law of the Sea, a number of states created various forms of exclusive economic zones, usually 200 nautical miles in breadth, to protect living resources and to regulate fishing. The Soviet Union, among those states, on 10 December 1976 enacted an Edict on Provisional Measures for the Preservation of the Living Resources and for the Regulation of Fishing in Marine Areas

Adjacent to the Coast of the USSR (Butler 1983: *Vedomosti SSSR*, 1976; 1982). With the signature of the 1982 LOS, the Soviet Union repealed the 1976 Edict as amended and adopted a series of enactments introducing and defining the exclusive economic zone of the USSR.

On 28 February 1984 an Edict 'On the Economic Zone of the USSR' created the economic zone in marine areas beyond the territorial waters of the USSR and adjacent thereto, including the areas around islands which belong to the USSR, the seaward boundary of which is 200 nautical miles from the same baselines used to calculate the territorial waters of the USSR. The boundaries of the economic zone between the USSR and adjacent States are to be delimited 'by taking into account USSR legislation through an agreement on the basis of international law with a view to achieving a just solution' (point 1).

Within the economic zone the Soviet Union draws a distinction between the exercise of sovereign rights and of jurisdiction. It claims to exercise sovereign rights for the purposes of the exploration, exploitation, conservation and management of natural resources, whether living or nonliving, on the seabed, in the subsoil, and in the superjacent waters thereof, and likewise sovereign rights with respect to other types of activity regarding the economic exploration and exploitation of the zone. Jurisdiction is claimed with regard to the establishment and use of artificial islands, installations, and structures; marine scientific research; and the protection and preservation of the marine environment; and other rights provided for by Soviet legislation or generally recognized norms of international law.

Unauthorized fishing has been the principal source of conflict under Soviet economic-zone legislation, chiefly in the Soviet Far East and, to a lesser extent, the Baltic and Barents seas. More than 600 instances have been reported, a sufficient number to oblige the Plenum of the USSR Supreme Court to issue a Guiding Explanation to lower courts on the application of economic-zone legislation. Most of the offences probably appertain to anadromous species of fish over which, as the coastal state, the Soviet Union claims exclusive rights within its economic zone and beyond, subject to special treaty arrangements.

Details regarding the issuance of fishing permits and the rules governing fishing or the taking of living resources within and beyond the economic zone are governed by a Statute confirmed by the USSR Council of Ministers on 17 February 1986 (Butler 1983: *SP SSSR*, 1986) and a list of statutory prices as the basis for calculating harm caused to fish stocks, confirmed on 10 March 1986 (Butler 1983: *SP SSSR*, 1986).

All states enjoy within the Soviet economic zone, on condition of observing Soviet law and generally recognized norms of international law, the freedoms of navigation, of overflight, of laying submarine cables and pipelines and other forms of using the sea related to such freedoms which are lawful under international law. Western airlines have since 1986 successfully negotiated agreements with the Soviet Union that allow the Northern Sea Route to be used between Western Europe and Japan.

With respect to artificial islands or any installations or structures intended to carry on scientific research within the economic zone or to explore and exploit the natural resources within that zone, or for any other purposes, the Soviet Union has the exclusive right to construct them or to authorize and regulate their construction, operation and use. It follows that such artificial islands, installations and structures are within the exclusive jurisdiction of the USSR, including with respect to customs, fiscal, sanitary, and safety laws, rules and regulations. Safety zones not exceeding 500 metres from each outer edge may be created for each such island, installation or structure unless another distance has been authorized by generally recognized international standards or recommended by a competent international organization. Notification of artificial islands, installations, structures and their attendant safety zones is effected through *Izveshcheniia moreplavateliam*.

Marine scientific research in the economic zone

While shipping, resource and other commercial opportunities on the part of foreigners are chiefly a matter for the future, albeit the near future perhaps, marine scientific research has been an important Western activity in the waters north of the Soviet Union for many decades. Appreciable portions of those waters now fall within the economic zone of the USSR.

Within that zone marine scientific research may be conducted by foreign states and competent international organizations only with the consent of Soviet agencies. Under ordinary circumstances that consent will be given to foreign states on condition that such research is to be carried out exclusively for peaceful purposes and to increase scientific knowledge about the marine environment for all mankind. Complete information about the planned research must be submitted to the competent Soviet agencies at least 6 months prior to the proposed date of commencing the research; consent may be withheld if the data submitted is incomplete or if that state or international organization has failed in the past to honour obligations arising out of marine scientific research. Likewise consent may be refused if the research is directly significant to the exploration or exploitation of living or nonliving resources of the Soviet economic zone; involves boring into the seabed of the economic zone, the use of explosives or the introduction of harmful substances into the marine environment; or includes the construction, operation or utilization of artificial islands, installations or structures.

Certain further requirements are imposed on foreign states or international organizations who are permitted to conduct marine scientific research. Soviet representatives must take part, especially on board research vessels and other research structures or installations. Preliminary reports, final results and conclusions are to be submitted to competent Soviet agencies as soon as becomes practicable or after completing the research. The same agencies are to be given access at their request to all data and samples obtained in the research and are to be provided with a copy of the data and a share of the samples that can be divided without prejudicing their scientific value. Evaluations of such data, samples and research results are to be provided upon request, and there is to be no interference with activities carried on in the economic zone as an exercise of the sovereign rights and jurisdiction of the USSR. Any material changes in the research programme are to be advised at once to the competent Soviet agencies. Once the research is completed, any scientific research installations or equipment are to be promptly removed (Butler 1983: *SP SSSR*, 1986).

Environmental protection

Soviet conservation and environmental legislation is a vast subject. All general environmental legislation is applicable as appropriate to the Arctic. On 26 November 1984 a special Edict was enacted on intensifying nature protection 'in areas of the Far North and marine areas adjacent to the Northern Coast of the USSR' (Butler 1983: *Vedomosti SSSR*, 1984). The 1984 Edict acknowledges the special ecological situation in the Far North and adjacent marine areas, the vulnerability of objects of nature and the length of time needed to restore disturbances of the ecological balance.

Accordingly, provision is made for expanding the system of game preserves, reservations and other specially protected areas; for the introduction of special requirements for the navigation of vessels and other floating means, aircraft and means of land transport; special rules for the design, construction and operation of enterprises, installations, structures and technical devices, as well as for carrying on geological survey, scientific research, and other work; stricter requirements for the protection of the land, subsoil, water, the atmosphere, flora and fauna; and restrictions on tourism in the area. It is important to note that the creation of game preserves and the like may encompass marine areas, and in that event vessels may be required to navigate only along the sea lanes specified by competent Soviet agencies and published in *Izveshcheniia moreplavateliam*. Indeed, the same applies to ice: within ice-covered marine areas of game preserves, reservations and other specially protected territories other means of transport may be required to pass along routes specified by the competent Soviet authorities. Forced entry into protected areas would be permitted on condition of notifying the nearest Soviet port. Further, vessels, other floating means, equipment, supplies and crew may be required to satisfy higher requirements. Compulsory pilotage and icebreaker escort may be imposed and certain periods or areas may be closed for navigation.

Environmental considerations also affect overflight in the Soviet Arctic. The direction and breadth of air lanes, the flight paths and the altitude of aircraft are to have regard to the requirements of nature protection. And as in the case of sea and ice areas, certain areas may be temporarily closed to overflight.

Any construction or renovation in the Far North or adjacent marine areas of enterprises, installations, artificial islands, cable-laying and the like may be authorized only if there is a positive ecologically substantiated opinion from those agencies charged with exercising state control over nature protection and the rational use of national resources. Any prospecting, geological survey, mining, construction and other work must be carried on so as to have the least adverse effect on the natural environment. Scientific and expedition activities incompatible with nature conservation requirements are prohibited.

The discharging of sewage waters not purified up to the established standards or of wastes, materials and articles in northern marine areas, whether ice-covered or not, is prohibited, and the burial within those marine areas of such items requires the authorization of Soviet agencies and must be carried out under their control. Similarly, other forms of human activities — tourism, hunting, fishing etc. — may be restricted or prohibited in the interests of the ecological balance in the region. These provisions of the 1984 Edict must be read against a Statute on the Protection and Preservation of the Marine Environment in the Economic Zone of the USSR confirmed on 15 July 1985 (Butler 1983: *SP SSSR*, 1985). The Statute extends to the Soviet economic zone in the Arctic and introduces a number of minimum environmental standards. In particular, the Statute authorizes the USSR Ministry of Soil Conservation and Water Conservancy, the USSR Ministry of Fisheries and the USSR Ministry of Public Health to establish a list of substances whose discharge into the economic zone from vessels, other floating means, artificial islands, devices and installations is either prohibited or must satisfy standards for maximum admissible concentrations. Masters of passing vessels, or persons in charge of installations, are required to notify the nearest Soviet port about any such discharges.

Similarly, special areas and measures may be designated to reduce or eliminate vessel-source pollution, and the burial of wastes and other materials is to be authorized so as to conform to Soviet obligations arising out of the 1972 Convention on the Prevention of Pollution of the Sea by Discharge of Wastes and Other Materials. If a vessel is grounded, involved in a collision or suffers other marine distress within or beyond the economic zone and there may be harmful consequences to the Soviet coast or Soviet coastal interests, including fishing, designated agencies of the USSR have the right to take necessary measures in accordance with international law and proportionate to the actual or imminent damage with a view to protection against the pollution. The limits of shipowner liability for losses caused by pollution of the sea by oil are fixed maximally at 120 roubles multiplied by each registered gross ton of the vessel, not exceeding 12,500,000 roubles for each instance of pollution. The limits are not applicable if the losses were caused directly through the shipowner's fault. Soviet criminal legislation makes provision for other types of pollution of the sea (Butler 1983: *Vedomosti SSSR*, 1974, 1981).

Continental shelf

Soviet legislation governing the continental shelf dates back to 1968, following ratification by the USSR of the 1958 Geneva Convention on the

227

Continental Shelf. That Edict was amended on 9 April 1982 in order to reflect certain changes in Soviet law introduced by the 1977 USSR Constitution and by 1979 legislation on the law of treaties (Butler 1969:103–7). There has been much speculation about the resource potential of the Soviet arctic continental shelf, but adverse climatic conditions and available technology have combined to confine exploratory efforts to shallow areas close to the coast. Sand and mineral concentrations have proved to be promising in some localities, but to date the extent of commercial exploitation has been extremely modest. Oil deposits are especially attractive. In 1987, experimental industrial oil extraction was begun on Kolguev Island in the Barents Sea; one drilling station began operations as far north as the 75th parallel in the Barents Sea and another commenced drilling in the shelf of the Kara Sea off the Yamal peninsula (*Izvestiya*, 14 and 30 September 1987) . In August 1989, 2 massive natural gas and oil fields were discovered in the Barents and Kara seas (Butler 1990).

Recent Soviet legislation appertaining to the continental shelf regulates the procedure for conducting work on the shelf and the labour conditions of individuals employed in the exploitation of oil and gas resources or engaged in geological survey work for hard minerals (Butler 1983; legislation on the continental shelf). The lateral boundaries of the continental shelf in the Arctic with Norway and the United States remain to be demarcated precisely. The living organisms of the Soviet continental shelf which are deemed to be natural resources of the shelf were enumerated by the USSR Ministry of Fisheries on 29 October 1968 (Butler 1983).

Straits

The straits along the Northeast Arctic Passage have been treated thoroughly by Butler (1978) (see Figure 14.3). Soviet legislation demarcating straight baselines has enclosed several of those linking seas north of the Soviet coast, notably the Vil'kitskii, Shokal'skii, Sannikov and Dmitriy Laptev straits (see Figure 14.3). Inasmuch as these are straits used for international navigation, however, under the 1982 LOS the rights of innocent passage through those straits would not be prejudiced, although there are Soviet doctrinal views to the contrary.

Deep seabed

Some months before the 1982 LOS was signed, the Soviet Union adopted an Edict on provisional measures to regulate the activities of Soviet enterprises relating to the exploration and exploitation of seabed mineral resources beyond the continental shelf (Butler 1983: *Vedomosti SSSR*, 1982). The Edict is 'provisional' until the 1982 LOS enters into force. Under the Edict competent agencies of the USSR may issue permits to Soviet enterprises for the exploration or exploitation of seabed mineral resources and may

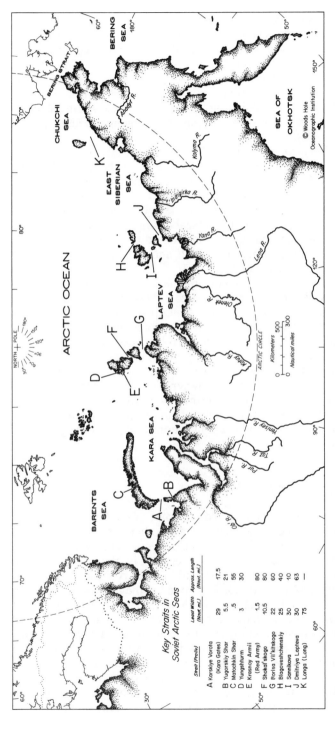

Key Straits in
Soviet Arctic Seas

Strait (Proliv)	Least Width (Naut. mi.)	Approx. Length (Naut. mi.)
A Karskiye Vorota (Kara Gates)	29	17.5
B Yugorskiy Shar	5.5	21
C Matochkin Shar	.5	55
D Yungshturm	3	30
E Krasnoy Armii (Red Army)	1.5	80
F Shokal'skogo	10.5	80
G Borisa Vil'kitskogo	22	60
H Blagoveshchenskiy	25	40
I Sannikova	30	10
J Dmitriya Lapteva	30	63
K Longa (Long)	75	—

Figure 14.3 Key straits in Soviet Arctic seas (adapted from Butler 1978).

229

determine the size and geographic coordinates of the seabed plots for which the permits are issued. No claim of sovereignty, of sovereign or exclusive rights, jurisdiction or ownership with respect to any seabed area or its resources is involved in the issuance of a permit, nor would the USSR recognize claims of that nature advanced by other states. However, the Soviet Union retains jurisdiction over any Soviet juridical persons who take part in such exploration or exploitation, as well as any vessels or installations used by Soviet enterprises in such work and the persons situated on those vessels or installations.

On the basis of reciprocity the Soviet Union is prepared to cooperate with those states which recognize the permits issued under the Edict. A Soviet enterprise applying for a permit must specify 2 seabed plots believed to have mineral resource potential. If the permit is issued, the applicant enterprise may use one of the 2 plots and the second is reserved for possible exploration and exploitation by a future international seabed organization. All proposed plots should be reasonable in size, having regard to the legal interests of other states. The actual exploitation of plots under the edict may not have commenced before 1 January 1988.

Foreign national and juridical persons may, on the basis of treaties between the USSR and interested states, become involved in the exploration and exploitation of seabed mineral resources carried on by Soviet enterprises, and vice versa . Any such work carried on should not create unjustified obstacles to the exercise of other freedoms of the sea or to lawful activities on the high seas. Any minerals extracted by Soviet enterprises from the deep seabed are owned by the Soviet state, but if there is foreign involvement in seabed mining ownership, what is extracted may be shared. A special fund is to be created by the Soviet government from part of the seabed mining proceeds and eventually transferred to a future international seabed organization in connection with Soviet obligations to that body.

Strategic policy and the Soviet Arctic

The military perception of the Arctic on the part of the Great Powers has been that the northern regions are peripheral to other theatres where issues of deterrence are more vital. The vast vulnerable northern coastlines of the arctic powers have been protected more, perhaps, by the terrain, ice and weather conditions than massive investment in military installations. Only submarines can operate more or less year round in the polar seas, and even then at risk. Western and Soviet concerns focus chiefly on the large Soviet naval base at Murmansk and the access routes into the Atlantic Ocean and North Sea or on early-warning systems to detect possible missile attacks. There is no reason to believe the military factor in the Arctic is likely to become more significant relatively than it has been when measured against other global considerations, whereas technological and economic advances in the region carry increasingly greater weight in policy deliberations on arctic policy. What in the past by way of developing arctic potential were merely 'pipe dreams', have become or are becoming a reality. In the mid-1950s the United States offered proposals for transforming the Arctic into an 'atom-free-zone', Three decades later, the Soviet Union has put forward analogous suggestions that go far beyond the strategic factor. Whether these ultimately find favour or not, the peripheral nature of the strategic factor in the Arctic makes that region an ideal forum for exploring approaches and solutions that may have broader application elsewhere.

The legal regime and future of the Arctic

Soviet legislation giving effect to the 1982 LOS in general and with regard to the Arctic in particular has made clear beyond all doubt that the international regime of the seas is applicable to the marine areas adjacent to Soviet arctic coasts and that doctrinal claims to those expanses as internal historic waters do not have (and never had) any basis in state practice. Widely misunderstood outside the Soviet Union, they were products of a balance of power now obsolete and have been supplanted by a body of international and national legal rules that are in much greater harmony with the status and potential of the region.

But arctic developments from a regional perspective have proceeded piecemeal. Individual states in the area promoted economic, cultural and other measures in their own interests, often with little regard to the larger welfare of the region. Cooperation, such as it has existed in a formal sense, has been confined to a few ecological and resource agreements. Even the principal lateral boundaries between the arctic powers require further clarification. Marine and polar research, so vital to the region and the planet as a whole, often has been frustrated by jurisdictional claims or ambiguities or simply foundered on mutual suspicion and unhelpful bureaucratic procedures. Sundry initiatives for regional conferences capable of taking a comprehensive view of arctic needs and prospects have met with little encouragement.

It is against this background that the Murmansk Speech by M. S. Gorbachev, on 1 October 1987, takes on such significance, for it is the first by any leader of an arctic power to suggest specific proposals for collaboration and development in the region on what appear to be the virtual full range of salient arctic concerns (Gorbachev 1987). Moreover, the proposals offered could only be viable against the type of legal regime that has crystallized in the Arctic under the 1982 LOS.

Gorbachev linked the land and marine interests of the arctic powers. The Arctic, he said, 'is not merely the northern Arctic Ocean, but also the northern territories of three continents: Europe, Asia and America. It is enclosed by the Euro-Asian, North American and Asian Pacific regions, frontiers meet there and the interests of States which belong to adversary military blocs and those which are not members of them cross there'. Noting the security interests of the Soviet Union in the region and the experiences of 2 world wars, he also commented on the positive role in world affairs played by the northern capitals — Helsinki, Stockholm, Reykjavik — and lamented Denmark's and Norway's NATO affiliation. This was followed by an invitation to 'the States of this region to discuss the issues of security that have long since matured there'. Whether cooperation in the area is to be bilateral, multilateral or both simultaneously, the Soviet Union favours a 'radical reduction in the level of military confrontation in the region'. He adds: 'Let the north of the planet, the Arctic, become a zone of peace. Let the North Pole become a pole of peace'. Specifically Gorbachev put forward 6 proposals:

1. *A nuclear-free zone in Northern Europe.* The Soviet Union would be willing to act as a guarantor of such an arrangement in whatever form it took: multilateral or bilateral agreements, governmental declarations or other form of agreement. At the same time the Soviet Union would be prepared to discuss with interested states or groups of states all problems related to a nuclear-free zone, including measures applicable to Soviet territory. The latter might include removing from the Soviet Baltic fleet all submarines equipped with ballistic missiles.

2. *Limitation of naval operations in seas adjacent to Northern Europe.* This amounts to endorsement of a Finnish initiative and might involve consultations between NATO and the Warsaw Pact to reduce operations in the Baltic Sea, North Sea, Norwegian Sea and Greenland Sea, together with the implementation of other measures of trust which might be extended to the entire Arctic in both hemispheres. A meeting is suggested, perhaps in Leningrad, to discuss the prohibition of naval activities in mutually agreed zones of international straits.

3. *Peaceful cooperation in the exploitation of arctic resources.* Here an exchange of knowledge and experience, President Gorbachev suggests, is essential in order to work out a common notion for the rational development of the northern regions. An example might be a unified energy programme for Northern Europe. The reserves of oil and gas are virtually boundless but their extraction exceedingly difficult and expensive. It would be reasonable to cooperate in this matter and to 'involve, for example, Canada and Norway in the creation of mixed firms and enterprises' to produce oil and gas on the Soviet northern continental shelf.

4. *Scientific study of the Arctic.* The rich Soviet experience, Gorbachev offered, in arctic research can be shared, and there is Soviet interest in doing research in other arctic states. A conference of arctic states is proposed to coordinate scientific research in the Arctic and consider the possibility of establishing a joint arctic scientific council.

5. *Environmental protection.* Cooperation in environmental protection is deemed absolutely essential. The Soviet Union suggests that a combined integrated plan for the environmental protection of the North be prepared and a control system be agreed for monitoring the state of the environment and radiation safety in the region.

6. *Opening of the Northern Sea Route.* The Northern Sea Route, extending from Leningrad to Vladivostok, is a cabotage route which only Soviet vessels or vessels under charter to Soviet agencies may use unless special

authorization is given. It is distinct from the Northeast Passage as a sea-link between the Atlantic and Pacific Oceans which vessels must navigate without assistance from the coastal state (*Izvestiya*, 2 October 1987).

In 1967 for a brief period the Soviet Union opened the Northern Sea Route to foreign vessels, but the offer was never taken up and apparently was tacitly withdrawn. President Gorbachev's offer is a qualified one: 'I believe that, depending on how the normalization of international relations goes, we might open the Northern Sea Route to foreign vessels with the provision by us of icebreaker escort'. On 7 September 1989 a foreign flag vessel chartered to carry Soviet cargo completed a successful transit of the Northeast Passage from Hamburg to the Soviet Far East (Butler 1990).

The willingness of the Soviet Union to discuss 'any counter-suggestions and proposals' as well as their own places arctic relationships, including legal relationships, on an entirely different footing. It now remains to be seen what the Arctic Powers can make of this.

References

Butler, W.E., 1969. 'The Soviet Union and the continental shelf.' *American Journal of International Law* 66:103-7.
— 1971., 'New Soviet legislation on straight baselines.' *International Comparative Law Quarterly* 20:750-52.
— 1978. *Northeast Arctic Passage*. Alphen aan den Rijn, The Netherlands:Sijthoff and Noordhoff.
— (1983–). Translations in: *The USSR, Eastern Europe and the Development of the Law of the Sea*, various booklets. Dobbs Ferry:Oceana.
SP SSSR. 1985. No. 22, item 112.
　　　　1986. No. 4, item 22; no. 10, item 66; no. 12, item 75.
Vedomosti SSSR. 1974. No. 10, item 161.
　　　　1976. No. 50, item 728 (amended 9 April 1982).
　　　　1980. No. 22, item 425.
　　　　1981. No. 11, item 284.
　　　　1982. No. 15, item 238; no. 16, item 254;
　　　　　　No. 48, item 891.
　　　　1984. No. 48, items 863 and 856.
— 1987a. 'The restructuring of Soviet foreign economic relations.' *Connecticut Journal of International Law* 2:215-60.
— 1987b. 'Innocent passage and the 1982 Convention: the influence of Soviet law and policy.' *American Journal of International Law* 81:331-47.
— 1989a. 'Mirnyi prokhod i Konventsiia OON po morskomu pravu: vliianie Sovetskogo zakonodatel'stva i politiki.' [Innocent passage and the United Nations Convention on the Law of the Sea: the influence of Soviet legislation and policy] *Sovetskii ezhegodnik morskogo prava*:19-33.
— 1989b. 'Innocent passage and the 1982 UNCLOS: the influence of Soviet Law and policy.' *Soviet Yearbook of Maritime Law*:19-31.
— 1990. 'Joint ventures and the Soviet Arctic.' *Marine Policy* 14(2).
Gorbachev, M.S. 1987. Speech at Murmansk. FBIS-SOV-87-191. 2 October, 42. (see Appendix I)

International Legal Materials. 1989. 'Uniform interpretation of rules of international law governing innocent passage.' 28:1444-47.

Izvestiya. 1987. 14 September:1 (columns 1-2); 30 September:6 (columns 1-6).

Johnston, D.M. 1982. *Arctic Ocean Issues in the 1980s*. Honolulu: Law of the Sea Institute, University of Hawaii.

Kolodkin, A.L., and M.E. Volosov. 1990. 'The legal regime of the Soviet Arctic.' *Marine Policy* 14(2).

Lukashin, V. 1986. 'Flot proiavil vyderzhku.' [The fleet displayed restraint.] *Izvestiya* 23 March:3 (columns 5-7).

United Nations. 1983. *The Law of the Sea: United Nations Convention on the Law of the Sea*. New York: United Nations Publications.

Vestnik Ministerstva inostrannykh del SSSR. 1989. Russian text of Joint Statement. 21(55):25.

15

Canada-USSR Arctic Science Exchange Programme: An historical perspective of arctic cooperation

Walter Slipchenko

This historical perspective reviews the highlights in the development of the bilateral Arctic Science Exchange Programme between Canada and the Soviet Union. The chapter outlines events in the history of the Programme from a Canadian perspective.

Resolute Canadian and Soviet interest in an Arctic Science Exchange Programme set the stage for early, tentative agreements in the form of memoranda in 1972 and discussions in Moscow in 1973 and 1974. After a lapse of relations owing to an inability to recognize each other's priorities, by 1984 both countries realized the imminent benefits for arctic exchange and developed significant protocols in 1984 and 1987. A mature agreement finally evolved in 1990, primarily dedicated to technical and scientific cooperation, economic cooperation and social and cultural exchanges for native people.

Early agreements

Since the early 1960s, the Department of Indian Affairs and Northern Development (IAND) has been open to an exchange programme with Soviet agencies, especially in the areas of scientific and technical exchanges, and northern socioeconomic development. In fact, the basis of the Canada–USSR Arctic Science Exchange can be traced back to 1965 when Arthur Laing, minister of Indian Affairs and Northern Development, accepted an invitation to visit the Soviet North. In return, a Soviet delegation, made up primarily of representatives from the USSR State Committee on Construction (GOSSTROY), toured northern Canada the same year.

An effective exchange, between the Soviet Union and Canada would be beneficial to Canada as a whole given IAND's policy on exchange programmes as of December 1969. Simply put, the Soviet Union and Canada were the 2 largest nations with sizeable territories north of the Arctic Circle and faced many common problems. To confirm these sentiments, the Interdepartmental Advisory Committee on Northern Development (ACND) took an active role in the coordination of scientific exchanges with the Soviet Union.

By January 1971, Jean-Luc Pepin, minister of Industry, Trade and Commerce, and V.A. Kirillin, chairman of the State Committee for Science and Technology of the USSR Council of Ministers, signed the Canada–Soviet Agreement for Cooperation in the Industrial Application of Science and Technology. The Agreement was aimed 'at encouraging cooperation between the 2 countries in the field of industrial science and technology...and could take the form of exchanges of information, and visits of businessmen and experts. It could also lead to licensing agreements in specific areas of technology' (Pepin 1971). Under this Agreement, 6 working groups were formed to identify areas for mutually beneficial exchanges in electric power; architecture, construction and building materials; forest-based industries; nonferrous metals industry; oil industry; and gas industry. This was later expanded to include other working groups, each focusing on northern applied technology.

In the summer of 1971, Jean Chrétien, minister of Indian Affairs and Northern Development, travelled to the Soviet North as a guest of I.T. Novikov, deputy chairman of the USSR Council of Ministers and chairman of the State Committee on Construction. While in the Soviet Union, Chrétien focused on the importance of exchanges between both countries, particularly under the Canada–USSR Agreement on the Industrial Application of Science and Technology and the General Exchanges Agreement, under which he suggested cooperation in the area of arctic scientific research.

The Canadian government envisioned arctic science exchanges dealing primarily with scientific research, a theme already covered under the General Exchanges Agreement (signed at Ottawa on 20 October 1971). The Agreement provided for the establishment of a Mixed Commission that met for the first time in Moscow during 7–9 June 1972. They agreed on a programme of exchanges in 7 thematic areas: science and education, arts, cinematography, television and radio, sports, exchanges between nongovernmental bodies and other exchanges, and tourism. Arctic cooperation fell under science and education, which stated that 'both parties confirmed that cooperation will be established on a regular- and long-term basis in arctic science, resources and development, in accordance with the joint memorandum agreed in Moscow on 24 February 1972' (Science and Education, 1972). Various Soviet scientists and officials expressed the view, at the conclusion of Chrétien's visit, that an effective social, technological and scientific exchange programme with Canada would indeed be most desirable (Slipchenko 1972:95).

Discussions between L.N. Yefremov, first deputy chairman of the USSR State Committee for Science and Technology, and Chrétien introduced the subject of a joint working group in the area of arctic scientific research. At this meeting, it was decided that a cooperative basis to arctic research was necessary, but that the mechanics of the exchange would be determined at a later date. In Chrétien's final meeting with his Soviet host, I.T. Novikov, he stated, 'I am also pleased that I was able to reach an agreement with Yefremov...to establish a working group on arctic science research. In this connection, we shall be interested to explore further the suggestion by Yefremov with respect to joint scientific expeditions in the north' (Slipchenko 1972:86). By September 1971, when Yefremov visited Canada, both sides agreed upon the formation of an *ad hoc* working group to determine areas of arctic research.

After Yefremov's visit, the Executive Group of the ACND Subcommittee on Science and Technology met on 22 September 1971. They identified the following areas of scientific exchanges with responsible departments: *atmospheric sciences* (Atmospheric Environmental Service, Department of the Environment); *biological sciences* (Department of the Environment in consultation with the National Research Council (NRC) and the Canadian Committee for International Biological Programme); *earth sciences* (Department of Energy, Mines and Resources in consultation with NRC); *northern education* (Department of Indian Affairs and Northern Development); *health sciences* (Department of National Health and Welfare); *hydrologic sciences* (Department of Environment); and *social sciences* (Department of Indian Affairs and Northern Development).

Dr J.M. Harrison, assistant deputy minister of Energy, Mines and Resources, and chairman of the Committee stressed that in the selection of topics under each theme, the underlying principle should be 'importance to Canada, activities in which the USSR appears to have the lead in knowledge and activities in which Canada has special knowledge and may be of interest to the USSR' (Harrison 1971). This committee became the central Canadian coordinating agency for the negotiation of a package deal with Soviet scientists and for the implementation of the entire programme during the 1970s.

Prospects for a worthwhile scientific exchange programme between both countries seemed extremely favourable after the visits of Chrétien and Yefremov. In spite of procedural difficulties, negotiations began almost immediately with meetings in Moscow, 21–4 February 1972 and in Ottawa, 16–20 November 1972.

Memorandum for identifyng exchange areas

A meeting of Canadian and Soviet scientists took place in Moscow 21–24 February 1972 (Memorandum of 24 February 1972). The purpose of the meeting was to identify areas of common interest in arctic science, research and development, and to study possible forms of future cooperation. There seemed to be great expectations on both sides that a programme of exchanges could be developed.

The Canadian group of experts was led by J.M. Harrison, the Soviet group was led by E.I. Sklyarov, Member of the Collegium of the State Committee for Science and Technology. Both groups agreed that cooperation between Canadian and Soviet organizations would be established on a regular and long-term basis in arctic science, research and development. Initial steps would be taken in 5 fields of cooperation (see Themes I, II, III, V, and VI, p. 239).

The scientists agreed that specific programmes of research, with terms of reference and methods of implementation, should be established for the fields of cooperation. The forms of cooperation could be in joint scientific experiments and research, bilateral symposia and seminars, reciprocal exchange of research workers and specialists, joint field trips, exchange of scientific and technological information, as well as other forms to be agreed upon additionally in the course of cooperation.

The next step in Canadian–Soviet cooperation would be the designation of responsible individuals and organizations for coordination of cooperative programmes in each of the selected fields. When the programmes in each field were defined, further study would be given to coordination of the cooperative programme as a whole, including the possibility of establishing a Canadian–Soviet working group on arctic science and research. At the conclusion of the meeting, both sides confirmed that a further meeting should be held in Ottawa, at the earliest convenience in order to develop a comprehensive, workable programme of arctic science, research and development exchanges based on the subject areas outlined in the Memorandum of 24 February 1972.

Memorandum for developing an arctic science programme

The second meeting of Canadian and Soviet experts dealing with arctic science, research, and development took place 16–20 November 1972 in Ottawa (Memorandum of 20 November, 1972). The groups were again led by J.M. Harrison and E.I. Sklyarov. The prime purpose of the second meeting was to discuss the programme of Canadian-Soviet Cooperation in arctic science, research, and development in accordance with the terms of the joint Memorandum of 24 February 1972.

The experts agreed that a major purpose of the Canadian–USSR Arctic Science Cooperation was to improve the quality of life of the native populations, of the North. They confirmed the desire of both sides to further the cooperation in the indicated fields and agreed on the organizations in both countries that would implement the programme. The next stage of cooperation would be the development of specific programmes on each of the agreed problems, taking into consideration the wishes and suggestions of the specialists. The experts also agreed that in developing specific programmes of cooperation, questions of nature protection should be taken into account, including the influence of different pollutants. It was decided that the activities related to the programme of Canadian–Soviet Cooperation in arctic science, research and development would commence in Canada and in the USSR not later than 1973 and the first phase of activities would be completed by 1980.

The Cooperation would take into account the wishes of the Canadian delegation to organize an exchange of experience for the work done in the two countries with regard to the development of native peoples. It would specifically include the problems of involvement in government, education, conservation and rational exploitation of renewable natural resources, adaptation to new occupations and public health and hygiene. The experts agreed on the need to organize a joint group of scientists and specialists for the purpose of mutual familiarization of measures taken in the fields of direction. In their opinion, this would define the subjects for more detailed study. The composition of the group and the geographical locations for reciprocal visits would be determined without delay and, if possible, exchanges would begin in 1973.

In reviewing the results of these discussions, not only were the subject areas within the original 5 themes expanded, but they now included 2 more. Themes IV and VII were newly added in the Memorandum of 20 November 1972, while Themes I, II, III, V, and VI were agreed upon earlier in the Memorandum of 24 February 1972. The Themes from the earlier Memorandum were almost an exact replication of the subsequent expanded Themes:

I. Stratigraphy, structural evolution and deep structures of northern regions, including methods and means of investigations. Permafrost studies, glaciology, geochemistry, and geomorphology of the northern regions.

II. Hydrology, meteorology, and oceanography studies for better understanding and more accurate forecasting of ice, hydrological and meteorological phenomena.

III. Arctic and subarctic freshwater and marine ecosystems and their biological processes, including the ecology of fish and marine mammals, the effect of human activity and other factors on these ecosystems. (The specialists agreed that the original Theme III, which included marine and terrestrial ecosystems, should be divided into two separate areas, one dealing with freshwater, marine fauna and ecosystems and the other with terrestrial fauna and ecosystems.)

IV. Terrestrial fauna and ecosystems. Arctic and subarctic terrestrial ecosystems. Development of methods of protection, conservation and rational utilization of terrestrial mammals and birds, including the effect of human activity on these ecosystems.

V. Studies of medical and nutritional problems specific for the northern regions.

VI. Ethnography and adaptation of indigenous people in the North to a new way of life resulting from the development of northern regions.

VII. Experience in training specialists from among native people of the North.

The Memorandum of 20 November 1972 also outlined administrative procedures involved in carrying out the exchange and the need for a meeting in Moscow by the end of 1973 to work out the final details. By then, the groups would have developed specific programmes and would exchange information on the progress made in the themes of cooperation.

Reconciling themes

It became clear by the end of 1974 that discussions on several themes had reached an impasse despite continued meetings between Canadian and Soviet specialists. They discussed cooperation under Themes VI and VII in Moscow during November 1973. During February and March 1974, again in Moscow, they considered a detailed programme for Themes I to IV, and in Yellowknife and Jasper during July 1974, they completed a programme in medical sciences. In addition, there was a flurry of letters and meetings with ambassadors on both sides that continued well into 1975. Although a programme of activities was generally agreed upon, with certain reservations on both sides for Themes I to V, unfortunately, at that particular time, the Soviet side was not prepared to discuss an exchange programme for the social sciences covered under Themes VI and VII. The main problem appeared to be the inability of the USSR State Committee on Science and Technology to coordinate a programme dealing with the social, educational and environmental sciences, particularly in coordinating the interests of the Soviet Academy of Sciences and the ministries of the Russian Republic, which had northern responsibilities.

There was also the issue of carrying out research in each other's northern territories. This seemed to provide more of a dilemma to the Soviets than to the Canadians. Dr Harrison, in his opening remarks in November 1972, had emphasized that for any cooperation to succeed, both countries would have to agree to two basic points. The first dealt with reciprocity and the need for both countries to agree upon an equivalent exchange of information, scientists and visits to specific northern and arctic geographical areas. The second was the result of a conference in the latter part of October 1972, at Mont Gabriel, which stressed that the needs of the people in the North were more important than resource development and that the maintenance of ecological balance was essential (Greenaway 1973).

Jean Chrétien endorsed these points in a report to Canada's Standing Committee and IAND concerning the government's northern objectives, priorities and strategies for the 1970s and noted that they would have to be reflected in the research programme (Greenaway 1973:272–80). A temporary impasse occurred when the inability of the Soviets to come up with a solution to include a programme for the social sciences became unacceptable to the Canadians in view of the Canadian government's

240

priority for the social development of its northern people. As a result, no further action was taken on the other themes.

Although there was relatively little activity from 1975 to 1978, both sides 'continued to agree to discuss programmes of cooperation' under the Canada-USSR General Exchanges Agreement. In spite of the lack of progress under the Arctic Science Programme, some northern exchanges did occur between both countries between 1972 and 1979. These were under the auspices of other sections of the Canada–USSR General Exchanges Agreement and also under the Canada–USSR Industrial Application of Science and Technology Agreement. By the end of 1979, however, Soviet intervention in Afghanistan and the imposition of martial law in Poland caused the majority of the bilateral programmes, under both agreements, to be suspended. These were relegated then to the same inactive status as the Arctic Science Programme.

Resuming discussions in the 1980s

Once more, the need for a bilateral, scientific exchange programme dealing with the Arctic began to gain momentum when a Soviet *Aide-Mémoire* presented to the Canadian government in the latter part of 1981 noted the importance of arctic scientific and technical cooperation between both countries. It outlined 6 specific study areas: sea ice, tectonic mapping of the Arctic Ocean, arctic petroleum exploration and development, climate, permafrost and construction of ships. Soon after, in the early part of 1982, the Canadians received a Soviet Draft Text of a programme of exchanges under the Canada–USSR Exchange Agreement that had been dormant over the previous 3 years.

In addition to the possibility of cooperation dealing with scientific and technical aspects, the Soviet Draft Text noted that 'both sides also agreed to hold at mutually acceptable times, talks aimed at considering specific proposals on possible cooperation in the social and ethnographic aspects of northern development' (Soviet Draft Text, 1982). The Soviet Draft Text revitalized the following exchanges:

1. Both sides acknowledged their interest *in problems of studying and developing the Arctic* on a regular and long-term basis and expressed readiness to consider specific proposals on the scientific and technical aspects of cooperation;
2. The USSR State Committee for Science and Technology was prepared to receive in the first half of 1982 an appropriate Canadian delegation to conduct negotiations. The Soviets wanted to conclude, possibly, a bilateral agreement on scientific and technical cooperation in studying and developing the Arctic; and
3. Both sides also agreed to hold talks at mutually acceptable times aimed at considering specific proposals on possible cooperation concerning social and ethnographic aspects of northern development.

This was the commitment that the Canadians had been seeking from the Soviet officials for nearly 10 years.

It was during this same period that the Canadian government reviewed the possibility of opening up relations with the Soviet government. Relations were based primarily on areas of particular interest to Canadians, such as northern scientific and technical exchanges. There was a general agreement among Canadian scientists and officials, who were interested in having bilateral relations with the Soviet Union, that any exchange had to ensure reciprocity and should not interfere with existing scientist-to-scientist contacts and/or any international agreements. Furthermore, the social and environmental sciences had to be an integral part of any agreement, together with the full involvement of northern natives. In light of this decision by the Canadian government to negotiate a mutually beneficial arctic exchange programme with the Soviet Union, extensive interdepartmental consultations took place throughout 1982 and 1983. As a result of the diminishing role of the ACND, IAND continued with the provision of the secretariat and coordination, while the NRC took over the chairmanship of the 'new *ad hoc*' General Committee. The main federal component in the development of an exchange programme included the Departments of Energy, Mines and Resources; Environment; External Affairs; Fisheries and Oceans; Indian Affairs and Northern Development; National Research Council; Public Works and from the Government of the Northwest Territories, the Departments of Education, Public Works, and Renewable Resources.

A number of subject areas of particular interest to Canada were identified under 4 main themes dealing with geoscience and arctic petroleum, northern and arctic environments, northern construction and ethnography. Canadian and Soviet delegations exchanged proposals in February 1983, with both delegations meeting in Ottawa, 14–16 March 1983.

Protocol outlining consultations

Further consultations on arctic cooperation took place in Ottawa during 14–16 March 1983, based on the 1971 Agreement on General Exchanges (Protocol of Consultation 1983). Dr Bernard Gingras, vice-president (external relations) of the National Research Council of Canada, led the Canadian delegation. Dr Yuri Rybakov, director of the Treaty and Legal Department, Ministry of Foreign Affairs of the USSR, led the Soviet delegation.

During the course of the consultations, the Canadian and Soviet delegations worked out the main areas of cooperation concerning problems of study and development of arctic regions in 25 subject areas that fulfilled Canadian and Soviet interests and merited further consideration. This was no mean accomplishment since both started with individual shopping lists, each with more than 40 subject areas. For the Canadians, most of their priorities were met with only minor changes. The selected subject areas

Table 15.1 Main areas of cooperation between Canada and the USSR on problems of study and development of northern and arctic regions

---

Theme I: Geoscience and arctic petroleum

1. Preparing regional geological maps of dry land in the arctic latitudes.

2. Preparing a tectonic map of the Amerasian subbasin in the North Arctic Ocean, including the adjacent shelf and a historical analysis of its development.

3. Studying the formation and the structure of the largest platforms in the Arctic (West and East Siberian and Canadian) and the formation of the arctic fold belt (Inuit and Novosibirsk–Chukhotsk fold systems).

4. Preparing correlational stratigraphic diagrams of Precambrian and phanerozoic deposits in the Soviet and Canadian Arctic.

5. Studying the geological formation of the largest asphalt and heavy crude-oil deposits in the Arctic (Olenek deposit in the USSR and Athabasca group in Canada). A study of the methods used for their development, including the mining method.

6. Methods of discovery and study of petroleum-related hydrates.

Theme II: Northern and arctic environment

7. Studying the Arctic.

8. Methods of detecting and managing oil and gas pollution in the arctic environment.

9. Conservation policies.

10. Preventing, detecting and fighting forest fires. Improving detection and technical methods of fire fighting. Increasing efficiency and technical equipment used.

11. Raising domesticated reindeer, wild reindeer and caribou. Caribou management and processing of reindeer industry products.

12. Farm breeding of furbearing animals.

13. Studying population dynamics, life cycles, rational utilization, scientific management methodologies and mitigation methods of industrial impacts relating to arctic ecosystems and food chains, specifically: marine animals, furbearers, polar bears, rare and endangered species and fish.

Theme III: Northern construction

14. Studying construction problems under permafrost conditions.

15. Principals of planning and building northern communities, including settlements intended for short-term usage.

16. Principles of planning and engineering services for residential and public buildings, including energy conservation.

17. Foundation methods for building and engineering structures on permafrost.

18. Monitoring services for permafrost soil condition and for operation and maintenance of buildings, engineered structures and roads.

19. Residential construction in remote regions with difficult access. Transportation problems.

20. Exchanging experience in the field of housing utility management. Developing measures for the improvement of water supply and sewage systems, and structures and treatment of domestic sewage for towns and communities in the regions of Siberia, the Far East, and the Far North, and in the Canadian North.

Theme IV: Ethnography and education

21. Social and economic changes.

22. Ethnography — traditional and contemporary culture, traditions and way of life of the native people of the Soviet North and northern Canada. Research in the field of languages and culture of northern native people.

23. Ethnography — ancient history, ethnogenesis and ethnic processes taking place among native peoples in the Soviet north and northern Canada.

24. Joint or parallel publication of folk tales by northern peoples in Russian, Yakut, English, French and Eskimo languages.

25. Theory and practice of achieving an equal level of education under the conditions of a multinational country, using the peoples of the Soviet North and northern Canada as examples. These include the implementation of modern technical aids for education in the schools of the North and criteria for the specific items of equipment in northern Canada. A study of the means of preserving native languages in the school system.

---

became the basis of the exchange programme, which has been in effect over 4 years. Early in the deliberation, there was mutual agreement that the programme must be simplified, and existing bilateral and international agreements that already covered subject areas were to be avoided (see Table 15.1). It was understood that Canadian and Soviet arctic cooperation could include joint scientific research; exchanges of research workers and scientific and technical information; bilateral meetings and seminars; as well as other forms to be agreed upon in respect to specific projects. In regard to future action, the Canadians proposed that the 2 groups meet again when specific project proposals for cooperation on topics had been defined and exchanged for discussion (see Table 15.1). The purpose of the next meeting would be to agree on priorities and methods for implementation of selected projects.

The Soviet delegation, for its part, stated its readiness to meet again with Canadian representatives as soon as possible and invited the Canadian delegation to Moscow in May 1983. They proposed to elaborate specific programmes of cooperation in developing the Arctic within the framework of agreed-upon main areas and in order to achieve other arrangements. These included the establishment of a Soviet and Canadian Mixed

Commission on problems of the Arctic and the North and also the embodiment of these arrangements in an appropriate document.

At the conclusion of these discussions, there was a sense of optimism that after all these years the exchange was proceeding in the right direction.

Protocol of detailing scientific and technical cooperation

Building on the consultations in Ottawa, a meeting of Canadian and Soviet specialists took place in Moscow at the USSR State Committee for Science and Technology during 2–16 April 1984 (Protocol of Consultation, 1984). The specialists met to develop and to agree on the implementation of a programme of scientific and technical cooperation between Canada and the USSR in the Arctic and in the North.

At the end of this meeting, which witnessed some interesting and, at times, quite lively deliberations, B.A. Gingras and A.K. Romanov, deputy chairman of the USSR State Committee on Science and Technology, signed a *Protocol of Canadian Soviet Discussions on the Development of a Programme of Scientific and Technical Cooperation in the Arctic and the North*. In Canada, this Protocol became known as the Canada–USSR Arctic Science Exchange Programme. During the course of the consultations, the Canadian and Soviet delegations agreed on a detailed two-year programme of activities in 4 thematic areas of scientific and technical cooperation: Geoscience and Arctic Petroleum, Northern Environment, Northern Construction and Ethnography and Education. The agreed-upon programme of scientific research in the North included, among others, exchanges of experts and delegations to the Canadian Arctic and Soviet Arctic and exchanges of information.

Both delegations agreed that the programme would take effect immediately upon signature of the Protocol and would be implemented in the framework of the General Exchanges Agreement. They further agreed to establish a coordinating group, composed of the programme co-chairmen and the 4 theme chairmen from each side. It was understood that the coordinating group would meet alternately in Ottawa and Moscow at least once every 2 years (under the financial arrangements of the General Exchanges Agreement); coordinate the activities of the separate theme programmes; monitor their progress; and agree, when necessary, to add or to change the agreed programme of cooperation. The coordinating group was responsible for developing subsequent bilateral programmes of cooperation. Theme chairmen could also, through meetings or correspondence, undertake reviews of progress in their areas.

One interesting aspect raised in the final paragraph of the Protocol stated:

> Recognizing the special significance of cooperation in the Arctic and the North, both sides agreed that one of the purposes of the first meeting of the coordinating group is to consider the possibility of concluding a special agreement for cooperation in this area, including the possibility of reaching such an agreement under the auspices of the General Exchanges Agreement.

Although this programme was placed under the Canada—USSR General Exchanges Agreement when reactivated in October 1986, the question of a separate arctic agreement was again raised when a Soviet bilateral draft agreement on cooperating in the Arctic was presented to the Canadian government in February 1987. The Canadian government responded in a positive way to this Soviet initiative and a bilateral agreement was signed between both countries in November 1989.

Resulting arctic themes

In reviewing the various results during the two-year Protocol of Scientific and Technical Cooperation, some activities were carried over well into 1987 with the following actions occurring under each theme:

Theme I: Geoscience and arctic petroleum

Agreement on most aspects of standards, formats, time scales for legends and correlation for both bedrock and quaternary maps; joint field studies on the Aldan Shield and Wrangel Island in the USSR, and Melville Island, Somerset Island and Boothia peninsula in Canada; discussions for the compilation of lithostratigraphic and biostratigraphic correlation charts for Lower and Middle Paleozoic Triassic, Jurassic, and Cretaceous periods; and joint meetings in Canada and the USSR for the preparation of a programme dealing with geological and geophysical research on natural gas hydrates.

Theme II: Northern environment

Joint visits for preparation of a programme dealing with theoretical models of climate and of general atmospheric circulation, including air pollution in arctic regions; visit of Canadian specialists to Komi USSR, to discuss prevention of oil spills; exchange of legislation and standards dealing with environmental policy; Soviet participation at the Conservation Task Force workshop in Yellowknife, Canada; joint field trips concerned with reindeer and caribou management in Yukon and Northwest Territories, and Yakut ASSR; and joint visits to fur-farming operations in Ontario, New Brunswick and Nova Scotia, and Moscow, Leningrad and Murmansk.

Theme III: Northern construction

Joint visits to Yakut ASSR, and Komi ASSR and Northwest Territories, in subject areas dealing with the design, building and construction of private and public buildings, and water supply and sewage disposal for towns and development projects.

Theme IV: Ethnography and education

Joint visits to northern communities in the Yakut ASSR, Tyumen Oblast' (Khanty-Mansiysk Okrug) and Novosibirsk Oblast, and Northwest Territories and northern Quebec to review the social, cultural and economic development of native people; their traditional ethnography and archaeology, and native education, including exchange of northern school texts, teachers manuals and current aboriginal literature.

In the operation of the programme on the Canadian side the *ad hoc* General Committee, which had been operating since 1982, made up of an overall chairman and coordinator, four theme chairmen and deputy chairmen, all with their individual working groups, became the official Canadian coordinating body for this exchange. Moreover, since the federal government allocated no funds, the responsibility for carrying out the exchange programme came primarily from the chairmen of the individual themes and any agency involved with the programme. Needless to say, this lack of funding created difficulties, but in spite of this the Canadian side met its obligations in carrying out the programme of activities during 1984–6.

Realities of the cooperative programme

At the conclusion of the Protocol of Scientific and Technical Cooperation (it did not truly start until 1985 and continued well into 1987), 14 Canadian and 15 Soviet delegations had been exchanged with a total involvement of over 80 Canadian and Soviet scientists, teachers, specialists and engineers, some of whom were native. Most of the Canadian participants were satisfied with the programme, expressing specific benefits for themselves and for Canada. Although the prime purpose of this first exchange was primarily to become familiar with and to review current northern developments, the participants cited other benefits: excellent new contacts between specialists from the all-Union, republic and local levels; closer personal ties and good working relationships between the participants; access to information which had not been previously available; firsthand exposure to the situation in northern areas — in the areas of geology, wildlife, environment and/or social and economic development; better understanding of the administrative, regulatory and management practices; possible commercial spin-offs, especially in northern construction; and the involvement of native people on both sides. This involvement, primarily of Inuit educators, demonstrated the importance of the participation of native people in the exchange and was well received among the natives from both countries.

There were also difficulties on both sides with the programme. Many of these were minor irritants and dealt with administrative and financial procedures, but others were more serious and could be placed under the general category of reciprocity, whether in the actual exchange of information or data or contact time with specialists. As the first step, however, the initial phase of this programme was highly successful and certainly contributed to better and broader Canadian–Soviet relations. As both groups approached the upcoming joint meetings in Ottawa, there was a feeling that this initial programme had been a success and would be extended.

Ensuring scientific and technical cooperation

At the meeting of the Canadian and Soviet Coordinating Group during 23–6 February 1987, the exchange programme was extended until 1989 under a new *Protocol of the Meeting of the Coordinating Group in Scientific and Technical Cooperation between Canada and the USSR in the Arctic and the North* dated 26 February 1987. The Protocol underlined the success of the past programme, not only in the area of expanding contacts between scientists of both countries but also 'for broadening and deepening bilateral cooperation in arctic and northern problems' (DEA 1987). A detailed two-year programme of activities based upon the same themes as outlined in the 1984 Protocol was provided and the main subject areas were expanded to 30 with a corresponding increase in the subject areas. The Protocol also mentioned the possibility of joint projects and joint research on selected topics.

The new programme covered activities in the following areas:

Theme I: Regional geological maps, history of development of arctic platform structures and structures of arctic folded belts; stratigraphic charts of Precambrian and phanerozoic deposits; geological and geophysical research or gas hydrates; and geologically identifying prospective coal and natural-gas areas

Theme II: Study of climate; monitoring environmental oil and gas pollution; oil and gas transport technology; diffusion of petroleum hydrocarbons and other pollutants; advanced methods of protecting internal waters from pollution in arctic and northern water bodies; domesticated reindeer husbandry; wild reindeer and caribou harvesting; commercial breeding of northern furbearing animals; dynamics of the musk-ox populations; dynamics and migrations of snow geese; adaptation of northern living organisms; northern environmental protection policies; physical and mechanical properties of ice; and environmental effects of changes in northern hydrological systems.

Theme III: Design and construction techniques for residential and public buildings; water supply and sewage disposal systems; heating systems for housing and public utilities; and construction and maintenance of highways.

Theme IV: Contemporary situation and way of life for aboriginal people; traditional ethnography, including archaeology and education (training teaching personnel for the native schools, preparing curricula and textbooks, preservation and expansion of traditional occupations and traditional artistic occupations).

This second phase of the exchange programme had many interesting and significant activities. It proved a valuable agreement on the issues of scientific exchanges and participation by native people.

Successful arctic exchange

The success of the Protocol on Scientific and Technical Cooperation in the Arctic and the North with its exchanges was noted in the Report of the Special Joint Committee of the Senate and of the House of Commons on Canada's International Relations. It stated that 'the Committee considers that an arctic exchange programme with the Soviet Union is an effective way to increase Canadian knowledge of the North as well as to provide a basis for improving East–West relations. We recommend that the existing programme be properly funded' (Simard and Hockin 1986). The importance of this exchange was further emphasized when Joe Clark, secretary of state for external affairs responded:

> The government believes that its existing Arctic Exchange Programme is a unique and valuable arrangement, providing contacts between scientists of both countries, and giving Canadian scientists improved access to Soviet research and experience in the Arctic. The Department of Indian Affairs and Northern Development is now committed to strengthening the funding structure of the Canada–USSR Arctic Sciences Exchange Programme. Officials from both governments will be meeting early next year to review past programmes and future cooperation in areas such as economic development, protection of the environment, and exchanges among the indigenous people involved in traditional pursuits [Clark 1986].

For Canada, there was and presently is active support for this exchange both in and outside of government with good representation from the federal and territorial governments, and some aboriginal organizations. The next step was to have broader Canadian representation, which included greater aboriginal participation as well as the direct involvement of provinces, universities, industry and other agencies having northern interests.

From a Soviet viewpoint, President Mikhail Gorbachev in his Murmansk speech on 1 October 1987 reflected on the Soviet commitment to the importance of scientific exchanges and the interests of indigenous people. He made several proposals on international cooperation in Northern Europe and the Arctic, and in his fourth proposal he stressed the following:

> Scientific study of the Arctic is of huge importance for all mankind. We have very rich experiences here. We are prepared to share them. For our part, we are interested in research being conducted by other Arctic and northern states. We already have a program of scientific exchanges with Canada. We propose the holding in 1988 of a conference of arctic states to coordinate scientific research in the Arctic. It would be possible to examine there the subject of establishing a joint Arctic scientific council. If the partners agree, Murmansk could be the venue for holding the conference. Issues connected with the interests of indigenous population of the north and with the study of their ethnic peculiarities and the

development of cultural links among the northern ethnic groups demand special attention [Gorbachev 1987].

The 1972 expectations of scientists from both countries had become reality with these announcements.

Recent developments

In reviewing the last two years of activities under the Protocol of Scientific and Technical Cooperation Exchange Programme, direct benefits to both countries may be observed. Generally, this exchange was instrumental in accomplishing the following:

1. Establishing contact between Canadian and Soviet northern universities;
2. Helping to arrange Soviet Yuit participation at the Inuit Circumpolar Conference;
3. Supporting the proposed International Arctic Science Committee (IASC);
4. Establishing direct contact between the Government of the Northwest Territories and Soviet northern agencies and ministries within the Russian Federated Soviet Socialist Republic; and
5. Increasing contacts between Canadian and Soviet native people, scientists and officials.

Specifically, several direct results associated with the programme during this period included the following:

1. Publication of a circumpolar geological map of the Arctic;
2. Successful scientific research programme concerned with the snow geese project;
3. Design of a school/day-care centre in the Northwest Territories and a new town (Votcha) in the Komi ASSR;
4. Direct participation of Northwest Territories' businessmen with Soviet northern agencies in joint ventures; and
5. Signing of the Canada–USSR Arctic Science Cooperation Agreement.

Of paramount importance was the last item (see Appendix III). This agreement was a direct result of the success of the Arctic Science Exchange Programme. Canadian Prime Minister Brian Mulroney and Nikolai I. Ryzhkov, chairman of the USSR Council of Ministers signed the agreement on 20 November 1989. It shows clearly the importance that both countries place on ensuring good relations in the Arctic. Under this agreement, programmes of cooperation include a programme of scientific and technical cooperation, including geology, meteorology, climatology, environmental protection, construction, arctic marine, land and air technology and other agreed fields; a programme of economic cooperation, including the development of renewable and nonrenewable resources; and programmes of cooperation on social and cultural questions, including ethnography,

Table 15.2
List of Canadian and Soviet participants and their representative agencies

Canadian participants

Name	Agency	Meetings						
		1	2	3	4	5	6	7
Barrette, R.G.	Department of Energy, Mines and Resources				X			
Berry, M.J.	Department of Energy, Mines and Resources				X			
Breton, G.	Canadian Embassy, Moscow						X	X
Brown, C.	Department of External Affairs					X		
Cameron, H.	Department of the Environment	X			X			
Cooch, F.G.	Department of the Environment				X			X
Elkin, L.	Department of Education, Government of the Northwest Territories					X	X	X
Faulkner, G.N.	Department of Indian Affairs and Northern Development					X	X	
Fraikin, E.	Department of Indian Affairs and Northern Development					X	X	
Gingras, B.A.	National Research Council					X	X	X
Grey, M.	Makivik Corporation					X	X	X
Grey, S.	Canadian Embassy, Moscow		X				X	
Gryndahl, I.	Interpreter						X	
Halpin, R.R.	Canadian Embassy, Moscow	X					X	
Hancock, P.J.A.	Canadian Embassy, Moscow	X						
Handley, J.	Department of Education, Government of Northwest Territories							X
Hannigan, J.	Department of Indian Affairs and Northern Development		X					X
Harrison, J.M.	Department of Energy, Mines and Resources	X				X	X	
Hobson, G.D.	Department of Energy, Mines and Resources	X				X	X	X

Name	Affiliation							
Hotz, M.C.B.	Department of Environment	X	X	X		X	X	X
Hoyt, N.	Department of Public Works		X					X
Hunter, J.G.	Fisheries Research Board of Canada							X
Hutchison, W.W.	Department of Energy, Mines and Resources	X	X	X	X	X		X
Kerr, A.J.	Department of Indian Affairs and Northern Development				X			X
Keys, J.D.	National Research Council				X			X
Kiriloff, N.	Interpreter		X					
Lafferty, V.	Department of Energy, Mines and Resources	X	X			X		
Langtry, E.K.	Department of Indian Affairs and Northern Development		X			X		
Lewis, B.W.	Department of Education, Government of the Northwest Territories		X			X		
Loughrey, A.G.	Department of the Environment		X	X	X	X		X
MacDonald, G.	National Museum of Civilization (Man)		X			X		
Mace, M.	Department of External Affairs							
Macpherson, A.	Department of Indian Affairs and Northern Development	X						
Martin, W.R.	Department of Environment		X					
Mokievsky-Zubok, O.	Interpreter		X					
Monaghan, H.J.	Department of Renewable Resources, Government of the Northwest Territories							
Nassichuk, W.M.	Department of Energy, Mines and Resources	X	X	X	X	X	X	
Naysmith, P.	Department of Fisheries and Marine Service	X	X	X	X	X		
Paganuzzi, V.	Interpreter		X					
Pervushin, N.	Interpreter		X					
Poppe, V.P.	Interpreter		X		X			
Renaud, A.	University of Saskatchewan		X		X			
Roots, E.F.	Department of Environment		X		X	X	X	X
Rowley, G.W.	Department of Indian Affairs and Northern Development	X	X	X	X	X		X

Name	Affiliation
Salsky, G.	Interpreter
Schaefer, O.	Department of Health and Welfare
Slipchenko, W.	Department of Indian Affairs and Northern Development
Stone, J.M.	National Research Council
Thorpe, T.	Interpreter
Tsivunin, S.	Interpreter
Walker, P.F.	Canadian Embassy, Moscow
Wielgosz, R.	Department of External Affairs
Wright, J.	Department of External Affairs

Soviet participants

Name	Affiliation
Antoniuk, B.D.	USSR State Committee for Science and Technology
Bannikov, A.G.	USSR Academy of Veterinary Sciences
Baydikov, Yu.N.	USSR Ministry of Geology
Boldireff, V.G.	USSR State Committee for Hydrometeorology and Environmental Control
Bromley, Yu.V.	USSR Institute of Ethnography, AS
Crichyagin, V.I.	USSR State Committee for Science and Technology
Denisov, V.D.	USSR Ministry of Agriculture
Derevianko, A.P.	Institute of History, Philology and Philosophy, AS, SIB
Dorogartsev, S.M.	USSR State Committee for Hydrometeorology and Environmental Control
Dralkin, A.G.	USSR State Committee for Science and Technology
Dyin, V.M.	RSFSR State Committee on Construction (GOSSTROY)
Fedinskyij, V.V.	USSR Ministry of Geology
Fertikov, V.I.	RSFSR Council of Ministers
Galmissarov, V.P.	USSR State Committee for Science and Technology

Name	Affiliation							
Gavrin, V.F.	Central Research of Wildlife Management and Nature Reserves				X			
Golovin, V.P.	Hydrographic Service	X	X				X	
Gramberg, I.S.	USSR Ministry of Geology	X	X				X	X
Grosswald, M.G.	Geological Institute, AS	X			X		X	
Gurevich, I.S.	USSR Institute of Ethnography, AS		X				X	
Imerekov, B.I.	USSR State Committee for Science and Technology			X			X	X
Kashtanev, S.M.	Soviet Embassy, Ottawa				X			
Kasyanov, M.M.	RSFSR State Planning Committee (GOSPLAN)				X			
Kazakov, Y.E.	USSR State Committee for Hydrometeorology and Environmental Control				X			
Kaznacheyev, V.P.	USSR Medical Academy of Sciences, Siberian Branch (Akademgorodok)	X			X			
Kontramavikis, V.L.	Institute of Biological Northern Problems, AS (Magadan)	X	X					
Kopeleva, R.M.	USSR State Committee for Science and Technology	X			X		X	X
Koretsky, V.P.	USSR State Committee for Science and Technology		X		X		X	
Kosminskaya, I.P.	Institute of Physical and Mineral Sciences, AS	X						
Krutskikh, B.A.	Arctic and Antarctic Scientific Research Institute							X
Krylov, V.N.	USSR State Committee for Science and Technology	X						X
Kudinov, V.M.	USSR State Committee for Science and Technology							X
Kulebiakin, V.N.	USSR Ministry of Foreign Affairs			X				
Kuzin, V.A.	USSR State Committee on Science and Technology	X						
Kzasnoschakov, G.	Institute of Biological Northern Problems, AS (Magadan)				X			
Loginov, Yu.I.	RSFSR Council of Ministers				X		X	
Makarov, A.P.	Soviet Embassy, Ottawa			X			X	
Makogan, Yu.F.	USSR Ministry of Gas				X			
Markevich	USSR Ministry of Fisheries							
Melnikov, B.P.	USSR State Committee for Science and Technology	X			X		X	
Melnikov, P.I.	Permafrost Institute, SIB, AS (Yakutsk)	X			X		X	X

Name	Organization						
Metalnikov, A.P.	USSR State Committee for Science and Technology					X	
Moiseyev, P.A.	USSR Institute for Scientific Research and Oceanography (UNERO)	X	X				
Nazarov, I.M.	USSR State Committee for Hydrometeorology and Environmental Control					X	X
Novosselov, V.I.	Soviet Embassy, Ottawa					X	
Ostisty, B.K.	USSR Ministry of Gas					X	X
Patin	USSR Ministry of Fisheries			X			
Pavlenko, Yu.A.	Soviet Embassy, Ottawa					X	X
Pegov, S.A.	USSR State Committee for Science and Technology			X	X		
Petrov	Geological Institute, AS			X			
Pogribitsky	USSR Ministry of Geology			X		X	
Poryadin, A.F.	RSFSR State Committee on Construction (GOSSTROY)		X	X		X	
Pushcharovsky, Y.M.	Geological Institute, AS			X		X	
Pushkar	USSR Ministry of Agriculture			X			
Revina	USSR Ministry of Fisheries					X	
Romanov, A.K.	USSR State Committee for Science and Technology	X			X		
Ruptsov, I.F.	USSR State Committee for Science and Technology						
Rybakov, Y.M.	USSR Ministry of Foreign Affairs			X	X		
Ryzanstev	USSR Ministry of Fisheries			X			
Semikhatov, Y.	Geological Institute, AS		X				
Shaporenko, N.A.	RSFSR State Planning Committee (GOSPLAN)			X			
Shekhovtsev, A.A.	USSR State Committee for Hydrometeorology and Environmental Control					X	
Sherim-Zade, S.A.S.O.	USSR Ministry of the Oil Industry					X	
Sherinsky, A.E.	RSFSR Ministry of Education					X	
Shipkov, A.I.	RSFSR State Committee on Construction (GOSSTROY)					X	
Shvemberger, Yu.N.	USSR State Committee for Science and Technology		X			X	
Sklyarov, E.I.	USSR State Committee for Science and Technology	X	X			X	
Sokolovskii, V.G.	USSR State Committee for Science and Technology					X	
Sukhanov, N.V.	RSFSR State Committee on Construction (GOSSTROY)						
Syroechekovsky, E.E.	USSR Academy of Agricultural Sciences			X			X

Name	Institution	1	2	3	4	5	6	7
Tikimiroff	USSR Ministry of Agriculture					X		X
Tishkov, V.A.	USSR Institute of Ethnography, AS					X	X	X
Treshnikov, A.F.	Arctic and Antarctic Institute	X	X					
Tretiakov, A.F.	Soviet Embassy, Ottawa					X		X
Uspensky, S.M.	USSR Ministry of Agriculture			X				
Vekilov, E.Kh.	USSR Ministry of Gas					X		X
Vladimirov	USSR Ministry of Fisheries					X		
Volgin, V.V.	USSR Ministry of Agriculture					X	X	
Yagodnitsyn, N.G.	Hydrographic Service					X	X	X
Yakovlev, A.V.	USSR Council of Ministers							X
Zabrodin, V.A.	Institute of Polar Agriculture					X		
Zemskov, V.N.	USSR Ministry of Foreign Affairs					X	X	X
Zemsky	USSR Ministry of Fisheries					X		
Zotov, V.P.	USSR State Committee for Science and Technology							X

The USSR Academy of Sciences is designated as AS and the Siberian Branch of the USSR Academy of Sciences is designated as SIB, AS.

Meetings

1. Memorandum of 24 February 1972
2. Memorandum of 20 November 1972
3. Discussions in Moscow — 1973
4. Discussions in Moscow — 1974
5. Protocol — 1983
6. Protocol — 1984
7. Protocol — 1987

Note: This appendix provides a list of the individuals who were involved in the negotiations from 1972 to 1987. An attempt has been made to provide the names of all the negotiators, however, it is possible that some names have been missed and the author regrets these omissions.

education, public health, the socioeconomic problems of native people of the North and northern territories, cultural and academic exchanges and contacts between native people.

Consequently, the Arctic Science Exchange Programme no longer exists as a separate entity; the new Canada–USSR Arctic Science Cooperation Agreement subsumes it. It is a fitting tribute to the many people from both Canada and the Soviet Union who believed in the importance of arctic exchanges and at times continued to persevere during insurmountable odds (see Table 15.2).

References

Clark, J. 1986. *Canada's International Relations: Response of the Government of Canada to the Report of the Special Joint Committee of the Senate and the House of Commons*, December 1986. Ottawa:Minister of Supply and Services.

Department of External Affairs (DEA). 1987. Press release, 26 February 1987, Ottawa.

Gorbachev, M.S. 1987. Speech at Murmansk. FBIS-SOV-87-191, 2 October 2:42. (see Appendix I)

Greenaway, K.R. 1973. *Science and the North: A Seminar on Guidelines for Scientific Activities in Northern Canada*, 272-80. Ottawa:Queen's Printer.

Harrison, J.M. 1971. Executive Group Meeting. Department of Energy, Mines and Resources. Ottawa, 22 September.

Memorandum of 24 February. 1972. Most material for this section was taken directly from the Memorandum.

Memorandum of 20 November. 1972. Most material for this section was taken directly from the Memorandum.

Pepin, J. *House of Commons Debate*, 4 February 1971:3057. The Honourable Jean-Luc Pepin, Ministry of Indian Trade and Commerce, presented at the House of Commons, Ottawa.

Protocol of Consultation. 1983. *Protocol of Consultation Between the Delegation of Canada and the Delegation of the Union of Soviet Socialist Republics on Arctic Cooperation*. Most material for this section was taken directly from the Protocol signed in Ottawa on 16 March 1983.

Protocol of Consultation. 1984. *Protocol of Canadian Soviet Consultations on the Development of a Programme of Scientific and Technical Cooperation in the Arctic and the North*. Most material for this section was taken directly from the Protocol signed in Moscow on 16 April 1984.

Science and Education. 1972. *General Exchanges Agreement*. Signed in Ottawa, 20 October 1971:I(A)(3).

Simard, J., and T. Hockin. 1986. *Independence and Internationalism: Report of the Special Joint Committee of the Senate and of the House of Commons on Canada's International Relations*, June:129-130. Ottawa:Queen's Printer of Canada.

Slipchenko, W. 1972. *Siberia 1971*, 86, 95. Ottawa:Information Canada.

Soviet Draft Text. Canada-USSR Exchange Agreement. 1982. [Delivered to Department of External Affairs via Soviet Embassy. Ottawa].

16

International cooperation in the Arctic: Soviet attitudes and actions

Oran R. Young and Gail Osherenko

> What everyone can be absolutely sure of is the Soviet Union's deep and undoubted interest in ensuring that the north of the planet, its own polar and subpolar regions, and all the northern countries never again become an arena of war, and that a genuine zone of peace and fruitful cooperation will be created here.
> President M.S. Gorbachev,
> Murmansk, 1 October 1987

Until recently, Westerners desiring to enhance international cooperation in the Arctic often worried about persuading the Soviet Union to participate in the formation and implementation of cooperative regimes for the region. They believed that the Soviets regarded the Arctic as too sensitive to be an appropriate focus for international cooperation and that, in any case, a general Soviet preference for bilateral over multilateral agreements would obstruct the formation of arctic regimes. Does the actual performance of the Soviet Union support such a pessimistic assessment?

In fact, the Soviet Union already belongs to 3 arctic-specific regimes (the conservation regimes for fur seals and polar bears and the management regime for the Svalbard Archipelago) as well as an array of broader multilateral regimes (for example, the international whaling regime and the emerging arrangements aimed at the protection of stratospheric ozone) applicable to the Arctic as elsewhere. Prior to Gorbachev's Murmansk speech, the Soviets had also exhibited considerable interest in new cooperative arrangements covering commercial, environmental, scientific and social matters in the Arctic.

In his speech, Gorbachev set forth a six-point program for arctic cooperation including:

1. A nuclear-free zone in Northern Europe which might involve withdrawal of ballistic missile nuclear submarines from the Soviet Baltic Fleet;
2. East–West consultation on reducing military activities and limiting military forces in the Baltic, Northern, Norwegian and Greenland seas, consideration of a total ban on naval activity in mutually agreed zones of international straits and major shipping routes and discussion of measures to limit competition in antisubmarine weapons;
3. Joint efforts to exploit natural resources, especially offshore oil and gas, coupled with a unified energy program for the north of Europe;
4. 'A conference of arctic states to coordinate scientific research in the Arctic' in 1988 where parties could consider establishing a joint arctic scientific council, discussing issues related to northern indigenous peoples and developing cultural links among northern ethnic groups;
5. 'A united, comprehensive plan for protecting the environment of the North', including an extension of protections under the 1974 Convention on the Protection of the Marine Environment of the Baltic Sea to the maritime areas of the North and a joint system for monitoring radiation safety and the condition of the environment in the Arctic; and
6. A possible opening of the Northern Sea Route to foreign shipping with Soviet icebreaker escorts (Gorbachev 1987).

No other arctic leader has proposed such comprehensive cooperative arrangements for the Arctic.

The goal of this chapter, then, is to set aside conventional Western stereotypes regarding Soviet behavior and to probe beneath the surface in examining the determinants of Soviet attitudes and actions regarding international cooperation in the Arctic.

Our examination of the Soviet record is not limited to activities occurring in maritime areas for the simple reason that arctic issues ripe for international cooperation do not stop at the coastline. In the Arctic, water behaves like land for much of the year and land like water. For purposes of assessing the prospects for international cooperation, we must look at the Arctic as a whole rather than focusing exclusively on maritime areas (Osherenko and Young 1989).

Potential areas for international cooperation

If we employ a polar projection in thinking about the Arctic, it is immediately apparent that the Arctic Ocean is a mediterranean surrounded by land belonging to 8 countries: Canada, Denmark/Greenland; Finland; Iceland; Norway; Sweden; the Soviet Union; and the United States.

Broadly speaking, these arctic-rim or ice states, together with a few other countries possessing significant arctic interests (for example, Japan) now face a growing need for cooperation in 4 areas: security and arms control; industry and commerce, environment and conservation; and culture and science.

Security and arms control

As the role of the Arctic as a theater of operations for major weapons systems continues to grow, we need to think seriously about confidence building and arms-stabilization measures that would lessen the risk of incidents occurring in the Arctic. Because physical conditions in the Arctic interfere with communication systems and increase the risks of inadvertent or unintentional clashes, special consideration of arms-control measures tailored to arctic conditions is essential (Johnson *et al.* 1984:268–94).

At the same time, the relative concealment enjoyed by submarines operating in the Arctic helps to stabilize the military balance between the superpowers and may improve the chances for arms reductions elsewhere in the world. Additional possibilities include the establishment of submarine sanctuaries, limited nuclear-free zones or special arrangements to protect ecologically sensitive areas from the impacts of military activities in the Arctic (Young 1986).

Industry and commerce

The outlook for joint development projects in the Arctic featuring a pooling of capital, technology or markets is increasingly favorable. Projects of this type could lead not only to more rapid development of northern resources and transportation networks but to safer and more environmentally sound development as well.

Arctic transportation (shipping, air traffic, pipelines and powerlines) might benefit especially from increased international cooperation. The prospects for year-round transport through ice-infested waters may be enhanced by joint scientific and technical research. Even futuristic dreams of underwater transport using submarine tankers may materialize with cooperative research and development. The exploitation of offshore hydrocarbons in the Arctic, now underway in Soviet, Norwegian, Canadian and American waters, has benefited already from technical exchanges and has much to gain from increased cooperation (Bergesen *et al.* 1987).

Jurisdictional complications could be handled effectively through the initiation of joint exploration and development arrangements in areas like the Navarin Basin in the central Bering Sea or the continental shelf adjacent to Svalbard. The multilateral regime covering satellite-assisted search and rescue (SARSAT/COSPAS) is already applicable to the Arctic and could be expanded (Office of Technology Assessment, 1985:109–13). As well, preparations must be made for a substantial growth of tourism in the world's last great wilderness, sometimes called the *Serengeti of the North*. Whale watching, already a multimillion dollar industry in the United States, is bound to expand northward. Transit of the Northwest Passage, with day trips to the North Pole, has recently become a tourist attraction. Undoubtedly, there will be interest in opening the Arctic to more visitors as well as in achieving freer exchange among arctic residents (Francis 1987:1–32).

Environment and conservation

The Arctic is not only a meeting ground and common highway for the ice states, it is also a common dumping ground. Ocean currents carry pollutants long distances from the coastal waters of one state to those of its circumpolar neighbors. Marine pollution in the Arctic can be catastrophic given the large concentrations of relatively few species coupled with extremely slow regenerative processes. Hence, international cooperation to prevent and cope with chronic discharges of pollutants is needed, as well as early warning and effective responses in connection with oil, chemical or toxic spills emanating from oil rigs and ships or from northward-flowing rivers (Osherenko and Young 1989).

Multilateral cooperation (encompassing a number of the industrialized nations of the northern hemisphere) is also required to control the long-range transport of air pollutants which has already become severe in the form of arctic haze. That brownish substance, visible in the arctic air when the sun returns in the spring, is the only Distant Early Warning or DEW Line of environmental degradation in the North — an early warning of an array of unseen but measurable toxins, pesticides and greenhouse gases building up in the arctic atmosphere (Stonehouse 1986). Finally, international regimes to protect transboundary habitats and ecosystems and to secure the welfare of migratory species are required for the Arctic.

Culture and science

Scientific collaboration is relevant to all the areas mentioned. It is not surprising, therefore, that in the 1980s a rapid growth of interest in international cooperation among scientists working on arctic topics occurred (Roots 1984:127–56). In December 1988, representatives of the 8 arctic states met in Leningrad to continue negotiation of specific terms for an International Arctic Science Committee (IASC). This committee is expected to have ongoing responsibility to promote and to coordinate arctic research. IASC is designed to be a nongovernmental organization composed of delegates from national scientific bodies. In Leningrad, representatives agreed to a set of 'founding articles', which, at this date, are the subject of continuing negotiation over questions of voting as well as a method to ensure proper liaison between IASC and governments of the arctic states.

Arctic residents, for their part, share common problems of health, education and economics. The inhabitants of the remote communities of the circumpolar North are subject to high rates of suicide, accidents and alcoholism — the outward indicators of anomie and abrupt social change. They face similar problems of community development and share a desire to establish independent economic bases and to increase self-government.

Arctic-rim states with indigenous populations all recognize, today, a pressing need to protect distinctive native languages and cultures and might well benefit from collaboration in pursuit of this goal. Native residents of the Arctic have expressed a desire to enjoy freer movement of people and ideas across national boundaries.

The Soviet record

To evaluate the actual record of the Soviet Union and to assess the prospects for future international cooperation in the Arctic, we assembled several lists of existing arrangements to which the Soviet Union is a party. The tables containing these lists conform to the 4 areas for potential international cooperation outlined above. Included in the lists are the following:

1. multilateral agreements concerned explicitly with Arctic areas and resources;
2. broader multilateral agreements relevant to the Arctic as elsewhere;
3. bilateral agreements with circumpolar neighbors (the lists are not exhaustive in this area but rather suggestive of the range and extent of cooperation between the Soviet Union and its arctic neighbors); and
4. private agreements involving nongovernmental players and specific agencies within the Soviet bureaucracy.

The category of private agreements has been included to allow consideration of the potential for international cooperation initiated by corporations, non-governmental organizations and individuals. Whatever the pros and cons of specific arrangements of this type, the category as a whole is important. Private individuals have long served as go-betweens or intermediaries in efforts to improve Soviet–American relations (Hammer 1987). Commerce involving corporations located in different nations can ameliorate tensions, improve communication and create stakes in the maintenance of peaceful coexistence. The establishment of an International Union for Circumpolar Health (IUCH) is an obvious example of private players initiating cooperation focused on the Arctic and including the Soviet Union.

The Nuclear Test Ban Verification Demonstration Agreement, worked out between the Natural Resources Defense Council (NRDC) in the United States and the Institute of Physics of the Earth within the Soviet Academy of Sciences, is more controversial. But it also demonstrates clearly the potential role of private players. While newspapers called the agreement remarkable and Frank Press, at that time president of the National

Academy of Sciences, termed it 'an extraordinary event', critics asserted that the NRDC was improperly interfering in foreign policy. Regardless of the ultimate success of this venture in securing a moratorium on all nuclear testing (the goal of the participants), the agreement demonstrates the potential importance of scientific exchanges in laying a foundation for international cooperation on security issues. The rapport between Soviet and American seismologists, developed over 2 decades of cooperative research on understanding and predicting earthquakes, enabled both parties to move rapidly to install seismic monitoring equipment at three sites surrounding the Semipalatinsk testing grounds in Kazakhstan. Under the circumstances, scientific exchanges that are seemingly remote from larger goals of peace and security may become precursors to important cooperative activities, whether promoted by private or public entities (Palca 1986:638; Broad 1986:1; Lin 1987:34; Broad 1987:A3).

When we assembled these lists of cooperative arrangements to which the Soviet Union is a party, we naturally hoped to shed light on larger concerns: are the Soviets interested in international cooperation in the Arctic? how likely are they to participate in efforts that other nations or private parties initiate?

At the same time, we sought answers to several more specific questions:

1. Are the prospects for bilateral agreements better than the prospects for multilateral agreements?
2. Are the opportunities for cooperation greater in one functional area than another (for example, environmental protection as opposed to security)?
3. Can we identify areas where international cooperation is already so extensive that new arrangements are not necessary?
4. Can we pinpoint major gaps in existing international regimes for the Arctic?

In the remainder of this chapter, we discuss the evidence regarding the first 2 of these questions in some detail. We also offer preliminary observations concerning the remaining questions, but do not include an exhaustive response to the questions concerning coverage and gaps in existing international regimes for the Arctic.

Inferences and trends

When the welter of details is arranged (see Appendix IV), some generalizations begin to emerge about the Soviet record. We can quickly dispose of the notions that the Soviet Union shows little interest in international cooperation in the Arctic and that any interest Soviets do exhibit is confined to bilateral arrangements. As of November 1988, the Soviet Union was a party to 95 treaties relevant to the Arctic because of their subject matter or geographic coverage. Of these, more than 45 percent are multilateral (see Figure 16.1).

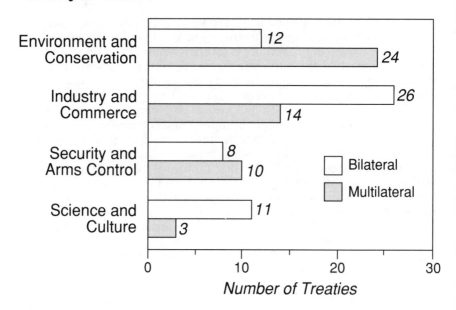

Figure 16.1 Level of Soviet participation in bilateral and multilateral international arrangements, 1911-88.

The Soviet Union is an active participant in 3 arctic-specific multilateral regimes as well as a number of international organizations dealing with arctic issues: for example, the International Permafrost Association and the International Union for Circumpolar Health. In addition, the Soviet Union belongs to a number of broader multilateral arrangements, which, while more general in geographic scope, are especially important to the Arctic. These include the International Whaling Convention, the Convention on International Trade in Endangered Species (CITES), the Convention on Wetlands (the Ramsar Convention) and several agreements dealing with marine pollution. The Soviet Union has ratified Annex 5 of the MARPOL Convention which restricts the dumping of pollutants from ships.

Though there are only a few arctic-specific multilateral agreements, these agreements do create significant international regimes. The 1920 Treaty of Spitsbergen, which came into force in 1925, establishes a unique and comprehensive regime for the Svalbard Archipelago. While the regime recognizes Norwegian sovereignty over the Archipelago, it also requires Norway to maintain the area in a demilitarized state and to grant non-discriminatory access to the natural resources of the Archipelago to nationals of the other regime parties. As Willy Østreng, director of the Fridtjof Nansen Institute in Norway, has pointed out:

'...the Svalbard Treaty was one of the few international agreements made at [the Peace Conference at] Versailles, which was not wiped out by National Socialism; it also survived World War II, and the subsequent Cold War. Not only did the

Svalbard regime survive the postwar period; but alongside the confrontation of the two major power blocs, it held out hope for peaceful coexistence. While politicians from the East and the West found it difficult to sit down and negotiate, Norwegians and Russians worked side by side in Svalbard without any signs of discord' [Østreng 1977:13].

The Convention on the Conservation of North Pacific Fur Seals (1957), amended and extended from an earlier agreement involving the same parties in 1911, brought Canada, Japan, the Soviet Union and the United States together to put an end to pelagic sealing and to manage the harvest of seals from American and Soviet rookeries in the Bering Sea in a carefully controlled manner (Lyster 1985). The fur seal regime has been widely praised as a successful venture in international conservation, but it came under attack in the early 1980s because the fur seal population was experiencing marked declines and because many animal protectionists objected to the provisions for commercial harvesting built into the regime. Though this arrangement is no longer in effect as a result of the failure of the US Senate to ratify a 1984 Protocol extending the Convention, the Soviet Union has continued to express clearcut interest in the retention of the fur seal regime or some revised international arrangement for the management of this species.

The more recent Agreement on the Conservation of of Polar Bears (1973) among Canada, Denmark/Greenland, Norway, the Soviet Union and the United States imposes restrictions on killing or capturing polar bears throughout their range. It also calls on all the range states to protect bear habitat within their jurisdictions (Gorbachev 1986:7–22; Stirling 1986:167–76). This regime has led to extensive cooperative research and protection of some important denning areas in the USSR and elsewhere as well as improved management of this highly mobile species. In short, though arctic-specific multilateral agreements are few in number, the Soviet Union is an active participant in all three.

The Soviet Union has also demonstrated a definite interest in arctic cooperation by entering into bilateral arrangements with its circumpolar neighbors. The Soviets have negotiated extensive agreements with Canada concerning scientific and cultural exchanges. The Mulroney–Gorbachev meeting in November 1989 produced a number of bilateral agreements, including 2 specific to the Arctic and a third of great importance to the region. The umbrella Agreement on Cooperation in the Arctic and the North calls for a Canadian–Soviet Mixed Commission to implement the agreement, which covers cooperation in science and technology, economic development and social and cultural questions. A second agreement deals with prevention and control of arctic marine pollution and a third addresses environmental cooperation more generally.

Under a cooperative arrangement between the Institute of Ethnography of the Soviet Academy of Sciences and the Smithsonian Institution in the United States, a circum-Bering Sea ethnographic exhibit with contributions of archaeological and cultural materials from both nations opened in the United States in 1988 and was shown later in the Soviet Union. The bilateral

US–USSR Agreement on Cooperation in Environmental Protection (1972, 1979, 1985) has provided a framework for extensive cooperative research on arctic topics (Fay and Fedoseev 1984; 1977).

Nor are these bilateral arrangements confined to scientific and cultural matters. An informal Soviet–American agreement in the fall of 1986 resolved (at least for the near future) a controversy over crab fishing in the Bering Sea that flared in August 1986 when Soviet patrol boats chased an American crabber off fishing grounds near the long-disputed border (*Pacific Fishing*, 1987a). Executives of 6 American fishing companies operating in the North Pacific toured the Soviet Union in the spring of 1987 and discussed a variety of northern fishing issues with high-level officials of the Soviet Ministry of Fisheries (*Pacific Fishing*, 1987b).

The Soviet Union is heavily involved in joint enterprises with its Nordic neighbors, including a 3-year contract (1987–1990) with Wartsila Marine Industries (a Finnish company) to construct 11 icebreaking transport vessels for Arctic use (see Chapter 8). A recent agreement regarding cooperation on oil and gas technology and research between the Soviet Union and the United Kingdom emphasizes subsea technology, pipeline design and deepwater and harsh environment technology (*Oil and Gas Journal Newsletter*, 1987). Additionally, the Soviets have entered into numerous bilateral agreements with Finland, Denmark, Iceland, Japan and Norway covering Arctic fishing, sealing, energy development, transportation, search and rescue, education and culture.

Partly as a result of this newfound Soviet interest, no doubt, efforts to stimulate international cooperation in the Arctic have flourished on a number of fronts. With regard to multilateral arrangements, the Soviet Academy of Sciences hosted a large Conference of Arctic and Nordic Countries on Coordination of Research in the Arctic in December 1988, as suggested by Gorbachev in his Murmansk speech (see Appendix I). The Conference, attended by roughly 500 scientists from 15 countries, enabled participants to foster contacts that are leading to new cooperative and collaborative research on the Arctic.

All this activity hardly suggests a feeling on the part of the Soviets that the Arctic is too sensitive to be an appropriate focus for international cooperation. For the first time, aboriginal delegates from the Soviet Union participated in the Inuit Circumpolar Conference's General Assembly, held in Sisimiut, Greenland, in the summer of 1989 (Armstrong 1986:141–54). Cultural and commercial exchanges are rapidly expanding, especially across the Bering Sea between Alaska and the Soviet Far East. Scheduled air service between Nome, Alaska and cities of the Soviet Far East, like Provideniya and Magadan, is likely to become a reality in the 1990s. US Secretary of State James Baker and Soviet Foreign Minister Schevardnadze made arrangements to initiate visa-free travel for indigenous people residing on both sides of the Bering Strait during their meeting in Jackson Hole, Wyoming in September 1989. This evidence suggests that the USSR is rapidly becoming enmeshed in a dense network of transboundary arrangements dealing with arctic issues.

The Soviets certainly do place heavy reliance on bilateral agreements in the areas of industry and commerce and of culture and science. It appears that this often has more to do with the intrinsic character of the issues at stake than with any generalized Soviet preference for bilateral over multilateral arrangements. With the advent of exclusive economic zones, for example, fishing agreements and joint enterprises directed toward offshore oil and gas development naturally call for bilateral arrangements. Much the same is true of many exchange agreements involving scientific research or education.

Where issues are truly international in scope, like the management of the Svalbard Archipelago and the protection of migratory species, the Soviets have long exhibited a willingness to participate in multilateral regimes. In fact, the Soviet Union is party to twice as many multilateral as bilateral treaties in the field of environment and conservation. President Gorbachev in his major address to the 27th Party Congress in 1986 stressed the need for international cooperation on global problems, referring particularly to environmental pollution and 'exhaustion of natural resources' (Gorbachev 1986:7–22; Twenty-seventh Party Congress, 1986). In cases where it seems more appropriate to rely on bilateral arrangements (for example, fishing, oil and gas development or technology transfer), by contrast the Soviets have proceeded to enter into an array of specific agreements with individual circumpolar neighbors.

In these respects, the Soviet record of cooperation on arctic issues is much like the records of the other arctic-rim states. Accordingly, we should not discount prospects for new multilateral regimes in the Arctic which would encompass participation on the part of the Soviet Union. Rather, we need to take a hard look at the specific problems arising in the region to determine which of them really require multilateral regimes in contrast to bilateral regimes.

Environmental issues: a starting point?

Analysis of yet another group of contradictions — those on a global scale, affecting the very foundations of the existence of civilization, leads to serious conclusions. This refers first of all to pollution of the environment, the air and oceans, and to the exhaustion of natural resources...The need for effective international procedures and mechanisms that would make for the rational use of the world's resources as an asset belonging to all humanity is becoming increasingly apparent. The global problems, affecting all humanity, cannot be resolved by the efforts of one state or a group of states. This calls for cooperation on a worldwide scale, for close and constructive joint action by the majority of countries.

Mikhail S. Gorbachev,
Report to 27th CPSU Congress

The comparatively long list of environmental and conservation agreements indicates not only that transboundary environmental problems affecting the Arctic are real but also that the Soviet Union has a serious interest in participating in cooperative arrangements to cope with these problems (see Appendix IV). This, together with Gorbachev's own recognition of the importance of international cooperation on environmental problems, suggests that environmental issues may constitute an attractive starting point for any effort to expand the scope of international cooperation in the Arctic. To explore this idea in greater depth, we focus in this section on the attitudes and actions of the Soviet Union regarding arctic environmental concerns (Ziegler 1987; Osherenko 1989:144–57).

The Soviets have signaled a growing interest in bilateral cooperation with circumpolar neighbors, like Canada and the United States, regarding environmental issues (Environmental Protection Agency 1986a, 1986b). To illustrate, cooperative Soviet and American efforts during 1987 under the provisions of the Environmental Protection Agreement included collaborative research on polar bears in the Chukchi Sea and adjacent Arctic Ocean as well as participation by American scientists in Soviet research cruises in the Bering and Chukchi seas. The US Fish and Wildlife Service has engaged in extensive cooperative efforts with Soviet specialists in the Bering Sea to construct periodic profiles of the marine environment, carry out whale and walrus surveys and conduct shore-based pinniped rookery studies as well as small projects on bear and caribou interactions and relic steppe arctic flora. Exchange of information on the specific problem of arctic haze began in the late 1980s, although efforts carried out under the Environmental Protection Agreement have included studies of the influence of environmental changes on climate for a number of years. The Soviet Union and the United States initiated a joint study of ozone conditions over Antarctica in June 1987 (*New York Times* 1987). A team of 300 scientists conducted arctic stratospheric studies early in 1989 (*International Environmental Reporter* 1989:55–7). Moreover, the US Coast Guard is working with a Soviet marine pollution-control authority on responses to oil pollution in cold environments (Jones 1987). The 2 sides have created a joint US and USSR oil-spill contingency plan for the Bering and Chukchi seas.

To counter these indicators of Soviet interest, critics often argue that Soviet participation in various multilateral environmental arrangements is perfunctory and that the Soviet Union seeks party status in these regimes solely to protect its interests from the actions of others. In some cases, the Soviet performance seems to reinforce these suspicions. The USSR is a party to the CITES regime dealing with endangered species, for example, but the Soviets send only low-level technical representatives to the biennial conferences and they have refused to pay their share of the cost of operating the CITES secretariat (McKeon 1987). Soviet concern about the financial implications of membership may also be an impediment to Soviet membership in the World Heritage Convention which, like CITES, requires parties to contribute to a trust fund for implementation of the Convention. Yet, this hardly reflects the general pattern of Soviet participation in multilateral environmental arrangements.

In 1987, we suggested that environmental issues constitute an appropriate starting point for expanded multilateral cooperation in the Arctic. In 1989, the Finnish foreign ministry apparently agreed and invited the 7 other arctic states to participate in a meeting on the protection of the arctic environment.

The impetus for this meeting was, at least in part, the Finnish foreign ministry's desire to be responsive to Gorbachev's Murmansk initiative. Representatives from foreign ministries, and environment and energy agencies from the 8 arctic states participated in the Consultative Meeting on the Protection of the Arctic Environment in Rovaniemi, Finland (20–6 September 1989). They established 2 working groups — one to review the state of the environment in the Arctic and the need for further action and a second to consider existing international legal instruments for the protection of the arctic environment and the organization of future cooperation. A second ambassadorial-level meeting was held in Yellowknife, Northwest Territories, Canada in April 1990.

The Finnish foreign ministry anticipated that the process would result in a ministerial-level meeting where the 8 states would conclude a framework agreement for environmental cooperation in the Arctic. At this point, it seems just as likely that the process will result in an ongoing forum or standing conference in which representatives of the 8 arctic states can meet to discuss regional environmental problems and issues. Proposals for an Arctic Basin Council or some other regional forum have surfaced sporadically since the late 1960s. The most recent formulation is contained in a Canadian report prepared in response to Gorbachev's Murmansk speech. The Report of the Panel on Arctic Arms Control recommends establishing a Conference on Arctic Security and Cooperation (CASC), modeled on the Conference on Security and Cooperation in Europe, with several 'baskets' of arctic issues including: 'indigenous peoples' affairs; scientific cooperation; economic and cultural development; constitutional development; environmental studies; and defense and arms control' (Cox and Rauf 1989:8, 25). Actual events to date, however, substantiate that environmental issues constitute an attractive starting point for any effort to expand the scope of international cooperation in the Arctic.

The Soviet Union, along with Canada and the United States, was among the first to ratify the 1985 Vienna Convention on ozone. It was an active participant in negotiations culminating in the signing of a protocol in Montreal on 16 September 1987 to freeze and eventually to reduce the production and consumption of chlorofluorocarbons (CFCs) that threaten ozone in the upper atmosphere (Butcher 1987; Aeppel 1987; Shabecoff 1987a:A11; Shabecoff 1987b:A6). Although the Soviets negotiated an exception that would allow them to freeze CFC production at 1990 rather than 1986 levels (to account for expansion underway in their current five-year plan), they are clearly committed to understanding and to solving this environmental problem, a fact of some importance since the Soviet Union produces about 10 percent of the world's CFCs. By way of comparison, the United States produces about 30 percent of the world's CFCs.

Of course, ozone depletion is a global concern. Many observers believe that the hole in the ozone layer over Antarctica may be mirrored in the Arctic, so the issue is one of special concern to major arctic states like the Soviet Union. A similar story emerges from examinations of efforts to devise contingency plans to cope with nuclear accidents under the 1986 Vienna Conventions on emergency relief and early notification regarding nuclear accidents likely to produce transboundary radioactive fallout. The list of bilateral cooperation agreements between the Soviet Union and its arctic and nordic neighbors has also grown. In 1988, Norway and the Soviet Union signed agreements covering environmental protection and notification of nuclear accidents as well as an agreement calling for scientific and technological cooperation on problems of the study of the Arctic and the North. The Soviet Union also agreed to bilateral cooperation regarding atomic power-plant engineering and safety with Finland and prompt notification of nuclear accidents with Sweden.

Though an active member of the international whaling regime, the Soviet Union, along with Japan and Norway, registered an objection to the 1982 amendment to the schedule of whaling regulations calling for a moratorium on all commercial whaling starting in 1986. In fact, the USSR suspended its own commercial whaling activities in 1987 and no longer mounts any commercial whaling efforts. Yet, the Soviets assert that this action was unrelated to the International Whaling Commission (IWC) ban and have not withdrawn their objection to the moratorium. Animal protectionist groups, especially Sea Shepherd, have directed public attention to the annual Soviet take of gray whales in the Bering Sea under the whaling regime's exception for indigenous harvesting. Whether this take violates the terms of the IWC is a matter of controversy. Since parties that do not engage in whaling now far outnumber the whaling nations in this regime, continued Soviet participation in the IWC demonstrates a preference on the part of the USSR for international cooperation over isolation, even in international regimes dominated by opposing interests.

The Soviet record with regard to Antarctic treaties is similarly mixed. The Soviet Union is a strong supporter of the Antarctic Treaty of 1959 and a vigorous player in the Antarctic Treaty system. As well, the USSR is a party to the Antarctic Sealing Convention of 1972 (as amended) and was quick to ratify the 1980 Convention for the Conservation of Antarctic Marine Living Resources (CCAMLR), (Lyster 1985). Even so, the reluctance of the Soviet Union to inform fully other parties regarding Soviet fishing and sealing activities in Antarctica concerned American environmentalists. In 1987, the Soviets confirmed a report from New Zealand that the USSR took 4,000 – 5,000 Antarctic seals for 'experimental' purposes. They discontinued sealing after one season. Sometimes, environmentalists also portray the Soviets as intransigent regarding the regulation under CCAMLR of finfishing and krill fishing in Antarctic waters, a matter of some importance since Soviet vessels harvest these resources more heavily than American scientists believe is compatible with proper conservation measures (Manheim 1987; Scully 1987).

Overall, the Soviet record of compliance with the terms of international environmental arrangements is a complex one. Like other states, the Soviet Union has a mix of interests regarding these arrangements which yields a pattern of behavior that varies from case to case. But in some cases, the USSR is a strong proponent of the provisions of these regimes. Given the Soviet record in conjunction with both arctic-specific agreements and broader environmental accords, we believe that the environmental issue area may well constitute an appropriate place to begin, in any effort, to stimulate an expansion of international cooperation in the Arctic with Soviet participation.

This conclusion is reinforced by the recent loosening of controls in the Soviet Union which has encouraged increased public discussion and has even opened criticism of environmentally harmful development plans in the USSR, particularly oil and gas development, hydroelectric power projects and large-scale water diversion schemes (*New York Times*, 1986:A13; *Winnipeg Free Press*, 1984:15). Under the leadership of President Gorbachev, the Soviet Union has cancelled long-debated plans for massive diversions of northward-flowing rivers from Siberia to central Asia (Micklin 1984:261–63). The shelving of these plans is attributable to the loss of power by its chief proponents, government leaders in Uzbekistan accused of widespread corruption, the rising power of the green movement and a growing environmental ethic among Soviet leaders.

Gorbachev has surrounded himself with an imaginative group of policy advisers, some of whom, like the economist Abel Aganbegyan, have extensive personal experience in dealing with northern environments. In 1987, Sergei Zalegan, an expert on the Siberian water diversion plans and one of the chief critics of these plans, became head of a newly created environmental organization, Ecology and Peace (Williams 1987; McTaggert 1987). Originally named *Zelyony Mir*, which can be translated either as 'Greenpeace' or 'Greenworld', the organization's name was changed to avoid confusion with Greenpeace International which hopes to open its own office in the Soviet Union. Some outsiders regarded the founding of this Soviet environmental organization as a mere propaganda ploy since the organization is a subsidiary body of the Soviet Committee for the Defense of Peace, the Soviet Union's officially sanctioned peace movement under the direction of the CPSU (US Department of State, 1987:1–8). Though it is never easy to separate propaganda from substantive initiatives, there is mounting evidence that Gorbachev concerns himself with environmental matters. In his address to the 27th Party Congress, Gorbachev stated, 'The task of conserving nature and rationally utilizing its resources confronts us acutely...[I]n a number of regions the condition of the natural environment gives cause for concern, and the public and our writers are correct to raise the question of a solicitous attitude to the land, to the resources of the earth, to its lakes and rivers, and to the world of plants and animals' (Gorbachev 1986:7–22). In November 1986, Gorbachev reported that he was reading one of the more controversial novels about the impact of humans on nature (Quinn-Judge 1987:10). Further, he appears to listen to advisers who are aware of the writings of Soviet ecologists on the importance of ecosystem protection (Clawson and Kolarik 1978:105–22).

This emerging Soviet concern for ecosystem protection could lead to an expansion of bilateral arrangements or even multilateral regimes dealing with arctic environmental issues. An interesting place to start with such an expansion would be a consideration of a broader multilateral regime governing arctic oil pollution as an outgrowth of the emerging Soviet and American cooperative arrangement covering oil pollution in the Bering Sea.

The Soviets have a well-documented interest in offshore oil development (Bergesen *et al.* 1987), and they are clearly interested in improving their ability to cope with oil spills under arctic conditions. Under the terms of the 1985 renewal of the USSR and US Environmental Protection Agreement, for example, a group of Soviet experts on marine pollution viewed American equipment available commercially and subsequently purchased over $1 million worth of the equipment from American manufacturers (US –USSR Joint Report, 1979; *Oil and Gas Newsletter*, 1987). The Reagan– Gorbachev Summit statement in December 1987 recognized the unique conditions and opportunities for arctic cooperation. US Secretary of State Baker and Soviet Foreign Minister Schevardnadze signed a bilateral oil-spill contingency agreement on 11 May 1989. This agreement concerned cooperation in combatting pollution in the Bering and Chukchi seas in emergency situations. In the spring of 1989, the Soviet government halted new development in the giant gas fields on the Yamal peninsula in northwestern Siberia pending further study of environmental and social impacts of such development — a strong indication that the growing 'green wave' has reached the Soviet Arctic. The Soviet interest in international cooperation to deal with environmental and social problems of arctic development was evident in August 1989 at an International Symposium on Geocryological Studies in Arctic Regions in Yamburg. This symposium included field trips to view the Yamburg gas fields as well as the Gdan and Yamal peninsulas. The Ministry of Oil and Gas Construction Industry invited a group of American environmental experts to the same region immediately following the symposium to advise on environmental problems related to development of the gas fields of northwestern Siberia. In January 1990, the US and USSR agreed to a number of specific arctic and subarctic ecological cooperation projects to be carried out under the US and USSR Agreement on Cooperation in the Field of Environmental Protection. As the Soviet Union becomes more involved in offshore oil and gas development in the Arctic and as similar developments occur in the maritime Arctic adjacent to Canada, Norway and the United States, the Soviets may welcome increased cooperation to prevent oil pollution and become more sensitized to the implications of oil spills emanating from their own arctic waters as well as the waters of their circumpolar neighbors.

Taking stock

It is fair to say, overall, that the Soviets have exhibited a cautious pattern of behavior regarding international cooperation in the Arctic. This may seem to justify the concerns of those who see the Soviet Union as an obstacle to the expansion of effective cooperative arrangements in the Arctic. However, we are struck, even more forcefully, by the exceptions to this generalization and by trends suggesting a growing Soviet interest in cooperative arrangements for the Arctic.

The Soviet Union behaves much like its circumpolar neighbors in this realm, calculating its interests on a case-by-case basis and choosing among options for arctic cooperation on the basis of these calculations. To grasp the significance of these observations consider the following concrete illustrations.

Until recently, the Soviet Union certainly exhibited a preference for formal state-to-state relations in the Arctic, just as it did in other areas. In effect, the Soviets resisted being drawn into the web of complex interdependence that has spread rapidly through international society in recent years (Keohane and Nye 1977). This probably goes far toward explaining the past reluctance of the Soviet Union to allow Soviet Eskimosi to participate in the activities of the Inuit Circumpolar Conference or to respond enthusiastically to proposals for an Arctic-wide scientific organization resembling the Scientific Committee for Antarctic Research (SCAR) (Roots and Rogne 1986).

Yet the Soviets now find themselves drawn willy-nilly into an array of comparatively informal arctic activities transcending national boundaries. Soviet scientists have participated actively in IUCN-sponsored meetings on polar bears, the International Permafrost Association and the agreement covering atmospheric research between the Murmansk Geophysics Institute and the Geophysical Institute of the University of Alaska, Fairbanks. The medical section of the Siberian branch of the Soviet Academy of Sciences represents the Soviet Union in the International Union for Circumpolar Health (IUCH). The Academy's Institute of Ethnography is the Soviet counterpart of the Smithsonian Institution in organizing the circum-Bering Sea exhibit. The Institute on Physics of the Earth has joined the Natural Resources Defense Council (NRDC) in the agreement on monitoring nuclear tests. Such comparatively informal linkages are growing rapidly as Gorbachev's policies of openness and restructuring have stimulated a shower of new proposals for relatively informal linkages regarding arctic issues between Soviet groups and groups in other arctic-rim states.

Traditionally, the Soviets, like other arctic states, have also favored arctic arrangements restricted in terms of membership or functional scope in contrast to a multipurpose or comprehensive arctic regime. Thus, they have exhibited a distinct preference for limited arrangements focusing on polar bears, fur seals or migratory birds. They have accepted arrangements involving larger numbers of parties only when they are sharply restricted in their geographical domain, as in the case of the regime for Svalbard. There are numerous signs that this form of Soviet conservatism, too, is giving way to emerging pressures for broader international cooperation on arctic issues. The latest version of the Environmental Protection Agreement with the United States has become a vehicle for cooperative work on issues with unusually broad implications such as arctic haze and ozone depletion in the polar regions. The 1989 science exchange agreement with Canada is remarkably broad in its coverage (see Slipchenko, 1987:12–13; see Chapter 15).

More broadly, the Soviet Union now participates in the Northern Science Network, an enterprise Unesco sponsors, which certainly takes an ecosystems' approach in contrast to a species-specific approach to environmental concerns (Roots 1985). It is also reasonable to suppose that the growing influence of ecology will show up in the form of increased concern for the dangers of oil pollution in the maritime Arctic as well as in more traditional realms like efforts to protect habitat that wild animals require.

There is no question that the Soviet Union has been concerned with the establishment of arctic zones demarcated in jurisdictional terms in contrast to the development of cooperative international regimes covering arctic matters. This is especially true of the marine areas adjacent to the arctic coastline (the Barents, Kara, East Siberian, and Chukchi seas). Here, the Soviets have extensive commercial interests involving the Northern Sea Route and offshore development as well as critical security interests involving the deployment of nuclear-powered submarines (Armstrong 1980:86–130).

Even so, the record does *not* indicate that the Soviets are any more sensitive about jurisdictional issues in the Arctic than the other ice states. The Soviet Union has not emulated Canada in employing unusually expansive baselines to enclose the maximum amount of arctic waters as internal waters or in turning to Article 234 of the 1982 Law of the Sea Convention to justify far-reaching unilateral initiatives in the Arctic concerning pollution control (see Chapter 14; Dehner 1972:271–88). The Soviets have not followed the American lead in using domestic legislation, like the Marine Mammal Protection Act of 1972, to supplant existing international regimes for migratory species (for example, fur seals) in the Arctic.

The USSR has vigorously opposed Norwegian efforts to minimize the reach of the international regime for the Svalbard Archipelago with regard to the continental shelves adjacent to the Archipelago (Østreng 1984:866–87). Given the fact that the Soviet Union is the pre-eminent arctic state not only in terms of its geographical presence in the region, but also in terms of its military and industrial activities in the Arctic, it is remarkable that the Soviets have not been more insistent in pursuing an array of jurisdictional claims in the Arctic or in simply treating the Arctic as part of the Soviet sphere of influence. If anything, those interested in the formation of international regimes in the Arctic should probably be more concerned about the problems posed by the jurisdictional ambitions of Canada, Norway and the United States than those of the Soviet Union.

In line with its generally cautious approach to international cooperation, the Soviet Union has been reluctant to participate actively in supranational organizations designed to administer cooperative regimes for the Arctic or in more general international regimes applying in the Arctic as elsewhere. Though the Soviets rely heavily on centralized organizations at the municipal level, Soviet foreign policymakers have generally exhibited a clearcut preference for decentralized coordination requiring little administrative apparatus at the international level. Thus, the Soviet Union would surely reject any proposal for an elaborate International Arctic Authority in conjunction with a comprehensive international regime for the Arctic. Yet, this does not mean that the Soviets are unwilling to accept more limited international organizations involved with arctic issues when it is in their interest to do so.

The USSR has participated actively in the work of the International North Pacific Fur Seal Commission, the IUCN specialists group on polar bears, and the International Permafrost Association. It is worth noting that the Soviets did not oppose the comparatively elaborate administrative apparatus created under the terms of the CCAMLR agreement for Antarctic marine living resources. Of course, it would be naïve to expect any radical change in Soviet attitudes toward supranational organizations in connection with the formation of international regimes for the Arctic during the immediate future. However, it is reasonable to expect the USSR, much like the other ice states, to behave pragmatically in this realm, accepting the establishment of limited organizational arrangements to handle well-defined tasks.

Finally, the Soviet Union has long exhibited a lack of interest in resorting to supranational mechanisms, like the International Court of Justice (ICJ), to settle disputes relating to the Arctic. No doubt, this has much to do with a (probably accurate) perception the Soviets have had that such mechanisms would display a pronounced anti-Soviet bias not only in the sense of relying on Western or Western-trained personnel but also in the more subtle sense of reflecting predominantly Western concepts and legal doctrines.

At the same time, it is important to note that the Soviets are not alone when it comes to adopting a wary attitude toward resorting to supranational mechanisms in connection with arctic disputes. Canada openly announced that it would not accept the jurisdiction of the ICJ over any disputes resulting from the enactment of the Canadian Arctic Waters Pollution Prevention Act of 1971 (Bilder 1970:1–54; Dosman 1976). Interestingly, following the articulation of Article 234 and other measures supporting more expansive jurisdictional claims on the part of coastal states, Canada has come to feel secure enough to suggest that Canadian and American differences regarding arctic waters should be turned over to the ICJ for resolution (Clark 1986). The American position, by contrast, has evolved in precisely the opposite direction. In the early 1970s, the United States remained confident that the Court would view American concerns in a sympathetic light. Yet today, in the aftermath of the Nicaragua Harbor case and the Gulf of Maine case as well as the articulation of Article 234, the United States has become decidedly unenthusiastic about any move to turn to the ICJ in connection with its dispute with Canada over arctic waters. The point of all this is that Soviet attitudes in this realm are, on balance, normal rather than peculiar.

Prospects for the future

Today, the ice states no longer line up regarding arctic issues on strictly opposing sides with the NATO allies arrayed against the Soviet Union. Perceiving this, Gorbachev is appealing to the lesser arctic-rim states' interests in avoiding being caught in the crossfire of Soviet and American confrontation. In the process, he undoubtedly hopes to diffuse the problems posed for the Soviet Union by the American maritime strategy which calls for a build-up of anti-submarine warfare capabilities in the Arctic. The existence of these Soviet interests does not lead us to doubt Gorbachev's sincerity or commitment in proposing arctic international cooperation. On the contrary, his Murmansk speech has initiated progress toward improved relations among all arctic-rim nations that can eventuate in the Arctic's becoming, in Gorbachev's words, 'a zone of peace'.

The wild card in this picture is surely the course of domestic political and economic developments within the Soviet Union. It is apparent that the version of *perestroika* introduced in the 1980s will not suffice to root out the sources of economic stagnation in the Soviet economy and make it more productive. If Gorbachev or his successors respond to this emerging domestic crisis by instituting more radical forms of restructuring, the Soviet desire for international cooperation in the Arctic may grow. The need to cut back even further on military spending and a desire to attract Western capital and technology in the drive to develop arctic resources could fuel initiatives in arctic cooperation. A dramatic failure of *perestroika*, on the other hand, might well be followed either by civil strife resulting in political fragmentation or by some sort of authoritarian (not necessarily Communist) regime. In either case, it seems probable that a dramatic failure of the Gorbachev reforms would put a damper on the growth of Soviet interest in international cooperation concerning the Arctic.

Naturally, we cannot make specific predictions regarding Soviet behavior, much less anticipate how and when particular international regimes will emerge in the Arctic. However, we can pinpoint the key factors likely to influence the attitudes and actions of the Soviet Union. These include cross-pressures regarding maritime issues, the Soviet Union's geopolitical position as the paramount arctic state, the international political picture, economic conditions and development of new Soviet domestic policies of devolution and decentralization.

Above all, we can anticipate that the Soviet Union will experience cross-pressures with regard to maritime issues in the Arctic, just as it has become cross-pressured concerning such matters in other parts of the world. The posture of the USSR increasingly reflects the interests of a distant-water state concerned about freedom of transit and access to marine resources in far-away places. Yet the Soviet stance continues to exhibit the imprint of the interests of a coastal state concerned with exercising exclusive management authority in a broad maritime band adjacent to its own coastline. The result is a set of attitudes and actions regarding arctic issues that displays internal inconsistencies and even contradictions. Thus, the Soviets supported the inclusion of Article 234 in the Law of the Sea Treaty, but the USSR has not yet ratified the Treaty nor taken any vigorous steps to implement the provisions of Article 234 in their sector of the Arctic (see Chapter 14).

The Soviet Union has expressed some support for recent Canadian moves to enclose the waters of the Canadian Arctic Archipelago as internal waters. Even so, the Soviets themselves have been distinctly cautious in advancing expansive jurisdictional claims in their own sector of the Arctic, and they are clearly concerned about developments that could impede the access of

Soviet vessels elsewhere in the Arctic basin. Similarly, the USSR has periodically indicated an interest in opening the Northern Sea Route to international shipping while simultaneously making controversial jurisdictional claims regarding some of the key straits used by the Northern Sea Route (Butler 1978). These inconsistencies are easy enough to understand in terms of the cross-pressures affecting Soviet policy regarding the maritime Arctic. They suggest an important lesson for those endeavoring to predict future Soviet attitudes toward international cooperation in the region.

Analysts who take an optimistic view of such matters are apt to place heavy emphasis on the distant-water interests influencing Soviet policy, while those who expect the Soviet Union to pose obstacles to cooperative arrangements tend to stress the coastal state interests affecting Soviet policy. In fact, both sets of interests will surely continue to shape Soviet actions in the Arctic during the foreseeable future. Accordingly, we must approach Soviet positions on cooperative arrangements on a case-by-case basis, neither drawing unduly optimistic conclusions from Soviet willingness to cooperate in some areas nor extrapolating excessively pessimistic conclusions from Soviet reluctance to cooperate in other areas.

The geopolitical position of the Soviet Union in the Arctic is another factor that will determine Soviet attitudes and actions regarding international cooperation in the region (Gibson 1986:14–20). About half the coastline of the Arctic basin is under Soviet jurisdiction. The major urban centers in the Arctic (for example, Murmansk, Arkhangel'sk and Noril'sk) are located in the Soviet Union. About 75 percent of the human residents of the Far North are Soviet citizens. The USSR has proceeded farther than any of the other arctic-rim states with northern development, as exemplified by the fact that over 60 percent of the oil and gas currently produced in the Soviet Union comes from northwestern Siberia (Hannigan 1986).

The Arctic is of critical importance to the Soviet Union militarily as a theater of operations for nuclear-powered submarines, manned aircraft and even nuclear tests (Bergesen *et al.* 1987; Critchley 1984:828–65). It follows that proposals for international cooperation in the region must be sensitive to these geopolitical realities, if they are to be treated as serious initiatives rather than mere propaganda moves. This factor undoubtedly accounts for the reluctance of the Soviet Union to participate in certain types of cooperative research programs focusing on the central Arctic basin in contrast to the marginal seas (for example, the Bering Sea). This suggests that the Soviets could not seriously discuss nuclear-free zones in the arctic region that would place restrictions on the deployment of their nuclear-powered submarines in the Arctic Basin. American scientists, in particular, have sometimes complained about Soviet unwillingness to participate in cooperative scientific research on atmospheric and oceanographic issues relating to the central Arctic Basin. It should be apparent, however, that these are among the most sensitive issues arising in the Arctic and that the United States, too, is likely to be extremely careful about sharing information concerning such matters.

Equally significant is the international political picture in the Arctic. Until recently, this factor was undoubtedly a deterrent to international cooperation from the Soviet point of view. While the Soviet Union controlled a large sector of the arctic coastline, the other arctic coastal states (that is, Canada, Denmark and Greenland, Iceland, Norway and the United States) were all arrayed in opposition to Soviet interests as members of the NATO alliance. It is hardly surprising, then, that the Soviets tended to react to proposals for international cooperation in the Arctic skeptically, perceiving an 'us versus them' dichotomy in most initiatives of this type. Today, however, there are signs of change in the international politics of the arctic states which has led Gorbachev to initiate proposals for increased arctic international cooperation.

The Home Rule Government in Greenland is wary of any involvement in security arrangements; Canada shows signs of wanting to distance itself somewhat from the United States regarding security issues and none of the arctic states is enthusiastic about the implications for the Arctic of the American maritime strategy or the Strategic Defense Initiative (Ross 1986). For the first time in a generation, therefore, the Soviets have reason to think seriously about the possibility of significant shifts in the international politics of the Arctic. It should come as no surprise that the USSR has begun to explore this development, making overtures to the Canadians and others about expanded cooperation in the Arctic (Denton 1987:8A). Whatever the results of this movement with respect to specific issues, it seems generally positive in terms of the prospects for international cooperation in the Arctic. The Soviet Union no longer finds itself perpetually on the defensive in the region, a fact that can only make the Soviets more interested in arctic cooperation.

The recent emergence of the Arctic as an important arena for the operations of major military systems may well reinforce this trend in Soviet attitudes toward international cooperation in the region (Byers and Slack 1986; Bassett 1986). For reasons referred to above, the Soviet Union cannot agree to any sweeping proposals for demilitarization or even nuclear-free zones in the Arctic. Nevertheless, the Soviets have real incentives to treat the Arctic as a key arena in efforts to stabilize the global strategic balance and to take an interest in arms-stabilization measures tailored to arctic conditions.

It is not hard, for example, to see why the Soviets may become interested in agreements to minimize the dangers of accidental or inadvertent clashes in the Arctic (for example, coordinated air-traffic-control arrangements), to establish secure zones for nuclear-powered ballistic missile submarines (SSBNs) in the Arctic basin or to forego elaborate and costly defenses against manned bombers carrying cruise missiles over polar routes. It is possible that a stable balance of deterrence in the Arctic could contribute to the creation of a strategic environment that would encourage the superpowers to go forward with plans for sizeable mutual reductions in their inventories of intercontinental ballistic missiles (ICBMs). This follows along the lines of proposals under consideration in the strategic arms reduction talks (START) in Geneva. None of this, of course, is likely to happen without a sustained effort and a willingness to participate in protracted negotiations. Still, recent political and military developments in the Arctic do suggest that the prospects for international cooperation regarding arms-control measures for the region are better today than they have been at any previous time in the postwar era (Young 1986; Bloomfield 1981:87–105; Osherenko and Young 1989).

To the extent that the Soviet Union continues to develop the nonrenewable resources of the Soviet North (including the offshore Arctic) on a large scale, it is reasonable to expect that economic considerations, too, will contribute to a growing Soviet responsiveness regarding international cooperation in the Arctic during the foreseeable future. The Soviets have a well-known need for Western technologies as well as outside sources of capital in connection with northern development (Whiting 1981). Exports of hydrocarbons from northwestern Siberia have already become the principal source of hard currency available to the USSR (Hannigan 1986; Hewett 1984).

For their part, the Western Europeans and the Japanese have clearcut incentives to look to the Soviet Union for some of their energy supplies as a means of reducing their dependence on Middle Eastern oil. The Soviets are already supplying natural gas from northwestern Siberia to several European countries, and they have recently indicated a distinct interest in negotiating joint enterprises in connection with northern resource development (Bergesen et al. 1987; see Chapter 14). Therefore, barring some dramatic political change, we can anticipate that the Soviet Union will become involved in an increasingly dense network of cooperative economic arrangements in the Arctic over the next several decades. Many of these arrangements are apt to feature private participants on the Western side and to take the form of bilateral in contrast to multilateral agreements. Taken together, however, they can only serve to draw the USSR into a more extensive pattern of complex interdependence in the Arctic. This could easily initiate a dynamic leading to broader cooperative arrangements in the Arctic, initially in the area of environmental protection and eventually in more sensitive political and military areas.

We cannot close this section on future prospects regarding Soviet attitudes toward international cooperation in the Arctic without more reference to the internal changes and domestic debates currently taking place within the Soviet Union. We know now that Gorbachev's efforts to promote domestic reforms are serious and that they go far beyond simple slogans referring to openness (Bialer 1987:59–87). Major efforts to revitalize the Soviet economy are clearly on the agenda, and those engaged in such efforts cannot fail to take a hard look at the constraints imposed by the massive Soviet defense budget.

A significant Soviet environmental movement has emerged in the 1980s and it has even succeeded in temporarily halting development in the supergiant arctic gas fields on the Yamal peninsula. Soviet scholars are generating new ideas for arctic cooperation especially in the field of environmental protection (see Chapter 5; Roginko 1989:133–43; Nikitina 1989:123–32). There is a striking receptivity to new cultural and intellectual ideas in Soviet society. Gorbachev himself has assembled a group of advisers

— Leonid Albalkin, Abel Aganbegyan, Tatyana Zaslavskaya and Yevgeny Primakov, for example — who are open to new ideas and who, in some cases, have considerable northern and Siberian experience. Needless to say, there are also groups opposing these trends within the Soviet Union, and we cannot simply assume that the Gorbachev reforms will unfold during the near future without a series of domestic struggles. What is new is the extent to which Gorbachev has taken the initiative in making the Soviet Union a leader in international affairs. At this juncture, therefore, it seems at least as appropriate to ask whether the other arctic states will respond favorably to Soviet initiatives aimed at enhancing international cooperation in the Arctic as it is to worry about the willingness of the Soviets to respond positively to the initiatives of others.

In short, the shifting pattern of political alignments in the Arctic itself together with the new receptivity to innovative policies among key Soviet decisionmakers augurs well for the prospects of devising mutually beneficial cooperative arrangements covering a number of economic, environmental and even security issues in the Arctic over the next decade.

Soviet international cooperation

Once we put aside ideologically based stereotypes regarding the Soviet Union, the examination of Soviet attitudes and actions toward international cooperation in the Arctic emerges as a complex and intriguing topic. As one would expect of a state possessing an array of sometimes contradictory interests, the Soviet record in this field is far from uniform. However, given the somewhat isolated position that the Soviet Union has occupied during most of the postwar era in the political alignments of the arctic states, it is remarkable that the Soviets have shown real interest in arctic international cooperation. Thus, it is hard to deny the genuineness of the Soviet interest in cooperative arrangements for seals, bears and migratory birds, certain broader environmental problems, economic development under arctic conditions and some types of scientific research.

While it is surely true that distinct elements of caution mark the Soviet record in this realm, these elements are no more pronounced in the Soviet case than they are in the behavior of the other leading arctic states. This brief analysis makes it clear that the Soviet Union has both major stakes and a complex array of interests in the Arctic and that Soviet policymakers are by no means insensitive to the attractions of international cooperation regarding some arctic issues. If anything, we would now stress Soviet leadership in the movement to enhance arctic cooperation as well as the indications of Soviet willingness to participate. This is sufficient to make it worth our while to undertake a concerted effort to identify cooperative initiatives likely to produce benefits for all of the major stakeholders in the Arctic.

References

Aeppel, T. 1987. 'Ozone accord shows concern over global climate.' *Christian Science Monitor* 17 September.

Armstrong, T. 1980. 'The Northeast Passage as a commercial waterway, 1879-1979.' *Ymer*:86-130.

— 1986. 'Soviet Government policy towards northern peoples of the USSR' *Arctic Policy*, ed. M.S. Stenbaek, 141–54. Montreal: McGill Centre for Northern Studies and Research.

Bassett, C., ed. 1986. *L'Arctique: Espace Strategique Vital Pour Les Grandes Puissances* [The Arctic: A Vital Strategic Space for the Great Powers]. Quebec City: Centre Quebecois de relations internationales.

Bergesen, H.O., A. Moe, and W. Østreng. 1987. *Soviet Oil and Security Interests in the Barents Sea.* New York: St. Martin's Press.

Bialer, S. 1987. 'Gorbachev's move.' *Foreign Policy* 68:59-87.

Bilder, R.B. 1970. 'The Canadian Arctic waters pollution prevention act: new stresses on the law of the sea.' *Michigan Law Review* 69:1-54.

Bloomfield, L.P. 1981. 'The Arctic: last unmanaged frontier.' *Foreign Affairs* 60:87-105. Compare with Young, O.R., 1986.

Broad, W.J. 1986. 'Westerners reach Soviet to check atom site.' *New York Times* 6 July:1.

— 1987. 'American scientists in Soviet getting ready to monitor atom tests.' *New York Times* 5 September:A3.

Butcher, 1987. Telephone interview with author. US Department of State. Washington, DC, August.

Butler, W. 1978. *Northeast Arctic Passage.* Alphen aan den Rijn:Sijthoff and Noordhoff.

Byers, R.B., and M. Slack, eds. 1986. *Strategy and the Arctic.* The Polaris Papers No. 4 of the Canadian Institute of Strategic Studies, Toronto, Canada.

Clark, J. 1986. House of Commons. Statement of the Secretary of State for External Affairs at the House of Commons on Canadian sovereignty, 10 September.

Clawson, R.W., and W. Kolarik. 1978. 'Soviet resource management: political aspects of water pollution control.' *In: Soviet Resource Management and the Environment*, ed. W.A. Douglas Jackson, 105-22. Columbus: American Association for the Advancement of Slavic Studies.

Cox, D., and T. Rauf. 1989. *Security Co-operation in the Arctic: A Canadian Response to Murmansk.* 24 October:8, 25. Ottawa: The Arms Control Center.

Critchly, H.W. 1984. 'Polar deployment of Soviet submarines.' *International Journal* 39:828-65.

Dehner, J.W. 1972. 'Creeping jurisdiction in the Arctic: Has the Soviet Union joined Canada?' *Harvard International Law Journal* 13:271-88.

Denton, H.H. 1987. 'Canada, Soviet Union discuss space ventures.' *Burlington Free Press* 8 February:8A.

Dosman, E.J., ed. 1976. *The Arctic in Question.* Toronto: Oxford University Press.

Environmental Protection Agency (EPA). 1986a. *Memorandum of the Tenth Meeting of the US - USSR Joint Committee on Cooperation in the Field of Environmental Protection* 14-18 December. Washington, DC: Environmental Protection Agency.

— 1986b. *Report on the Implementation of the US - USSR Agreement on Cooperation in the Field of Environmental Protection* 14-18 December. Washington, DC: Environmental Protection Agency.

Fay, F.H., and G. Fedoseev, eds. 1977. *Joint USA-USSR Ecosystem Investigation of*

the Bering Sea July-August, 1977. Washington, DC: US Department of the Interior.
— 1984. 'Soviet-American cooperative research on marine mammals.' *Pinnipeds* Vol. 1. Washington, DC: US Department of Commerce.
Francis, D.R. 1987. 'Skiing to N. Pole for adventure and peace.' *Christian Science Monitor*, 14 September:1-32.
Gibson, J.R. 1986. 'The geographical context: Canadian-Soviet comparisons.' *In*: *Strategy and the Arctic*, eds. R.B. Byers and M. Slack, 14-20. Toronto: Canadian Institute of Strategic Studies.
Gorbachev, M.S. 1986. 'Delivered to the 27th CPSU Congress.' *Political Report of the Communist Party of the Soviet Union (CPSU) Central Committee* FBIS-SOV-86-060. 28 March, 7-22.
— 1987. *Foreign Broadcast Information Service*, SOV-87–191. 2 October, 40-42. (See Appendix I).
Hammer, A. 1987. *Hammer*. New York: Putnam.
Hannigan, J. 1986. *Oil and Gas Development in the Soviet North: Exploration, Production, Transportation*. Ottawa: Department of Indian Affairs and Northern Development.
Hewett, E.A. 1984. *Energy Economics and Foreign Policy in the Soviet Union*. Washington, DC: Brookings Institution.
International Environmental Reporter. 1989. 'Investigation of ozone hole in Arctic begun by team of scientists, technicians.' 8 February:55-57.
Johnson, G.L., D. Bradley, and R.S. Winokur. 1984. 'United States security interest in the Arctic.' *In*: *United States Arctic Interests: The 1980s and 1990s*, eds. William E. Westermeyer and Kurt M. Shusterich, 268-94. New York: Springer-Verlag.
Jones, G. 1987. interview with author. US Coast Guard, Washington, DC, May.
Keohane, R.O., and J.S. Nye. 1977. *Power and Interdependence: World Politics in Transition*. Boston: Little Brown Books.
Lin, L.Y. 1987. 'Gaining ground zero.' *Sierra* January/February: 34.
Lyster, S. 1985. *International Wildlife Law*. Chapter 9. Cambridge: Grotius Publications.
Manheim, B. 1987. telephone interview with author. Environmental Defense Fund, Washington, DC, 4 August.
McKeon, E. 1987. telephone interview with author. US Department of State, Office of Ecology and Natural Resources, Washington, DC, August.
McTaggert, D. 1987. telephone interview with author. Greenpeace International, Lewes, East Sussex, UK, August.
Micklin, P.P. 1984. 'Recent developments in large-scale water transfers in the USSR.' *Soviet Geography* 25:261-63.
New York Times. 1986. 'Soviet drops diversion of river flow to south.' 5 March:A13.
— 1987. 'US and Soviet to study ozone in Antarctica.' 19 June:A13.
Nikitina, E.N. 1989. 'International mechanisms and arctic environmental research.' *Current Research in Peace and Violence* 12(3):123-32.
Office of Technology Assessment. 1985. *US -Soviet Cooperation in Space*, 109-113. Washington, DC: Government Printing Office.
Oil and Gas Journal Newsletter. 1987. 26 January.
Osherenko, G. 1989. 'Environmental cooperation in the Arctic: Will the Soviets participate?' *International Environmental Affairs*, summer. (Reprinted with alterations in *Current Research on Peace and Violence*, 12(3):144-57).
Osherenko, G., and O.R. Young. 1989. *The Age of the Arctic: Hot Conflicts and Cold Realities*. Cambridge: Cambridge University Press.

Østreng, W. 1977. *Politics in High Latitudes: The Svalbard Archipelago*: 13. London: C. Hurst.
— 1984. 'Soviet-Norwegian relation in the Arctic.' International Journal 39:866-87.
Pacific Fishing. 1987a. 'US lays down new strategy for fish talks.' 18 January.
— 1987b. 'US -Soviet fisheries leaders shake hands, see business relations.' 20 May.
Palca, J. 1986. 'Private diplomacy emergent.' *Nature* 12 June:638.
Quinn-Judge, P. 1987. 'Gorbachev maintains a hectic schedule.' *Christian Science Monitor*, 27 May:10.
Roginko, A. 1989. 'Arctic environmental cooperation — prospects and possibilities.' *Current Research on Peace and Violence* 12(3):133-43.
Roots, E.F. 1984. 'International and regional cooperation in Arctic science: A changing situation.' *Rapport fra Nordisk Vitenskapelig Konferanse om Arktisk Forsknine* 127-56. Trondheim: Universitet i Trondheim Press.
— 1985. 'The northern science network: Regional cooperation for research and conservation.' *Nature and Resources* April-June:21.
Roots, E.F., and O. Rogne. 1986. *Some Points for Consideration in Discussions on the Need for Feasibility, and Possible Role of an International Arctic Science Committee*, photocopied essay.
Ross, D. 1986. 'Canada, the Arctic and SDI: The case for early disengagement from integrated defense.' Paper delivered at the Conference on Sovereignty, Security, and the Arctic, York University, Toronto, May.
Scully, T. 1987. Telephone interview with author. US Department of State, Washington, DC, August.
Shabecoff, P. 1987a. 'Accord is reached to protect ozone.' *New York Times* 16 September:A11.
— 1987b. 'Dozens of nations approve accord to protect ozone.' *New York Times* 9 September:A6.
Slipchenko, W. 1987. 'Co-operation in Arctic science.' *Northern Perspective* 15:12-13.
Stirling, I. 1986. 'Research and management of polar bears.' *Polar Record* 143:167-76.
Stonehouse, B., ed. 1986. *Arctic Air Pollution*. Cambridge: Cambridge University Press.
Twenty-Seventh Party Congress. 1986. 'Environmental protection in the Party Program adopted at the Congress.' FBIS-SOV-86–046. 10 March:Supplement 051.
US Department of State. 1987. 'Moscow and the peace movement.' *Foreign Affairs Note* May:1-8.
US-USSR Joint Report. 1979. *Report on the Joint US-USSR Task Group on Prevention and Cleanup of Pollution of the Marine Environment from Shipping*. Washington, DC: US Coast Guard.
Whiting, A.S. 1981. *Siberian Development and East Asia: Threat or Promise?* Stanford: Stanford University Press.
Williams, N. 1987. interview with author. Greenpeace USA, Washington, DC, 11 August.
Winnipeg Free Press. 1984. '*Pravda* says Siberia plant pollutes atmosphere.' 18 October:15.
Young, O.R. 1986. 'The Militarization of the Arctic: Political consequences and prospects for arms control.' Paper delivered at the Conference on Sovereignty, Security and the Arctic, York University, Toronto, May.
Ziegler, C.E. 1987. *Environmental Policy in the USSR*. Amherst: University of Massachusetts Press.

17

A comparison of Soviet Arctic and Antarctic policies

Christopher C. Joyner

The Soviet Union is a polar state, with multiple polar interests. Significantly, these interests apply not only to the arctic region in the north, but also to the antarctic area in the south. Yet, policy attitudes and preferences regarding the Soviet Union's geopolitical, strategic and legal interests vary markedly, depending upon the pole in question and the national interests at stake.

A reasonable explanation for the disparities in the Soviet Union's policy attitudes towards the polar regions lies in the obvious physical distinctions associated with each pole's geostrategic circumstances. Popular misconception to the contrary, the Arctic and Antarctic actually have little in common geographically. The central Arctic is a deep, superincumbent ice-covered ocean — in essence a mediterranean sea, surrounded by national land regions of North America, Europe and Asia. The circumpolar northern rimland is not a frozen wasteland. Temperatures often climb above freezing in the summer, and native peoples have inhabited the region for thousands of years. More than 400 species of flowering plant life are found there, as are some of the largest known land mammals (CIA 1978:4–5).

For the Soviet Union, the Arctic is considered to be geostrategically critical. While the Arctic overlooks the Soviet homeland from the north — the shortest flight path for intercontinental ballistic missiles to travel from the United States — it also bears remembering that more than one-half of the arctic shoreland falls under Soviet sovereignty.

Antarctica is subglacially an archipelagic-like continent, conjoined and cemented together by a massive mantle of ice and snow. Approximately the size of the United States and Mexico combined, the south polar region is a high, perpetually ice-covered landmass, isolated from the world's other land areas by the waters of the Southern Ocean (ie, the southernmost reaches of the Atlantic, Pacific and Indian Oceans). Antarctica is the most lifeless of all the continents — in essence, a frozen desert. Ice-free areas cover only 2 percent of the continent, and man never has been a permanent settler there. Only 2 species of flowering plants have been discovered, and there are no trees, no reptiles, no freshwater fish and no true land mammals. The largest species of terrestrial animal life is a wingless mosquito (CIA 1978:4–5).

For the Soviet Union, the Antarctic lies more than 10,000 miles distant, and not surprisingly, was largely neglected as a geopolitical foreign-policy concern up until the mid-1950s. Since then, Antarctic policies have figured more prominently in the Soviet Union's foreign-policy calculus, but still pale in comparison to the predominant national interest priority afforded to the superjacent Arctic.

Given these clear geophysical polar contrasts, 3 issues lend particular insight into the Soviet government's perception of its national interest priorities for the respective poles, the evolution of policies formulated to attain those priorities and the geostrategic importance which subsequently has become affixed to them. First, there is the Soviet Union's legal attitude towards territorial claims and sovereignty considerations in both polar regions. Second, there is the process and means of conducting scientific research activities and the respective rationale for undertaking those activities in each pole. Third, there is the package of policies formulated to deal with managing and exploiting both living and non-living natural resources in the polar regions. When taken together, these issues indicate that certain geostrategic and geopolitical objectives are implicit in the Soviet Union's disparate polar policy. The nature of those policies and the implications they pose for international relations are addressed here.

Territorial and sovereignty claims

The Arctic

The Soviet Union has projected its sovereignty into the Arctic by means of the so-called 'sector theory of territorial demarcation'. In fact, the Soviet Union was the first and has been the only government to do so in the Arctic by formally applying, albeit not officially endorsing, the sector device as an instrument for delineating claims there (Butler 1978:71–7).

The Soviet government's decision to resort to the sector means for validating assertion of title to territory in the Arctic evolved over nearly a decade. On 20 September 1916, the Russian Imperial government gave notification that it recognized the doctrine of sectors, or 'territorial gravitation', which acknowledged the right of a state to claim territories beyond the boundaries of any other state, but lying within a particular geographical relationship to that state (Lakhtine 1930:703–17). On 4

November 1924, the People's Commissary for Foreign Affairs of the Soviet Union issued a memorandum addressed to US Secretary Charles Evans Hughes and diplomatic representatives of several other states, ostensibly to clarify the Soviet position on the status of its territorial claims in the Arctic. This memorandum in effect reiterated notification of the Russian Imperial Government's 1916 Decree and explicitly asserted that islands in the Arctic, north of the Soviet Union's coast, were Soviet territory (Lakhtine 1930:703–17). Less than 2 years later, on 15 April 1926, the Presidium of the Central Executive Committee of the USSR issued another special decree which designated the sector principle as the legal basis for the Soviet claim in the Arctic. In a relevant part, the decree asserted that:

> ...all lands and islands located in Arctic to the North, between the coastline of the USSR and the North Pole, both already discovered or to be discovered in the future, which at the time of the publication of the present decree are not recognized by the Soviet government as the territory of any foreign state... are part of the Soviet territory [*Journal of the Laws of the USSR*, 1926].

This 1926 decree in effect established a polar sector — that is, a triangular area of 'terrestrial gravitation', or region of attraction — for the Soviet state on grounds of its propinquity to the Arctic. Boundaries for the sector would be formed by using the northern coast of the Soviet Union as the baseline, with meridian lines running from the eastern and western extremities to the North Pole. As thus designated, the Soviet Union's arctic sector encompassed all arctic lands and islands lying between the Arctic coast of the Soviet Union, the North Pole and meridians 32° 4' 35" E and 168° 49' 30' W. As intended by the decree, this area under international law should be considered Soviet territory, under Soviet sovereignty and national jurisdiction.

The Soviet Union's political application and legal interpretation of the sector device in the Arctic entailed a radical modification of the traditional legal doctrine of discovery. The Soviet sector policy asserted in no uncertain terms that, regardless of the nationality of future explorers, sovereignty to any lands discovered within the compass of the declared sector of 'terrestrial gravitation' would belong to the Soviet Union. For all intents and purposes, then, the international legal doctrine of discovery was perforce rendered moot and inapplicable to lands in the Soviet Arctic. Not to be overlooked, the exact converse attitude has earmarked the Soviet Union's policy position for antarctic lands.

Importantly, as originally promulgated, the 1926 Decree extended Soviet claims only to land areas in the Arctic; sea ice and ocean space were to remain open to free navigation for all states (Butler 1978:73). Nevertheless, Soviet jurists have since argued that not only lands and islands, but also sea ice and frozen seas, within the sector ought to be included within the ambit of Soviet sovereignty (Svalien 1960:248, 257). Likewise, the Soviet press in 1928 and 1950 advanced the notion that Soviet claims actually extended to the polar seas contained within the 1926 sector boundaries (CIA 1978:32). While the Soviet government has refrained from supporting these assertions with official decrees, state practice by the Soviet Union as it has evolved over the last 6 decades clearly reveals an increasingly nationalistic attitude towards its arctic waters. Freedom of navigation for international shipping in the Soviet Arctic sector has become increasingly restricted in recent years, both by the promulgation of new legislation extending territorial jurisdiction seaward, as well as by heightened national defense and security considerations.

Intimately related to Soviet jurisdiction in the Arctic is control over foreign vessels transiting those waters. The focus of arctic shipping for the Soviet Union is the Northern Sea Route. The Northern Sea Route, which runs some 2,800 kilometers along the Soviet Arctic coastline, extends from Novaya Zemlya to the Bering Strait, forming the principal links between Murmansk in the west and the Pacific ports in the east (CIA 1978:26). As such, it is considered essential to economic development in the Soviet Arctic. The Soviet government, not surprisingly, has sought to maintain restrictive control over the shipping traffic using it, and any activities conducted within its vicinity.

The Soviet Union effects legal authority over the Northern Sea Route by claiming and enforcing maritime jurisdictional zones offshore its arctic coast. The Soviet Union claims a 12-nautical mile territorial limit (Vedomosti SSR 1982), which brings under Soviet jurisdiction prominent straits encountered in the passage. Relatedly, the Soviet Union does not recognize an international regime for straits in their portion of the Arctic. This policy was pointedly demonstrated when the Soviet government adopted legislation in 1984 establishing an exclusive economic zone (EEZ) that included the arctic coast and effectively subsumed within it all local straits within 200 nautical miles of shore (Vedomosti SSR 1984). Control over offshore navigation is further enhanced by Article 234 in the 1982 Law of the Sea Convention which would permit the Soviet Union 'to adopt and enforce non-discriminatory laws and regulations for the prevention, reduction and control of marine pollution from vessels in ice-covered areas within the limits of the exclusive economic zone... ' (United Nations 1982). In addition, at various times, Soviet legal commentators have claimed 'internal waters status' — that is, the status of being under complete Soviet sovereignty — for the arctic seas. Included among these are all the waters of the Kara, Laptev, White and East Siberian seas, as well as significant portions of the Barents and Chukchi seas. Legal justification for these claims has been predicated on so-called 'historic factors', coupled with the contention that ice on the seaward side of these water bodies is purportedly characterized by certain land-like qualities (Breitfuss 1929:467–69).

By asserting regulatory control over this Northern Sea Route, the Soviet Union has effectively established a national security zone along its northern coastal border. In the global context, the Soviet Union generally has opposed broad, very restrictive offshore maritime zones, simply to maximize its naval mobility and to ensure wider access for its fleet to global fisheries. For the Arctic, however, national security interests plainly have come to prevail over an open-access regime. The Soviet Union in recent years has increasingly sought to tighten its control over the arctic region, and in the process, to regulate a semi-closed transit regime for foreign shipping in the North.

The Antarctic

Russian involvement in Antarctica can be traced back to the controversy over who actually first discovered the continent. The Soviet Union is quick to claim that F.F. Bellinghausen and M.P. Lazarev sailing on board *Vostok* and *Mirnyy* were the first to sight Antarctica in their voyage during 1819–21, though that 'first' is still debated (Armstrong 1977:887). What remains undisputed is that Bellinghausen was the first to circumnavigate the southern continent and that he discovered Peter I Island, Alexander I Island and the South Shetland Islands group. These accomplishments have prompted the Soviet Union to declare officially that Russian navigators deserve chief credit for 'discovering Antarctica and [for] ushering in an era of scientific investigation and exploration of the new continent....' (UN Secretariat 1984:82).

Since early this century, the Antarctic continent has been subjected to claims of sovereign title asserted by 7 states: the United Kingdom, to the British Antarctic Territory, in 1908 and 1917; New Zealand, to the Ross Dependency, in 1923; France, to Adelie Land, in 1924; Australia, to the Australian Antarctic Territory, in 1933; Norway, to Dronning Maud Land, in 1939; Chile, to Territorio Chileno Antartico, in 1940; and Argentina, to Antartida Argentina, in 1943 (Auburn 1982) (see Figure 17.1). The Soviet Union has not recognized the lawful validity of any of these claims, and for that matter, neither has any other state. More significant than this, however, the Soviet Union has reserved for itself, 'all rights based on discoveries and explorations of Russian navigators and scientists, including the right to present corresponding territorial claims in the Antarctic' (UN Secretariat, 1984:95). As early as 1950, the Soviet press put forth that contingency, as *Komsomolskaya Pravada* declared:

> Our country is the lawful heir to the outstanding Russian geographical discoveries made in the South Polar Seas at the beginning of the 19th century. Historically the right of priority in the discovery and exploration of a number of antarctic lands remains eternally with Russia, and by succession, with the U.S.S.R. [Komsomolskaya Pravada, 1950:4].

It is important to realize that mere discovery in international law lacks the requisite legal force to validate a claim of title to territory. Appropriation is required, usually demonstrated by effective occupation through permanent settlement within a reasonable, albeit unspecified period of time. Interestingly enough, Soviet legal commentators reject the validity of the principle of effective occupation as legitimate expression of international law. Their rationale for this rejection is twofold. First, the theory of effective occupation derives from the Berlin Conference of 1885, which is viewed by the Soviets as a situation concerned with imperialist states exercising unlawful control over African territory. The second argument against the

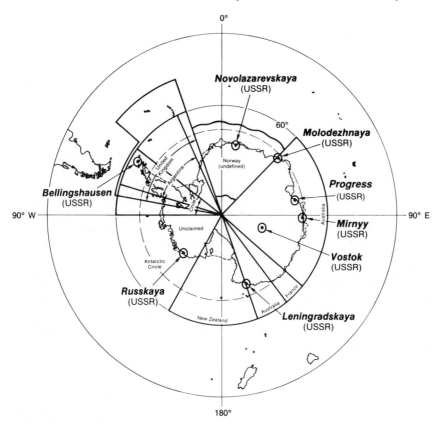

Figure 17.1 National claims and permanent Soviet research stations in Antarctica.

principle of effective occupation rests with its particular application to the polar regions. The unique physical conditions of the Arctic and Antarctic render it both impractical and unjustifiable to impose demands of 'effectiveness', given the harsh environmental factors and climatic conditions there [Molodtsov 1954:30–2].

For the Arctic, at least one prominent Soviet legal commentator has suggested that 'effective occupation' may be obtained with the establishment of scientific stations, or regularized patrols by government vessels or the siting of meteorological, radio or aviation facilities in the region (Taracouzio 1938:320). One may logically infer that this legal deduction would carry southward to Soviet activities in the Antarctic as well. Performance of the same criteria by the 7 claimant states in Antarctica, however, has not been recognized by the Soviet Union as constituting anything like lawful 'effective occupation' such that it could give rise to substantiating their claims. In sum, the Soviet Union repudiates the notion of fully effective occupation for validating claims to sovereignty in Antarctica. All that is required is the exercise of minimal administrative control over the region. Thus, minimal control, bolstered by discovery, presumably could be submitted to yield a future Soviet claim to some part of Antarctica.

Since promulgation of the Antarctic Treaty in 1959, the Soviet Union has not claimed specific or preferential sovereignty rights over any territory within the Antarctic area. Undoubtedly, much of this restraint can be attributed to the fiat contained in Article IV of the Treaty, which in part provides that, 'No acts or activities taking place while the present Treaty is in force shall constitute a basis for asserting, supporting or denying a claim to territorial sovereignty in Antarctica or create any rights of sovereignty in Antarctica' (The Antarctic Treaty, 1959). The Soviet Union has preferred to act within the Antarctic Treaty framework. In that capacity, the Soviet government has participated as an active member of the Antarctic Treaty Consultative Party group (ATCPs) — the administrative decision-making body created by the Treaty — and has contributed to the formulation of policies for all Treaty parties within ambit of the agreement, namely, the area south of 60°S (Joyner 1989a:83–104).

In contrast with its *de facto* position towards the Arctic, the Soviet Union has consistently refused to accept sector solutions for partitioning territory in the Antarctic. Application of the sector theory to Antarctica is rejected by the Soviet Union largely because of the obvious geographical distinctions between the Arctic and the Antarctic. While true, this rationale is probably more politically convenient than legally pertinent. Even so, as suggested by V. Durdenevsky,

> In the north, there are narrow 'ice' seas... close to the population centers of Europe and America, representing for the coast lands, aside from an economic, also a strategic interest... In the south, there is a special ice-bound unpopulated continent... distant from population centers but important in an industrial sense even for remote countries, particularly for Russia, who has discovered it, and for the Soviet Union, according to the right of succession [Toma 1956:611–19].

In short, Soviet claims to the Arctic by means of the sector device essentially employ the doctrines of contiguity and proximity for underpinning their legal support. As viewed by the Soviets, the situation in the Antarctic is radically different, as the continent is separated from its nearest landmass — South America — by some 550 miles of ocean space. Interestingly enough, it is worth noting that both Argentina and Chile, the 2 states closest to Antarctica, base their claims to the continent in part on these very same legal arguments of contiguity and proximity.

Scientific research activities

The Arctic

The Soviet Union has long recognized the importance of arctic science in its national ambitions, and, accordingly, has vigorously pursued policies to put those priorities into effect. Perhaps not surprisingly, much of the Soviet

Union's precise arctic science activities remain classified for military purposes.

Responsibility for Soviet arctic research in large part falls to the Arctic and Antarctic Scientific Research Institute (AASRI) in Leningrad which is staffed by some 1,800 research personnel. The AASRI operates more than 100 designated polar stations in the Soviet Arctic, as well as some 12 oceanographic vessels and several aircraft, which collect data about weather, ocean and ice conditions in the northern Soviet Union. In addition, numerous other scientific institutions are engaged in research operations in the Arctic, including the Scientific Research Institute of Arctic Geology in Leningrad and Murmansk, the Permafrost Institute in Yakutsk and the Polar Research Institute of Marine Fisheries and Oceanography in Murmansk. With respect to programs, much scientific research concerns climate studies and geophysical phenomena of the polar environment, including, for example, permafrost conditions, cold region engineering and human adaptation in frigid climes (CIA 1978:30).

Available information suggests that the Soviet scientific effort in studying the Arctic Ocean supercedes by far national programs of other arctic States. With respect to marine scientific research, the Soviet Union's official attitude towards the most appropriate type of international legal regime underwent a notable transformation during the 1970s, a process that doubtlessly can be attributable in part to security concerns over their northern border region. At the outset of the Third United Nations Conference on the Law of the Sea (UNCLOS III), the Soviet Union initially favored a regime that appeared reasonably balanced between freedom of research and coastal state consent. Towards this end, in 1974 the Soviet Union introduced to UNCLOS III a draft proposal that advocated freedom of scientific research unrelated to natural resources within the exclusive economic zone area, with coastal state consent required for research related to natural resources in the zone (United Nations, 1974). Such an approach would work well for the Soviet Union, both to preserve its coastal defense priorities, as well as to maintain the perceived benefits of being able to participate more freely in marine scientific research around the world. By 1976, however, the Soviet Union had moved to embrace a consent regime for all scientific research conducted offshore within a state's EEZ, that is, within 200 nautical miles of its coast. This policy was officially endorsed with the promulgation of the 'Temporary Measures for Conservation of Living Resources and Regulation of Marine Fishing' in December 1976, and was fully effected by special Soviet legislation adopted in 1984 (USSR Council of Ministers, 1985; Vedomosti SSR, 1984). That this shift in Soviet legal thinking occurred may be ascribed partially to the rise of defense concerns over protecting Soviet coasts and offshore regions, especially those in the north (Allison 1986:124–8). However, it is also significant to realize that motivation for the Soviet's initial acceptance in 1976 of the extended offshore jurisdiction in arctic waters, with its restrictive implications for foreign marine scientific research there, was also lodged in angry reaction to the unilateral adoption by the United States of a 200-mile fisheries management zone earlier that same year (Allison 1986:123).

Christopher C. Joyner

The Antarctic

Considerable experience in scientific research and polar exploration in the Arctic helped to prepare the Soviet Union for the leading role it has assumed since 1960 in scientific investigation of the Antarctic. The scientific facet of Soviet polar research is coordinated by the Arctic and Antarctic Scientific Research Institute of the Soviet Committee on Antarctic Research of the Academy of Sciences of the USSR. As officially stated, the Soviets see Antarctica as a 'zone reserved for peaceful research and scientific cooperation between States' (UN Secretariat, 1984:85). To this end, the Soviet government regards Article II of the Antarctic Treaty, which embodies the principle of freedom of scientific investigation in Antarctica, to be of utmost importance' (UN Secretariat, 1984:87). Unlike the arctic situation, the Soviet Union embraces absolute freedom of scientific research in the south. That is, the Soviet government recognizes no jurisdictional zones emanating offshore from any of the claimant states' territories, and acknowledges no consent regime for conducting scientific research in the region — policy attitudes which are legally upheld for all parties by Articles IV and II, respectively, in the Antarctic Treaty. Freedom of scientific research is thus guaranteed for all parties within the ambit of the Treaty area, that is south of 60°S (The Antarctic Treaty, 1959). As clearly evidenced by the establishment of scientific stations, the Soviet Union has been a major actor in maximizing this opportunity throughout the continent.

The Soviet Union in 1990 operates 8 principal year-round scientific stations on Antarctica (see Figure 17.1). The first Soviet station, Mirnyy, was established in the coastal area of the larger Australian sector in February 1956. Today it serves as the main base for Soviet research, with special emphasis placed on monitoring meteorological, geomagnetic and seismological activities on the continent. In December 1957 the Vostok base opened at the south geomagnetic pole. Owing to its special location, some of the most important scientific activities are conducted here, including aerological, meteorological and glaciological studies, as well as experiments on radio wave propagation, and the aurora australis. It was at the Vostok base that on 21 July 1983 the lowest temperature on record, −89.2° centigrade (−128.6° Fahrenheit), was measured (Hoffman 1986:750). During the 1960s, 3 more Soviet bases were established. In February 1961, the Novolazarevskaya station was set up on the coast of the Norwegian sector. In 1963 the Molodyozhnaya base was built in Enderby Land, in the Australian sector. This has become the headquarters for Soviet stations in Antarctica and it is the largest national base on the continent, next to that operated by the United States at McMurdo. The Bellinghausen station was set up on King George Island in the South Shetlands in 1968. In 1970, the Leningradskaya station was established in the smaller Australian portion of claim. In 1980, the Russkaya station was sited in the unclaimed sector. An eighth station called Progress was opened in April 1988 in the Larsemann Hills on Prydz Bay in the larger Australian sector. These 8 stations operate year round, with a combined population of about 300–50 personnel whose mission is to conduct experiments on polar conditions and phenomena.

292

Foremost among these Soviet research programs are those dealing with surface and air meteorology, geomagnetics and ionospheric conditions. In addition, considerable attention is devoted to snow, meteor and hydrologic observations, as well as the tracking of geodetic satellites (CIA 1978:47).

In addition to these 8 permanent bases facilities, several summer stations have been operated in recent years by the Soviets in Antarctica. Perhaps the most notorious is Druzhnaya I, founded in 1976 on the Filchner Ice Shelf with the express purpose of conducting prospecting experiments on the mineral-rich Dufek Intrusion. It was this station which broke away from the continent in June 1986 on an iceberg. In February 1987, it was reported that a Soviet ship had caught up with that iceberg, and recovered the ice station (Shabad 1987). Seven Soviet seasonal stations are now considered operative. Three of these are located along the coast of the larger Australian sector. Soyuz was established in November 1982, Oasis II began operation in January 1987 and Druzhnaya IV was founded early in 1989. Another seasonal station, Druzhnaya II, operates on the Weddell Sea and a fifth called Druzhnaya III was set up in January 1987 on the coast of the Norwegianclaim. Two inland summer stations, Pionerskaya established in 1956, and Komosomol'skaya founded in 1980, also conduct scientific research during the austral summer. Of significant note, during 1984–5, the 29th Soviet Antarctic Expedition (that is the complement of personnel involved in all Soviet antarctic-related activities on the continent) numbered some 600 participants (UN Secretariat, 1984:95).

As regards marine research, the Soviet Union (along with the United States) is the only state that routinely conducts scientific surveys around the entire continent. The Soviets operate 3 or more research vessels during the austral summer, and they regularly are involved in oceanographic, meteorologic, hydrographic and biological investigations in the circumpolar waters. To reiterate, unlike the Arctic, these research activities offshore Antarctica in the Southern Ocean are not affected by any consent regime, territorial seas prohibitions or EEZ restrictions. Moreover, it is fair to conclude that, aside from the real scientific benefits acquired from this highly sophisticated, multi-dimensional program of research investigation in Antarctica, geopolitical considerations figure no less importantly in the promotion of these activities within the broader context of the Soviet Union's foreign policy calculus. This substantial program of scientific activities supplies the Soviet Union with an ongoing physical presence and hence an enhanced basis for some future legal claim to the region. Further, it permits the Soviets to maintain a transcontinental and oceanic presence, thereby affording wide access to both mineral and marine resources that may become available for exploitation in the coming years. These points should not be lost when appraising the Soviet government's adamant insistence for maintaining a free and open scientific research regime in the Antarctic.

Christopher C. Joyner

Natural resource policies

Arctic resources

The Soviet Arctic, including its continental margin, encompasses about one-third of the area of the Soviet Union, and contains superabundant deposits of mineral and hydrocarbon resources. In recent decades, the economics of northern resource development have become particularly important for Soviet industrialization, especially that relating to oil and gas development. The most prospective region for onshore hydrocarbon resources in the Soviet Union is in the arctic areas: About two-thirds of the Soviet Union's proven and probable hydrocarbon reserves are in arctic or sub-arctic fields, mainly in the lower Ob' basin of Western Siberia. Offshore, the most highly touted deposits are also in the Arctic, in the Barents and Kara seas (see Chapter 7).

With respect to mining, the Soviet Union is by far the most active mineral resource miner of the Arctic States — an accomplishment principally attributable to the vast deposits of nickel, copper, platinum, gold, tin and diamonds which have been discovered there. In the northwest Soviet Arctic, the Kola peninsula contains tremendous reserves of iron and the largest known deposits of apatite in the world. Noril'sk in Eastern Siberia is considered to be the most important mineral center in the Soviet Arctic, with great reserves of copper and nickel. The Chukotskiy region is well known for its rich gold fields. It is the arctic region which, in sum, supplies the Soviet Union with the strategic minerals necessary for fueling and building the industrial infrastructure of that society. For that reason alone the Arctic assumes special — and indeed critical — strategic importance for the Soviet Union as a national security concern.

Respective to living marine resources, the Arctic is among the world's oldest and richest commercial fishing grounds. For the Soviet Union, however, less than 15 percent of its world fish catch is taken from arctic waters. Most of this is capelin caught in the Barents Sea and pollock from the Bering Sea. The remainder of the Soviet Union's fish harvest comes from its global fishery activities in distant waters of the Pacific, Atlantic, Indian and Southern Oceans (CIA 1978:21). It is in this respect that the bountiful fishery resources of Antarctica's circumpolar waters receive salient foreign policy consideration by the Soviet Government.

Antarctic resources

During the 1960s, an immense build-up occurred of the Soviet Union's distant-water fishing fleet and its fishing capability. The great efficiency and remarkable volume of the Soviet fleet's world-wide harvesting capacity, however, produced an unintended reaction in the international community during the 1970s: it contributed to the rise of a conservation-minded attitude among many coastal states, in particular the United States, to adopt measures designed to secure exclusive control over fishing in their offshore coastal areas. This attitude eventually became translated internationally into the legal notion of the 200-mile exclusive economic zone during the UNCLOS III and thus confronted the Soviet distant water fleets with the uncomfortable situation of having severely reduced ocean space in which to fish. Soviet fisherman thus have become encouraged in recent years to look more intently at harvesting opportunities in unregulated high-seas areas, including the waters of the Antarctic.

The Soviet Union has actually operated commercial fishing in the southern seas since 1967. In one of its most active years, 1971, some 40 Soviet trawlers were sighted in antarctic waters. For that year, catches were recorded by the Soviets of some 300,000 metric tons — mostly cod, herring, whiting and Patagonian hake — in the region (CIA 1978:54). Since the early 1970s, however, Soviet fishery attention turned increasingly towards harvesting krill, a small shrimp-like crustacean that concentrates in swarms in nutrient-laden waters found throughout the Southern Ocean. The Soviet Union, in fact, has pioneered the way with krill-fishing techniques, krill research and product marketing efforts, and has become the leading krill-fishing nation (Armstrong 1974:171). Krill catches by the Soviet Union in the 1986–7 fishing season amounted to some 377,000 metric tons. To preserve these harvesting opportunities, the Soviet Union stands firmly against the imposition by any claimant state of any type of exclusive fishing zone in antarctic waters. This view applies not only to possible jurisdictional zones that hypothetically might someday be extended offshore the continent; it applies with equal adamancy against those exclusive economic zones that have already been declared by France over Kerguelen and Crozet Islands and by Australia over Heard and McDonald Islands. In fact, when the 1980 Convention on the Conservation of Antarctic Living Resources was being negotiated among the Antarctic Treaty Consultative Parties, the Soviet Union made it patently clear that while it did not dispute either French or Australian sovereignty over these islands, it refused to recognize the legitimacy of the 200-mile EEZs that had been proclaimed around them in 1978 and 1979, respectively. Significant to note, krill swarms swim profusely around these two islands' formations (Boczek 1984:848–9).

Since 1982, the ATCPs have been engaged in negotiations designed to produce a treaty regime for regulating minerals activities in the Antarctic. The Soviet Union clearly favors and supports creation of this minerals regime in Antarctica, particularly one that will 'exclude any type of arbitrary actions detrimental to the interests of other countries and peoples of the world' (UN Secretariat, 1984:92). For the Soviet government, this new minerals regime is heralded to work as 'a reliable barrier against any uncontrolled activity in the region, and to ensure the conservation of the unique Antarctic environment and its dependent ecosystems for present and future generations' (UN Secretariat, 1984:91).

While the Soviet government doubtlessly believes that these rationales may justify creation of such a minerals regime, it is similarly true that other, more self-serving motives are at work as well. The Soviet Union has been relatively open about desiring to exploit and use antarctic mineral resources for its own national economy (Boczek 1984). Such a regime might facilitate that objective and in the process give the Soviet government legal leverage to control United States' access to those same resources.

Closely related to these mineral-related considerations are Soviet scientific activities on and around Antarctica. The Soviet Union's 8 permanent research stations have been strategically located around the continent, such that one is situated in every sector, except for that claimed by New Zealand. Moreover, the Soviet Union sponsors one of the largest and most sophisticated geological research programs for Antarctica. Soviet geological interest is concentrated most heavily in 2 particular areas. First, in the Ross Sea, with its possible oil and gas potential, 2 permanent bases are situated, Leningradskaya and Russkaya. Appreciating their location, these two installations may coincidentally be viewed as geostrategically imposing upon United States' interests in the region, as they straddle McMurdo, the largest US base in Antarctica. Second, in the Weddell Sea are located Druzhnaya I (before it broke off from the ice shelf) and Druzhnaya II. These facilities are used to engage in prospecting activities throughout the Dufek Massif, a geological site where deposits of certain critical strategic minerals such as chromium, copper, nickel and platinum group metals may possibly be discovered.

When assessed synergistically, this package of strategically located geological activities suggests that such policies may be intended to furnish the Soviet Union with an enhanced negotiating position should mineral rights ever be allocated in the future. Since 1958, the Soviet Union has worked steadily to bolster and firm up the legal basis for a claim in Antarctica, if someday that development were to become warranted. This process has taken on a multifaceted character through more extensive and enhanced scientific, exploratory and research-related activities throughout the continent. The current operation of 8 major year-round stations, as well as seasonal stations and the various scientific research being conducted there, clearly indicates this commitment by the Soviet government.

It merits mention that so long as the Antarctic Treaty remains in force, Soviet scientific activities conducted thereunder ostensibly would be precluded from counting as substantive enhancement to a claim they might make in the Antarctic. Article IV prohibits assertions of new claims, or the enlargement or perfection of extant ones, during the life of the Treaty. If for some reason, however, the Antarctic Treaty were to break down or collapse, the Soviet Union, as any other state, would be legally eligible to assert a claim to part of the continent. In any event, one would be hard pressed to argue convincingly that all the Soviet Union's scientific efforts and accomplishments in the Antarctic since 1961 were of nugatory legal value. This difficulty becomes plainly evident with the simple realization that of all the states involved in antarctic affairs over the last 30 years, the Soviet Union has sponsored by far the most active scientific community, save for perhaps that of the United States (Joyner 1989b).

296

Conclusion

Soviet polar policies have been markedly affected by the development of that state's global interests over the last three decades. This process has been accelerated by the growth of the Soviet Union's maritime capability, as well as by adjustments to conditions in the international geopolitical situation and to changes in international law.

The Soviet Union has made the doctrine of discovery inapplicable to the Arctic through promulgation of a national decree which delimited the Soviet Arctic by a variant of the sector theory. Importantly, the arctic sector doctrine has neither been forthrightly heralded nor officially embraced by the Soviet Union in recent years; to do so would obviously pose a direct conflict with the Soviet Union's outspoken rejection of the sector theory's legitimacy for claims made by 7 other states to portions of the Antarctic. The Soviet Union has opted to apply the sector doctrine to the poles selectively. Where and when this application serves the Soviet government's national interests, such as clearly is the case in the Arctic, the legitimacy of that sectorization is recognized. When Soviet interests might be compromised or undercut, as in the Antarctic, the validity of that sectorial application is denied.

Soviet scientific activities have been undertaken in both the Arctic and Antarctic, ostensibly for the sake of conducting primary research into the nature of polar phenomena. However, Soviet scientific research in the Arctic appears more likely to contain defense-related components, as well as national security motives. In the same vein, it is not farfetched to suggest that Soviet scientific investigation in the Antarctic — while certainly contributing much to the body of knowledge relating to the cold continent — is also motivated by the prospects that these multifaceted activities will enhance the Soviet Union's future opportunities in securing access to hard minerals and hydrocarbons in the Antarctic, if indeed any are ever discovered and subsequently developed. Such pervasive activities, moreover, do supply additional evidence of the Soviet Union's continued 'occupation' of the continent, a consideration which might be used in support of staking and legally substantiating some future Soviet claim there, if indeed that strategic option ever became a realistic policy consideration.

In the Arctic, the Soviet Union unequivocally favors maintaining a nationalistic regime to regulate each arctic state's coastal regions. Soviet national legislation since the mid-1970s has underscored the import of this policy attitude, especially with regard to regulating foreign shipping sailing along the Northern Sea Route. On the other hand, in the Antarctic, the Soviet Union plainly supports the Antarctic Treaty System, and is 'vigorously opposed to [any] attempts to revise the Antarctic Treaty, regardless of the pretexts under which they are put forward' (UN Secretariat, 1984). The international stability promoted by this Treaty — including provisions which assure free scientific cooperation and exchange of information, peaceful uses only of the continent, non-militarization of the continent, denuclearization of the continent, unannounced on-site inspection and peaceful settlement of disputes in the region — unmistakably serve Soviet national interests far better than otherwise would be the case without a Treaty (Joyner 1989b). Similarly, the Soviet government believes that the present system for the Antarctic is far preferable to that of a radically revised universalistic arrangement, such as that envisioned under a 'Common Heritage of Mankind' regime. Especially in this context, the Soviet Union strongly supports establishment of an Antarctic Minerals Treaty Regime under ATCP control to regulate mineral activities on and around the continent, though prospects for this occurring soon are uncertain.

The Soviet Union's polar policies are products of its national interests. As such, they mirror the Soviet government's foreign policy objectives and international priorities. Clearly, the Arctic retains paramount priority for the Soviet Union because of the region's strategic proximity for national security and its economic value for supplying natural resources. Though of lesser import, the Antarctic still remains salient on the Soviet Union's foreign policy agenda. This consideration turns on the potential value which that continent may hold for Soviet interests in the future, rather than on any immediate gains which will be attained there today. If the past is viewed as a prologue, lessons for Soviet activities in Antarctic may be apparent from that state's historical experiences in the Arctic. In any event, one fact seems plainly evident. In both arctic and antarctic politics, as well as in any diplomatic efforts to fashion international legal regimes for regulating polar activities, the Soviet Union will remain a key national player in formulating and determining policy outcomes.

References

Allison, A.P. 1986. 'The Soviet Union and UNCLOS III: pragmatism and policy evolution.' *Ocean Development and International Law* 16:109, 123-8.
Antarctic Treaty, The. 1959. 12 U.S.T. 794, 797, TIAS No. 4780, 492 UNTS 71, 76, Article II, Article IV.
Armstrong, T. 1974. 'Soviet equipment for processing krill.' *Polar Record* 17:171.
— 1977. 'Bellinghausen and the discovery of Antarctica.' *Polar Record* 15:887.
Auburn, F.M. 1982. *Antarctic Law and Politics*, 5-84. Bloomington:Indiana University Press.
Boczek, B.A. 1984. 'The Soviet Union and the Antarctic region.' *American Journal of International Law* 78:834, 848-9, 851.
Breitfuss, L. 1929. 'Territorial division of the Arctic.' *Dalhousie Review* 8:457, 467-9.
Butler, W.E. 1978. *Northeast Arctic Passage*, 71-77. Alphen aan den Rijn, The Netherlands:Sijthoff & Noordhoff.
— ed. 1983. *The USSR, Eastern Europe and the Development of the Law of the Sea.* Dobbs Ferry:Oceana.
Central Intelligence Agency (CIA). 1978. *Polar Regions Atlas*, 4-5, 21, 26, 32, 47, 54. Washington, DC:CIA.
Hoffman, M.S., ed. 1986. *The World Almanac and Book of Facts 1987*, 750. New York:Ballantine Books.
Journal of the Laws of the USSR. 1926. See Sec. 1:586, Sec. 2. 'Sobranie-zakonov i

rasporiazhanii Raboche-Krestianskogo Pravitelstva SSSR 1923-37,' Otd. I, Otd. II.

Joyner, C. 1989a. 'Nonmilitarization of the Antarctic: The interplay of law and politics.' *Naval War College Review* 42: 83-104.

— 1989b. 'US-Soviet cooperative diplomacy: The case of Antarctica.' *In: US-Soviet Cooperation: A New Future*, ed. Nsh Jamgotch, Jr. New York:Praeger.

Komsomolskaya Pravada. 1950. 'Russkie Ofkryli Antarktiku' [Russians discovered the Antarctic], 28 January, 4.

Lakhtine, V.L. 1930. 'Rights over the Arctic.' *American Journal of International Law* 25:703-17.

Molodtsov, S.V. 1954. *Contemporary International Legal Status of the Antarctic*, 30-32. Moscow:Gosynrizdat.

Shabad, T. 1987. 'Russians recover lost ice station.' *New York Times*, 22 February, 4.

Svalien, O. 1960. 'The sector principle in law and practice.' *Polar Record* 10:248, 257.

Taracouzio, T.A. 1938. *Soviets in the Arctic*, 320, 348-9. New York.

Toma, P.H. 1956. 'Soviet attitude towards the acquisition of territorial sovereignty in the Antarctic.' *American Journal of International Law* 50:611, 619.

United Nations. 1974. Doc. A/CONF.62/C 2/L38, Article 5.

— 1982. *Convention on the Law of the Sea*. Doc. A/CONF.62/122, Article 234.

United Nations Secretariat. 1984. *Question of Antarctica: Study Requested Under General Assembly Resolution 38/77, Report of the Secretary-General, Part Two, (Views of States)*. Doc. A/39/583, Part II, 9 November 1984:82, 91-92, 95.

USSR Council of Ministers. 1985. *Statute on the Procedure for Conducting Marine Scientific Research in the Economic Zone of the USSR*. Conferred by Decree of the USSR Council of Ministers, 19 December 1985, No. 1272. [Translated in *The USSR, Eastern Europe, and the Development of the Law of the Sea*, ed. W.E. Butler, 1983. Dobbs Ferry:Oceana.]

Vedomosti SSR. 1982. 'Law on the State Boundary.' Entered into force March 1, 1983. No. 48, item 891. [Translated in *The USSR, Eastern Europe, and the Development of the Law of the Sea*, ed. W.E. Butler, 1983. Dobbs Ferry:Oceana.]

— 1984. 'Edict on the Economic Zone.' Entered into force March 1, 1984. No. 9, item 137. [Translated in *The USSR, Eastern Europe, and the Development of the Law of the Sea*, ed. W.E. Butler, 1983. Dobbs Ferry:Oceana.]

Part V
Appendices

Appendix I

Excerpt on international arctic affairs/foreign policy taken from the speech in Murmansk by General Secretary Mikhail S. Gorbachev

Ceremonial Meeting on the presentation of the Order of Lenin and the Gold Star Medal to the City of Murmansk, 1 October 1987

Comrades, millions of people throughout the world are watching the restructuring process in our country with immense interest. Our bold embarking on large-scale constructive work and revolutionary change demanding consolidation of all the country's efforts is convincing evidence of our confidence that peace can be preserved, that mankind does have a future.

Indeed, the international situation is still complicated. The dangers to which we have no right to turn a blind eye remain. There has been some change, however, or, at least, change is starting. Certainly, judging the situation only from the speeches made by top Western leaders, including their 'program' statements, everything would seem to be as it was before; the same anti-Soviet attacks, the same demands that we show our commitment to peace by renouncing our order and principles, the same confrontational language: 'totalitarianism', 'communist expansion', and so on.

Within a few days, however, these speeches are often forgotten, and, at any rate, the theses contained in them do not figure during businesslike political negotiations and contacts. This is a very interesting point, an interesting phenomenon. It confirms that we are dealing with yesterday's rhetoric, while real-life processes have been set into motion. This means that something is indeed changing. One of the elements of the change is that it is now difficult to convince people that our foreign policy, our initiatives, our nuclear-free world program are mere 'propaganda'.

A new, democratic philosophy of international relations, of world politics is breaking through. The new mode of thinking with its humane, universal criteria and values is penetrating diverse strata. Its strength lies in the fact that it accords with people's common sense. Considering that world public opinion and the peoples of the world are very concerned about the situation in the world, our policy is an invitation to dialogue, to a search, to a better world, to normalization of international relations. This is why despite all attempts to besmirch and belittle our foreign policy initiatives, they are making their way in the world, because they are consonant with the moods of the broad masses of working people and realistically-minded political circles in the West.

Favorable tendencies are gaining ground in international relations as well. The substantive and frank East–West dialogue, far from proving fruitless for both sides, has become a distinguishing feature of contemporary world politics. Just recently the entire world welcomed the accord reached at the talks in Washington to promptly complete drafting an agreement on medium- and shorter-range missiles to be later signed at the top level. Thus, we are close to a major breakthrough in the field of actual nuclear disarmament. It happens, it will be the first such breakthrough to be achieved in the post-war years. So far, the arms race has proceeded either unimpeded or with some limitations, but no concrete move has as yet been made towards disarmament, towards eliminating nuclear weapons.

The road to the mutual Soviet–American decision was hard. Reykjavik was a crucial event along that road. Life has confirmed the correctness of our assessment of the meeting in the Icelandic capital. Contrary to panic wavering of all sorts, skeptical declarations and the propaganda talk about the 'failure', developments have borne out the correctness of the assessment we made, as you remember, just 40 minutes after the dramatic end of the meeting.

Reykjavik indeed became a turning point in world history, it showed a possibility of improving the international situation. A different situation has developed, and no one could act after Reykjavik as if nothing had happened. It was for us an event that confirmed the correctness of our course, the need for the constructiveness of new political thinking.

Full use of the potential created in Reykjavik is yet to be made. Gleams of hope have emerged, however, not only in the field of medium- and shorter-range missiles. Things have started moving in the field of banning nuclear testing. Full-scale talks on these problems will soon be held. It is obvious that our moratorium was not in vain. This was not an easy step for us either. It engendered and intensified worldwide demands for an end to the tests.

I can't undertake to predict the course of events. By no means everything depends on us. There is no doubt that the first results achieved in Washington recently and the forthcoming meeting with the President of the United States may cause a kind of peaceful 'chain reaction' in the field of strategic offensive arms and non-launching of weapons into outer space as well as in many other issues which insistently call for international dialogue.

It would be irresponsible on our part to underestimate the forces of resistance to change. Those are influential and very aggressive forces blinded by hatred for everything progressive. they exist in various quarters of the Western world, but the largest concentration of them is observed among those who cater directly for the military–industrial complex, both ideologically and politically, and who live on it.

Here it is a recent and fine example. A series of hearings on the subject 'Gorbachev's Economic Reforms' began at the Joint Economic Committee of the US Congress on September 10, with Senators and Congressmen participating. The hearings are both open and closed-door ones. Speakers include representatives of the Administration and Sovietologists from the Central Intelligence Agency, the US Defense Department and from various scientific centres. In general, it is quite normal and even good that in America officials of such a level should want to gain a thorough understanding of what is taking place in the Soviet Union and what our restructuring means for the rest of the world and for the United States itself.

But different kinds of recommendation are also being made at these hearings to the Administration and to Congress. Here is one such, almost word for word; if the Soviet Union attains the targets planned by the 27th Congress of the CPSU, that will, first of all, raise its prestige in the international arena and heighten the CPSU authority in the country and abroad and..., thereby, increase the threat to US national security. Who would ever have thought of such a conclusion? Moreover, success of the restructuring may weaken the political and economic unity of Western Europe, for the USSR will reach its market. The USSR will exert greater political influence on the developing countries, since Soviet military and other aid to them may be increased, and some of them will want to adopt the model of the Soviet economy if it proves competitive *vis-à-vis* the US economy.

And still further, the restructuring is dangerous because it will strengthen the Soviet Union's positions in international financial and economic organizations. Those analysts see a particular threat in the Soviet Union's increased influence in the world arena due to its initiatives in the field of arms control and the prospect of signing a treaty on medium-range missiles.

Just listen what conclusion they draw as a result: the failure of the socio-economic policy being pursued by the Soviet Union under the leadership of the CPSU and the Soviet government would accord with US national interests.

In order to 'facilitate' such a failure the following is recommended: to speed up the programs of costly ABM systems under SDI and draw the USSR into the arms race in order to hinder its restructuring; to allocate still more funds for the development of expensive high-accuracy weapons and space-based military systems; for the same purpose to increase the amount of military and other aid to groups and regimes which are actively fighting against the governments of the countries supported by the Soviet Union; to hinder the establishment of economic and trade contacts by the USSR with other countries and international organizations; fully to rule out the possibility of the transfer of advanced technology to the USSR and other socialist countries, and to tighten control over the activities of COCOM and of its member countries.

Such are the views expressed overtly and cynically. We cannot but take into account such a stance. The more so as assurances of peace intentions, which we often hear from US officials are immediately accompanied, at one go, so to speak, by the lauding of 'power politics' and by arguments very similar to those being used by the authors of the recommendations which I just mentioned.

Militarist and anti-Soviet forces are clearly concerned lest the interest among the people and political quarters of the West in what is happening in the Soviet Union today and the growing understanding of its foreign policy erase the artificially created 'image of the enemy', an image which they have been exploiting unshamedly for years. Well, it's their business after all. But we shall firmly follow the road of restructuring and new thinking.

Comrades, speaking in Murmansk, the capital of the Soviet Polar Region, it is appropriate to examine the idea of cooperation between all people also from the standpoint of the situation in the northern part of this planet. In our opinion, there are several weighty reasons for this.

The Arctic is not only the Arctic Ocean, but also the northern tips of three continents; Europe, Asia and America. It is the place where the Euroasian, North American and Asian Pacific regions meet, where the frontiers come close to one another and the interests of states belonging to mutually opposed military blocs and non-aligned ones cross.

The North is also a problem of security of the Soviet Union's northern frontiers. We have had some historical experience which cost us dearly. The people of Murmansk remember well the years 1918–19 and 1941–45.

The wars fought during this century were severe trials for the countries of Northern Europe. It seems to us they have drawn some serious conclusions for themselves. And this is probably why the public climate in those countries is more receptive to the new political thinking.

It is significant that the historic Conference on Security and Cooperation in Europe was held in one of the northern capitals — Helsinki. It is significant that another major step in the development of that process — was achieved in another northern capital — Stockholm. Reykjavik has become a symbol of hope that nuclear weapons are not an eternal evil and that mankind is not doomed to live under that sword of Damocles.

Major initiatives in the sphere of international security and disarmament are associated with the names of famous political figures of northern Europe. One is Urho Kekkonen. Another is Olaf Palme, whose death at the hand of a vile assassin shocked Soviet people. Then there is Kalevi Sorsa, who has headed the Socialist International Advisory Council for many years now. And we applaud the activities of the authoritative World Commission on Environment and Development headed by Prime Minister Gro Harlem Brundtland of Norway.

The Soviet Union duly appreciates the fact that Denmark and Norway, while being members of NATO, unilaterally refused to station foreign military bases and deploy nuclear weapons on their territory in peacetime. This stance, if consistently adhered to, is important for lessening tensions in Europe.

However, this is only part of the picture.

The community and interrelationship of the interests of our entire world is felt in the northern part of the globe, in the Arctic, perhaps more than anywhere else. For the Arctic and the North Atlantic are not just the 'weather kitchen', the point where cyclones and anticyclones are born to influence the climate in Europe, the USA and Canada, and even in south Asia and Africa. One can feel here freezing breath of the 'Arctic strategy' of the Pentagon. An immense potential of nuclear destruction concentrated aboard submarines and surface ships affects the political climate of the entire world and can be detonated by an accidental political–military conflict in any other region of the world.

The militarization of this part of the world is assuming threatening dimensions. One cannot but feel concern over the fact that NATO, anticipating an agreement on medium- and shorter-range missiles being reached, is preparing to train military personnel in the use of sea- and air-based cruise missiles from the North Atlantic. This would mean an additional threat to us and to all the countries of northern Europe.

A new radar station, one of the Star Wars elements, has been made operational in Greenland in violation of the ABM Treaty. US cruise missiles are being tested in the north of Canada. The Canadian government has recently developed a vast program for a build-up of forces in the Arctic. The US and NATO military activity in areas adjoining the Soviet Polar Region is being stepped up. The level of NATO's military presence in Norway and Denmark is being built up.

Therefore, while in Murmansk, and standing on the threshold of the Arctic and the North Atlantic, I would like to invite, first of all, the countries of the region to a discussion on the burning security issues.

How do we visualize this? It is possible to take simultaneously the roads of bilateral and multilateral cooperation. I have had the opportunity to speak on the subject of 'our common European home' on more than one occasion. The potential of contemporary civilization could permit us to make the Arctic habitable for the benefit of the national economies and other human interests of the near-Arctic states, for Europe and the entire international community. To achieve this, security problems that have accumulated in the area should be resolved above all.

The Soviet Union is in favor of a radical lowering of the level of military confrontation in the region. Let the north of the globe, the Arctic, become a zone of peace. Let the North Pole be a pole of peace. We suggest that all interested states start talks on the limitation and scaling down of military activity in the north as a whole, in both the Eastern and Western Hemispheres.

What, specifically, do we mean?

Firstly, a nuclear-free zone in northern Europe. If such a decision were adopted, the Soviet Union, as has already been declared, would be prepared to act as a guarantor. It would depend on the participating countries how to formalize this guarantee; by multilateral or bilateral agreements, governmental statements or in some other way.

The Soviet Union simultaneously reaffirms its readiness to discuss with each of the interested states, or with a group of states, all the problems related to the creation of a nuclear-free zone, including possible measures applicable to the Soviet territory. We could go so far as to remove submarines equipped with ballistic missiles from the Soviet Baltic Fleet.

As it is known, the Soviet Union earlier unilaterally dismantled launchers of medium-range missiles in the Kola Peninsula and the greater part of launchers of such missiles on the remaining territory of the Leningrad and Baltic military areas. A considerable number of shorter-range missiles was removed from those districts. The holding of military exercises was restricted in areas close to the borders of Scandinavian countries. Additional opportunities for military *détente* in the region will open up after the conclusion of the agreement on 'global double zero'.

Secondly, we welcome the initiative of Finland's President Mauno Koivisto on restricting naval activity in the seas washing the shores of northern Europe. For its part, the Soviet Union proposes consultations between the Warsaw Treaty Organization and NATO on restricting military activity and scaling down naval and airforce activities in the Baltic, Northern, Norwegian and Greenland Seas, and on the extension of confidence-building measures to these areas.

These measures could include arrangements on the limitation of rivalry in anti-submarine weapons, on the notification of large naval and airforce exercises, and on inviting observers from all countries participating in the European process to large naval and airforce exercises. This could be an initial step in the extension of confidence-building measures to the entire Arctic and to the northern areas of both hemispheres.

At the same time we propose considering the question of banning naval activity in mutually agreed-upon zones of international straits and in intensive shipping lanes in general. A meeting of representatives of interested states could be held for this purpose, for instance, in Leningrad.

The following thought suggests itself in connection with the idea of a nuclear-free zone. At present the northern countries, that is Iceland, Denmark, Norway, Sweden and Finland have no nuclear weapons. We are aware of their concern over the fact that we have a testing range for nuclear explosions on Novaya Zemlya.

We are thinking how to solve this problem, which is a difficult one for us because so much money has been invested in the testing range. But, frankly speaking, the problem could be solved once and for all if the United States agreed to stop nuclear tests or, as a beginning, to reduce their number and yield to the minimum.

Thirdly, the Soviet Union attaches much importance to peaceful cooperation in developing the resources of the North, the Arctic. Here an exchange of experience and knowledge is extremely important. Through joint efforts it could be possible to work out an overall concept of rational development of northern areas. We propose, for instance, reaching agreement on drafting an integral energy program for the north of Europe.

According to existing data, the reserves there of such energy sources as oil and gas are truly boundless. But their extraction entails immense difficulties and the need to create unique technical installations capable of withstanding the Polar elements. It would be more reasonable to pool efforts in this endeavor, which would cut both material and other outlays. We have an interest in inviting, for instance, Canada and Norway to form mixed firms and enterprises for developing oil and gas deposits of the shelf of our northern seas. We are prepared for relevant talks with other states as well.

Fourthly, the scientific exploration of the Arctic is of immense importance for the whole of mankind. We have a wealth of experience here and are prepared to share it. In turn, we are interested in the studies conducted in other sub-arctic and northern countries. We already have a program of scientific exchanges with Canada.

We propose holding in 1988 a conference of sub-Arctic states on coordinating research in the Arctic. The conference could consider the possibility of setting up a joint Arctic Research Council. Should the partners agree, Murmansk could host the conference.

Questions bearing on the interests of the indigenous population of the North, the study of its ethnic distinctions and the development of cultural ties between northern peoples require special attention.

Fifthly, we attach special importance to the cooperation of the northern countries in environmental protection. The urgency of this is obvious. It would be well to extend joint measures for protecting the marine environment of the Baltic, now being carried out by a commission of seven maritime states, to the entire oceanic and sea surface of the globe's north.

The Soviet Union proposes drawing up jointly an integrated comprehensive plan for protecting the natural environment of the north. The north European countries could set an example to others by reaching an agreement on establishing a system to monitor the state of the natural environment and radiation safety in the region. We must hurry to protect the nature of the tundra, forest tundra, and northern forest areas.

Sixthly, the shortest sea route from Europe to the Far East and the Pacific Ocean passes through the Arctic. I think that depending on progress in the normalization of international relations we could open the North Sea Route to foreign ships, with ourselves providing the services of ice-breakers.

Such are our proposals. Such is the Concrete meaning of Soviet foreign policy with regard to the North. Such are our intentions and plans for the future. Of course, safeguarding security and developing cooperation in the North is an international matter and by no means depends on us alone. We are ready to discuss any counter proposals and ideas. The main thing is to conduct affairs so that the climate here is determined by the warm Gulfstream of the European process and not by the Polar chill of accumulated suspicions and prejudices.

What everybody can be absolutely certain of is the Soviet Union's profound and certain interest in preventing the North of the planet, its polar and sub-polar regions and all Northern countries from ever again becoming an arena of war, and in forming there a genuine zone of peace and fruitful cooperation.

This is how, Comrades, we approach internal and international issues, how we understand the connection between the former and the latter. In both, our policy has proven its viability and constructive spirit. We are convinced that there is no other way to security and social progress but creative labor in the name of happiness and freedom of man inside the country and the development of equal cooperation between states on the world scene.

We are legitimately proud of the fact that our country has always stood at the sources of socialist practice and new thinking. In the last 70 years the world has changed beyond recognition—materially, spiritually and politically. The impact made by the Great October Revolution on the social and ideological progress of mankind is the greatest contribution to contemporary and future civilization. It is within our powers and in our interests to multiply this contribution by the practical results of restructuring.

May I wish you, your families and all working people of the region success in all your efforts to transform our country, in studies and life and to congratulate you once again on the 70th anniversary of the Great October Revolution which you are celebrating in your Hero City.

[Novosti Agency Publishing House, Moscow, 1987]

Appendix II

Decree of the Presidium of the Supreme Soviet of the USSR to Improve the Protection of Nature in the Regions of the Far North and in the Sea Areas Adjacent to the Northern Coastline of the USSR (26 November 1984)

In the Soviet Union's Far North large territorial centers of production are being established, industrial plants and centers of population are being built, the economic exploitation of the USSR's continental shelf is in progress, shipping, air and overland transport are being developed. The northern peoples continue to live in these regions, pursuing their traditional activities of reindeer breeding, fishing, hunting and the trapping of marine animals.

In the regions of the Far North and the sea areas adjacent to the USSR's northern coastline the severe climatic conditions (lack of heat and light, a significantly long season covered by snow and ice, the permafrost), render natural life highly vulnerable and lengthen the time of recovery of damaged ecological systems.

All these factors require that special attention be paid to the protection of nature in the above regions.

The Presidium of the Supreme Soviet of the USSR decrees that:

1.   To assure the better protection of nature; the preservation and study of natural life in the regions of the Far North and the sea areas adjacent to the USSR's northern coastline; the provision of the best conditions for the lives of the peoples; the maintenance of the health of the citizens; the satisfaction of their material and cultural needs in every possible way:

reserves, sanctuaries, and other specially protected territories be set apart (in the sea areas also) with the creation of protected zones within them as necessary;

special requirements be introduced to regulate the movement of ships and other craft, the flights of aircraft and the operation of land transport;

special regulations be drawn up to govern the exploitation of enterprises, the design, construction and operation of equipment, installations and other equipment as well as the conduct of geological surveys, scientific research and other work;

stricter requirements be introduced for the protection of the oil, its substrata, waters, atmospheric air, plant and animal life;

tourism be limited;

other measures be taken for the protection of nature.

2. The reserves, sanctuaries and other specially protected territories in the regions of the Far North and the sea areas adjacent to the USSR's northern coastline are created for: the conservation and restoration of natural life chains; the elaboration of scientific bases for the protection of nature in those regions; the conservation of genetic stocks of plants and animals; to provide the means and subsistence, the conditions of procreation and the paths of migration of animals, especially of species that are rare and threatened by extinction.

Within the reserves, sanctuaries, and other specially protected territories are included continental (including river deltas) and lake areas as well as the sea bed and the areas of water adjacent to the USSR's northern coastline, including sea areas covered by ice. The procedure for the creation of specially protected territories in the above regions is established by the Council of Ministers of the USSR.

Every activity within the boundaries of the above reserves, sanctuaries and other specially protected territories and their protected zones that destroys natural life chains, or threatens the conservation of natural life that is part of them is forbidden.

3. In the sea areas adjacent to the USSR's northern coastline where climatic conditions are particularly severe and the presence of ice constitutes an obstacle or an increased danger to the navigation of ships, or where pollution of the marine environment could entail serious harm to the ecological equilibrium or break it irreversibly, special regulations are laid down by the competent Soviet authorities for the navigation of ships and other craft. These regulations incorporate stricter requirements for the design of ships and other craft, for their equipping, the supplies and gear that they carry, for the composition and qualification of their crews, including the interdiction of navigating without a pilot and under other circumstances, the imposition of periods and areas closed to navigation as well as other measures to assure the safety of shipping operations and the prevention, reduction and control of pollution of the marine environment. The above regulations are promulgated in 'Notices to Mariners'.

4. The navigation of ships and other craft within the bounds of the sea areas

of reserves, sanctuaries and other specially protected territories and their protected zones is confined to the sea corridors laid down by the competent Soviet authority. Information about the laying down of such corridors is promulgated in 'Notices to Mariners'.

The movement of any means of transport across the surface of the ice within the bounds of the sea areas of reserves, sanctuaries and other specially protected territories and their protected zones takes place only along routes laid down by the competent Soviet authorities. Information about such routes is promulgated in accordance with established procedure.

The crossing, by ships and other craft, of the bounds of the sea areas of reserves, sanctuaries and other specially protected territories and their protected zones and the penetration of these areas from within the sea corridors or routes may, in some instances, be disastrous to the safety of people, ships and other means of transport as well as, in other cases, in contravention of the prevailing legislation of the Union of the SSR. The administration of the nearest Soviet port must be swiftly informed of every case of an unavoidable entry into the above areas or the convoying of ships and other transport craft through them and action taken strictly in accordance with the relevant competent Soviet authorities.

5. The direction and width of the aerial corridors of the USSR, of local air corridors and flight routes as well as the flying altitude of aircraft in regions of the Far North and sea areas adjacent to the USSR's northern coastline are established with regard for the needs of the protection of nature.

Aircraft should not fly at low altitude over reserves, sanctuaries and other specially protected territories, nor over localities in which animals habitually herd together, nor above the paths of their migration.

In order not to harm the natural environment of the regions of the Far North and sea areas adjacent to the USSR's northern coastline, regions may be temporarily closed to the flights of aircraft in accordance with established procedure. Information about the closing of such regions is promulgated in the 'Air Navigation Information' series.

Exceptions to the regulations provided for in the second and third parts of this article are permitted in the event of direct danger to the safety of flight, for the saving of human life and in other circumstances provided for in the legislation of the Union of the SSR.

6. The construction (reconstruction), in the regions of the Far North and sea areas adjacent to the USSR's northern coastline, of enterprises and other facilities; the creation, operation and utilization of artificial islands of any kind or any installation or structure in the sea; the laying out and development of population settlements; the laying of pipe and transmission lines is permitted subject to an ecologically favorable decision by the authority exercising state control for the protection of nature and the rational use of natural resources.

7. Prospecting, geological surveying, mining, construction and other work in the regions of the Far North and sea areas adjacent to the USSR's northern

coastline should be performed using methods that are the least harmful to the surrounding natural environment.

Installations, gear, equipment, mechanisms, constructions, transport vehicles and materials are to be accommodated only within the limits of the tracts and areas of land allotted for the above purposes.

It is forbidden to move across the tundra or the forest tundra outside the limits of the roads and other routes specially allotted in accordance with established procedure using mechanized transport which destroys the soil and plant cover.

8. Standard technical documentation for equipment, installations, machines, mechanisms, gear, transport vehicles and materials intended for employment in the regions of the Far North and the sea areas adjacent to the USSR's northern coastline as well as documentation concerning the implementation of constructional, geological surveying and other work in the above regions should be prepared taking account of the necessity for the protection of nature in these regions and the need to take measures for the restoration of renewable natural resources.

9. The creation, exploitation, use and demolition of artificial islands, installations and structures in the sea areas adjacent to the USSR's northern coastline, as well as the creation of safety zones around them, are performed with the permission of the competent Soviet authority.

10. Scientific and expeditionary activity in regions of the Far North and the sea areas adjacent to the USSR's northern coastline that is incompatible with requirements for the protection of nature in these regions is forbidden.

Scientific and expeditionary activity, including marine scientific research, in the above regions takes place subject to permission granted by the competent Soviet authority in accordance with the procedure established by the Council of Ministers of the USSR.

11. In the sea areas adjacent to the USSR's northern coastline, whether covered or not covered by ice, the discharge of waste water that has not been cleaned to the established standards, as well as the discharge of waste, materials and objects, is forbidden.

The burying, within the above sea areas, of waste, materials and objects can take place only with permission from, and under the control of, the competent Soviet authorities.

The storing, distribution, utilization and burying of waste, materials and objects on dry land in the regions of the Far North as well as the cleaning of waste water and discharges into the atmosphere are conducted with regard for the heightened vulnerability of nature in these regions.

12. In the regions of the Far North and the sea areas adjacent to the USSR's northern coastline the legislation of the Union of the SSR and of the RSFSR, in conformity with international agreements with the USSR, provides for particular restrictions on the hunting of wild animals, birds and other creatures.

13. Tourism and other forms of recreation in the regions of the Far North and the sea areas adjacent to the USSR's northern coastline take place with regard for the necessity for the protection of nature.

For this purpose, legislation may be enacted by the Union of the SSR and the RSFSR to restrict the tourist season, access to local territories and water areas, the use of means of transport (including small ships) as well as the imposition of other restrictions.

14. Persons guilty of contravening the present Decree bear criminal, administrative and other responsibilities in accordance with the prevailing legislation.

In the event of contravention, in the sea areas adjacent to the USSR's northern coastline of the provisions of: article 3; the first and second clauses of article 4; the second and third clauses of article 5; articles 9 and 10; the first and second clauses of article 11 of the present Decree; and regulations issued on the basis of it, guilty parties will be liable to an administrative penalty in the form of a fine of up to 10,000 roubles imposed at the place of discovery of the offense.

If the contraventions referred to in the second clause of the present article cause substantial damage or give rise to other serious consequences, or are repeated offenses, or are accompanied by obstruction of the lawful acts of persons acting on behalf of the authorities responsible for the defense of nature in the sea areas adjacent to the USSR's northern coastline, the guilty parties will be liable to a fine of up to 100,00 roubles imposed by the regional (municipal) people's court. In the case of contraventions referred to in article 9 and the second clause of article 10 of the present Decree the court may impose, as an additional administrative penalty, the seizing of the ship, installation, equipment, instruments and other objects used by the guilty party.

For contraventions referred to in the second and third clauses of the present article, the guilty parties bear administrative responsibility for contraventions whose nature does not entail action under the USSR's prevailing legislation for criminal responsibility.

15. For the purpose of forestalling contraventions of the regulations referred to in the second and third clauses of article 14 of the present Decree and to assure the timely and proper inspection of procedures and the implementation of resolutions concerning these contraventions, the competent Soviet authorities have the right to inspect ships and to detain and seize them.

In the event of the seizure or detention of a foreign ship, the corresponding competent Soviet authorities notify the country of its flag, without delay, of the action taken and of the ensuing penalties. The detained ship and its crew are released without delay on the deposit of a reasonable surety or other security.

16. The taking of the administrative measures provided for in the present Decree does not absolve the contravener from liability for indemnification,

in accordance with the prevailing legislation, of the damage he has caused to natural resources.

17. The scope of the present Decree extends to islands in the Arctic ocean and its seas, islands in the Bering and Okhotsk Seas, to other territories of the USSR that the USSR Council of Ministers assigns to the regions of the Far North as well as to sea areas adjacent to the USSR's northern coastline (including areas around islands belonging to the USSR) whose condition affects the ecological well-being of the northern parts of the territory of the USSR.

The conditions and the date of entry into force of the provisions of the present Decree within delineated sea areas adjacent to the USSR's northern coastline as well as ways of implementing the present Decree and assuring its observance are laid down by the Council of Ministers of the USSR.

18. Questions concerning the protection of nature in the regions of the Far North and the sea areas adjacent to the USSR's northern coastline that are not provided for in the present Decree will be subject to the legislation of the Union of SSR and of the RCFSR concerning the protection of nature and the legislation of the Union of the SSR concerning the economic zone and the continental shelf of the USSR.

[Alexei Y. Roginko, Research Fellow,Institute of World Economy and International Relations, Moscow; translation by Gordon Watson, President, East–West Technical Services, Montreal]

Appendix III

Agreement Between the Government of Canada and the Government of the Union of Soviet Socialist Republics on Cooperation in the Arctic and the North (Signed 20 November 1989)

The Government of Canada and the Government of the Union of Soviet Socialist Republics hereinafter referred to as 'the Parties':

Noting the unique features of the Arctic region, its population and its environment,

Guided by the desire to broaden and deepen mutually beneficial cooperation between the two countries in accordance with existing agreements and understandings,

Convinced that the development of such cooperation makes a constructive contribution to the relaxation of international tensions and to the consolidation of the principles of long-term fruitful and mutually beneficial cooperation among states on the basis of equality, non-interference in internal affairs and mutual respect for the interests of the Parties,

Taking into account that Canada and the USSR, as Arctic states, play leading roles in Arctic studies and development and that the Arctic region is of particular importance for both countries,

Bearing in mind the rights and obligations of Canada and the USSR, in accordance with international law, as Arctic rim countries,

Drawing on the experience gained in bilateral contacts and exchanges on the Arctic and the North under the Canada–USSR General Exchanges Agreement of 20 October, 1971, the Long-Term Program of Economic, Industrial, Scientific and Technical Cooperation between Canada and the

USSR of 26 October, 1978, and the Canadian–Soviet Protocols on Scientific and Technical Cooperation in the Arctic and the North of 16 April, 1984, and 26 February, 1987,

Have agreed as follows:

ARTICLE 1

1.The Parties shall promote mutually beneficial cooperation between Canada and the USSR on matters relating to the Arctic and the North, considering it an important factor conducive to all-round development of their bilateral relations on a stable and long-term basis in the interests of promoting a lasting peace and good neighbourliness in the region.

2.The Parties will develop the following programmes, inter alia:

(a) a program of scientific and technical cooperation, including geology, meteorology, climatology, environmental protection, construction, Arctic marine, land and air technology and other agreed fields;

(b) a program of economic cooperation, including the development of renewable and non-renewable resources; and

(c) programs of cooperation on social and cultural questions, including ethnography, education, public health, the socio-economic problems of native peoples of the North and Northern territories, cultural and academic exchanges, and contacts between native peoples.

ARTICLE 2

1. The Parties will engage in bilateral cooperation on matters relating to the Arctic and the North on the basis of mutual benefit, equality and reciprocity.

2.Cooperation between the Parties may take the following forms:

(a) exchange of delegations;

(b) exchange of information and documentation;

(a) joint research, development and exchange of the results;

(d) joint symposiums, conferences and seminars for specialists;

(e) joint preparation for publication and publication of scientific and technical materials;

(f) appropriate assistance on both sides in establishing contacts and reaching agreements between Canadian and Soviet organizations and firms on the development of the Arctic and the North;

(g) exchange of information on matters of general policies and development of national legislation with respect to the Arctic and the North; and

(h) other mutually agreed forms of cooperation.

ARTICLE 3

1. For the purpose of this Agreement and in accordance with the agreed programs, the Parties will promote, facilitate and encourage the development of cooperative and direct contacts between governmental and

non-governmental establishments, scientific research and other organizations, trade associations and firms of the two countries, including the conclusion of working arrangements or contracts on implementation of specific projects and programs in accordance with this Agreement.

2. Each Party will provide assistance for travel to areas, institutions and organizations of the other country appropriate for the conduct of the agreed programs.

3. Information obtained as a result of joint research and activities will be accessible to the participants and be transmitted between them as soon as practicable. Such information may be freely used by the participants unless specific otherwise.

4. The cooperation provided for in this Agreement shall be subject to the laws and regulations of the Parties.

ARTICLE 4

1. To implement this Agreement, a Canadian–Soviet Mixed Commission on cooperation in the Arctic and the North shall be established. Sub-commissions shall also be established, as appropriate, with respect to scientific and technical cooperation, economic cooperation and cooperation on social and cultural questions, *inter alia*. The Commission will meet at least once every two years, alternately in Canada and the USSR. Each Party will designate its representatives to the Commission's sessions in accordance with its own procedures and practices.

2. The Commission will:

(a) work out programs of cooperation between Canada and the USSR in the Arctic and the North;
(b) review the implementation of the programs and ensure that the activities approved are properly carried out; and
(c) consider proposals of the Parties for the development of cooperation in specific fields and for amendment of existing programs and activities.

3. The Parties will name co-chairmen of the Commission and of the sub-commissions, as well as organizations and agencies responsible for the implementation of activities provided for in the programs.

4. The co-chairmen of the Commission and of the sub-commissions will be permanent members of the Commission.

5. For the purpose of the implementation of the programs, working groups may be set up and working plans for separate activities may be elaborated by mutual consent between the co-chairmen of the sub-commissions.

6. The following organizations will be responsible for the implementation of this Agreement; for the Government of Canada — the Department of Indian Affairs and Northern Development, and for the Government of the USSR — the USSR State Committee for Science and Technology.

7. The programme of cooperation agreed to under the Protocol of the

Meeting of the Coordinating Group on Scientific and Technical Cooperation between Canada and the USSR in the Arctic and the North of 26 February, 1987, will be maintained and fall under the general supervision of the Canada–USSR Mixed Commission on Cooperation in the Arctic and the North.

ARTICLE 5

1. Each Party shall bear the expenses of its participation in the activities carried out unless otherwise agreed.

2. During the exchange of delegations in the course of programs, the sending Party shall bear the expenses of two-way travel to a mutually agreed point and the receiving Party shall bear the expenses during the stay of the delegations in the receiving country, unless otherwise agreed.

3. Duration of the stay in the receiving country and the number of persons in each delegation will be agreed prior to their departure from the sending country. The exchanges will be based on the principle of equal number of delegations and equal durations of stay.

4. Matters of a commercial or juridical character that may arise during cooperation shall be resolved by special agreements or contracts, or both.

ARTICLE 6

1. This Agreement shall enter into force on the date of its signature.

2. This Agreement shall remain in force for a period of five years, and thereafter it shall be extended automatically for further periods of five (5) years unless either Party gives notice of termination not less than six months prior to the expiration of the initial period or of any extension thereof.

[Walter Slipchenko, Director of Circumpolar Affairs, Government of the Northwest Territories, Ottawa]

Appendix IV

USSR PARTICIPATION IN SELECTED INTERNATIONAL
ARRANGEMENTS

Security and arms control arrangements

Multilateral

*1920 Treaty of Spitsbergen
 1958 Convention of the Territorial Sea and Contiguous Zone
 1958 Convention on the High Seas
 1959 Antarctic Treaty
 1963 Partial Nuclear Test Ban Treaty
 1967 A Treaty on Principles Governing the Activities of States in the
       Exploration and Use of Outer Space
 1968 Nuclear Non-Proliferation Treaty
 1971 Seabed Treaty
 1977 Convention on the Prohibition of Military or Any Other Hostile
       Use of Environmental Modification Techniques
 1982 Convention on the Law of the Sea [not in force]
 1985 Japan/US/USSR Air Traffic Control Agreement

Bilateral

 1955 USSR/Finland Military Protocol

1971   USSR/US Agreement on Measures to Reduce the Risk of
       Outbreak of Nuclear War
1972   USSR/US Incidents at Sea Agreement (INCSEA)
1972   USSR/US Strategic Arms Limitation Treaty I (SALT I) and
       Antiballistic Missile Treaty (ABM Treaty)
1972   USSR/US Agreement on the Prevention of Nuclear War
1974   USSR/Norway Military Protocol
1976   USSR/US Treaty on the Limitation of Underground Nuclear
       Tests (TTBT) [not ratified by US]
1979   USSR/US SALT II [not ratified by US]
1987   USSR/US Agreement on Crisis Control Centers
1988   USSR/US Reciprocal Observation of Nuclear Tests

Private

1986   Soviet Academy of Sciences/NRDC Agreement on Nuclear Test
       Monitoring

Industry and commerce arrangements

Multilateral

*1920   Treaty on Spitsbergen
1944   International Civil Aeronautics Organization — ICAO
1948   International Maritime Organization — IMO
1958   Convention of the Territorial Sea and Contiguous Zone
1958   Convention on the Continental Shelf
1958   Convention on the High Seas
1959   Northeast Atlantic Fishing Convention
1965   Convention on Facilitation of International Maritime Traffic
1967   Convention on Conduct of Fishing Operations in the North
       Atlantic (ICNAF)
1972   Convention on the International Regulations for Preventing
       Collisions at Sea
1974   International Convention for the Safety of Life at Sea (SOLAS)
       (as amended by 1978 Protocol); Protocol for Global Maritime
       Distress and Safety System [negotiated in November 1988]
*1974   Regulation of the Fishing of North-East Arctic Cod [1974 but
       USSR withdrew 15 August, 1974]
1979   COSPAS-SARSAT Memorandum [amended in 1984,
       superseded by 1988 agreement]
1982   Convention on the Law of the Sea [not in force]
1988   International COSPAS–SARSAT Programme Agreement
       [signed 1 July, 1988]

Bilateral¹

*1956   USSR/Norway Search and Rescue Cooperation in the Barents Sea
*1957   & 1973 USSR/Norway Sea Boundary Demarcation Agreements
1967   USSR/Finland IGO Establishment
1971   USSR/Finland Rescue Operations in Finnish and Soviet Territorial Waters
1972   USSR/Norway Technical Cooperation
1974   USSR/Norway Land Transportation
1974   USSR/Norway Water Transportation
1974   USSR/Finland Energy
1974   USSR/US Deep Sea Drilling
1974   USSR/US Agreement on Cooperation in Housing and Other Construction
1974   USSR/US Long-term Agreement to Facilitate Economic, Industrial, and Technical Cooperation
1977   USSR/Finland Industry
1979   USSR/Finland Boundary Maintenance
*1981   USSR/Finland Arctic Technology Committee
1987   USSR/UK Cooperation on Oil and Gas Research and Technology
1988   USSR/Norway Search and Rescue in Barents Sea
1988   USSR/Finland Program of Cooperation in Atomic Power Plant Engineering and Safety

Bilateral Fisheries

       USSR/Japan Fisheries (numerous agreements)
*1824   USSR/US Convention Regarding Navigation, Fishing, and Trading on the Pacific Ocean and Along the Northwest Coast of America
1922   USSR/Finland Fishing and Sealing in Territorial Waters
*1957   USSR/Norway Regulation and Conservation of Seals in the Northeast Atlantic
1959   USSR/Finland Fishing and Sealing
1965   USSR/Finland Fishing and Seal Hunting
1969   USSR/Finland Fisheries and Sealery
1973   USSR/US Agreement Relating to the Consideration of Claims Resulting from Damage to Fishing Vessels or Gear and Measures to Prevent Fishing Conflicts
*1975   USSR/Norway Fisheries
1976   USSR/Finland Fisheries
1976   USSR/Canada Agreement on Fisheries Relations
*1977   USSR/Iceland Science and Technology in Fisheries and Living Resources of the Sea
1988   USSR/US Agreement on Mutual Fisheries Relations [May 1988,

upon entry into force, supersedes agreements of 1976 as extended and amended 1982, 1985, and February 1988]
* USSR/Denmark Faeroe Islands Agreement

Private

*1987 USSR/Wartsila Marine Industries, Inc. Contract for Delivery of 11 Arctic Class Tankers and 1 Barge Carrier

Culture and science arrangements

Multilateral

1959 Antarctic Treaty
1964 Convention for the International Council for the Exploration of the Sea (ICES)
1972 Convention Concerning the Protection of World Cultural and Natural Heritage [USSR ratified in 1988]
*1982 Northern Science Network, UNESCO Man in the Biosphere Project

Bilateral

1961 USSR/Iceland Cultural and Scientific Cooperation
1972 USSR/US Agreement on Cooperation in Medical Science and Public Health [extended]
1972 USSR/US Agreement on Cooperation in the Field of Environmental Protection [as amended and extended]
1973 USSR/US Agreement on Cooperation in Studies of the World Ocean
*1977 USSR/US Soviet Academy of Sciences (Institute of Ethnography/Smithsonian Institute joint exhibit 'Crossroads of Continents: Traditional Cultures and peoples of the North Pacific Rim')
1978 USSR/Finland Agreement on Culture
1979 USSR/Finland Agreement on Education
*1984/ USSR/Canada Protocol of Consultations on the Development of
1987 a Program of Scientific and Technical Cooperation in the Arctic and the North
1985 USSR/US General Agreement on Contacts, Exchanges, and Cooperation in Scientific, Technical, Educational, Cultural and Other Fields
1985 USSR/US Program of Cooperation and Exchanges for 1986–1988
*1988 USSR/Norway Agreement Concerning Scientific-Technological

Cooperation on Problems of the Study of the Arctic and of the
North for 1988–1992

Private

*1983	International Permafrost Association
*1984	Polar Geophysical Institute of the Soviet Academy of Sciences/ Geophysical Institute, University of Alaska Collaborative Research
*1986	International Union of Circumpolar Health (IUCH)
*	Siberian Branch of the Soviet Academy of Sciences/Nordic Council for Arctic Medical Research Agreement to Produce *Arctic Medical Research*

Environment and conservation arrangements

Multilateral

*1911	Treaty for the Preservation and Protection of Fur Seals [Terminated in 1941, replaced in 1957, see below]
1946	International Whaling Convention
1954	International Convention for the Prevention of Pollution of the Sea by Oil [1958], with amendments of 1962 [1967] and 1969 [1978], superseded by MARPOL 1973/78 (listed below)
1956	Treaty Establishing the International Atomic Energy Agency (IAEA)
*1957	Interim Convention on the Conservation of North Pacific Fur Seals [extended and amended 1963, 1969, 1976, 1980, but 1984 Protocol not ratified by US]
1959	Antarctic Treaty
1969	International Convention Relating to Intervention on the High Seas in Cases of Oil Pollution Casualties
1969	Brussels International Convention on Civil Liability for Oil Pollution Damage (Protocols of 1976 and 1984)
1969	Developmental Studies of the Effects of Radioactivity in the Sea (and 1975)
1971	Ramsar Convention on Wetlands of International Importance, Especially as Water Fowl Habitat (Protocol of 1982)
1972	Convention for the Conservation of Antarctic Seals
1972	Convention on the Prevention of Marine Pollution by Dumping of Wastes and Other Matter [1975]
1972	Paris Convention Concerning the Protection of World Cultural and Natural Heritage
1973	Protocol Relating to Intervention on the High Seas in Cases of Pollution by Substances Other Than Oil

1973   Convention on Fishing and Conservation of Living Resources in the Baltic Sea and the Belts

*1973   Agreement on the Conservation of Polar Bears

1973   Convention on International Trade in Endangered Species of Wild Fauna and Flora (CITES) [1975]

1974   Convention for the Protection of the Marine Environment of the Baltic Sea Area

1974   International Convention for the Safety of Life at Sea (SOLAS) [1980], with Protocol of 1978 [1981] and amendments of 1983 giving effect to International Bulk Chemicals Code and 1984 amendments regarding subdivision, stability, and fire protection (re: USSR acceptance of 1983 and 1984 amendments)

1977   Convention on the Prohibition of Military or any Other Hostile Use of Environmental Modification Techniques

1978   Protocol Relating to the International Convention for the Prevention of Pollution from Ships (MARPOL '73/'78) [1983]

1979   Convention on Long-Range Transboundary Air Pollution [1983] (with 1984 Protocol on Long-Term Financing of the Co-operative Programme for Monitoring and Evaluation of Long-Range Transmission of Air Pollution in Europe [1988], 1985 Protocol on Reduction of Sulphur Emissions or their Transboundary Fluxes by at least 30 percent, Helsinki [1987])

1980   Convention on the Conservation of Antarctic Marine Living Resources [1982]

1982   Convention on the Law of the Sea (not in force)

1985   Vienna Convention for the Protection of the Ozone Layer [1988] (Montreal Protocol of September 1987, signed but not yet ratified by USSR, not in force)

1986   Convention on Early Notification of a Nuclear Accident

1986   Convention on Assistance in the Case of a Nuclear Accident or Radiological Emergency

Bilateral

*1957   USSR/Norway Agreement on Measures to Regulate Sealing and to Protect Seal Stocks in the Northeastern Part of the Atlantic Ocean

1972   USSR/US Agreement on Cooperation in the Field of Environmental Protection [extended]

1973   USSR/US Agreement on Cooperation in Studies of the World Ocean

*1976   USSR/US Convention Concerning the Conservation of Migratory Birds and Their Environment [1978]

*1978   USSR/US Bering Sea Surface Ice and Air Tracking

*1984   USSR/Canada Protocol on the Development of a Programme of Scientific and Technical Cooperation in the Arctic and the North

*1988   USSR/Norway Agreement Concerning Scientific-Technological

Cooperation on Problems of the Study of the Arctic and of the
North for 1988-1992 (See section IV, Arctic Biology)
*1988   USSR/Norway Agreement on Environmental Protection
1988   USSR/Norway Agreement on Notification of Nuclear Accidents
1988   USSR/Sweden Agreement on Prompt Notification of Nuclear
Accidents
1988   USSR/Finland Program of Cooperation in Atomic Power Plant
Engineering and Safety (1988–1990)
*1990   USSR/US Agreement on Mutual Assistance in the Event of a
Large-Scale Oil Spill in the Bering and Chuckchi Sea area

NOTES
Year in square brackets = dates of entry into force
* = arctic-specific arrangements
[1] The listing of bilateral conventions is not exhaustive. It simply indicates
the range of concerns covered by cooperative arrangements. We have not
verified which of these agreements remain in force or have been
superceded by more current agreements.

[Oran Young and Gail Osherenko, Institute for Arctic Studies,
Dartmouth College, Hanover, New Hampshire]

Index

biogenic hydrocarbons, 66
biological sciences, 237, 239, 243, 248
birds, nature reserves for, 70, 72, 73
bituminous shale, 111
Black Sea, 221–2
black shales, 114
Boguchany, 181
Bol'shoy Pit river, 188
boundaries and territorial waters, 216–18, 287
brash ice, 165
Bratsk, 181
breccia ice fields, 43
Britain (UK), 17–20 *passim,* 92, 266, 288
building work *see* construction
Burroughs, Stephen, 11

cake zones, ice, 43
Canada, 278
  arctic areas, of, 16, 84
  and international artic cooperation, 77, 265
  with USSR, 235–57, 273
  territorial waters of, 223, 274, 275, 276
Carboniferous rocks, 112, 114
cargo ships *see* freighters
Catherine the Great, 16, 17
Central Barents high, 113
Central Hydrographic Administration, 22
Chattanooga shale, 113
Chekanovskiy, A. L., 19
Chelyuskin, Semen, 15
Chelyuskin, Cape, 12, 15
Cherskiy, I. D., 19
Cheshkaya polynya, 73
Chichagov, Vasiliy Yakovlevich, 16
Chief Northern Sea Route Agency, 140–2
Chile, 288, 290
Chilingarov, A., 34
China, 182
chlorinated hydrocarbons, 65
Chrétien, Jean, 236–7, 240
Chukchi people, 14, 16, 17
Chukchi Sea, 17, 18
  ice distribution in, 59–60
  geology of, 119
  pollution problems in, 65
  transport on, 154
Chukotka, 17, 294
CITES (Convention on International Trade in Endangered Species), 264, 268
Civil Aviation, USSR Ministry of, 141, 143
Civil War, Russian, 24–5
Clark, Joe, 249
close-coupled tow technique, 166
coal, 119
Communist Part of the Soviet Union, 75

conservation *see* environment protection
construction work, 75, 195, 226
  international cooperation, in, 243–4, 246, 248
  on jetties, 172–5
containerization, 192
continental shelf, legislation on, 227–8
convoy system, 159–60, 163–7
Cook, James, 17, 18
cooperation *see* international cooperation
copper, 188, 294
cost-accounting system, 136
Council of Ministers, USSR, 75, 143, 219, 220
Cretaceous rocks, 111, 116–17, 118, 119
crustaceans, 67, 266, 295
currents, sea, and ice formation
  in Barents Sea, 47, 49–50
  in Chukchi Sea, 59–60
  in E. Siberian Sea, 58
  in Kara Sea, 54
  in Laptev Sea, 56

dams, 70, 174, 181
De Long, George W., 20
Delta class submarines, 202, 206, 208, 211
Denmark, 265, 266
deterrence *see* security
Devonian rocks, 112, 113, 114
Dezhnev, Semen, 13–14
Dezhnev, Cape, 14
diamonds, 189, 294
Diomede Islands, 14, 15
Directorate of the Northern Sea Route *see* Administration of ...
Dmitrii Donskoi class freighters, 160, 162
Domanik calcareous shales, 113
drift ice, 49, 51, 54, 56
drifting stations, 28–9, 36
Drizhenko, F. K., 22
Druzhnaya Antarctic bases, 293, 296
Dudinka, 152, 153, 164, 174, 181, 188, 190
Durdenevsky, V., 290

eagles, 70
earth sciences, 237, 239, 243, 246, 248
  see also geological structures
East Siberian regional economic complex, 63
East Siberian Sea
  geology of, 119
  ice conditions in, 58
  pollution problems in, 65
  transport on, 154
East Taymyr Current, 56
echelon towing, 163–4
ecological concerns *see* environment protection

Index

Lena river, 13, 20, 181–2
  and ice conditions, 56, 57, 179
  transport on, 138, 153, 186, 189–90, 192–3
Lenin, Vladimir Ilyich, 88, 92
Lenin (icebreaker), 126, 135, 151
Leningrad gas field, 118
Leningradskaya Antarctic base, 292, 296
Leonid Brezhnev (icebreaker), 151
Leont'yev, I., 17
Leskov, M., 163–4
Lied, Jonas, 24
Litke, Fedor Petrovich, 19
Lomonosov, M. V., 16, 87
Long strait, 59
Lukin, V., 37
Lyakhov, Ivan, 17

Magadan, 189
Makarov, Stephan Osipovich, 22
Makarov, Ye., 36
Malygin, Stepan, 15
Malygin (icebreaker), 27
Malyye Karmakulyy, 19
Mangazeya, 12
marine transport *see* Northern Sea Route
Maritime Ice Operations, Department of, 141
MARPOL Convention, 78, 264
massifs, ice, 49, 56, 57, 58, 134, 155
Matochkin Shar strait, 17
Max Waldeck (icebreaker), 167
medical (health) science, 237, 239
Medvezh'i Islands, 17, 18
Merchant Marine, USSR Ministry of, 74, 89, 142, 143, 148, 154–5, 193
metallurgical slag, transport of, 186
meteorological data *see* weather
Middendorf, A. F., 19
Middleton, Christopher, 16
Mikhail Fedorovich, Tsar, 12, 92
Mikhailichenko, V., 167–9
Minin, Fedor, 15
mining, 75, 294
Mirnyy Antarctic base, 292
missiles, 201, 278
Molodyozhnaya Antarctic base, 292
monuments, 73, 98, 155
Morskoy flot (journal), 158
Moskva class icebreakers, 126, 128
Moskvitin, Ivan Yur'yev, 12
Mudyug (icebreaker), 167
Mudyug class icebreakers, 132, 151
Mulroney, Brian, 250, 265
multi-year ice *see* old ice
Murmansk gas field, 114, 209
Murmansk shipping agency, 156

Nansen, Fridtjof, 20
narwhals, 73

nationalism, 84, 85–6, 88, 93, 97–100
native peoples
  and early discoverers, 12, 14, 16, 17
  ethnography of, 244, 247, 248, 265
  and international cooperation, 78, 238, 239–40, 250, 262, 266
NATO (North Atlantic Treaty Organization), 232, 278
natural resources, 294–6
  see also fish; oil and gas
nature conservation *see* environment protection
Nature Conservation Laboratory, 69
nature reserves, 70–4, 75
naval operations and strategies
  proposed limitation on, 232, 259
  of USA, 90, 204, 210–11, 278
  of USSR, 91, 201–13
navigation
  and environmental protection, 75, 78
  and ice conditions, 61–2, 135
  ice forecasts for, 40–1, 145–6
  under-ice, of submarines, 205–13
  see also Northern Sea Route— river transport
Neogene sediments, 111
new ice, 49
New Zealand, 288
nickel, 188, 294
Nikolaya II Island, 24
Nizhnyaya Tunguska river, 188
Nordenskiöld, A. E., 20
Noril'sk class freighters, 133, 136–7, 162, 193
Noril'sk economic complex, 63, 188, 294
North Cape Current, 49
North Cape downwarp, 113
North Novaya Zemlya downwarp, 113
North Pole, 16, 28, 33–4, 261
North Pole I (drifting station), 28
North Pole 27 (drifting station), 36
North Pole 29 (drifting station), 37
North Sea, oil pollution from, 64
North Siberian sill, 116
Northeast Siberia Arctic Shelf, 119–20, 121
Northern Science Network, 273
Northern Sea Route (NSR, Northeast Passage), 74
  foreign exploration of, 17, 19–22
  future prospects for, 136–8, 175–6
  ice distribution in, 47–62, 134
  legal authority over, 287
  management of, 140–9
  operation of, 150–7, 159–75
  overlap with river transport of, 190–5
  proposed opening of, to foreign shipping, 232–3, 259
  Russian exploration of, 11–19, 22–4
  Soviet development of, 25–9, 89–90, 125

332

Index